Praise for *Docker: Up & Running*

Docker: Up & Running moves past the Docker honeymoon and prepares you for the realities of running containers in production.

—*Kelsey Hightower, Principal Developer Advocate,*
Google Cloud Platform

Docker: Up & Running takes you from the basics underlying concepts to invaluable practical lessons learned from running Docker at scale.

—*Liz Rice, Chief Open Source Officer*
with eBPF specialists, Isovalent

Docker: Up & Running will steer you toward building modern, reliable, and highly available distributed systems.

—*Mihai Todor, Senior Principal Engineer, TLCP*

A few years ago, I had to switch my workflow away from virtual machines and start focusing on containers. For me, the best way to understand how something works is by getting hands-on experience as a user, and only then diving into the technology. *Docker: Up & Running* made the process of getting hands-on with Docker and containers a smooth process, allowing me to easily get up to speed with containers.

—*Fabiano Fidêncio, Cloud Orchestration*
Software Engineer, Intel Corporation

THIRD EDITION

Docker: Up & Running

Shipping Reliable Containers in Production

Sean P. Kane

with Karl Matthias

Beijing · Boston · Farnham · Sebastopol · Tokyo

Docker: Up & Running

by Sean P. Kane with Karl Matthias

Published by O'Reilly Media, Inc., 1005 Gravenstein Highway North, Sebastopol, CA 95472.

O'Reilly books may be purchased for educational, business, or sales promotional use. Online editions are also available for most titles (*https://oreilly.com*). For more information, contact our corporate/institutional sales department: 800-998-9938 or *corporate@oreilly.com*.

Acquisitions Editor: John Devins	**Indexer:** Sue Klefstad
Development Editor: Michele Cronin	**Interior Designer:** David Futato
Production Editor: Elizabeth Faerm	**Cover Designer:** Randy Comer
Copyeditor: Sonia Saruba	**Illustrator:** Kate Dullea
Proofreader: Piper Editorial Consulting, LLC	

April 2023: Third Edition

Revision History for the Third Edition

2023-04-13: First Release

See *https://oreilly.com/catalog/errata.csp?isbn=9781098131821* for release details.

978-1-098-13182-1

[LSI]

For my wife and children, who make everything worth it.

For my parents, who pointed me toward the beautiful intersection between logic and passion.

And for my sister, who challenges me to explore the world through the perception of others.

—Sean P. Kane

For my mom, who got me to read, and my dad, who read to me.

And for my wife and daughters, who are my bedrock.

—Karl Matthias

Table of Contents

Foreword

Containers are ubiquitous. From local development, to continuous integration, to managing large-scale production workloads, containers are everywhere. Why did this come about, where is it going, and what do you, the reader, need to know about this revolution that has taken over our industry?

Many older technologies offer the promise of "write once, run anywhere." However, not all runtimes offered this facility, and even those that did still required the runtime (and any additional dependencies) to be available in order for an application to run. Containers offer the promise of "build once, run anywhere." They allow you to package your applications, the runtime required to run it, configuration files, and any and all file dependencies it needs into one artifact. As long as you have a container runtime on the target machine, your application just works. This allows your infrastructure to be truly application agnostic. "It works on my machine," begone!

Containers offer a standard application programming interface (API) to manage the lifecycle of a container and the applications packaged within the container. This API provides a homogenous interface to an otherwise heterogeneous deployment landscape, relieving operations teams from having to know the nitty-gritty of deploying and running applications and, consequently, being able to focus on the what they do best—managing infrastructure, enforcing security and compliance, and keeping the lights on.

This interface also forms the basis for a ton of innovation. Container orchestrators like Kubernetes and Nomad leverage this control plane to raise the level of abstraction, making it easier to manage containerized workflows at scale. Service mesh technologies, like Istio, work hand in glove with orchestrators, decoupling cross-cutting concerns like service discovery and security from the application stack.

All the benefits of a standard interface also flow upstream, making the daily lives of developers easier. A single command can produce an entire development environment. Within continuous integration (CI), containers can be easily spun up to house databases, queues, or whatever dependencies your application needs to allow for integration, smoke, and end-to-end tests to check and verify your work. And finally, the portability of containers allows development teams to take ownership of their work in production, making many facets of DevOps a reality.

In a world where runtimes upgrade major versions regularly, teams and organizations are polyglot, DevOps practices like blue-green and canary releases are the norm, and scale is unprecedented, the technology that teams throughout the world are using to build and deploy their applications is containers. Containers are no longer new or novel—rather, they represent the rule of how organizations are packaging and deploying applications.

However, working with containers isn't easy. Having used containers for almost a decade, and having spent time teaching it to audiences around the world, I can attest to how nuanced this subject is.

Sean and Karl have distilled years of experience into a highly readable, yet comprehensive guide to using containers with Docker. Everything you need to get started and be productive with Docker can be found within the pages of this book—from installation, to understanding how to use and build images, to working with containers, introspecting builds and the runtime, as well as productionizing containers, can be all found here.

And that's not all—Sean and Karl aren't afraid to dive into microscopic details—elaborating on how simple Linux primitives like cgroups and namespaces make this magical thing called containers a reality. Finally, the Docker ecosystem is ever growing and expanding—and you'll find coverage on that landscape as well.

In the foreword of *Docker: Up & Running*, second edition, Laura Tacho made an astute observation—cloud native technologies like VMs and containers are not exclusive. Rather, they are additive. This statement couldn't be truer today—the rise of technologies like Kata Containers (*https://katacontainers.io*) that combine the use of lightweight virtual machines to run containers, thus allowing us to have the best of both worlds (the isolation of VMs with the portability of containers), are an attestation to Laura's commentary.

Containers are ubiquitous. A journey of a thousand miles begins with a single step—and indeed, the journey to truly grokking containers is a long one. If this book is your first step, you've made the right choice. You have two very experienced guides showing you the way, and while I realize you don't need it, I still wish you the very best of luck.

Happy containerizing.

— Raju Gandhi
Founder, DefMacro Software, LLC,
and author of Head First Software Architecture,
Head First Git, *and* JavaScript Next
@looselytyped (https://twitter.com/looselytyped)
Columbus, Ohio
April 2023

Preface

This book is designed for anyone who needs a practical understanding of Linux containers and how they can be used to improve development and production practices. Most modern integration workflows and production systems require developers and operations engineers to have a firm understanding of Linux containers and how they can be leveraged to significantly improve repeatability and predictability across the system. Along the way we'll explore how to build, test, deploy, and debug Linux containers within the Docker ecosystem. We'll also cover a few of the significant orchestration tools that leverage Linux containers. And finally, we'll round all of that out with some guidance on security and best practices for your container environment.

Who Should Read This Book

This book is intended for anyone who is looking to solve the complex workflow problems involved in developing and deploying software to production at scale. If you're interested in Linux containers, Docker, Kubernetes, DevOps, and large, scalable, software infrastructures, then this book is for you.

Why Read This Book?

Today there are many conversations, projects, and articles on the internet about Docker, and some of them have even started predicting the demise of Docker.

So why should you devote precious hours to reading this book?

Although there are other alternatives today, Docker single-handedly made Linux containers accessible to all engineers. Before Docker created the container image format and helped build many of the core libraries used in containerization systems today, Linux containers were very difficult to use and primarily remained the tools of very large cloud-hosting companies that needed to provide scalability while also protecting their systems from untrusted user code.

Docker changed all of that.

Even though there is a lot of information about Docker and Linux containers out there, the landscape is still actively evolving, and best practices are shifting. Imagine that you just read a blog post, published four years ago, about Docker. It might still work, but it might not be the best approach anymore. During the time it took us to write the first edition of this book, Docker, Inc., released four versions of Docker plus a few major tools into their ecosystem. In the seven years between the first and third editions of this book, the landscape has changed significantly. Docker has stabilized, and there are now many additional tools that fill similar roles. Instead of suffering from a complete lack of tools, there are now many robust choices for almost every aspect of the DevOps workflow. Wrapping your arms around the scope of what Linux containers and Docker provide, understanding how they fit into your workflow, and getting all the various integrations right are not trivial tasks.

We have worked with multiple companies for over nine years building and operating a mix of production Linux container platforms, including Docker, Mesos, and Kubernetes. We originally implemented Docker in production only months after its release and can share with you some of the experience we gained from evolving our production platforms since then. Our goal with this book is for you to benefit from this experience by avoiding many of the bumps in the road that we suffered through. Even though the online documentation for the Docker project (*https://docs.docker.com*) is very useful, we will attempt to give you a much bigger picture and expose you to many of the best practices that we have learned along the way.

When you finish this book, you should have enough information to understand what Linux containers are, what Docker provides, why they are important, and how you can leverage them to streamline everything from local development through production. It should be a fascinating trip through a few interesting technologies that have some very practical applications.

Navigating This Book

This book is organized as follows:

- Chapters 1 and 2 provide an introduction to Docker and explain what it is and how you can use it.
- Chapter 3 takes you through the steps required to install Docker.
- Chapters 4 through 6 dive into the Docker client, images, and containers, exploring what they are and how you can work with them.
- Chapter 7 discusses how to debug your images and containers.
- Chapter 8 introduces Docker Compose and how it can be used to significantly simplify the process of developing complex container-based services.

- Chapter 9 explores the considerations that are important to ensure a smooth transition into production.

- Chapter 10 delves into deploying containers at scale in public and private clouds.

- Chapter 11 dives into advanced topics that require some familiarity with Docker and can be important as you start to use Docker in your production environment.

- Chapter 12 explores a few alternative tools that can be useful in containerized Linux environments.

- Chapter 13 explores some of the core concepts that have solidified in the industry about how to design the next generation of internet-scale production software.

- Chapter 14 wraps everything up and ties it with a bow. It includes a summary of what has been covered and how it should help you improve the way you deliver and scale software services.

We realize that many people don't read technical books front to back and that something like the preface is incredibly easy to skip, but if you're still with us, here is a quick guide to some different approaches to reading this book:

- If you are new to Linux containers, start at the beginning. The first two chapters are intended to help you get your head around the basics of Docker and Linux containers, including what they are, how they work, and why you should care.

- If you want to jump right in and install and run Docker on your workstation, then skip to Chapters 3 and 4, which show you how to install Docker, create and download images, run containers, and much more.

- If you are familiar with the Docker basics but would like to learn more about how to utilize it for development, take a look at Chapters 5 through 8, which go over a lot of the skills that will make working with Docker on a day-to-day basis easy, and conclude with a thorough exploration of Docker Compose.

- If you are already using Docker for development but need some help getting it into production, consider starting with Chapter 9 and continuing on through Chapter 12. These sections delve into deploying containers, leveraging advanced container platforms, and many other advanced topics.

- If you are a software or platform architect, you might find Chapter 13 an interesting place to investigate, as we dive into some of the current thinking regarding containerized applications and horizontally scalable service design.

Conventions Used in This Book

The following typographical conventions are used in this book:

Italic
> Indicates new terms, URLs, email addresses, filenames, and file extensions.

`Constant width`
> Used for program listings, as well as within paragraphs to refer to program elements such as variable or function names, databases, data types, environment variables, statements, and keywords.

`Constant width bold`
> Shows commands or other text that should be typed literally by the user.

`<Constant width in angle brackets>`
> Shows text that should be replaced with user-supplied values or by values determined by context.

 This element signifies a tip or suggestion.

 This element signifies a general note.

 This element indicates a warning or caution.

Using Code Examples

Supplemental material (code examples, exercises, etc.) is available for download at *https://github.com/bluewhalebook/docker-up-and-running-3rd-edition*.

This book is here to help you get your job done. In general, if there is code that is offered along with this book, you may use it in your programs and documentation. You do not need to contact us for permission unless you're reproducing a significant portion of the code. For example, writing a program that uses several chunks of code from this book does not require permission. Selling or distributing a collection of examples from O'Reilly books does require permission. Answering a question by citing this book and quoting example code does not require permission. Incorporating a significant amount of example code from this book into your product's documentation does require permission.

We appreciate but do not require attribution. An attribution usually includes the title, author, publisher, and ISBN. For example: "*Docker: Up & Running*, 3e, by Sean P. Kane with Karl Matthias (O'Reilly). Copyright 2023 Sean P. Kane and Karl Matthias, 978-1-098-13182-1."

If you feel your use of code examples falls outside fair use or the permission given above, feel free to contact us at *permissions@oreilly.com*.

O'Reilly Online Learning

 For more than 40 years, *O'Reilly Media* has provided technology and business training, knowledge, and insight to help companies succeed.

Our unique network of experts and innovators share their knowledge and expertise through books, articles, and our online learning platform. O'Reilly's online learning platform gives you on-demand access to live training courses, in-depth learning paths, interactive coding environments, and a vast collection of text and video from O'Reilly and 200+ other publishers. For more information, visit *https://oreilly.com*.

How to Contact Us

Please address comments and questions concerning this book to the publisher:

O'Reilly Media, Inc.
1005 Gravenstein Highway North
Sebastopol, CA 95472
800-998-9938 (in the United States or Canada)
707-829-0515 (international or local)
707-829-0104 (fax)

We have a web page for this book, where we list errata, examples, and any additional information. You can access this page at *https://oreil.ly/docker-up-and-running-3e*.

Email *bookquestions@oreilly.com* to comment or ask technical questions about this book.

For news and information about our books and courses, visit *https://oreilly.com*.

Find us on LinkedIn: *https://linkedin.com/company/oreilly-media*.

Follow us on Twitter: *https://twitter.com/oreillymedia*.

Watch us on YouTube: *https://youtube.com/oreillymedia*.

Acknowledgments

We'd like to send a heartfelt thanks to the many people who helped make each edition of this book possible:

- Nic Benders, Bjorn Freeman-Benson, and Dana Lawson at New Relic, who went far above and beyond in supporting the first edition, and who ensured that we had time to pursue it.

- Roland Tritsch and Nitro Software for supporting Karl's efforts on the second edition.

- Laurel Ruma at O'Reilly, who initially reached out to us about writing a Docker book, and Mike Loukides who helped get everything on track.

- A special thanks to our first-edition editor, Brian Anderson, who ensured that we knew what we were getting into and guided us along every step of the way.

- Nikki McDonald and Virginia Wilson, who helped shepherd us through the process of creating a much-needed second edition of this book.

- And to John Devins, Michele Cronin, and Elizabeth Faerm who worked incredibly hard to make sure that this third edition saw the light of day.

- Thank you to Yevgeniy (Jim) Brikman, the author of the excellent *Terraform: Up & Running*, who graciously let us heavily base the website design for *https://dockerupandrunning.com* on his previous work.

- Introducing a new audience to a new technology succinctly takes a special talent. We are very grateful to Lars Herrmann, Laura Frank Tacho, and Raju Ghandi for taking the time to create a foreword for one of the releases.

- Our draft reviewers, who helped ensure that we were on the right track at various points throughout the writing process: Ksenia Burlachenko, who gave us our very first review as well as a full tech review, Andrew T. Baker, Sébastien Goasguen, Henri Gomez, Chelsey Frank, Rachid Zarouali, Werner Dijkerman, Predrag Knežević, and Vishwesh Ravi Shrimali.

- A special call-out is due to Alice Goldfuss and Tom Offermann, who gave us detailed and consistently useful feedback when we wrote the first edition, and to Mihai Todor for his encouragement, tech review, and full feedback on the second edition.

- Gillian McGarvey, Melanie Yarbrough, Justin Billing, Rachel Monaghan, and Sonia Saruba for their efforts in copyediting the manuscript and making it appear like we were paying attention in our high school English classes. 517 commas added and counting….

- Sue Klefstad, who helped us ensure that the 3e index was a useful reference for all of our readers, and to Wendy Catalano and Ellen Troutman for their efforts in indexing the earlier editions.

- A special thanks to Nick Adams and everyone who worked behind the scenes at O'Reilly Media to help ensure that everything appeared just right in all of the distribution formats.

- All of our peers at New Relic and Nitro who have been along for the whole Docker ride. They provided us with much of the experience that's reflected here.

- Grains of Wrath Brewery, World Cup Coffee, McMenamins Ringlers Pub, Old Town Pizza, A Beer at a Time!, Taylor's Three Rock pub, and others who kindly let us use their tables and power long after our dishes were empty.

- Our families, for being supportive and giving us the required quiet time when we needed it.

- And finally to everyone else who encouraged us, gave us advice, or supported us in any way throughout this process.

## CHAPTER 1

Introduction

Docker was first introduced to the world—with no pre-announcement and little fan-fare—by Solomon Hykes, founder and CEO of a company then called dotCloud, in a five-minute lightning talk (*https://youtu.be/wW9CAH9nSLs*) at the Python Developers Conference (*https://us.pycon.org*) in Santa Clara, California, on March 15, 2013. At the time of this announcement, only about 40 people outside of dotCloud had been given the opportunity to play with Docker.

Within a few weeks of this announcement, there was a surprising amount of press. The source code was quickly released on GitHub (*https://github.com/moby/moby*) as a public and fully open source project. Over the next few months, more and more people in the industry started hearing about Docker and how it was going to revolutionize the way software was built, delivered, and run. And within a year, almost no one in the industry was unaware of Docker, but many were still unsure what it was exactly, and why people were so excited about it.

Docker is a tool that promises to easily encapsulate the process of creating a distrib-utable artifact for any application, deploying it at scale into any environment, and streamlining the workflow and responsiveness of Agile software organizations.

The Promise of Docker

Initially, many people who were unfamiliar with Docker viewed it as some sort of virtualization platform, but in reality, it was the first widely accessible tool to build on top of a much newer technology called *containerization*. Docker and Linux containers have had a significant impact on a wide range of industry segments that include tools and technologies like Vagrant, KVM, OpenStack, Mesos, Capistrano, Ansible, Chef, Puppet, and so on. There is something very telling about the list of products that have had their market share directly impacted by Docker, and maybe you've spotted it already. Looking over this list, most engineers would recognize that these tools span a lot of different use cases, yet all of these workflows have been forever changed by Docker. This is largely because Docker has significantly altered everyone's expectations of how a continuous integration and continuous delivery (CI/CD) workflow should function. Instead of each step involving a time-consuming process managed by specialists, most people expect a DevOps pipeline to be fully automated and flow from one step to the next without any human intervention. The technologies in that list are also generally acclaimed for their ability to improve productivity, and that's exactly what has given Docker so much buzz. Docker sits right in the middle of some of the most enabling technologies of the last decade and can bring significant improvements to almost every step of the pipeline.

If you were to do a feature-by-feature comparison of Docker and the reigning champion in any of these individual areas (e.g., configuration management), Docker would very likely look like a middling competitor. It's stronger in some areas than others, but what Docker brings to the table is a feature set that crosses a broad range of workflow challenges. By combining the ease of application testing and deployment tools like Vagrant and Capistrano with the ease of administrating virtualization systems, and then providing interfaces that make workflow automation and orchestration easy to implement, Docker provides a very enabling feature set.

Lots of new technologies come and go, and a dose of skepticism about the newest rage is always healthy. When Docker was a new technology, it would have been easy to dismiss Docker as just another technology that solves a few very specific problems for developers or operations teams. If you look at Docker as a pseudovirtualization or deployment technology alone, it might not seem very compelling. But Docker is much more than it seems on the surface.

It is hard and often expensive to get communication and processes right between teams of people, even in smaller organizations. Yet we live in a world where communicating detailed information between teams is increasingly required to be successful. Discovering and implementing a tool that reduces the complexity of that communication while aiding in the production of more robust software is a big win. And that's exactly why Docker merits a deeper look. It's no panacea, and the way that you implement Docker within your organization requires some critical thought, but Docker and Linux containers provide a good approach to solving some real-world organizational problems and helping enable companies to ship better software faster. Delivering a well-designed Linux container workflow can lead to happier technical teams and real savings for the organization's bottom line.

So where are companies feeling the most pain? Shipping software at the speed expected in today's world is hard to do well, and as companies grow from one or two developers to many teams of developers, the burden of communication around shipping new releases becomes much heavier and harder to manage. Developers have to understand a lot of complexity about the environment they will be shipping software into, and production operations teams need to increasingly understand the internals of the software they ship. These are all generally good skills to work on because they lead to a better understanding of the environment as a whole and therefore encourage the designing of robust software, but these same skills are very difficult to scale effectively as an organization's growth accelerates.

The details of each company's environment often require a lot of communication that doesn't directly build value for the teams involved. For example, requiring developers to ask an operations team for release 1.2.1 of a particular library slows them down and provides no direct business value to the company. If developers could simply upgrade the version of the library they use, write their code, test with the new version, and ship it, the delivery time would be measurably shortened, and fewer risks would be involved in deploying the change. If operations engineers could upgrade software on the host system without having to coordinate with multiple teams of application developers, they could move faster. Docker helps to build a layer of isolation in software that reduces the burden of communication in the world of humans.

Beyond helping with communication issues, Docker is opinionated about software architecture in a way that encourages more robustly crafted applications. Its architectural philosophy centers on atomic or throwaway containers. During deployment, the whole running environment of the old application is thrown away with it. Nothing in the environment of the application will live longer than the application itself, and that's a simple idea with big repercussions. It means that applications are not likely to accidentally rely on artifacts left by a previous release. It means that ephemeral debugging changes are less likely to live on in future releases that picked them up from the local filesystem. And it means that applications are highly portable between servers because all of the state has to be included directly into the deployment artifact and be immutable, or sent to an external dependency like a database, cache, or file server.

All of this leads to applications that are not only more scalable but more reliable as well. Instances of the application container can come and go with little impact on the uptime of the frontend site. These are proven architectural choices that have been successful for non-Docker applications, but the design choices enforced by Docker mean that containerized applications are *required* to follow these best practices. And that's a very good thing.

Benefits of the Docker Workflow

It's hard to cohesively categorize all of the things Docker brings to the table. When implemented well, it benefits organizations, teams, developers, and operations engineers in a multitude of ways. It makes architectural decisions simpler because all applications essentially look the same on the outside from the hosting system's perspective. It makes tooling easier to write and share between applications. Nothing in this world comes with benefits and no challenges, but Docker is surprisingly skewed toward the benefits. Here are some more of the benefits you get with Docker and Linux containers:

Packaging software in a way that leverages the skills developers already have
Many companies have had to create positions for release and build engineers in order to manage all the knowledge and tooling required to create software packages for their supported platforms. Linux tools like `rpm`, `mock`, `dpkg`, and `pbuilder` can be complicated to use, and each one must be learned independently. Docker wraps up all your requirements together into one packaging format, known as the Open Container Initiative (OCI) (*https://opencontainers.org*) standard.

Bundling application software and required OS filesystems together in a single standardized image format
In the past, you typically needed to package not only your application but also many of the dependencies that it relied on, including libraries and daemons. However, you could never ensure that 100% of the execution environment was identical. For natively compiled code, this meant that your build system needed to have exactly the same shared library versions as your production environment. All of this made packaging difficult to master, and hard for many companies to accomplish reliably. Often someone running Scientific Linux (*https://scientificlinux.org*) would resort to trying to deploy a community package tested on Red Hat Enterprise Linux (*https://www.redhat.com/en/technolo gies/linux-platforms/enterprise-linux*), hoping that the package was close enough to what they needed. With Docker, you deploy your application along with every single file required to run it. Docker's layered images make this an efficient process that ensures that your application is running in the expected environment.

Using packaged artifacts to test and deliver the exact same artifact to all systems in all environments
When developers commit changes to a version control system, a new Docker image can be built, which can go through the whole testing process and be deployed to production without having to be recompiled or repackaged at any step in the process, unless that is specifically desired.

Abstracting software applications from the hardware without sacrificing resources
Traditional enterprise virtualization solutions like VMware are typically used when someone needs to create an abstraction layer between the physical hardware and the software applications that run on it, at the cost of resources. The hypervisors that manage the VMs and each VM's running kernel use a percentage of the hardware system's resources, which are then no longer available to the

hosted applications. A container, on the other hand, is just another process that typically talks directly to the underlying Linux kernel and therefore can utilize more resources, up until the system or quota-based limits are reached.

When Docker was first released, Linux containers had been around for quite a few years, and many of the other technologies that Docker is built on are not entirely new. However, Docker's unique mix of strong architectural and workflow choices combines into a whole that is much more powerful than the sum of its parts. Docker single-handedly made Linux containers, which have been publicly available since 2008, approachable and useful for all computer engineers. Docker fits containers relatively easily into the existing workflow and processes of real companies. And the problems discussed earlier have been felt by so many people that interest in the Docker project accelerated much faster than anyone could have reasonably expected.

From a standing start in 2013, Docker has seen rapid iteration and now has a huge feature set and is deployed in a vast number of production infrastructures across the planet. It has become one of the foundation layers for any modern distributed system and has inspired many others to expand on the approach. A large number of companies now leverage Docker and Linux containers as a solution to some of the serious complexity issues that they face in their application delivery processes.

What Docker Isn't

Docker can be used to solve a wide range of challenges that other categories of tools have traditionally been enlisted to fix; however, Docker's breadth of features often means that it lacks depth in specific functionality. For example, some organizations will find that they can completely remove their configuration management tool when they migrate to Docker, but the real power of Docker is that although it can replace some aspects of more traditional tools, it is also usually compatible with them or even enhanced in combination with them. In the following list, we explore some of the tool categories that Docker doesn't directly replace but that can often be used in conjunction to achieve great results:

Enterprise virtualization platform (VMware, KVM, etc.)
> A container is not a virtual machine in the traditional sense. Virtual machines contain a complete operating system, running on top of a hypervisor that is managed by the underlying host operating system. Hypervisors create virtual hardware layers that make it possible to run additional operating systems on top of a single physical computer system. This makes it very easy to run many virtual machines with radically different operating systems on a single host. With containers, both the host and the containers share the same kernel. This means that containers utilize fewer system resources but must be based on the same underlying operating system (e.g., Linux).

Cloud platform (OpenStack, CloudStack, etc.)
Like enterprise virtualization, the container workflow shares a lot of similarities—on the surface—with more traditional cloud platforms. Both are traditionally leveraged to allow applications to be horizontally scaled in response to changing demand. Docker, however, is not a cloud platform. It only handles deploying, running, and managing containers on preexisting Docker hosts. It doesn't allow you to create new host systems (instances), object stores, block storage, and the many other resources that are often managed with a cloud platform. That being said, as you start to expand your Docker tooling, you should start to experience more and more of the benefits that one traditionally associates with the cloud.

Configuration management (Puppet, Chef, etc.)
Although Docker can significantly improve an organization's ability to manage applications and their dependencies, it does not directly replace more traditional configuration management. *Dockerfiles* are used to define how a container should look at build time, but they do not manage the container's ongoing state and cannot be used to manage the Docker host system. Docker can, however, significantly lessen the need for complex configuration management code. As more and more servers simply become Docker hosts, the configuration management codebase that a company uses can become much smaller, and Docker can be used to ship the more complex application requirements inside of standardized OCI images.

Deployment framework (Capistrano, Fabric, etc.)
Docker eases many aspects of deployment by creating container images that encapsulate all the dependencies of an application in a manner that can be deployed in all environments without changes. However, Docker can't be used to automate a complex deployment process by itself. Other tools are usually still needed to stitch together the larger workflow. That being said, because Docker and other Linux container toolsets, like Kubernetes (k8s), provide a well-defined interface for deployment, the method required to deploy containers will be consistent on all hosts, and a single deployment workflow should suffice for most, if not all, of your Docker-based applications.

Development environment (Vagrant, etc.)
Vagrant is a virtual machine management tool for developers that is often used to simulate server stacks that closely resemble the production environment in which an application will be deployed. Among other things, Vagrant makes it easy to run Linux software on macOS and Windows-based workstations. Virtual machines managed by tools like Vagrant assist developers in trying to avoid the common "it worked on my machine" scenario that occurs when the software runs fine for the developer but does not run properly elsewhere. However, as with many of the previous examples, when you start to fully utilize Docker, there

is a lot less need to mimic a wide variety of production systems in development, since most production systems will simply be Linux container servers, which can easily be reproduced locally.

Workload management tool (Mesos, Kubernetes, Swarm, etc.)
An orchestration layer (including the built-in Swarm mode) must be used to coordinate work across a pool of Linux container hosts, track the current state of all the hosts and their resources, and keep an inventory of running containers. These systems are designed to automate the regular tasks that are needed to keep a production cluster healthy while also providing tools that help make the highly dynamic nature of containerized workloads easier for human beings to interact with.

Each of these sections point out an important function that Docker and Linux containers disrupted and improved. Linux containers provide a way to run software in a controlled and isolated environment, while the easy-to-use command line interface (CLI) tooling and container image standard that Docker introduced made working with containers much easier and ensured that there was a repeatable way to build software across the whole fleet.

Important Terminology

Here are a few terms that we will continue to use throughout the book and whose meanings you should become familiar with:

Docker client
This is the `docker` command used to control most of the Docker workflow and talk to remote Docker servers.

Docker server
This is the `dockerd` command that is used to start the Docker server process that builds and launches containers via a client.

Docker or OCI images
Docker and OCI images consist of one or more filesystem layers and some important metadata that represent all the files required to run a containerized application. A single image can be copied to numerous hosts. An image typically has a repository address, a name, and a tag. The tag is generally used to identify a particular release of an image (e.g., *docker.io/superorbital/wordchain:v1.0.1*). A Docker image is any image that is compatible with the Docker toolset, while an OCI image is specifically an image that meets the Open Container Initiative standard and is guaranteed to work with any OCI-compliant tool.

Linux container
This is a container that has been instantiated from a Docker or OCI image. A specific container can exist only once; however, you can easily create multiple containers from the same image. The term *Docker container* is a misnomer since Docker simply leverages the operating system's container functionality.

Atomic or immutable host
An atomic or immutable host is a small, finely tuned OS image, like Fedora CoreOS (*https://getfedora.org/en/coreos*), that supports container hosting and atomic OS upgrades.

Wrap-Up

Completely understanding Docker can be challenging when you are coming at it without a strong frame of reference. In the next chapter, we will lay down a broad overview of Docker: what it is, how it is intended to be used, and what advantages it brings to the table when implemented with all this in mind.

## CHAPTER 2

The Docker Landscape

Before you dive into configuring and installing Docker, a broad survey is in order to explain what Docker is and what it brings to the table. It is a powerful technology but not a tremendously complicated one at its core. In this chapter, we'll cover the generalities of how Docker and Linux containers work, what makes them powerful, and some of the reasons you might use them. If you're reading this, you probably have your reasons to use containers, but it never hurts to augment your understanding before you jump in.

Don't worry—this chapter should not hold you up for too long. In the next chapter, we'll dive right into getting Docker installed and running on your system.

Process Simplification

Because Docker is a piece of software, it may not be obvious that it can also have a big positive impact on company and team processes if it is adopted and implemented well. So, let's dig in and see how Docker and Linux containers can simplify both workflows and communication. This usually starts with the deployment story. Traditionally, the cycle of getting an application to production often looks something like the following (illustrated in Figure 2-1):

1. Application developers request resources from operations engineers.

2. Resources are provisioned and handed over to developers.

3. Developers script and tool their deployment.

4. Operations engineers and developers tweak the deployment repeatedly.

5. Additional application dependencies are discovered by developers.

6. Operations engineers work to install the additional requirements.

7. Loop over steps 5 and 6 n more times.

8. The application is deployed.

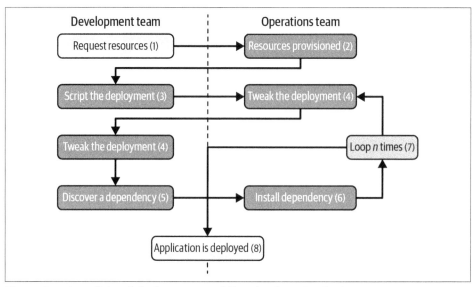

Figure 2-1. A traditional deployment workflow (without Docker)

Our experience has shown that when you are following traditional processes, deploying a brand-new application into production can take the better part of a week for a complex new system. That's not very productive, and even though DevOps practices work to alleviate many of the barriers, it often still requires a lot of effort and communication between teams of people. This process can be both technically challenging and expensive, but even worse, it can limit the kinds of innovation that development teams will undertake in the future. If deploying new software is hard, time-consuming, and dependent on resources from another team, then developers may just build everything into the existing application in order to avoid suffering the new deployment penalty, or even worse, they may simply avoid solving problems that require new development efforts.

Push-to-deploy systems like Heroku (*https://www.heroku.com*) have shown developers what the world can look like if you are in control of your application and a majority of your dependencies. Talking with developers about deployment will often turn up discussions of how easy things are on Heroku or similar systems. If you're an operations engineer, you've probably heard complaints about how much slower your internal systems are compared with "push-button" solutions like Heroku, which are built on top of Linux container technology.

Heroku is a whole environment, not just a container engine. While Docker doesn't try to be everything that is included in Heroku, it provides a clean separation of responsibilities and encapsulation of dependencies, which results in a similar boost in productivity. Docker also allows even more fine-grained control than Heroku by putting developers in control of everything, down to the exact files and package versions that ship alongside their application. Some of the tooling and orchestrators that have been built on top of Docker (e.g., Kubernetes, Docker Swarm mode, and Mesos) aim to replicate the simplicity of systems like Heroku. But even though these platforms wrap more around Docker to provide a more capable and complex environment, a simple platform that uses only Docker still provides all of the core process benefits without the added complexity of a larger system.

As a company, Docker adopts an approach of "batteries included but removable." This means that its tools come with everything most people need to get the job done while still being built from interchangeable parts that can easily be swapped in and out to support custom solutions. By using an image repository as the hand-off point, Docker allows the responsibility of building the application image to be separated from the deployment and operation of the container. What this means in practice is that development teams can build their application with all of its dependencies, run it in development and test environments, and then just ship the exact same bundle of application and dependencies to production. Because those bundles all look the same from the outside, operations engineers can then build or install standard tooling to deploy and run the applications. The cycle described in Figure 2-1 then looks somewhat like this (illustrated in Figure 2-2):

1. Developers build the Docker image and ship it to the registry.

2. Operations engineers provide configuration details to the container and provision resources.

3. Developers trigger deployment.

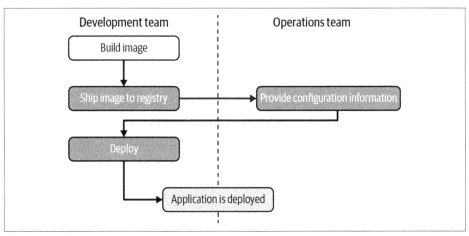

Figure 2-2. A Docker deployment workflow

This is possible because Docker allows all of the dependency issues to be discovered during the development and test cycles. By the time the application is ready for its first deployment, that work has already been done. And it usually doesn't require as many handoffs between the development and operations teams. In a well-refined pipeline, this can completely alleviate the need for anyone other than the development team to be involved in the creation and deployment of a new service. That's a lot simpler and saves a lot of time. Better yet, it leads to more robust software through testing of the deployment environment before release.

Broad Support and Adoption

Docker is well supported, with the majority of the large public clouds offering some direct support for it. For example, Docker and Linux containers have been used in Amazon Web Services (AWS) via multiple products like Amazon Elastic Container Service (Amazon ECS), Amazon Elastic Kubernetes Service (Amazon EKS), Amazon Fargate, and Amazon Elastic Beanstalk. Linux containers can also be used on Google App Engine (GAE), Google Kubernetes Engine, Red Hat OpenShift, IBM Cloud, Microsoft Azure, and many more. At DockerCon 2014, Google's Eric Brewer announced that Google would be supporting Docker as its primary internal container format. Rather than just being good PR for these companies, what this meant for the Docker community was that a lot of money began to back the stability and success of the Docker platform.

Further building its influence, Docker's image format for Linux containers has become the lingua franca among cloud providers, offering the potential for "write once, run anywhere" cloud applications. When Docker released its `libswarm` development library, an engineer from Orchard demonstrated deploying a Linux container to a heterogeneous mix of cloud providers at the same time. This kind of orchestration had not been easy before because every cloud provider offered a different API or toolset for managing instances, which were usually the smallest item you could manage with an API. What was only a promise from Docker in 2014 has since become fully mainstream as the largest companies continue to invest in the platform, support, and tooling. With most providers offering some form of Docker and Linux container orchestration as well as the container runtime itself, Docker is well supported for nearly any kind of workload in common production environments. If all of your tooling is built around Docker and Linux containers, then your applications can be deployed in a cloud-agnostic manner, allowing for new flexibility that was not previously possible.

In 2017, Docker donated its `containerd` runtime (*https://thenewstack.io/docker-donate-container-runtime-containerd-cloud-native-computing-foundation*) to the Cloud Native Computing Foundation (CNCF) (*https://www.cncf.io*), and in 2019, it was elevated to the graduated project status.

Today, the use of Linux containers in development, delivery, and production is bigger than ever. In 2022, we saw that Docker started to lose a share of the server market to the newest versions of Kubernetes that no longer require the Docker daemon, but even these releases of Kubernetes rely very heavily on the `containerd` runtime, which was initially developed by Docker. Docker also continues to have a very strong presence in many developer and CI/CD workflows.

So, what about OS vendor support and adoption? The Docker client runs directly on most major operating systems, and the server can run on Linux or Windows Server. The vast majority of the ecosystem is built around Linux servers, but other platforms are increasingly being supported. The beaten path is and will likely continue to revolve around Linux servers running Linux containers.

It is possible to run Windows containers natively (without a VM) on 64-bit versions of Windows Server 2016+. However, 64-bit versions of Windows 10+ Professional still require Hyper-V to provide the Windows Server kernel that is used for Windows containers. We will dive into a little more detail about this in "Windows Containers" on page 131.

It is also worth noting here that Windows can run Linux containers outside a virtual machine by leveraging WSL 2 (Windows Subsystem for Linux, version 2).

To support the growing demand for Docker tooling in development environments, Docker has released easy-to-use implementations for macOS and Windows. These appear to run natively but are still utilizing a small Linux virtual machine to provide the Docker server and Linux kernel. Docker has traditionally been developed on the Ubuntu Linux distribution, but most Linux distributions and other major operating systems are now supported where possible. Red Hat, for example, has gone all in on containers, and all of its platforms have first-class support for Docker. With the near-ubiquity of containers in the Linux realm, we now have distributions like Red Hat's Fedora CoreOS, which is built entirely for Linux container workloads.

In the first years after Docker's release, a set of competitors and service providers voiced concerns about Docker's proprietary image format. Containers on Linux did not have a standard image format, so Docker, Inc., created its own according to the needs of its business.

Service providers and commercial vendors were particularly reluctant to build platforms that might be subject to the whims of a company with overlapping interests to their own. Docker as a company faced some public challenges in that period as a result. To gain some goodwill and support wider adoption in the marketplace, Docker, Inc., decided to help sponsor the Open Container Initiative (OCI) (*https://www.opencontainers.org*) in June of 2015. The first full specification from that effort was released in July 2017 and was based in large part on version 2 of the Docker image format. It is now possible to apply for OCI certification for both container images and container runtimes.

This is the primary high-level OCI-certified runtime:

- `containerd` (*https://containerd.io*), which is the default high-level runtime in modern versions of Docker and Kubernetes.

These lower-level OCI-certified runtimes can be used by `containerd` to manage and create containers:

- `runc` (*https://github.com/opencontainers/runc*) is often used as the default lower-level runtime by `containerd`.
- `crun` (*https://github.com/containers/crun*) is written in C and designed to be fast and have a small memory footprint.
- Kata Containers (*https://katacontainers.io*) from Intel, Hyper, and the OpenStack Foundation is a virtualized runtime that can run a mix of containers and virtual machines.
- gVisor (*https://github.com/google/gvisor*) from Google is a sandboxed runtime, implemented entirely in user space.
- Nabla Containers (*https://nabla-containers.github.io*) provide another sandboxed runtime designed to significantly reduce the attack surface of Linux containers.

The space around deploying containers and orchestrating entire systems of containers continues to expand, too. Many of these are open source and available both on premises and as cloud or software as a service (SaaS) offerings from various providers, either in their clouds or yours. Given the amount of investment continuing to pour into the Linux container space, it's likely that Docker will continue to have an important role in the modern internet.

Architecture

Docker is a powerful technology, and that often indicates both tools and processes that come with a high level of complexity. And, under the hood, Docker is fairly complex; however, its fundamental user-facing structure is indeed a simple client/server model. Several pieces are sitting behind the Docker API, including `containerd` and `runc`, but the basic system interaction is a client talking over an API to a server. Underneath this simple exterior, Docker heavily leverages kernel mechanisms such as iptables, virtual bridging, Linux control groups (cgroups), Linux namespaces, Linux capabilities, secure computing mode, various filesystem drivers, and more. We'll talk about some of these in Chapter 11. For now, we'll go over how the client and server

---

work and give a brief introduction to the network layer that sits underneath a Linux container in Docker.

Client/Server Model

It's easiest to think of Docker as consisting of two parts: the client and the server/ daemon (see Figure 2-3). Optionally there is a third component called the *registry*, which stores Docker images and their metadata. The server does the ongoing work of building, running, and managing your containers, and you use the client to tell the server what to do. The Docker daemon (*https://en.wikipedia.org/wiki/Daemon_(com puting)*) can run on any number of servers in the infrastructure, and a single client can address any number of servers. Clients drive all of the communication, but Docker servers can talk directly to image registries when told to do so by the client. Clients are responsible for telling servers what to do, and servers focus on hosting and managing containerized applications.

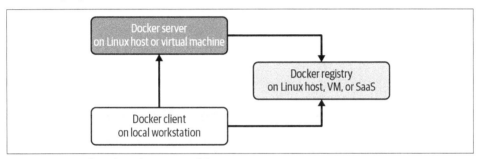

Figure 2-3. Docker client/server model

Docker is a little different in structure from some other client/server software. It has a docker client and a dockerd server, but rather than being entirely monolithic, the server then orchestrates a few other components behind the scenes on behalf of the client, including containerd-shim-runc-v2, which is used to interact with runc and containerd. Docker cleanly hides any complexity behind the simple server API, though, so you can just think of it as a straightforward client and server for most purposes. Each Docker host will normally have one Docker server running that can manage any number of containers. You can then use the docker command-line tool to talk to the server, either from the server itself or, if properly secured, from a remote client. We'll talk more about that shortly.

Network Ports and Unix Sockets

The docker command-line tool and dockerd daemon can talk to each other over Unix sockets and network ports. Docker, Inc., has registered three ports with the Internet Assigned Numbers Authority (IANA) (*https://www.iana.org*) for use by the Docker daemon and client: TCP port 2375 for unencrypted traffic, port 2376 for encrypted SSL connections, and port 2377 for Docker Swarm mode. Using a different port is easily configurable for scenarios where you need to use different settings. The default setting for the Docker installer is to only use a Unix socket for communication with the local Docker daemon. This ensures that the system defaults to the most secure installation possible. This is also easily configurable, but it is highly recommended that network ports are not used with Docker, due to the lack of user authentication and role-based access controls within the Docker daemon. The Unix socket can be located in different paths on different operating systems, but in most cases, it can be found here: */var/run/docker.sock*. If you have strong preferences for a different location, you can usually specify this at install time or simply change the server configuration afterward and restart the daemon. If you don't, then the defaults will probably work for you. As with most software, following the defaults will save you a lot of trouble if you don't need to change them.

> Recent versions of Docker Desktop may create the *docker.sock* file in the user's home directory inside *.docker/run/* and then simply link *_/var/run/docker.sock* to this location.

Robust Tooling

Among the many things that have led to Docker's strong adoption is its simple and powerful tooling. Since its initial release, its capabilities have been expanding ever wider, thanks to efforts from the Docker community at large. The tooling that Docker ships with supports building Docker images, basic deployment to individual Docker daemons, a distributed mode called Swarm mode, and all the functionality needed to manage a remote Docker server. Beyond the included Swarm mode, community efforts have focused on managing whole fleets (or clusters) of Docker servers and scheduling and orchestrating container deployments.

> When we talk about Docker Swarm or Swarm mode (*https:// docs.docker.com/engine/swarm*) in this book, we are referring to the built-in Swarm functionality in the Docker client and server, which leverages another underlying library called SwarmKit. When searching for articles on the internet, you may find references to an older standalone version of Docker Swarm, which is often referred to as Docker Swarm "Classic" (*https://github.com/docker-archive/ classicswarm*) nowadays.

Docker has also launched its own orchestration toolset, including Compose (*https://github.com/docker/compose*), Docker Desktop (*https://www.docker.com/prod ucts/docker-desktop*), and Swarm mode (*https://docs.docker.com/engine/swarm*), which creates a cohesive deployment story for developers. Docker's offerings in the production orchestration space have been largely overshadowed by Google's Kubernetes, although it should be noted that Kubernetes relied heavily on Docker until v1.24 was released in early 2022 (*https://kubernetes.io/blog/2020/12/02/dockershim-faq*). But Docker's orchestration tools remain useful, with Compose being particularly handy for local development.

Because Docker provides both a command-line tool and a remote REST API, it is easy to add further tooling in any language. The command-line tool lends itself well to shell scripting, and anything the client can do can also be done programmatically via the REST API. The Docker CLI is so well-known that many other Linux container CLI tools, like podman (*https://podman.io*) and nerdctl (*https://github.com/contain erd/nerdctl*), mimic its arguments for compatibility and easy adoption.

Docker Command-Line Tool

The command-line tool docker is the main interface that most people will have with Docker. The Docker client is a Go program (*https://golang.org*) that compiles and runs on all common architectures and operating systems. The command-line tool is available as part of the main Docker distribution on various platforms and also compiles directly from the Go source. Some of the things you can typically do with the Docker command-line tool include, but are not limited to, the following:

- Building a container image
- Pulling images from a registry to a Docker daemon or pushing them up to a registry from the Docker daemon
- Starting a container on a Docker server either in the foreground or background
- Retrieving the Docker logs from a remote server
- Interactively running a command inside a running container on a remote server
- Monitoring statistics about your container
- Getting a process listing from your container

You can probably see how these can be composed into a workflow for building, deploying, and observing applications. But the Docker command-line tool is not the only way to interact with Docker, and it's not necessarily the most powerful.

Docker Engine API

Like many other pieces of modern software, the Docker daemon has an API. This is in fact what the Docker command-line tool uses to communicate with the daemon. But because the API is documented and public, it's quite common for external tooling to use the API directly. This provides a convenient mechanism that allows any tool to create, inspect, and manage all of the images and containers that are under the Docker daemon's management. While it's unlikely that beginners will initially want to talk directly to the Docker API, it's a great tool to have available. As your organization embraces Docker over time, you will increasingly find the API to be a good integration point for this tooling.

Extensive documentation for the API (*https://dockr.ly/2wxCHnx*) is on the Docker site. As the ecosystem has matured, robust implementations of Docker API libraries have emerged for all popular languages. Docker maintains SDKs for Python and Go (*https://dockr.ly/2wxCHnx*), and there are additional libraries maintained by third parties that are worth considering. For example, over the years we have used these Go (*https://github.com/fsouza/go-dockerclient*) and Ruby (*https://github.com/upserve/docker-api*) libraries and have found them to be both robust and rapidly updated as new versions of Docker are released.

Most of the things you can do with the Docker command-line tooling are supported relatively easily via the API. Two notable exceptions are the endpoints that require streaming or terminal access: running remote shells or executing the container in interactive mode. In these cases, it's often easier to use one of these solid client libraries or the command-line tool.

Container Networking

Even though Linux containers are largely made up of processes running on the host system itself, they usually behave quite differently from other processes at the network layer. Docker initially supported a single networking model but now supports a robust assortment of configurations that handle most application requirements. Most people run their containers in the default configuration, called *bridge mode*. So let's take a look at how it works.

To understand bridge mode, it's easiest to think of each of your Linux containers as behaving like a host on a private network. The Docker server acts as a virtual bridge, and the containers are clients behind it. A bridge is just a network device that repeats traffic from one side to another. So you can think of it like a mini virtual network, with each container acting like a host attached to that network. The actual implementation (see Figure 2-4) is that each container has a virtual Ethernet interface connected to the Docker bridge and an IP address allocated to the virtual interface. Docker lets you bind and expose individual or groups of ports on the host to the container so that the outside world can reach your container on those ports. The traffic is largely managed by the vpnkit (*https://github.com/moby/vpnkit*) library.

Docker allocates the private subnet from an unused RFC 1918 (*https://www.rfc-editor.org/rfc/rfc1918*) private subnet block. It detects which network blocks are unused on the host and allocates one of those to the virtual network. That is bridged to the host's local network through an interface on the server called docker0. This means that, by default, all of the containers are on a network together and can talk to one another directly. But to get to the host or the outside world, they go over the docker0 virtual bridge interface.

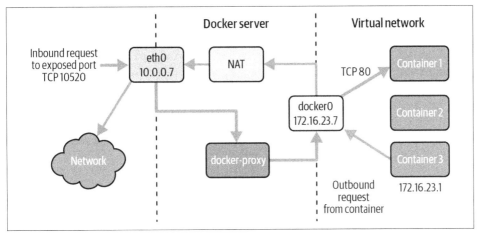

Figure 2-4. The network on a typical Docker server

There is a dizzying array of ways in which you can configure Docker's network layer, from allocating your own network blocks to configuring your own custom bridge interface. People often run with the default mechanisms, but there are times when something more complex or specific to your application is required. You can find much more detail about Docker networking in the documentation (*https://dockr.ly/2otp461*), and we will cover more details in Chapter 11.

When developing your Docker workflow, you should get started with the default networking approach. You might later find that you don't want or need this default virtual network. Networking is configurable per container, and you can switch off the whole virtual network layer entirely for a container using the --net=host switch to docker container run. When running in that mode, Linux containers use the host's own network devices and addresses, and no virtual interfaces or bridges are provisioned. Note that host networking has security implications you might need to consider. Other network topologies are possible and discussed in Chapter 11.

Getting the Most from Docker

Like most tools, Docker has a number of great use cases, and others that aren't so good. You can, for example, open a glass jar with a hammer. But that has its downsides. Understanding how to best use the tool, or even simply determining if it's the right tool, can get you on the correct path much more quickly.

To begin with, Docker's architecture is aimed squarely at applications that are either stateless or where the state is externalized into data stores like databases or caches. Those are the easiest to containerize. Docker enforces some good development principles for this class of application, and we'll talk later about how that's powerful. But this means that doing things like putting a database engine inside Docker is a bit like swimming against the current. It's not that you can't do it, or even that you shouldn't do it; it's just that this is not the most obvious use case for Docker, so if it's the one you start with, you may find yourself disappointed early on. Databases that run well in Docker are now often deployed this way, but this is not the simple path. Some good applications for beginning with Docker include web frontends, backend APIs, and short-running tasks like maintenance scripts that might normally be handled by `cron`.

If you focus first on building an understanding of running stateless or externalized-state applications inside containers, you will have a foundation on which to start considering other use cases. We strongly recommend starting with stateless applications and learning from that experience before tackling other use cases. The community is continuously working on how to better support stateful applications in Docker, and there are likely to be many developments in this area.

Containers Are Not Virtual Machines

A good way to start shaping your understanding of how to leverage Docker is to think of Linux containers not as virtual machines (VMs) but as very lightweight wrappers around a single Unix process. During actual implementation, that process might spawn other processes, but on the other hand, one statically compiled binary could be all that's inside your container (see "Outside Dependencies" on page 234 for more information). Containers are also ephemeral: they may come and go much more readily than a traditional virtual machine.

Virtual machines are by design a stand-in for real hardware that you might throw in a rack and leave there for a few years. Because a real server is what they're abstracting, virtual machines are often long-lived in nature. Even in the cloud where companies often spin virtual machines up and down on demand, they usually have a running life span of days or more. On the other hand, a particular container might exist for months, or it may be created, run a task for a minute, and then be destroyed. All of that is OK, but it's a fundamentally different approach than the one virtual machines are typically used for.

To help drive this differentiation home, if you run Docker on a mac or Windows system, you are leveraging a Linux virtual machine to run `dockerd`, the Docker server. However, on Linux, `dockerd` can be run natively, and therefore there is no need for a virtual machine to be run anywhere on the system (see Figure 2-5).

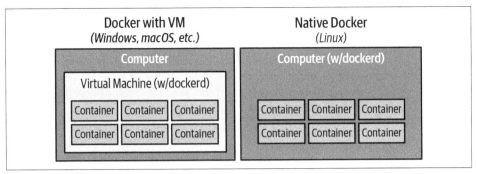

Figure 2-5. Typical Docker installations

Limited Isolation

Containers are isolated from one another, but that isolation is probably more limited than you might expect. While you can put limits on their resources, the default container configuration just has them all sharing CPU and memory on the host system, much as you would expect from colocated Unix processes. This means that unless you constrain them, containers can compete for resources on your production machines. That might be fine for your use case, but it impacts your design decisions. Limits on CPU and memory use are encouraged through Docker, but in most cases, they are not the default like they would be with a virtual machine.

It's often the case that many containers share one or more common filesystem layers. That's one of the more powerful design decisions in Docker, but it also means that if you update a shared image, you may also need to rebuild and redeploy containers that are still utilizing the older image.

Containerized processes are just processes on the Docker server itself. They are running on the same instance of the Linux kernel as the host operating system. All container processes show up in the normal ps output on the Docker server. That is utterly different from a hypervisor, where the depth of process isolation usually includes running an entirely separate instance of the operating system kernel for each virtual machine.

This light containment can lead to the tempting option of exposing more resources from the host, such as shared filesystems to allow the storage of state. But you should think hard before further exposing resources from the host into the container unless they are used exclusively by the container. We'll talk about the security of containers later, but generally, you might consider helping to enforce isolation further by applying Security-Enhanced Linux (SELinux) (*https://www.redhat.com/en/topics/linux/what-is-selinux*) or AppArmor (*https://apparmor.net*) policies rather than compromising the existing barriers.

By default, many containers use UID 0 to launch processes. Because the container is *contained*, this seems safe, but in reality, it isn't very safe. Because everything is running on the same kernel, many types of security vulnerabilities or simple misconfiguration can give the container's root user unauthorized access to the host's system resources, files, and processes. Refer to "Security" on page 303 for a discussion of how to mitigate this.

Containers Are Lightweight

We'll get more into the details of how this works later, but creating a new container can take up very little disk space. A quick test reveals that a newly created container from an existing image takes a whopping 12 kilobytes of disk space. That's pretty lightweight. On the other hand, a new virtual machine created from a golden image might require hundreds or thousands of megabytes, since at a minimum it requires a full operating install to exist on that disk. The new container, on the other hand, is so small because it is just a reference to a layered filesystem image and some metadata about the configuration. By default, no copy of the data is allocated to the container. Containers are just processes on the existing system that may only need to read information from the disk, so there may not be a need to copy any data for the exclusive use of the container, until a time when it needs to write data that is unique to that container instance.

The lightness of containers means that you can use them for situations where creating another virtual machine would be too heavyweight or where you need something to be truly ephemeral. You probably wouldn't, for instance, spin up an entire virtual machine to run a curl command to a website from a remote location, but you might spin up a new container for this purpose.

Toward an Immutable Infrastructure

By deploying most of your applications within containers, you can start simplifying your configuration management story by moving toward an immutable infrastructure, where components are replaced entirely rather than changed in place. The idea of an immutable infrastructure has gained popularity in response to how difficult it is, in reality, to maintain a truly idempotent configuration management codebase. As your configuration management codebase grows, it can become as unwieldy and unmaintainable as large, monolithic legacy applications.

With Docker, it is possible to deploy a very lightweight Docker server that needs almost no configuration management, or in many cases, none at all. You handle all of your application management simply by deploying and redeploying containers to the server. When the server needs an important update to something like the Docker daemon or the Linux kernel, you can simply bring up a new server with the changes, deploy your containers there, and then decommission or reinstall the old server.

Container-based Linux distributions like Red Hat's Fedora CoreOS (*https://getfe dora.org/en/coreos*) are designed around this principle. But rather than requiring you to decommission the instance, Fedora CoreOS can entirely update itself and switch to the updated OS. Your configuration and workload largely remain in your containers, and you don't have to configure the OS very much at all.

Because of this clean separation between deployment and configuration of your servers, many container-based production systems are using tools such as Hashi-Corp's Packer (*https://www.packer.io/intro/index.html*) to build cloud virtual server images, and then leveraging Docker to nearly or entirely avoid configuration management systems.

Stateless Applications

A good example of the kind of application that containerizes well is a web application that keeps its state in a database. Stateless applications are normally designed to immediately answer a single self-contained request and have no need to track information between requests from one or more clients. You might also run something like ephemeral Memcached (*https://memcached.org*) instances in containers. If you think about your web application, though, it probably has some local state that you rely on, like configuration files. That might not seem like a lot of state, but if you bake that configuration into your images, it means that you've limited the reusability of your image and made it more challenging to deploy into different environments, without maintaining multiple images for different deployment targets.

In many cases, the process of containerizing your application means that you move configuration state into environment variables that can be passed to your application at runtime. Rather than baking the configuration into the container, you apply the configuration to the container when it is deployed. This allows you to easily do things like use the same container to run in either production or staging environments. In most companies, those environments would require many different configuration settings like the connection URLs for various external services that the application utilizes.

With containers, you might also find that you are always decreasing the size of your containerized application as you optimize it down to the bare essentials required to run. We have found that thinking of anything that you need to run in a distributed way as a container can lead to some interesting design decisions. If, for example, you have a service that collects some data, processes it, and returns the result, you might configure containers on many servers to run the job and then aggregate the response on another container.

Externalizing State

If Docker works best for stateless applications, how do you best store state when you need to? Configuration is typically passed by environment variables, for example. Docker supports environment variables natively, and they are stored in the metadata that makes up a container configuration. This means that restarting the container will ensure that the same configuration is passed to your application each time. It also makes the configuration of the container easily observable while it's running, which can make debugging a lot easier, although there are some security concerns around exposing secrets in environment variables. It is also possible to store and retrieve your application configuration inside an external datastore, like Consul (*https://www.con sul.io*) or PostgreSQL (*https://www.postgresql.org*).

Databases are often where scaled applications store state, and nothing in Docker interferes with doing that for containerized applications. Applications that need to store files, however, face some challenges. Storing things to the container's filesystem is not performant, will be limited by space, and will not preserve state when a container is re-created. If you redeploy a stateful service without utilizing storage external to the container, you will lose all of that state. Applications that need to store filesystem state should be carefully considered before you put them into Docker. If you decide that you can benefit from Linux containers in these cases, it's best to design a solution where the state can be stored in a centralized location that could be accessed regardless of which host a container runs on. In certain cases, this might mean using a service like Amazon Simple Storage Service (Amazon S3), OpenStack Swift, or a local block store, or even mounting EBS volumes or iSCSI disks inside the container. Docker volume plug-ins (*https://docs.docker.com/engine/extend/plugins_vol ume*) provide some additional options and are briefly discussed in Chapter 11.

Although it is possible to externalize state on the host's local filesystem, it is not generally encouraged by the community and should be considered an advanced use case. It is strongly recommended that you start with applications that don't need persistent state. There are multiple reasons why this is typically discouraged, but in almost all cases it is because it introduces dependencies between the container and the host that interfere with using Docker as a truly dynamic, horizontally scalable application delivery service. If your container maintains state on the local host filesystem, then it can only be deployed to the system that houses that local filesystem. Remote volumes that can be dynamically attached are a good solution but also an advanced use case.

The Docker Workflow

Like many tools, Docker strongly encourages a particular workflow. It's a very enabling workflow that maps well to how many companies are organized, but it's probably a little different than what you or your team are doing now. Having adapted our own organizations' workflows to the Docker approach, we can confidently say that this is a change that can have a wide-reaching positive impact on many teams in your organization. If the workflow is implemented well, it can help you realize the promise of reduced communication overhead between teams.

Revision Control

The first thing that Docker gives you out of the box is two forms of revision control. One of them is used to track the filesystem layers that each Docker image is comprised of, and the other is a tagging system for those images.

Filesystem layers

Linux containers are made up of stacked filesystem layers, each identified by a unique hash, where each new set of changes made during the build process is laid on top of the previous changes. That's great because it means that when you do a new build, you only have to rebuild the layers that follow the change you're deploying. This saves time and bandwidth because containers are shipped around as layers, and you don't have to ship layers that a server already has stored. If you've done deployments with many classic deployment tools, you know that you can end up shipping hundreds of megabytes of the same data to a server over and over with each deployment. That's incredibly inefficient, and worse, you can't be sure exactly what changed between deployments. Because of the layering effect, and because Linux containers include all of the application dependencies, with Docker you can be more confident about the changes that you are shipping to production.

To simplify this a bit, remember that a Docker image contains everything required to run your application. If you change one line of code, you certainly don't want to waste time rebuilding every dependency that your code requires into a new image. Instead, by leveraging the build cache, Docker can ensure that only the layers affected by the code change are rebuilt.

Image tags

The second kind of revision control offered by Docker makes it easy to answer an important question: what was the previous version of the application that was deployed? That's not always easy to answer. There are a lot of solutions for non-containerized applications, from Git tags for each release, to deployment logs, to tagged builds for deployment, and many more. If you're coordinating your deployment with Capistrano (*https://capistranorb.com*), for example, it will handle this for you by keeping a set number of previous releases on the server and then using symlinks to make one of them the current release.

But what you find in any scaled production environment is that each application has a unique way of handling deployment revisions. Many of them do the same thing, but some may be different. Worse, in heterogeneous language environments, the deployment tools are often entirely different between applications, and very little is shared. So the question "What was the previous version?" can have many answers depending on whom you ask and which application you're referring to. Docker has a built-in mechanism for handling this: image tagging a standard build step. You can easily leave multiple revisions of your application on the server so that performing a rollback is trivial. This is not rocket science, and it's not functionality that is hard to find in other deployment tooling, but with container images, it can easily be made standard across all of your applications, and everyone can have the same expectations about how things will be tagged for all applications. This makes communication easier between teams, and it makes tooling much simpler because there is one source of truth for application releases.

 In many examples online and in this book, you will see people use the latest tag for a container image. This is useful when you're getting started and when you're writing examples, as it will always grab the most recent build of an image. But since this is a floating tag, it is a really bad idea to use latest in most production workflows, as your dependencies can get updated out from under you, and it is impossible to roll back to latest because the old version is no longer the one tagged latest. It also makes it hard to verify if the same image is running on different servers. The rule of thumb is: don't use the latest tag in production. It's not even a good idea to use the latest tag from upstream images, for the same reasons.

It is highly recommended that you tag your CI/CD builds with something that uniquely identifies the exact source code commit that was used to build them. In a git workflow, this could be the git hash related to the commit. Once you are ready to release an image, the recommendation is that you use semantic versioning (*https://semver.org*) and provide your image with tags, like 1.4.3, 2.0.0, etc.

Pinning versions requires a bit more work to keep them current, but it will also prevent many unfortunate and poorly timed surprises during builds and deployments.

Building

Building applications is a black art in many organizations, where a few people know all the levers to pull and knobs to turn to spit out a well-formed, shippable artifact. Part of the heavy cost of getting a new application deployed is getting the build just right. Docker doesn't solve all of these problems, but it does provide a standardized tool configuration and toolset for builds. That makes it a lot easier for people to learn how to build your applications and to get new builds up and running.

The Docker command-line tool contains a `build` flag that will consume a *Dockerfile* and produce a Docker image. Each command in a *Dockerfile* generates a new layer in the image, so it's easy to reason about what the build is going to do by looking at the *Dockerfile* itself. The great part of all of this standardization is that any engineer who has worked with a *Dockerfile* can dive right in and modify the build of any other application. Because the Docker image is a standardized artifact, all of the tooling behind the build will be the same regardless of the development language or base image that is being used or the number of layers needed. The *Dockerfile* is usually checked into a revision control system, which also means that tracking changes to the build is simplified. Modern multistage Docker builds also allow you to define the build environment separately from the final artifact image. This provides huge "configure ability" for your build environment just like you'd have for a production container.

Many Docker builds are a single invocation of the `docker image build` command and generate a single artifact, the container image. Because it's usually the case that most of the logic about the build is wholly contained in the *Dockerfile*, it's easy to create standard build jobs for any team to use in build systems like Jenkins (*https:// jenkins-ci.org*). As a further standardization of the build process, many companies— eBay, for example—have standardized Linux containers to do the image builds from a *Dockerfile*. SaaS build offerings like Travis CI (*https://travis-ci.com*) and CodeShip (*https://codeship.com*) also have first-class support for Docker builds.

It is also possible to automate the creation of multiple images that support different underlying compute architectures, like x86 and ARM, by utilizing the newer BuildKit (*https://github.com/moby/buildkit*) support in Docker.

Testing

While Docker itself does not include a built-in framework for testing, the way containers are built lends some advantages to testing with Linux containers.

Testing a production application can take many forms, from unit testing to full integration testing in a semi-live environment. Docker facilitates better testing by guaranteeing that the artifact that passed testing will be the one that ships to production. This can be guaranteed because we can either use the Docker SHA for the container, or a custom tag to make sure we're consistently shipping the same version of the application.

Since, by design, containers include all of their dependencies, tests run on containers are very reliable. If a unit test framework says tests were successful against a container image, you can be sure that you will not experience a problem with the versioning of an underlying library at deployment time, for example. That's not easy with most other technologies, and even Java WAR (Java Web application ARchive) files, for example, don't include testing of the application server itself. That same Java application deployed in a Linux container will generally also include an application server like Tomcat, and the whole stack can be smoke tested before shipping to production.

A secondary benefit of shipping applications in Linux containers is that in places where there are multiple applications that talk to one another remotely via something like an API, developers of one application can easily develop against a version of the other service that is currently tagged for the environment they require, like production or staging. Developers on each team don't have to be experts in how the other service works or is deployed just to do development on their own application. If you expand this to a service-oriented architecture with innumerable microservices, Linux containers can be a real lifeline to developers or QA engineers who need to wade into the swamp of inter-microservice API calls.

A common practice in organizations that run Linux containers in production is for automated integration tests to pull down a versioned set of Linux containers for different services, matching the current deployed versions. The new service can then be integration-tested against the very same versions it will be deployed alongside. Doing this in a heterogeneous language environment would previously have required a lot of custom tooling, but it becomes reasonably simple to implement because of the standardization provided by Linux containers.

Packaging

Docker builds produce an image that can be treated as a single build artifact, although technically they may consist of multiple filesystem layers. No matter which language your application is written in or which distribution of Linux you run it on, you get a layered Docker image as the result of your build. And it is all built and handled by the Docker tooling. That build image is the shipping container metaphor that Docker is named for: a single, transportable unit that universal tooling can handle, regardless of what it contains. Like oceanic cargo ships that package everything into steel containers, your Docker tooling will only ever have to deal with one kind of package: the Docker image. That's powerful, because it's a huge facilitator of tool reuse between applications, and it means that someone else's off-the-shelf container tools will work with your build images.

Applications that traditionally took a lot of custom configuration to deploy onto a new host or development system become very portable with Docker. Once a container is built, it can easily be deployed on any system with a running Docker server on the same architecture.

Deploying

Deployments are handled by so many kinds of tools in different shops that it would be impossible to list them here. Some of these tools include shell scripting, Capistrano (*https://capistranorb.com*), Fabric (*https://www.fabfile.org*), Ansible (*https://www.ansible.com*), and in-house custom tooling. In our experience with multiteam organizations, there are usually one or two people on each team who know the magical incantation to get deployments to work. When something goes wrong, the team is dependent on them to get it running again. As you probably expect by now, Docker makes most of that a nonissue. The built-in tooling supports a simple, one-line deployment strategy to get a build onto a host and up and running. The standard Docker client handles deploying only to a single host at a time, but there is a large array of tools available that make it easy to deploy into a cluster of Docker or other compatible Linux container hosts. Because of the standardization Docker provides, your build can be deployed into any of these systems, with low complexity on the part of the development teams.

The Docker Ecosystem

Over the years, a wide community has formed around Docker, driven by both developers and system administrators. Like the DevOps movement, this has facilitated better tools by applying code to operations problems. Where there are gaps in the tooling provided by Docker, other companies and individuals have stepped up to the plate. Many of these tools are also open source. That means they are expandable and can be modified by any other company to fit its needs.

 Docker is a commercial company that has contributed much of the core Docker source code to the open source community. Companies are strongly encouraged to join the community and contribute back to the open source efforts. If you are looking for supported versions of the core Docker tools, you can find out more about its offerings at the Docker website (*https://www.docker.com/support*).

Orchestration

The first important category of tools that add functionality to the core Docker distribution and Linux container experience contains orchestration and mass deployment tools. Early mass deployment tools like New Relic's Centurion (*https://github.com/newrelic/centurion*), Spotify's Helios (*https://github.com/spotify/helios*), and the Ansible

Docker tooling (*https://oreil.ly/V8X_f*)[1] still work largely like traditional deployment tools but leverage the container as the distribution artifact. They take a fairly simple, easy-to-implement approach. You get a lot of the benefits of Docker without much complexity, but many of these tools have been replaced by more robust and flexible tools, like Kubernetes.

Fully automatic schedulers like Kubernetes (*https://kubernetes.io*) or Apache Mesos (*https://mesos.apache.org*) with the Marathon scheduler (*https://mesosphere.git hub.io/marathon*) are more powerful options that take nearly complete control of a pool of hosts on your behalf. Other commercial entries are widely available, such as HashiCorp's Nomad (*https://www.nomadproject.io*), Mesosphere's DC/OS (Datacenter Operating System) (*https://dcos.io*), and Rancher (*https://rancher.com*).[2] The ecosystems of both free and commercial options continue to grow rapidly.

Immutable atomic hosts

One additional idea that you can leverage to enhance your Docker experience is immutable atomic hosts. Traditionally, servers and virtual machines are systems that an organization will carefully assemble, configure, and maintain to provide a wide variety of functionality that supports a broad range of usage patterns. Updates must often be applied via nonatomic operations, and there are many ways in which host configurations can diverge and introduce unexpected behavior into the system. Most running systems are patched and updated in place in today's world. Conversely, in the world of software deployments, most people deploy an entire copy of their application, rather than trying to apply patches to a running system. Part of the appeal of containers is that they help make applications even more atomic than traditional deployment models.

What if you could extend that core container pattern down into the operating system? Instead of relying on configuration management to try to update, patch, and coalesce changes to your OS components, what if you could simply pull down a new, thin OS image and reboot the server? And then if something breaks, easily roll back to the exact image you were previously using?

This is one of the core ideas behind Linux-based atomic host distributions, like Red Hat's Fedora CoreOS (*https://getfedora.org/en/coreos*), Bottlerocket OS (*https://github.com/bottlerocket-os/bottlerocket*), and others. Not only should you be able to easily tear down and redeploy your applications, but the same philosophy should apply for the whole software stack. This pattern helps provide very high levels of consistency and resilience to the whole stack.

---

1 Full URL: *https://docs.ansible.com/ansible/latest/collections/community/docker/docsite/scenario_guide.html#ansible-collections-community-docker-docsite-scenario-guide*

2 Some of these commercial offerings have free editions of their platforms.

Some of the typical characteristics of an immutable or atomic host (*https://gist.git hub.com/jzb/0f336c6f23a0ba145b0a*) are a minimal footprint, a design focused on supporting Linux containers and Docker, and atomic OS updates and rollbacks that can easily be controlled via multihost orchestration tools on both bare-metal and common virtualization platforms.

In Chapter 3, we will discuss how you can easily use these immutable hosts in your development process. If you are also using these hosts as deployment targets, this process creates a previously unheard-of amount of software stack symmetry between your development and production environments.

Additional tools

Docker is not just a standalone solution. It has a massive feature set, but there is always a case where someone needs more than it can deliver on its own. There is a wide ecosystem of tools to either improve or augment Docker's functionality. Some good production tools leverage the Docker API, like Prometheus (*https://prom etheus.io*) for monitoring and Ansible (*https://www.ansible.com*) for simple orchestration. Others leverage Docker's plug-in architecture. Plug-ins are executable programs that conform to a specification for receiving and returning data to Docker.

 Many of the Docker plug-ins are considered legacy and are being replaced with better approaches. Make sure that you perform adequate research before deciding on a plug-in that you are going to utilize, to ensure that it is the best option and is not going to be unsupported or quickly replaced.

There are many more good tools that either talk to the API or run as plug-ins. Many of these have sprung up to make life with Docker easier on the various cloud providers. These help with seamless integration between Docker and the cloud. As the community continues to innovate, the ecosystem continues to grow. There are new solutions and tools available in this space on an ongoing basis. If you find you are struggling with something in your environment, look to the ecosystem!

Wrap-Up

There you have it: a quick tour through Docker. We'll return to this discussion later on with a slightly deeper dive into the architecture of Docker, more examples of how to use the community tooling, and an exploration of some of the thinking behind designing robust container platforms. But you're probably itching to try it all out, so in the next chapter, we'll get Docker installed and running.

## CHAPTER 3

Installing Docker

We're now at the point where you hopefully understand roughly what Docker is and what it isn't, and it's time for some hands-on work. Let's get Docker installed so we can work with it. The steps required to install Docker vary depending on the platform you use for development and the Linux distribution you use to host your applications in production.

In this chapter, we discuss the steps required to get a fully working Docker development environment set up on most modern desktop operating systems. First, we'll install the Docker client on your native development platform, and then we'll get a Docker server running on Linux. Finally, we'll test out the installation to make sure it works as expected.

Although the Docker client can run on Windows and macOS to control a Docker server, Linux containers can only be built and launched on a Linux system. Therefore, non-Linux systems will require a virtual machine or remote server to host the Linux-based Docker server. Docker Community Edition, Docker Desktop, and Vagrant, which are all discussed later in this chapter, provide some approaches to address this issue. It is also possible to run Windows containers natively on Windows systems, and we will specifically discuss this in "Windows Containers" on page 131, but most of the book's focus will be on Linux containers.

The Docker ecosystem is changing very rapidly as the technology evolves to become more robust and solve a broader range of problems. Some features discussed in this book and elsewhere may become deprecated. To see what has been tagged for deprecation and eventual removal, refer to the documentation (*https://docs.docker.com/engine/deprecated*).

We assume that you are using a traditional Unix shell in most of the code examples in the book. You can use PowerShell, but be aware that some commands will need adjusting to work in that environment.

If you are in an environment that requires you to use a proxy, make sure that it is properly configured for Docker (*https:// docs.docker.com/network/proxy*).

Docker Client

The Docker client natively supports 64-bit versions of Linux, Windows, and macOS.

The majority of popular Linux distributions can trace their origins to either Debian or Red Hat. Debian systems utilize the deb package format and Advanced Package Tool (apt) (*https://wiki.debian.org/AptCLI*) to install most prepackaged software. On the other hand, Red Hat systems rely on RPM Package Manager (rpm) files and Yellowdog Updater, Modified (yum) (*https://en.wikipedia.org/wiki/Yum_(software)*), or Dandified yum (dnf) (*https://goo.gl/TdkGRS*) to install similar software packages. Alpine Linux, which is often used in environments that require a very small Linux footprint, relies on the Alpine Package Keeper (apk) (*https://wiki.alpinelinux.org/wiki/ Package_management*) to manage software packages.

On macOS and Microsoft Windows, native GUI installers provide the easiest method to install and maintain prepackaged software. Homebrew for macOS (*https://brew.sh*) and Chocolatey for Windows (*https://chocolatey.org*) are also very popular options among technical users.

We will be discussing a few approaches to installing Docker in this section. Make sure that you pick the first one in this list that best matches your needs. Installing more than one may cause problems if you are not well versed in how to switch between them properly.

Choose one of these: Docker Desktop, Docker Community Edition, OS package manager, or Vagrant.

You can always find the most recent installation documentation (*https:// docs.docker.com/get-docker*) on the Docker website.

Linux

It is strongly recommended that you run Docker on a modern release of your preferred Linux distribution. It is possible to run Docker on some older releases, but stability may be a significant issue. Generally, a 3.8 or later kernel is required, and we advise you to use the newest stable version of your chosen distribution. The following directions assume you are using a recent stable release of the Ubuntu or Fedora Linux distributions.

Although we are not covering it here, Docker Desktop for Linux (*https://docs.docker.com/desktop/linux/install*) has been released and can be used on Linux if you would prefer running the Docker daemon on a local virtual machine instead of directly on your system.

Ubuntu Linux 22.04 (64-bit)

Let's take a look at the steps required to install Docker on the 64-bit version of Ubuntu Linux 22.04.

For up-to-date instructions or coverage of other versions of Ubuntu, see the Docker Community Edition for Ubuntu (*https://dockr.ly/2NwNbuw*).

These first two commands will ensure that you aren't running older versions of Docker. The packages have been renamed a few times, so you'll need to specify several possibilities here:

```
$ sudo apt-get remove docker docker.io containerd runc
$ sudo apt-get remove docker-engine
```

It is safe to ignore `apt-get` errors that say "Unable to locate package" or "Package is not installed."

Next, you will need to add the required software dependencies and *apt* repository for Docker Community Edition. This lets us fetch and install packages for Docker and validate that they are signed:

```
$ sudo apt-get update
$ sudo apt-get install \
    ca-certificates \
    curl \
    gnupg \
    lsb-release
$ sudo mkdir -p /etc/apt/keyrings
$ curl -fsSL https://download.docker.com/linux/ubuntu/gpg |\
    sudo gpg --dearmor -o /etc/apt/keyrings/docker.gpg
$ sudo chmod a+r /etc/apt/keyrings/docker.gpg
$ echo \
```

```
"deb [arch=$(dpkg --print-architecture) \
signed-by=/etc/apt/keyrings/docker.gpg] \
https://download.docker.com/linux/ubuntu \
$(lsb_release -cs) stable" |\
sudo tee /etc/apt/sources.list.d/docker.list > /dev/null
```

Now that you have the repository set up, run the following commands to install Docker:

```
$ sudo apt-get update
$ sudo apt-get install \
    docker-ce \
    docker-ce-cli \
    containerd.io \
    docker-compose-plugin
```

Assuming you don't get any error messages, you now have Docker installed!

Fedora Linux 36 (64-bit)

Now let's take a look at the steps needed to install Docker on the 64-bit version of Fedora Linux 36.

 For up-to-date instructions or coverage of other versions of Fedora, see the Docker Community Edition for Fedora (*https://dockr.ly/ 2NwNdTa*).

This first command will ensure that you aren't running older versions of Docker. As on Ubuntu systems, the package has been renamed a few times, so you'll need to specify several possibilities here:

```
$ sudo dnf remove -y \
    docker \
    docker-client \
    docker-client-latest \
    docker-common \
    docker-latest \
    docker-latest-logrotate \
    docker-logrotate \
    docker-selinux \
    docker-engine-selinux \
    docker-engine
```

Next, you will need to add the required software dependencies and *dnf* repository for Docker Community Edition:

```
$ sudo dnf -y install dnf-plugins-core
$ sudo dnf config-manager \
    --add-repo \
    https://download.docker.com/linux/fedora/docker-ce.repo
```

Now you can install the current version of Docker Community Edition:

```
$ sudo dnf install -y \
    docker-ce \
    docker-ce-cli \
    containerd.io \
    docker-compose-plugin
```

macOS, Mac OS X

To install Docker on macOS, you should use the official Docker Desktop installer.

GUI installer

Download the latest Docker Desktop for Mac installer (*https://dockr.ly/2wyTpCO*), and then double-click on the downloaded program icon. Follow all of the installer's prompts until the installation is finished. Docker Desktop for macOS relies on the xhyve (*https://github.com/machyve/xhyve*) project and Apple's Hypervisor framework (*https://developer.apple.com/documentation/hypervisor*) to provide a native lightweight virtualization layer for the Linux server component, which is required to launch Linux virtual machines that can build Docker images and run containers.

Homebrew installation

You can also install the Docker CLI tools using the popular Homebrew (*https://docs.brew.sh/Installation*) package management system for macOS. If you take this approach, you should consider installing Vagrant for creating and managing your Linux VM. We'll discuss that shortly in "Non-Linux VM-Based Server" on page 40.

Microsoft Windows 11

Here are the steps required to install Docker Desktop on Windows 11.

It is highly recommended that you set up the Windows Subsystem for Linux (WSL2) (*https://docs.microsoft.com/en-us/windows/wsl/install*) *before* installing Docker Desktop, and then select any available options in the Docker Desktop installer to enable and default to WSL2.

Docker Desktop for Windows can leverage Hyper-V (*https://oreil.ly/vt6-o*)[1] to provide a native virtualization layer for the Linux server components, but WSL2 (*https://docs.microsoft.com/en-us/windows/wsl/install*) should provide you with the smoothest experience when working with Linux containers.

---

1 Full URL: *https://learn.microsoft.com/en-us/virtualization/hyper-v-on-windows/about*

Download the latest Docker Desktop for Windows installer (*https://dockr.ly/2C0n7H0*), and then double-click on the downloaded program icon. Follow all of the installer prompts until the installation is finished.

Enabling Linux Container Mode for Windows

By default, your Docker Desktop installation on Windows should be set up for Linux containers, but if you ever get a message that says something like "no matching manifest for windows/amd64," then Docker Desktop is likely configured for Windows containers.

Linux containers are still the most common type of Linux container, and this book requires Linux container support. You can easily change your Windows setup by right-clicking on the Docker icon in the Windows taskbar and selecting "Switch to Linux containers…," as shown in Figures 3-1 and 3-2.

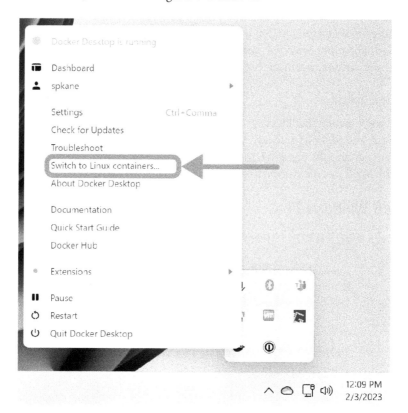

Figure 3-1. Switch to Linux containers

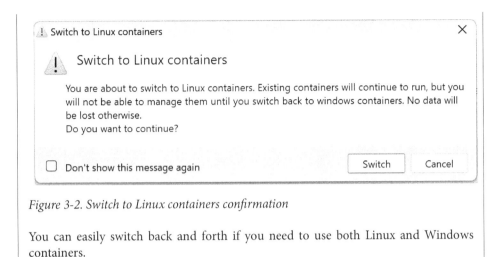

Figure 3-2. Switch to Linux containers confirmation

You can easily switch back and forth if you need to use both Linux and Windows containers.

Chocolatey installation

You can also install the Docker CLI tools using the popular Chocolatey (*https://docs.chocolatey.org/en-us/choco/setup*) package management system for Windows. If you take this approach, you should consider installing Vagrant for creating and managing your Linux VM. We'll discuss that shortly in "Non-Linux VM-Based Server" on page 40.

The Docker website (*https://docs.docker.com/engine/install*) has installation directions for additional environments online.

Docker Server

The Docker server is a separate binary from the client and is used to manage most of the work for which Docker is typically used. Next we will explore the most common ways to manage the Docker server.

Docker Desktop and Docker Community Edition already set up the server for you, so if you took that route, you do not need to do anything else besides ensuring that the server (dockerd) is running. On Windows and macOS, this typically just means starting the Docker application. On Linux, you may need to run the following systemctl commands to start the server.

systemd-Based Linux

Current Fedora and Ubuntu releases use systemd (*https://www.freedesktop.org/wiki/Software/systemd*) to manage processes on the system. Because you have already installed Docker, you can ensure that the server starts every time you boot the system by typing this:

```
$ sudo systemctl enable docker
```

This tells systemd to enable the docker service and start it when the system boots or switches into the default run level. To start the Docker server, type the following:

```
$ sudo systemctl start docker
```

Non-Linux VM-Based Server

If you are using Microsoft Windows or macOS in your Docker workflow, you will need a VM so that you can set up a Docker server for testing. Docker Desktop is convenient because it sets up this VM for you using the native virtualization technology on these platforms. If you are running an older version of Windows or cannot use Docker Desktop for other reasons, you should investigate Vagrant (*https://www.vagrantup.com*) to help you create and manage your Docker server Linux VM.

In addition to using Vagrant, you can also use other virtualization tools, like Lima on macOS (*https://github.com/lima-vm/lima*) or any standard hypervisor, to set up a local Docker server, depending on your preferences and needs.

Vagrant

Vagrant provides support for multiple hypervisors and can often be leveraged to mimic even the most complex environments.

A common use case for leveraging Vagrant during Docker development is to support testing on images that match your production environment. Vagrant supports everything from broad distributions like Red Hat Enterprise Linux (*https://www.redhat.com/en/technologies/linux-platforms/enterprise-linux*) and Ubuntu (*https://ubuntu.com*) to finely focused atomic host distributions like Fedora CoreOS (*https://getfedora.org/en/coreos*).

You can easily install Vagrant on most platforms by downloading a self-contained package (*https://www.vagrantup.com/downloads.html*).

This Vagrant example is not secure and is not intended to be a recommendation. Instead, it is simply a demonstration of the basic requirements needed to set up a *remote* Docker server VM and make use of it. Securing the server is of critical importance.

Using Docker Desktop for development is often a better option, when possible.

You will need to have a hypervisor, like one of the following, fully installed on your system:

- VirtualBox (*https://www.virtualbox.org/wiki/Downloads*)
  - — Freely available
  - — Supports multiplatforms on most architectures
- VMware Workstation Pro/Fusion (*https://oreil.ly/4uNsR*)[2]
  - — Commercial software
  - — Supports multiplatforms on most architectures
- HyperV (*https://oreil.ly/agPTI*)[3]
  - — Commercial software
  - — Supports Windows on most architectures
- KVM (*https://www.linux-kvm.org*)
  - — Freely available
  - — Supports Linux on most architectures

By default, Vagrant assumes that you are using the VirtualBox hypervisor, but you can change it by using the `--provider` flag (*https://learn.hashicorp.com/tutorials/vagrant/getting-started-providers*) when using the `vagrant` command.

In the following example, you will create a Ubuntu-based Docker host running the Docker daemon. Then you will create a host directory with a name similar to *docker-host* and move into that directory:

```
$ mkdir docker-host
$ cd docker-host
```

In order to use Vagrant, you need to find a Vagrant Box (VM image) (*https://app.vagrantup.com/boxes/search*) that is compatible with your provisioner and architecture. In this example, we will use a Vagrant Box for the Virtual Box hypervisor.

---

2 Full URL: *https://www.vmware.com/products/workstation-pro.html*

3 Full URL: *https://docs.microsoft.com/en-us/virtualization/hyper-v-on-windows/quick-start/enable-hyper-v*

Virtual Box only works on Intel/AMD x86(64) systems, and the Vagrant Box we are using is specifically built for AMD64 systems.

Go ahead and create a new file called *Vagrantfile* with the following contents in it:

```
puts (<<-EOT)
  ----------------------------------------------------------------
  [WARNING] This exposes an unencrypted Docker TCP port on the VM!!

  This is NOT secure and may expose your system to significant risk
  if left running and exposed to the broader network.
  ----------------------------------------------------------------

EOT

$script = <<-SCRIPT
echo \'{"hosts": ["tcp://0.0.0.0:2375", "unix:///var/run/docker.sock"]}\' | \
sudo tee /etc/docker/daemon.json
sudo mkdir -p /etc/systemd/system/docker.service.d
echo -e \"[Service]\nExecStart=\nExecStart=/usr/bin/dockerd\" | \
sudo tee /etc/systemd/system/docker.service.d/docker.conf
sudo systemctl daemon-reload
sudo systemctl restart docker
SCRIPT

Vagrant.configure(2) do |config|

  # Pick a compatible Vagrant Box
  config.vm.box = 'bento/ubuntu-20.04'

  # Install Docker if it is not already on the VM image
  config.vm.provision :docker

  # Configure Docker to listen on an unencrypted local port
  config.vm.provision "shell",
    inline: $script,
    run: "always"

  # Port-forward the Docker port to
  # 12375 (or another open port) on our host machine
  config.vm.network "forwarded_port",
    guest: 2375,
    host: 12375,
    protocol: "tcp",
    auto_correct: true

end
```

You can retrieve a complete copy of this file by running this:

```
$ git clone https://github.com/bluewhalebook/\
docker-up-and-running-3rd-edition.git --config core.autocrlf=input
$ cd docker-up-and-running-3rd-edition/chapter_03/vagrant
$ ls Vagrantfile
```

You may need to remove the "\" in the git clone command and reassemble the URL into a single line. It is there because the command is too long for the standard printed page, and this should work in a standard Unix shell as long as there are no leading or trailing spaces in either line.

Ensure that you are in the directory with the *Vagrantfile*, and then run the following command to start the Vagrant VM.

This setup is provided as a simple example. It is not secure and should not be left running without ensuring that the server cannot be accessed from the broader network.

Docker maintains documentation on how to secure your Docker endpoint with SSH or TLS client certificates (*https://docs.docker.com/engine/security/protect-access*) and provides some additional information about the attack surface of the Docker daemon (*https://docs.docker.com/engine/security/#docker-daemon-attack-surface*).

```
$ vagrant up
…
Bringing machine 'default' up with 'virtualbox' provider…
==> default: Importing base box 'bento/ubuntu-20.04'…
==> default: Matching MAC address for NAT networking…
==> default: Checking if box 'bento/ubuntu-20.04' version '…' is up to date…
==> default: A newer version of the box 'bento/ubuntu-20.04' for provider…
==> default: available! You currently have version '…'. The latest is version
==> default: '202206.03.0'. Run `vagrant box update` to update.
==> default: Setting the name of the VM: vagrant_default_1654970697417_18732
==> default: Clearing any previously set network interfaces…
…
==> default: Running provisioner: docker…
    default: Installing Docker onto machine…
==> default: Running provisioner: shell…
    default: Running: inline script
    default: {"hosts": ["tcp://0.0.0.0:2375", "unix:///var/run/docker.sock"]}
    default: [Service]
    default: ExecStart=
    default: ExecStart=/usr/bin/dockerd
```

On macOS, you may see an error like this:

```
VBoxManage: error: Details: code NS_ERROR_FAILURE
(0x80004005), component MachineWrap, interface IMachine
```

This is due to the security features in macOS. A quick search should lead you to an online post that describes the fix (*https://scriptcrunch.com/solved-vboxmanage-error-component-machinewrap*).

Once the VM is running, you should be able to connect to the Docker server by running the following command and telling the Docker client where it should connect to with the -H argument:

```
$ docker -H 127.0.0.1:12375 version
Client:
 Cloud integration: v1.0.24
 Version:           20.10.14
 API version:       1.41
 …

Server: Docker Engine - Community
 Engine:
  Version:          20.10.17
  API version:      1.41 (minimum version 1.12)
  …
```

The output will provide you with version information about the various components that make up the Docker client and server.

Passing in the IP address and port every time you want to run a Docker command is not ideal, but luckily Docker can be set up to know about multiple Docker servers by using the docker context command. To start, let's check and see what context is currently in use. Take note of the entry that has an asterisk (*) next to it, which designates the current context:

```
$ docker context list
NAME      TYPE … DOCKER ENDPOINT              …
default * moby … unix:///var/run/docker.sock …
…
```

You can create a new context for the Vagrant VM and then make it active by running the following sequence of commands:

```
$ docker context create vagrant --docker host=tcp://127.0.0.1:12375
vagrant
Successfully created context "vagrant"

$ docker context use vagrant
vagrant
```

If you re-list all the contexts now, you should see something like this:

```
$ docker context list
NAME        TYPE … DOCKER ENDPOINT          …
default     moby … unix:///var/run/docker.sock …
vagrant *   moby … tcp://127.0.0.1:12375      …
…
```

With your current context set to `vagrant`, running `docker version` without the additional `-H` argument will still connect to the correct Docker server and return the same information as before.

To connect to a shell on the Vagrant-based VM, you can run the following:

```
$ vagrant ssh
…
Welcome to Ubuntu 20.04.3 LTS (GNU/Linux 5.4.0-91-generic x86_64)
…
vagrant@vagrant:~$ exit
```

Until you have time to secure this setup, it is best to go ahead and shut down the VM and set your context back to its original state:

```
$ vagrant halt
…
==> default: Attempting graceful shutdown of VM…

$ docker version
Cannot connect to … daemon at tcp://127.0.0.1:12375. Is the … daemon running?

$ docker context use default
default
```

 If you are using macOS, you might want to take a look at Colima (*https://github.com/abiosoft/colima*), which makes it very easy to spin up and manage a flexible Docker or Kubernetes VM.

Testing the Setup

Once you have a working client and server set up, you are ready to test that everything is working. You should be able to run any one of the following commands on your local system to tell the Docker daemon to download the latest official container for that distribution and then launch it with a running Unix shell process.

This step is important to ensure that all the pieces are properly installed and communicating with one another as expected. It shows off one of the features of Docker: we can run containers based on any Linux distribution we like. In the next few steps, we'll run Linux containers based on Ubuntu, Fedora, and Alpine Linux. You don't need to run them all to prove that this works; running one of them will suffice.

If you are using the Docker client on a Linux system, you may need to prepend each docker command with sudo since the *root* user may be the only one with Docker access, by default.

Most Docker installs create a docker group that can be used to manage who has access to the dockerd Unix socket. You can add your user to that group so that you no longer need to use the sudo command (*https://man7.org/linux/man-pages/man8/sudo.8.html*).

Ubuntu

Let's try launching a container using the latest Ubuntu Linux base image:

```
$ docker container run --rm -ti docker.io/ubuntu:latest /bin/bash

root@aa9b72ae1fea:/#
```

Using docker container run is functionally the same as using docker run.

Fedora

In this example, we launch a container using the latest Fedora Linux base image:

```
$ docker container run --rm -ti docker.io/fedora:latest /bin/bash

[root@5c97201e827b /]# exit
```

Alpine Linux

And then finally, we can test launching a container using the latest Alpine Linux base image:

```
$ docker container run --rm -ti docker.io/alpine:latest /bin/sh

/ # exit
```

docker.io/ubuntu:latest, docker.io/fedora:latest, and docker.io/alpine:latest all represent a Docker image repository, followed by an image name and an image tag.

Exploring the Docker Server

Although the Docker server is often installed, enabled, and run automatically, it's useful to see that running the Docker daemon manually on a Linux system (*https://docs.docker.com/engine/reference/commandline/dockerd*) can be as simple as typing something like this:

```
$ sudo dockerd -H unix:///var/run/docker.sock \
  --config-file /etc/docker/daemon.json
```

 This section assumes that you are on the actual Linux server or VM that is running the Docker daemon. If you are using Docker Desktop on Windows or Mac, you won't be able to easily interact with the dockerd executable, as it is intentionally hidden from the end user, but we'll show you a trick in just a moment.

This command starts the Docker daemon, creates and listens to a Unix domain socket (`-H unix:///var/run/docker.sock`), and reads in the rest of the configuration from */etc/docker/daemon.json*. You're not likely to have to start the Docker server yourself, but that's what's going on behind the scenes. On non-Linux systems, you will typically have a Linux-based VM that hosts the Docker server. Docker Desktop sets up this VM for you in the background.

 If you already have Docker running, executing the daemon again will fail because it can't use the same network port twice.

In most cases, it is very easy to SSH into your new Docker server and take a look around, but the seamless experience of Docker Desktop on a non-Linux system means it is often not apparent that Docker Desktop is leveraging a local VM on which to run the Docker daemon. Because the Docker Desktop VM is designed to be very small and very stable, it does not run an SSH daemon and is, therefore, a bit tricky to access.

If you are curious or just ever have a need to access the underlying VM, you can do it, but it requires a little advanced knowledge. We will talk about the command nsenter in much more detail in "nsenter" on page 334, but for now, if you would like to see the VM (or underlying host), you can run these commands:

```
$ docker container run --rm -it --privileged --pid=host debian \
  nsenter -t 1 -m -u -n -i sh

/ # cat /etc/os-release
PRETTY_NAME="Docker Desktop"
```

```
/ # ps | grep dockerd
  1540 root      1:05 /usr/local/bin/dockerd
                        --containerd /var/run/desktop-containerd/containerd.sock
                        --pidfile /run/desktop/docker.pid
                        --swarm-default-advertise-addr=eth0
                        --host-gateway-ip 192.168.65.2

/ # exit
```

This command uses a privileged Debian container that contains the `nsenter` command to manipulate the Linux kernel namespaces so that we can navigate the filesystem of the underlying VM or host.

 This container is privileged to allow us to navigate the underlying host, but you should not get into the habit of using privileged containers when adding individual capabilities or system call privileges will suffice. We discuss this more in "Security" on page 303.

If you can use a Docker server endpoint, this command will give you access to the underlying host.

The Docker daemon configuration is typically stored in *etc/docker/daemon.json*, but you may notice that it exists somewhere like */containers/services/docker/rootfs/etc/ docker/daemon.json* in the Docker Desktop VM. Docker uses reasonable defaults for all its settings, so this file may be very small or even completely absent. If you are using Docker Desktop, you can edit this file by clicking on the Docker icon and selecting Preferences… → Docker Engine, as shown in Figure 3-3.

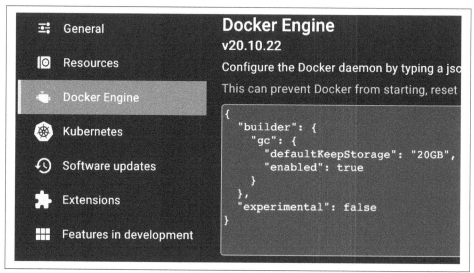

Figure 3-3. Docker Desktop server configuration

Wrap-Up

Now that you have a running Docker setup, you can start to look at more than the basic mechanics of getting it installed. In the next chapter, you'll explore how to build and manage Docker images, which provide the basis for every container you will ever launch with Docker.

 In the rest of the book, when you see docker on the command line, assume you will need to have the correct configuration in place either as a Docker context, environment variables, or via the -H command-line flag to tell the docker client how to connect to the dockerd server process.

## CHAPTER 4

Working with Docker Images

Every Linux container is based on an image. Images are the underlying definition of what gets reconstituted into a running container, much like a virtual disk becomes a VM when you start it up. Docker or Open Container Initiative (OCI) (*https://open containers.org*) images provide the basis for everything that you will ever deploy and run with Docker. To launch a container, you must either download a public image or create your own. You can think of the image as a single asset that primarily represents the filesystem for the container. However, in reality, every image consists of one or more linked filesystem layers that generally have a direct one-to-one mapping to each build step used to create that image.

Because images are built up from individual layers, they put special demands on the Linux kernel, which must provide the drivers that Docker needs to run the storage backend. For image management, Docker relies heavily on this storage backend, which communicates with the underlying Linux filesystem to build and manage the multiple layers that combine into a single usable image. The primary storage backends that are supported include the following:

- Overlay2 (*https://oreil.ly/r4JHY*)[1]
- B-Tree File System (Btrfs) (*https://btrfs.wiki.kernel.org/index.php/Main_Page*)
- Device Mapper (*https://www.sourceware.org/dm*)

Each storage backend provides a fast copy-on-write (CoW) system for image management. We discuss the specifics of various backends in Chapter 11. For now, we'll use the default backend and explore how images work, since they make up the basis for almost everything else that you will do with Docker, including the following:

---

[1] Full URL: *https://github.com/torvalds/linux/commit/e9be9d5e76e34872f0c37d72e25bc27fe9e2c54c*

- Building images
- Uploading (pushing) images to an image registry
- Downloading (pulling) images from an image registry
- Creating and running containers from an image

Anatomy of a Dockerfile

To create a custom Docker image with the default tools, you will need to become familiar with the *Dockerfile*. This file describes all the steps that are required to create an image and is usually contained within the root directory of the source code repository for your application.

A typical *Dockerfile* might look something like the one shown here, which creates a container for a Node.js-based application:

```
FROM node:18.13.0

ARG email="anna@example.com"
LABEL "maintainer"=$email
LABEL "rating"="Five Stars" "class"="First Class"

USER root

ENV AP /data/app
ENV SCPATH /etc/supervisor/conf.d

RUN apt-get -y update

# The daemons
RUN apt-get -y install supervisor
RUN mkdir -p /var/log/supervisor

# Supervisor Configuration
COPY ./supervisord/conf.d/* $SCPATH/

# Application Code
COPY *.js* $AP/

WORKDIR $AP

RUN npm install

CMD ["supervisord", "-n"]
```

Dissecting this *Dockerfile* will provide some initial exposure to a number of the possible instructions for controlling how an image is assembled. Each line in a *Dockerfile* creates a new image layer that is stored by Docker. This layer contains all of the changes that are a result of that command being issued. This means that when you build new images, Docker will only need to build layers that deviate from previous builds: you can reuse all the layers that haven't changed.

Although you could build a Node instance from a plain, base Linux image, you can also explore Docker Hub (*https://registry.hub.docker.com*) for official images for Node. The Node.js community maintains a series of Docker images (*https://registry.hub.docker.com/_/node*) and tags that allow you to quickly determine what versions are available. If you want to lock the image to a specific point release of Node, you could point it at something like `node:18.13.0`. The following base image will provide you with an Ubuntu Linux image running Node 11.11.x:

```
FROM docker.io/node:18.13.0
```

The `ARG` parameter provides a way for you to set variables and their default values, which are only available during the image build process:

```
ARG email="anna@example.com"
```

Applying labels to images and containers allows you to add metadata via key/value pairs that can later be used to search for and identify Docker images and containers. You can see the labels applied to any image using the `docker image inspect` command. For the maintainer label, we are leveraging the value of the `email` build argument that was defined in the previous line of the *Dockerfile*. This means that this label can be changed anytime we build this image:

```
LABEL "maintainer"=$email
LABEL "rating"="Five Stars" "class"="First Class"
```

By default, Docker runs all processes as `root` within the container, but you can use the `USER` instruction to change this:

```
USER root
```

 Even though containers provide some isolation from the underlying operating system, they still run on the host kernel. Due to potential security risks, production containers should almost always be run in the context of an unprivileged user.

Unlike the `ARG` instruction, the `ENV` instruction allows you to set shell variables that can be used by your running application for configuration, in addition to being available during the build process. The `ENV` and `ARG` instructions can be used to simplify the *Dockerfile* and help keep it DRYer (Don't Repeat Yourself):

```
ENV AP /data/app
ENV SCPATH /etc/supervisor/conf.d
```

In the following code, you'll use a collection of RUN instructions to start and create the required file structure that you need, and install some required software dependencies:

```
RUN apt-get -y update

# The daemons
RUN apt-get -y install supervisor
RUN mkdir -p /var/log/supervisor
```

 While we're demonstrating it here for simplicity, it is not recommended that you run commands like apt-get -y update or dnf -y update in your application's *Dockerfile*. This is because it requires crawling the repository index each time you run a build, which means that your build is not guaranteed to be repeatable since package versions might change between builds. Instead, consider basing your application image on another image that already has these updates applied to it and where the versions are in a known state. It will be faster and more repeatable.

The COPY instruction is used to copy files from the local filesystem into your image. Most often this will include your application code and any required support files. Because COPY copies the files into the image, you no longer need access to the local filesystem to access them once the image is built. You'll also start to use the build variables you defined in the previous section to save you a bit of work and help protect you from typos:

```
# Supervisor Configuration
COPY ./supervisord/conf.d/* $SCPATH/

# Application Code
COPY *.js* $AP/
```

 Remember that every instruction creates a new Docker image layer, so it often makes sense to combine a few logically grouped commands onto a single line. It is even possible to use the COPY instruction in combination with the RUN instruction to copy a complex script to your image and then execute that script with only two commands in the *Dockerfile*.

With the WORKDIR instruction, you change the working directory in the image for the remaining build instructions and the default process that launches with any resulting containers:

```
WORKDIR $AP

RUN npm install
```

 The order of commands in a *Dockerfile* can have a very significant impact on ongoing build times. You should try to order commands so that things that change between every single build are closer to the bottom. This means that adding your code and similar steps should be held off until the end. When you rebuild an image, every single layer after the first introduced change will need to be rebuilt.

And finally, you end with the CMD instruction, which defines the command that launches the process that you want to run within the container:

```
CMD ["supervisord", "-n"]
```

 Though not a hard-and-fast rule, it is generally considered a best practice to try to run only a single process within a container. The core idea is that a container should provide a single function so that it remains easy to horizontally scale individual functions within your architecture. In the example, you are using supervisord as a process manager to help improve the resiliency of the node application within the container and ensure that it stays running. This can also be useful for troubleshooting your application during development so that you can restart your service without restarting the whole container.

You could also achieve a similar effect by using the --init command-line argument to docker container run, which we discuss in "Controlling Processes" on page 179.

Building an Image

To build your first image, go ahead and clone a Git repo that contains an example application called *docker-node-hello*, as shown here:[2]

```
$ git clone https://github.com/spkane/docker-node-hello.git \
    --config core.autocrlf=input
Cloning into 'docker-node-hello'…
remote: Counting objects: 41, done.
remote: Total 41 (delta 0), reused 0 (delta 0), pack-reused 41
Unpacking objects: 100% (41/41), done.

$ cd docker-node-hello
```

---

2 This code was originally forked from GitHub (*https://github.com/enokd/docker-node-hello*).

Git is frequently installed on Linux and macOS systems, but if you do not already have Git available, you can download a simple installer from *git-scm.com* (*https://git-scm.com/downloads*).

The --config core.autocrlf=input option we use helps ensure that the line endings are not accidentally altered from the Linux standard that is expected.

This will download a working *Dockerfile* and related source code files into a directory called *docker-node-hello*. If you look at the contents while ignoring the Git repo directory, you should see the following:

```
$ tree -a -I .git
.
├── .dockerignore
├── .gitignore
├── Dockerfile
├── index.js
├── package.json
└── supervisord
    └── conf.d
        ├── node.conf
        └── supervisord.conf
```

Let's review the most relevant files in the repo.

The *Dockerfile* should be the same as the one you just reviewed.

The *.dockerignore* file allows you to define files and directories that you do not want to upload to the Docker host when you are building the image. In this instance, the *.dockerignore* file contains the following line:

```
.git
```

This instructs docker image build to exclude the *.git* directory, which contains the whole source code repository, from the build. The rest of the files reflect the current state of your source code on the checked-out branch. You don't need the contents of the *.git* directory to build the Docker image, and since it can grow quite large over time, you don't want to waste time copying it every time you do a build. *package.json* defines the Node.js application and lists any dependencies that it relies on. *index.js* is the main source code for the application.

The *supervisord* directory contains the configuration files for supervisord that you will use to start and monitor the application.

Using supervisord (*http://supervisord.org*) in this example to monitor the application is overkill, but it is intended to provide a bit of insight into some of the techniques you can use in a container to provide more control over your application and its running state.

As we discussed in Chapter 3, you will need to have your Docker server running and your client properly set up to communicate with it before you can build a Docker image. Assuming that this is all working, you should be able to initiate a new build by running the upcoming command, which will build and tag an image based on the files in the current directory.

Each step identified in the following output maps directly to a line in the *Dockerfile*, and each step creates a new image layer based on the previous step. The first build that you run will take a few minutes because you have to download the base node image. Subsequent builds should be much faster unless a new version of our base image tag has been released.

> The output that follows is from the new BuildKit included in Docker. If you see significantly different output, then you are likely still using the older image building code.
>
> You can enable BuildKit in your environment by setting the DOCKER_BUILDKIT environment variable to 1.
>
> You can find more details on the Docker website (*https:// docs.docker.com/build/buildkit*).

At the end of the build command, you will notice a period. This refers to the build context, which tells Docker what files it should upload to the server so that it can build our image. In many cases, you will simply see a . at the end of a build command, since a single period represents the current directory. This build context is what the *.dockerignore* file is filtering so that we don't upload more than we need.

> Docker assumes that the *Dockerfile* is in the current directory, but if it is not, you can point directly to it using the -f argument.

Let's run the build:

```
$ docker image build -t example/docker-node-hello:latest .

 => [internal] load build definition from Dockerfile
 => => transferring dockerfile: 37B
 => [internal] load .dockerignore
 => => transferring context: 34B
 => [internal] load metadata for docker.io/library/node:18.13.0
 => CACHED [1/8] FROM docker.io/library/node:18.13.0@19a9713dbaf3a3899ad…
 => [internal] load build context
 => => transferring context: 233B
 => [2/8] RUN apt-get -y update
 => [3/8] RUN apt-get -y install supervisor
```

```
=> [4/8] RUN mkdir -p /var/log/supervisor
=> [5/8] COPY ./supervisord/conf.d/* /etc/supervisor/conf.d/
=> [6/8] COPY *.js* /data/app/
=> [7/8] WORKDIR /data/app
=> [8/8] RUN npm install
=> exporting to image
=> => exporting layers
=> => writing image sha256:991844271ca5b984939ab49d81b24d4d53137f04a1bd…
=> => naming to docker.io/example/docker-node-hello:latest
```

To improve the speed of builds, Docker will use a local cache when it thinks it is safe. This can sometimes lead to unexpected issues because it doesn't always notice that something changed in a lower layer. In the preceding output, you will notice lines like ⇒ [2/8] RUN apt-get -y update. If instead you see ⇒ CACHED [2/8] RUN apt-get -y update, you know that Docker decided to use the cache. You can disable the cache for a build by using the --no-cache argument to the docker image build command.

If you are building your Docker images on a system that is used for other simultaneous processes, you can limit the resources available to your builds by using many of the same cgroup methods that we will discuss in Chapter 5. You can find detailed documentation on the docker image build arguments in the official documentation (*https://docs.docker.com/engine/reference/commandline/image_build*).

Using docker image build is functionally the same as using docker build.

If you have any issues getting a build to work correctly, you may want to skip ahead and read the sections "Multistage builds" on page 78 and "Troubleshooting Broken Builds" on page 92 in this chapter.

Running Your Image

Once you have successfully built the image, you can run it on your Docker host with the following command:

```
$ docker container run --rm -d -p 8080:8080 example/docker-node-hello:latest
```

This command tells Docker to create a running container in the background from the image with the example/docker-node-hello:latest tag, and then map port 8080 in the container to port 8080 on the Docker host. If everything goes as expected, the new Node.js application should be running in a container on the host. You can verify this by running `docker container ls`. To see the running application in action, you will need to open up a web browser and point it at port 8080 on the Docker host. You can usually determine the Docker host IP address by examining the entry from `docker context list` that is marked with an asterisk or checking the value of the `DOCKER_HOST` environment variable if it happens to be set. If the `DOCKER ENDPOINT` is set to a Unix socket, then the IP address is most likely `127.0.0.1`:

```
$ docker context list
NAME       TYPE … DOCKER ENDPOINT              …
default * moby … unix:///var/run/docker.sock …
…
```

Get the IP address and enter something like *http://127.0.0.1:8080/* (or your remote Docker address if it's different than that) into your web browser address bar, or use a command-line tool like `curl`. You should see the following text:

```
Hello World. Wish you were here.
```

Build Arguments

If you inspect the image that we built, you will be able to see that the maintainer label was set to `anna@example.com`:

```
$ docker image inspect \
   example/docker-node-hello:latest | grep maintainer
         "maintainer": "anna@example.com",
```

If we wanted to change the `maintainer` label, we could simply rerun the build and provide a new value for the `email ARG` via the `--build-arg` command-line argument, like so:

```
$ docker image build --build-arg email=me@example.com \
    -t example/docker-node-hello:latest .

…
 => => naming to docker.io/example/docker-node-hello:latest
```

After the build has finished, we can check the results by reinspecting the new image:

```
$ docker image inspect \
   example/docker-node-hello:latest | grep maintainer
         "maintainer": "me@example.com",
```

The `ARG` and `ENV` instructions can help make *Dockerfile*s very flexible while also avoiding a lot of repeated values that can be hard to keep up to date.

Environment Variables as Configuration

If you read the *index.js* file, you will notice that part of the file refers to the variable $WHO, which the application uses to determine who the application is going to say Hello to:

```
var DEFAULT_WHO = "World";
var WHO = process.env.WHO || DEFAULT_WHO;

app.get('/', function (req, res) {
  res.send('Hello ' + WHO + '. Wish you were here.\n');
});
```

Let's quickly cover how you can configure this application by passing in environment variables when you start it. First, you need to stop the existing container using two commands. The first command will provide you with the container ID, which you will need to use in the second command:

```
$ docker container ls
CONTAINER ID   IMAGE                             STATUS        …
b7145e06083f   example/centos-node-hello:latest  Up 4 minutes …
```

You can format the output of docker container ls by using a Go template (*https://developer.hashicorp.com/nomad/tutorials/tem plates/go-template-syntax*) so that you see only the information that you care about. In the preceding example, you might decide to run something like docker container ls --format "table {{.ID}}\t{{.Image}}\t{{.Status}}" to limit the output to the three fields you care about. Additionally, running docker con tainer ls --quiet with no format options will limit the output to only the container ID.

And then, using the container ID from the previous output, you can stop the running container by typing the following:

```
$ docker container stop b7145e06083f
b7145e06083f
```

Using docker container ls is functionally equivalent to using docker container list, docker container ps, or docker ps.

Using docker container stop is also functionally equivalent to using docker stop.

You can then restart the container after adding a single instance of the --env argument to the previous docker container run command:

```
$ docker container run --rm -d \
    --publish mode=ingress,published=8080,target=8080 \
    --env WHO="Sean and Karl" \
    example/docker-node-hello:latest
```

If you reload your web browser, you should see that the text on the web page now reads as follows:

```
Hello Sean and Karl. Wish you were here.
```

 You could shorten the preceding docker command to the following if you wanted:

```
$ docker container run --rm -d -p 8080:8080 \
    -e WHO="Sean and Karl" \
    example/docker-node-hello:latest
```

You can go ahead and stop this container now, by using docker container stop and passing in the correct container ID.

Custom Base Images

Base images are the lowest-level images that other Docker images will build upon. Most often, these are based on minimal installs of Linux distributions like Ubuntu, Fedora, or Alpine Linux, but they can also be much smaller, containing a single statically compiled binary. For most people, using the official base images for their favorite distribution or tool is a great option.

However, there are times when it is preferable to build your own base images rather than use an image created by someone else. One reason to do this is to maintain a consistent OS image across all your deployment methods for hardware, VMs, and containers. Another is to get the image size down substantially. There is no need to ship around an entire Ubuntu distribution, for example, if your application is a statically built C or Go application. You might find that you only need the tools you regularly use for debugging, and some other shell commands and binaries. Making the effort to build such an image could pay off in better deployment times and easier application distribution.

A common middle ground between these two approaches is to build images using Alpine Linux, which is designed to be very small and is popular as a basis for Docker images. To keep the distribution size very small, Alpine Linux is based on the modern, lightweight musl standard library (*https://musl.libc.org*), instead of the more traditional GNU C Library (glibc) (*https://www.gnu.org/software/libc*). In general, this is not a big issue, since many packages support *musl*, but it is something to be aware of. It has the largest impact on Java-based applications and DNS resolution. It's widely used in production, however, because of its diminutive image size. Alpine Linux is highly optimized for space, which is the reason that it ships with */bin/sh* instead of */bin/bash*, by default. However, you can also install *glibc and bash* in Alpine Linux if you need it, and this is often done in the case of JVM containers.

In the official Docker documentation, there is some good information about how you can build base images on the various Linux distributions (*https://dockr.ly/2N1FZcU*).

Storing Images

Now that you have created a Docker image that you're happy with, you'll want to store it somewhere so that it can be easily accessed by any Docker host that you want to deploy it to. This is also the normal hand-off point between building images and storing them somewhere for future deployment. You don't normally build the images on a production server and then run them. This process was described when we talked about handoff between teams for application deployment. Ordinarily, deployment is the process of pulling an image from a repository and running it on one or more Linux servers. There are a few ways you can go about storing your images into a central repository for easy retrieval.

Public Registries

Docker provides an image registry (*https://registry.hub.docker.com*) for public images that the community wants to share. These include official images for Linux distributions, ready-to-go WordPress containers, and much more.

If you have images that can be published on the internet, the best place for them is a public registry, like Docker Hub (*https://hub.docker.com*). However, there are other options. When the core Docker tools were first gaining popularity, Docker Hub did not exist. To fill this obvious void in the community, Quay.io (*https://quay.io*) was created. Since then, Quay.io has gone through a few acquisitions and is now owned by Red Hat. Cloud vendors like Google and SaaS companies like GitHub also have their own registry offerings. Here we'll talk about just the two of them.

Both Docker Hub and Quay.io provide centralized Docker image registries that can be accessed from anywhere on the internet, and provide a method to store private images in addition to public ones. Both have nice user interfaces and the ability to separate team access permissions and manage users. Both also offer reasonable commercial options for private SaaS hosting of your images, much in the same way that GitHub sells private registries on its systems. This is probably the right first step if you're getting serious about Docker but are not yet shipping enough code to need an internally hosted solution.

For companies that use Docker heavily, one of the biggest downsides to these registries is that they are not local to the network on which the application is being deployed. This means that every layer of every deployment might need to be dragged across the internet to deploy an application. Internet latencies have a very real impact on software deployments, and outages that affect these registries could have a very detrimental impact on a company's ability to deploy smoothly and on schedule. This is mitigated by good image design, where you make thin layers that are easy to move around the internet.

Private Registries

The other option that many companies consider is to host some type of Docker image registry internally, which can interact with the Docker client to support pushing, pulling, and searching images. The open source Distribution (*https://git hub.com/distribution/distribution*) project provides the basic functionality that most other registries build upon.

Other strong contenders in the private registry space include Harbor (*https://gohar bor.io*) and Red Hat Quay (*https://www.redhat.com/en/technologies/cloud-computing/ quay*). In addition to the basic Docker registry functionality, these products have solid GUI interfaces and many additional features, like image verification.

Authenticating to a Registry

Communicating with a registry that stores container images is a part of daily life with Docker. For many registries, this means you'll need to authenticate to gain access to images. But Docker also tries to make it easy to automate things so it can store your login information and use it on your behalf when you request things like pulling down a private image. By default, Docker assumes the registry will be Docker Hub, the public repository hosted by Docker, Inc.

 Although a bit more advanced, it is worth noting that you can also configure the Docker daemon to use a custom registry mirror (*https://oreil.ly/16Kns*)[3] or a pull-through image cache (*https:// oreil.ly/2Am1f*).[4]

Creating a Docker Hub account

For these examples, you will create an account on Docker Hub. You don't need an account to download publicly shared images, but you will need to be logged in to avoid rate limits and upload any containers that you build.

To create your account, use a web browser of your choice to navigate to Docker Hub (*https://hub.docker.com*).

---

3 Full URL: *https://docs.docker.com/registry/recipes/mirror/#configure-the-docker-daemon*

4 Full URL: *https://docs.docker.com/registry/recipes/mirror/#run-a-registry-as-a-pull-through-cache*

From there, you can log in via an existing account or create a new login based on your email address. When you create your account, Docker Hub sends a verification email to the address that you provided during sign-up. You should immediately log in to your email account and click the verification link inside the email to finish the validation process.

At this point, you have created a public registry to which you can upload new images. The Account Settings (*https://hub.docker.com/settings/default-privacy*) option under your profile picture has a `Default Privacy` section that allows you to change your registry default visibility to `private` if that is what you need.

 For much better security, you should create and log in to Docker Hub with a limited-privilege personal access token (*https://docs.docker.com/go/access-tokens*).

Logging in to a registry

Now let's log in to the Docker Hub registry using our account:

```
$ docker login
Login with your Docker ID to push and pull images from Docker Hub. If you
don't have a Docker ID, head over to https://hub.docker.com to create one.
Username: <hub_username>
Password: <hub_password/token>
Login Succeeded
```

 The command `docker login` is functionally the same command as `docker login docker.io`.

When you get `Login Succeeded` back from the server, you know you're ready to pull images from the registry. But what happened behind the scenes? It turns out that Docker has written a dotfile for you in your home directory to cache this information. The permissions are set to 0600 as a security precaution against other users reading your credentials. You can inspect the file with something like this:

```
$ ls -la ${HOME}/.docker/config.json
-rw-------@ 1 …  158 Dec 24 10:37 /Users/someuser/.docker/config.json

$ cat ${HOME}/.docker/config.json
```

On Linux you will see something like this:

```
{
    "auths": {
```

```
        "https://index.docker.io/v1/": {
          "auth":"cmVsaEXamPL3hElRmFCOUE=",
          "email":"someuser@example.com"
      }
    }
}
```

Docker is constantly evolving and has added support for many
OS native secret management systems like the macOS Keychain
or Windows Credential Manager. So, your *config.json* file might
look significantly different than the example. There is also a set of
credentials managers (*https://github.com/docker/docker-credential-
helpers*) for different platforms that can make your life easier here.

The auth value in the Docker client config file is only base64 enco-
ded. It is *not* encrypted. This is typically only a significant issue on
multiuser Linux systems, because there isn't a default system-wide
credential manager that just works, and other privileged users on
the system can likely read your Docker client config file and access
those secrets. It is possible to configure gpg pr pass to encrypt
these files on Linux.

Here you can see that the *${HOME}/.docker/config.json* file contains docker.io cre-
dentials for the user someuser@example.com in JSON. This configuration file supports storing credentials for multiple registries. In this case, you just have one entry,
for Docker Hub, but you could have more if you needed it. From now on, when the
registry needs authentication, Docker will look in *${HOME}/.docker/config.json* to see
if you have credentials stored for this hostname. If so, it will supply them. You will
notice that one value is completely lacking here: a timestamp. These credentials are
cached forever or until you tell Docker to remove them, whichever comes first.

As with logging in, you can also log out of a registry if you no longer want to cache
the credentials:

```
$ docker logout
Removing login credentials for https://index.docker.io/v1/
$ cat ${HOME}/.docker/config.json

{
  "auths": {
  }
}
```

Here you have removed the cached credentials and they are no longer stored by
Docker. Some versions of Docker may even remove this file if it is empty. If you were
trying to log in to something other than the Docker Hub registry, you could supply
the hostname on the command line:

```
$ docker login someregistry.example.com
```

This would then add another auth entry into your *${HOME}/.docker/config.json* file.

Pushing images into a repository

The first step required to push your image is to ensure that you are logged in to the Docker repository you intend to use. For this example, we will focus on Docker Hub, so ensure that you are logged in to Docker Hub with your preferred credentials:

```
$ docker login
Login with your Docker ID to push and pull images from Docker Hub. If you
don't have a Docker ID, head over to https://hub.docker.com to create one.
Username: <hub_username>
Password: <hub_password/token>
Login Succeeded

Logging in with your password grants your terminal complete access to
your account.
```

Once you are logged in, you can upload an image. Earlier, you used the command `docker image build -t example/docker-node-hello:latest .` to build the docker-node-hello image.

In reality, the Docker client, and for compatibility reasons, many other container tools, actually interpret `example/docker-node-hello:latest` as `docker.io/example/docker-node-hello:latest`. Here, `docker.io` signifies the image registry hostname, and `example/docker-node-hello` is the repository inside the registry that contains the images in question.

When you are building an image locally, the registry and repository name can be anything that you want. However, when you are going to upload your image to a real registry, you need that to match the login.

You can easily edit the tags on the image that you already created by running the following command and replacing ${<myuser>} with your Docker Hub username:

```
$ docker image tag example/docker-node-hello:latest \
    docker.io/${<myuser>}/docker-node-hello:latest
```

If you need to rebuild the image with the new naming convention or simply want to give it a try, you can accomplish this by running the following command in the *docker-node-hello* working directory that was generated when you performed the Git checkout earlier in the chapter.

 For the following examples, you will need to replace ${<myuser>} in all the examples with the user that you created in Docker Hub. If you are using a different registry, you will also need to replace `docker.io` with the hostname of the registry you are using.

```
$ docker image build -t docker.io/${<myuser>}/docker-node-hello:latest .
...
```

On the first build, this will take a little time. If you rebuild the image, you may find that it is very fast. This is because most, if not all, of the layers already exist on your Docker server from the previous build. We can quickly verify that our image is indeed on the server by running docker image ls ${<myuser>}/docker-node-hello:

```
$ docker image ls ${<myuser>}/docker-node-hello
REPOSITORY                   TAG      IMAGE ID       CREATED            SIZE
myuser/docker-node-hello     latest   f683df27f02d   About an hour ago  649MB
```

It is possible to format the output of docker image ls to make it more concise by using the --format argument, like this: docker image ls --format="table {{.ID}}\t{{.Repository}}".

At this point you can upload the image to the Docker repository by using the docker image push command:

```
$ docker image push ${<myuser>}/docker-node-hello:latest
Using default tag: latest
The push refers to repository [docker.io/myuser/docker-node-hello]
5f3ee7afc69c: Pushed
...
5bb0785f2eee: Mounted from library/node
latest: digest: sha256:f5ceb032aec36fcacab71e468eaf0ba8a832cfc8244fbc784d0…
```

If this image was uploaded to a public repository, anyone in the world can now easily download it by running the docker image pull command.

If you uploaded the image to a private repository, then users must log in with credentials that have access to those repositories using the docker login command before they will be able to pull the image down to their local system.

```
$ docker image pull ${<myuser>}/docker-node-hello:latest
Using default tag: latest
latest: Pulling from myuser/docker-node-hello
Digest: sha256:f5ceb032aec36fcacab71e468eaf0ba8a832cfc8244fbc784d040872be041cd5
Status: Image is up to date for myuser/docker-node-hello:latest
docker.io/myuser/docker-node-hello:latest
```

Exploring images in Docker Hub

In addition to simply using the Docker Hub website (*https://hub.docker.com*) to explore what images are available, you can also use the docker search command to find images that might be useful.

Running docker search node will return a list of images that contain the word node in either the image name or the description:

```
$ docker search node
NAME                      DESCRIPTION                   STARS OFFICIAL AUTOMATED
node                      Node.js is a JavaScript-ba… 12267 [OK]
mongo-express             Web-based MongoDB admin in… 1274  [OK]
nodered/node-red          Low-code programming for e… 544
nodered/node-red-docker   Deprecated - older Node-RE… 356           [OK]
circleci/node             Node.js is a JavaScript-ba… 130
kindest/node              sigs.k8s.io/kind node imag… 78
bitnami/node              Bitnami Node.js Docker Ima… 69            [OK]
cimg/node                 The CircleCI Node.js Docke… 14
opendronemap/nodeodm      Automated build for NodeOD… 10            [OK]
bitnami/node-exporter     Bitnami Node Exporter Dock… 9             [OK]
appdynamics/nodejs-agent  Agent for monitoring Node.… 5
wallarm/node              Wallarm: end-to-end API se… 5             [OK]
…
```

The OFFICIAL header tells you that the image is one of the official curated images (*https://docs.docker.com/docker-hub/official_images*) on Docker Hub. This typically means that the image is maintained by the company or official development community that oversees that application. AUTOMATED denotes that the image is automatically built and uploaded by a CI/CD process triggered via commits to the underlying source code repository. Official images are always automated.

Running a Private Registry

In keeping with the spirit of the open source community, Docker encourages the community to share Docker images via Docker Hub by default. There are times, however, when this is not a viable option due to commercial, legal, image retention, or reliability concerns.

In these cases, it makes sense to host an internal private registry. Setting up a basic registry is not difficult, but for production use, you should take the time to familiarize yourself with all the available configuration options for the open source Docker Registry (Distribution) (*https://docs.docker.com/registry*).

For this example, we are going to create a very simple secure registry using SSL and HTTP basic auth.

First, let's create a few directories and files on our Docker server. If you are using a VM or cloud instance to run your Docker server, then you will need to SSH to that

---

server for the next few commands. If you are using Docker Desktop or Community Edition, then you should be able to run these on your local system.

 Windows users may need to download additional tools, like `htppaswd`, or alter the non-Docker commands to accomplish the same tasks on your local system.

First let's clone a Git repository that contains the basic files required to set up a simple, authenticated Docker registry:

```
$ git clone https://github.com/spkane/basic-registry \
  --config core.autocrlf=input
Cloning into 'basic-registry'…
remote: Counting objects: 10, done.
remote: Compressing objects: 100% (8/8), done.
remote: Total 10 (delta 0), reused 10 (delta 0), pack-reused 0
Unpacking objects: 100% (10/10), done.
```

Once you have the files locally, you can change directories and examine the files that you just downloaded:

```
$ cd basic-registry
$ ls
Dockerfile          config.yaml.sample  registry.crt.sample
README.md           htpasswd.sample     registry.key.sample
```

The *Dockerfile* simply takes the upstream registry image from Docker Hub and copies some local configuration and support files into a new image.

For testing, you can use some of the included sample files, but *do not* use these in production.

If your Docker server is available via `localhost` (127.0.0.1), then you can use these files unmodified by simply copying each of them like this:

```
$ cp config.yaml.sample config.yaml
$ cp registry.key.sample registry.key
$ cp registry.crt.sample registry.crt
$ cp htpasswd.sample htpasswd
```

If, however, your Docker server is on a remote IP address, then you will need to do a little additional work.

First, copy *config.yaml.sample* to *config.yaml*:

```
$ cp config.yaml.sample config.yaml
```

Then edit *config.yaml* and replace 127.0.0.1 with the IP address of your Docker server so that:

```
http:
  host: https://127.0.0.1:5000
```

becomes something like this:

```
http:
  host: https://172.17.42.10:5000
```

 It is easy to create a registry using a fully qualified domain name (FQDN), like my-registry.example.com, but for this example, working with IP addresses is easier because no DNS is required.

Next, you need to create an SSL keypair for your registry's IP address.

One way to do this is with the following OpenSSL command. Note that you will need to set the IP address in this portion of the command, /CN=172.17.42.10, to match your Docker server's IP address:

```
$ openssl req -x509 -nodes -sha256 -newkey rsa:4096 \
  -keyout registry.key -out registry.crt \
  -days 14 -subj '{/CN=172.17.42.10}'
```

Finally, you can either use the example htpasswd file by copying it:

```
$ cp htpasswd.sample htpasswd
```

or you can create your own username and password pair for authentication by using a command like the following, replacing ${<username>} and ${<password>} with your preferred values:

```
$ docker container run --rm --entrypoint htpasswd g \
  -Bbn ${<username>} ${<password>} > htpasswd
```

If you look at the directory listing again, it should now look like this:

```
$ ls
Dockerfile        config.yaml.sample  registry.crt         registry.key.sample
README.md         htpasswd            registry.crt.sample
config.yaml       htpasswd.sample     registry.key
```

If any of these files are missing, review the previous steps to ensure that you did not miss one, before moving on.

If everything looks correct, then you should be ready to build and run the registry:

```
$ docker image build -t my-registry .
$ docker container run --rm -d -p 5000:5000 --name registry my-registry
$ docker container logs registry
```

If you see errors like "docker: Error response from daemon: Conflict. The container name "/registry" is already in use," then you need to either change the preceding container name or remove the existing container with that name. You can remove the container by running `docker container rm registry`.

Testing the private registry

Now that the registry is running, you can test it. The very first thing that you need to do is authenticate against it. You will need to make sure that the IP address in the `docker login` matches the IP address of your Docker server that is running the registry.

`myuser` is the default username, and `myuser-pw!` is the default password. If you generated your own `htpasswd`, then these will be whatever you choose.

```
$ docker login 127.0.0.1:5000
Username: <registry_username>
Password: <registry_password>
Login Succeeded
```

This registry container has an embedded SSL key and is not using any external storage, which means that it contains a secret, and when you delete the running container, all your images will also be deleted. This is by design.

In production, you will want to have your containers pull secrets from a secrets management system and use some type of redundant external storage, like an object store. If you want to keep your development registry images between containers, you could add something like `--mount type=bind,source=/tmp/registry-data,target=/var/lib/registry` to your `docker container run` command to store the registry data on the Docker server.

Now, let's see if you can push the image you just built into your local private registry.

In all of these commands, ensure that you use the correct IP address for your registry.

```
$ docker image tag my-registry 127.0.0.1:5000/my-registry
$ docker image push 127.0.0.1:5000/my-registry
Using default tag: latest
The push refers to repository [127.0.0.1:5000/my-registry]
f09a0346302c: Pushed
…
4fc242d58285: Pushed
latest: digest: sha256:c374b0a721a12c41d5b298930d11e658fbd37f22dc2a0fac7d6a2…
```

You can then try to pull the same image from your repository:

```
$ docker image pull 127.0.0.1:5000/my-registry
Using default tag: latest
latest: Pulling from my-registry
Digest: sha256:c374b0a721a12c41d5b298930d11e658fbd37f22dc2a0fac7d6a2ecdc0ba5490
Status: Image is up to date for 127.0.0.1:5000/my-registry:latest
127.0.0.1:5000/my-registry:latest
```

> It's worth keeping in mind that both Docker Hub and Docker
> Distribution expose an API endpoint that you can query for useful
> information. You can find out more information about the API
> via the official documentation (*https://github.com/distribution/distri
> bution/blob/main/docs/spec/api.md*).

If you have not encountered any errors, then you have a working registry for development and can build on this foundation to create a production registry. At this point, you may want to stop the registry for the time being. You can easily accomplish this by running the following:

```
$ docker container stop registry
```

> As you become comfortable with Docker Distribution, you may
> also want to consider exploring the Cloud Native Computing
> Foundation (CNCF) open source project, called Harbor (*https://
> goharbor.io*), which extends the Docker Distribution with a lot of
> security and reliability-focused features.

Optimizing Images

After you have spent a little bit of time working with Docker, you will quickly notice that keeping your image sizes small and your build times fast can be very beneficial in decreasing the time required to build and deploy new versions of your software into production. In this section, we will talk a bit about some of the considerations you should always keep in mind when designing your images and a few techniques that can help you achieve these goals.

Keeping Images Small

In most modern businesses, downloading a single 1 GB file from a remote location on the internet is not something that people often worry about. It is so easy to find software on the internet that people will often rely on simply re-downloading it if they need it again, instead of keeping a local copy for the future. This may often be acceptable when you truly need a single copy of this software on a single server, but it can quickly become a scaling problem when you need the same software on 100+ nodes and you deploy new releases multiple times a day. Downloading these large files can quickly cause network congestion and slower deployment cycles that have a real impact on the production environment.

For convenience, a large number of Linux containers inherit from a base image that contains a minimal Linux distribution. Although this is an easy starting place, it isn't required. Containers only need to contain the files that are required to run the application on the host kernel, and nothing else. The best way to explain this is to explore a very minimal container.

Go is a compiled programming language that can easily generate statically compiled binary files. For this example, we are going to use a very small web application written in Go that can be found on GitHub (*https://github.com/spkane/scratch-helloworld*).

Let's go ahead and try out the application so that you can see what it does. Run the following command, and then open up a web browser and point it to your Docker host on port 8080 (e.g., *http://127.0.0.1:8080* for Docker Desktop and Community Edition):

```
$ docker container run --rm -d -p 8080:8080 spkane/scratch-helloworld
```

If all goes well, you should see the following message in your web browser: "Hello World from Go in minimal Linux container." Now let's take a look at what files this container comprises. It would be fair to assume that at a minimum it will include a working Linux environment and all the files required to compile Go programs, but you will soon see that this is not the case.

While the container is still running, execute the following command to determine what the container ID is. The following command returns the information for the last container that you created:

```
$ docker container ls -l
CONTAINER ID IMAGE                      COMMAND        CREATED         …
ddc3f61f311b spkane/scratch-helloworld "/helloworld"  4 minutes ago   …
```

You can then use the container ID that you obtained from running the previous command to export the files in the container into a tarball, which can be easily examined:

```
$ docker container export ddc3f61f311b -o web-app.tar
```

Using the `tar` command, you can now examine the contents of your container at the time of the export:

```
$ tar -tvf web-app.tar
-rwxr-xr-x 0 0         0          0 Jan  7 15:54 .dockerenv
drwxr-xr-x 0 0         0          0 Jan  7 15:54 dev/
-rwxr-xr-x 0 0         0          0 Jan  7 15:54 dev/console
drwxr-xr-x 0 0         0          0 Jan  7 15:54 dev/pts/
drwxr-xr-x 0 0         0          0 Jan  7 15:54 dev/shm/
drwxr-xr-x 0 0         0          0 Jan  7 15:54 etc/
-rwxr-xr-x 0 0         0          0 Jan  7 15:54 etc/hostname
-rwxr-xr-x 0 0         0          0 Jan  7 15:54 etc/hosts
lrwxrwxrwx 0 0         0          0 Jan  7 15:54 etc/mtab -> /proc/mounts
-rwxr-xr-x 0 0         0          0 Jan  7 15:54 etc/resolv.conf
-rwxr-xr-x 0 0         0    3604416 Jul  2  2014 helloworld
drwxr-xr-x 0 0         0          0 Jan  7 15:54 proc/
drwxr-xr-x 0 0         0          0 Jan  7 15:54 sys/
```

The first thing you might notice here is that there are almost no files in this container, and almost all of them are zero bytes in length. All of the files that have a zero length are required to exist in every Linux container and are automatically bind-mounted (*https://unix.stackexchange.com/questions/198590/what-is-a-bind-mount*) from the host into the container when it is first created. All of these files, except for *.dockerenv*, are critical files that the kernel needs to do its job properly. The only file in this container that has any actual size and is related to our application is the statically compiled `helloworld` binary.

The takeaway from this exercise is that your containers are only required to contain exactly what they need to run on the underlying kernel. Everything else is unnecessary. Because it is often useful for troubleshooting to have access to a working shell in your container, people will often compromise and build their images from a very lightweight Linux distribution like Alpine Linux.

> If you find yourself exploring image files a lot, you might want to take a look at the tool dive (*https://github.com/wagoodman/dive*), which provides a nice CLI interface for understanding what an image contains.

To dive into this a little deeper, let's look at that same container again so that we can dig into the underlying filesystem and compare it with the popular `alpine` base image.

Although we could easily poke around in the `alpine` image by simply running `docker container run -ti alpine:latest /bin/sh`, we cannot do this with the `spkane/scratch-helloworld` image, because it does not contain a shell or SSH. This means that we can't use `ssh`, `nsenter`, or `docker container exec` to examine it, though there is an advanced trick discussed in "Debugging Shell-less Containers" on page 336. Earlier, we took advantage of the docker container export command to create a *.tar* file that contained a copy of all the files in the container, but this time around we are going to examine the container's filesystem by connecting directly to the Docker server and then looking into the container's filesystem itself. To do this, we need to find out where the image files reside on the server's disk.

To determine where on the server our files are actually being stored, run docker image inspect on the alpine:latest image:

```
$ docker image inspect alpine:latest
[
    {
        "Id": "sha256:3fd...353",
        "RepoTags": [
            "alpine:latest"
        ],
        "RepoDigests": [
            "alpine@sha256:7b8...f8b"
        ],
        ...
        "GraphDriver": {
            "Data": {
                "MergedDir":
                "/var/lib/docker/overlay2/ea8...13a/merged",
                "UpperDir":
                "/var/lib/docker/overlay2/ea8...13a/diff",
                "WorkDir":
                "/var/lib/docker/overlay2/ea8...13a/work"
            },
            "Name": "overlay2"
        ...
        }
    }
    ...
]
```

And then on the spkane/scratch-helloworld:latest image:

```
$ docker image inspect spkane/scratch-helloworld:latest
[
    {
        "Id": "sha256:4fa...06d",
        "RepoTags": [
            "spkane/scratch-helloworld:latest"
        ],
        "RepoDigests": [
            "spkane/scratch-helloworld@sha256:46d...a1d"
        ],
        ...
```

```
        "GraphDriver": {
            "Data": {
                "LowerDir":
                "/var/lib/docker/overlay2/37a…84d/diff:
                /var/lib/docker/overlay2/28d…ef4/diff",
                "MergedDir":
                "/var/lib/docker/overlay2/fc9…c91/merged",
                "UpperDir":
                "/var/lib/docker/overlay2/fc9…c91/diff",
                "WorkDir":
                "/var/lib/docker/overlay2/fc9…c91/work"
            },
            "Name": "overlay2"
    …
        }
    }
…
]
```

 In this particular example, we are going to use Docker Desktop running on macOS, but this general approach will work on most Docker servers. However, you can access your Docker server via whatever method is easiest.

Since we are using Docker Desktop, we need to use our `nsenter` trick to enter the SSH-less VM and explore the filesystem:

```
$ docker container run --rm -it --privileged --pid=host debian \
  nsenter -t 1 -m -u -n -i sh

/ #
```

Inside the VM, we should now be able to explore the various directories listed in the `GraphDriver` section of the `docker image inspect` commands.

In this example, if we look at the first entry for the `alpine` image, we will see that it is labeled `MergedDir` and lists the folder */var/lib/docker/overlay2/ea86408b2b15d33ee27d78ff44f82104705286221f055ba1331b58673f4b313a/merged*. If we list that directory, we will get an error, but from listing the parent directory, we quickly discover that we actually want to look at the *diff* directory:

```
/ # ls -lFa /var/lib/docker/overlay2/ea…3a/merged

ls: /var/lib/docker/overlay2/ea..3a/merged: No such file or directory

/ # ls -lF /var/lib/docker/overlay2/ea…3a/

total 8
drwxr-xr-x   18 root      root           4096 Mar 15 19:27 diff/
-rw-r--r--    1 root      root             26 Mar 15 19:27 link
```

```
/ # ls -lF /var/lib/docker/overlay2/ea…3a/diff

total 64
drwxr-xr-x     2 root     root          4096 Jan  9 19:37 bin/
drwxr-xr-x     2 root     root          4096 Jan  9 19:37 dev/
drwxr-xr-x    15 root     root          4096 Jan  9 19:37 etc/
drwxr-xr-x     2 root     root          4096 Jan  9 19:37 home/
drwxr-xr-x     5 root     root          4096 Jan  9 19:37 lib/
drwxr-xr-x     5 root     root          4096 Jan  9 19:37 media/
drwxr-xr-x     2 root     root          4096 Jan  9 19:37 mnt/
dr-xr-xr-x     2 root     root          4096 Jan  9 19:37 proc/
drwx------     2 root     root          4096 Jan  9 19:37 root/
drwxr-xr-x     2 root     root          4096 Jan  9 19:37 run/
drwxr-xr-x     2 root     root          4096 Jan  9 19:37 sbin/
drwxr-xr-x     2 root     root          4096 Jan  9 19:37 srv/
drwxr-xr-x     2 root     root          4096 Jan  9 19:37 sys/
drwxrwxrwt     2 root     root          4096 Jan  9 19:37 tmp/
drwxr-xr-x     7 root     root          4096 Jan  9 19:37 usr/
drwxr-xr-x    11 root     root          4096 Jan  9 19:37 var/

/ # du -sh  /var/lib/docker/overlay2/ea…3a/diff
4.5M    /var/lib/docker/overlay2/ea…3a/diff
```

Now, `alpine` happens to be a very small base image, weighing in at only 4.5 MB, and it is ideal for building containers on top of it. However, we can see that there is still a lot of stuff in this container before we have started to build anything from it.

Now, let's take a look at the files in the `spkane/scratch-helloworld` image. In this case, we want to look at the first directory from the `LowerDir` entry of the `docker image inspect` output, which you'll notice also ends in a directory called *diff*:

```
/ # ls -lFh /var/lib/docker/overlay2/37…4d/diff

total 3520
-rwxr-xr-x     1 root     root          3.4M Jul  2  2014 helloworld*

/ # exit
```

You'll notice that there is only a single file in this directory, and it is 3.4 MB. This `helloworld` binary is the only file shipped in this container and is smaller than the starting size of the `alpine` image before any application files have been added to it.

 It is possible to run the `helloworld` application from that directory on your Docker server because it does not require any other files. You really don't want to do this on anything but a development box, but it can help drive the point home about how useful these types of statically compiled applications can be.

Multistage builds

There is a way you can constrain containers to an even smaller size in many cases: multistage builds. This is how we recommend that you build most production containers. You don't have to worry as much about bringing in extra resources to build your application, and you can still run a lean production container. Multistage containers also encourage doing builds inside Docker, which is a great pattern for repeatability in your build system.

As the original author of the scratch-helloworld application has written (*https://medium.com/@adriaandejonge/simplify-the-smallest-possible-docker-image-62c0e0d342ef*), the release of multistage build support in Docker itself has made the process of creating small containers much easier than it used to be. In the past, to do the same thing that multistage delivers for nearly free, you were required to build one image that compiled your code, extract the resulting binary, and then build a second image without all the build dependencies that you would then inject that binary into. This was often difficult to set up and did not always work out of the box with standard deployment pipelines.

Today, you can now achieve similar results using a *Dockerfile* as simple as this one:

```
# Build container
FROM docker.io/golang:alpine as builder
RUN apk update && \
    apk add git && \
    CGO_ENABLED=0 go install -a -ldflags '-s' \
    github.com/spkane/scratch-helloworld@latest

# Production container
FROM scratch
COPY --from=builder /go/bin/scratch-helloworld /helloworld
EXPOSE 8080
CMD ["/helloworld"]
```

The first thing you'll notice about this *Dockerfile* is that it looks a lot like two *Dockerfiles* that have been combined into one. Indeed this is the case, but there is more to it. The FROM command has been extended so that you can name the image during the build phase. In this example, the first line, which reads FROM docker.io/golang as builder, means that you want to base your build on the golang image and will be referring to this build image/stage as builder.

On the fourth line, you'll see another FROM line, which was not allowed before the introduction of multistage builds. This FROM line uses a special image name, called scratch, that tells Docker to start from an empty image, which includes no additional files. The next line, which reads COPY --from=builder /go/bin/scratch-helloworld /helloworld, allows you to copy the binary that you built in the *builder* image directly into the current image. This will ensure that you end up with the smallest container possible.

The `EXPOSE 8080` line is documentation that is intended to inform users which port(s) and protocols (TCP is the default protocol) the service listens on.

Let's try to build this and see what happens. First, create a directory where you can work, and then, using your favorite text editor, paste the content from the preceding example into a file called *Dockerfile*:

```
$ mkdir /tmp/multi-build
$ cd /tmp/multi-build
$ vi Dockerfile
```

You can download a copy of this *Dockerfile* from GitHub (*https://oreil.ly/C1TSz*).[5]

We can now start the multistage build:

```
$ docker image build .
[+] Building 9.7s (7/7) FINISHED
 => [internal] load build definition from Dockerfile
 => => transferring dockerfile: 37B
 => [internal] load .dockerignore
 => => transferring context: 2B
 => [internal] load metadata for docker.io/library/golang:alpine
 => CACHED [builder 1/2] FROM docker.io/library/golang:alpine@sha256:7cc6257...
 => [builder 2/2] RUN apk update && apk add git && CGO_ENABLED=0 go install ...
 => [stage-1 1/1] COPY --from=builder /go/bin/scratch-helloworld /helloworld
 => exporting to image
 => => exporting layers
 => => writing image sha256:bb853f23418161927498b9631f54692cf11d84d6bde3af2d...
```

You'll notice that the output looks like most other builds and still ends by reporting the successful creation of our final, very minimal image.

> If you are compiling binaries on your local system that use shared libraries, you need to be careful to ensure that the correct versions of those shared libraries are also available to the process inside the container.

---

[5] Full URL: *https://github.com/bluewhalebook/docker-up-and-running-3rd-edition/blob/main/chapter_04/multi stage/Dockerfile*

You are not limited to two stages, and in fact, none of the stages need to even be related to one another. They will be run in order. You could, for example, have a stage based on the public Go image that builds your underlying Go application to serve an API, and another stage based on the Angular container to build your frontend web UI. The final stage could then combine outputs from both.

As you start to build more complex images, you may find that being limited to a single build context is challenging. The docker-buildx plug-in, which we discuss near the end of this chapter, is capable of supporting multiple build contexts (*https://www.docker.com/blog/dockerfiles-now-support-multiple-build-contexts*), which can be used to support some very advanced workflows.

Layers Are Additive

Something that is not apparent until you dig much deeper into how images are built is that the filesystem layers that make up your images are strictly additive by design. Although you can shadow/mask files in previous layers, you cannot delete those files. In practice, this means that you cannot make your image smaller by simply deleting files that were generated in earlier steps.

If you enable experimental features on your Docker server, it is possible to squash a bunch of layers into a single layer using docker image build --squash. This will cause all of the files that were deleted in the intermediate layers to actually disappear from the final image and can therefore recover a lot of wasted space, but it also means that the whole layer must be downloaded by every system that requires it, even when only a single line of source code was updated, so there are real trade-offs to using this approach.

The easiest way to explain the additive nature of image layers is by using some practical examples. In a new directory, download (*https://github.com/bluewhalebook/docker-up-and-running-3rd-edition/blob/main/chapter_04/additive*) or create the following file, which will generate an image that launches the Apache web server running on Fedora Linux:

```
FROM docker.io/fedora
RUN dnf install -y httpd
CMD ["/usr/sbin/httpd", "-DFOREGROUND"]
```

and then build it like this:

```
$ docker image build .
[+] Building 63.5s (6/6) FINISHED
 => [internal] load build definition from Dockerfile
```

```
=> => transferring dockerfile: 130B
=> [internal] load .dockerignore
=> => transferring context: 2B
=> [internal] load metadata for docker.io/library/fedora:latest
=> [1/2] FROM docker.io/library/fedora
=> [2/2] RUN dnf install -y httpd
=> exporting to image
=> => exporting layers
=> => writing image sha256:543d61c956778b8ea3b32f1e09a9354a864467772e6…
```

Let's go ahead and tag the resulting image so that you can easily refer to it in subsequent commands:

```
$ docker image tag sha256:543d61c956778b8ea3b32f1e09a9354a864467772e6… size1
```

Now let's take a look at our image with the `docker image history` command. This command will give us some insight into the filesystem layers and build steps that our image uses:

```
$ docker image history size1
IMAGE          CREATED            CREATED BY                              SIZE  …
543d61c95677 About a minute ago CMD ["/usr/sbin/httpd" "-DFOREGROU…"] 0B
<missing>      About a minute ago RUN /bin/sh -c dnf install -y httpd … 273MB
<missing>      6 weeks ago        /bin/sh -c #(nop)  CMD ["/bin/bash"]… 0B
<missing>      6 weeks ago        /bin/sh -c #(nop) ADD file:58865512c… 163MB
<missing>      3 months ago       /bin/sh -c #(nop)  ENV DISTTAG=f36co… 0B
<missing>      15 months ago      /bin/sh -c #(nop)  LABEL maintainer=… 0B
```

You'll notice that three of the layers added no size to our final image, but two of them increase the size a great deal. The layer that is 163 MB makes sense, as this is the base Fedora image that includes a minimal Linux distribution; however, the 273 MB layer is surprising. The Apache web server shouldn't be nearly that large, so what's going on here, exactly?

If you have experience with package managers like `apk`, `apt`, `dnf`, or `yum`, then you may know that most of these tools rely heavily on a large cache that includes details about all the packages that are available for installation on the platform in question. This cache uses up a huge amount of space and is completely useless once you have installed the packages you need. The most obvious next step is to simply delete the cache. On Fedora systems, you could do this by editing your *Dockerfile* so that it looks like this:

```
FROM docker.io/fedora
RUN dnf install -y httpd
RUN dnf clean all
CMD ["/usr/sbin/httpd", "-DFOREGROUND"]
```

and then building, tagging, and examining the resulting image:

```
$ docker image build .
[+] Building 0.5s (7/7) FINISHED
  …
```

```
 => => writing image sha256:b6bf99c6e7a69a1229ef63fc086836ada20265a793cb8f2d…

$ docker image tag sha256:b6bf99c6e7a69a1229ef63fc086836ada20265a793cb8f2d17…
IMAGE        CREATED           CREATED BY                                  SIZE  …
b6bf99c6e7a6 About a minute ago CMD ["/usr/sbin/httpd" "-DFOREGROU…"]      0B
<missing>    About a minute ago RUN /bin/sh -c dnf clean all # build… 71.8kB
<missing>    10 minutes ago    RUN /bin/sh -c dnf install -y httpd …  273MB
<missing>    6 weeks ago       /bin/sh -c #(nop)  CMD ["/bin/bash"]…  0B
<missing>    6 weeks ago       /bin/sh -c #(nop) ADD file:58865512c…  163MB
<missing>    3 months ago      /bin/sh -c #(nop)  ENV DISTTAG=f36co…  0B
<missing>    15 months ago     /bin/sh -c #(nop)  LABEL maintainer=… 0B
```

If you look carefully at the output from the docker image history command, you'll notice that you have created a new layer that adds 71.8kB to the image, but you have not decreased the size of the problematic layer at all. What is happening, exactly?

The important thing to understand is that image layers are strictly *additive* in nature. Once a layer is created, nothing can be removed from it. This means that you cannot make earlier layers in an image smaller by deleting files in subsequent layers. When you delete or edit files in subsequent layers, you're simply masking the older version with the modified or removed version in the new layer. This means that the only way you can make a layer smaller is by removing files before you save the layer.

The most common way to deal with this is by stringing commands together on a single *Dockerfile* line. You can do this very easily by taking advantage of the && operator. This operator acts as a Boolean AND statement and basically translates into English as "and if the previous command ran successfully, run this command." In addition to this, you can take advantage of the / operator, which is used to indicate that a command continues after the newline. This can help improve the readability of long commands.

With this knowledge in hand, you can rewrite the *Dockerfile* like this:

```
FROM docker.io/fedora
RUN dnf install -y httpd && \
    dnf clean all
CMD ["/usr/sbin/httpd", "-DFOREGROUND"]
```

Now you can rebuild the image and see how this change has impacted the size of the layer that includes the http daemon:

```
$ docker image build .
[+] Building 0.5s (7/7) FINISHED
…
 => => writing image sha256:14fe7924bb0b641ddf11e08d3dd56f40aff4271cad7a421fe…

$ docker image tag sha256:14fe7924bb0b641ddf11e08d3dd56f40aff4271cad7a421fe9b…
IMAGE        CREATED           CREATED BY                                  SIZE  …
14fe7924bb0b About a minute ago CMD ["/usr/sbin/httpd" "-DFOREGROUN"]…     0B
<missing>    About a minute ago RUN /bin/sh -c dnf install -y httpd &… 44.8MB
```

```
<missing>      6 weeks ago      /bin/sh -c #(nop)  CMD ["/bin/bash"] … 0B
<missing>      6 weeks ago      /bin/sh -c #(nop) ADD file:58865512ca… 163MB
<missing>      3 months ago     /bin/sh -c #(nop)  ENV DISTTAG=f36con… 0B
<missing>      15 months ago    /bin/sh -c #(nop)  LABEL maintainer=C… 0B
```

In the first two examples, the layer in question was 273 MB in size, but now that you have removed many unnecessary files that were added to that layer, you can shrink the layer down to 44.8 MB. This is a very large saving of space, especially when you consider how many servers might be pulling the image down during any given deployment.

Utilizing the Layer Cache

The final building technique that we will cover here is related to keeping build times as fast as possible. One of the important goals of the DevOps movement is to keep feedback loops as tight as possible. This means that it is important to try to ensure that problems are discovered and reported as quickly as possible so that they can be fixed when people are still completely focused on the code in question and haven't moved on to other unrelated tasks.

During any standard build process, Docker uses a layer cache to try to avoid rebuilding any image layers that it has already built and that do not contain any noticeable changes. Because of this cache, the order in which you do things inside your *Dockerfile* can have a dramatic impact on how long your builds take on average.

For starters, let's take the *Dockerfile* from the previous example and customize it just a bit so that it looks like this.

Along with the other examples, you can also find these files on GitHub (*https://github.com/bluewhalebook/docker-up-and-running-3rd-edition/blob/main/chapter_04/cache*).

```
FROM docker.io/fedora
RUN dnf install -y httpd && \
    dnf clean all
RUN mkdir -p /var/www && \
    mkdir -p /var/www/html
ADD index.html /var/www/html
CMD ["/usr/sbin/httpd", "-DFOREGROUND"]
```

Now, in the same directory, let's also create a new file called *index.html* that looks like this:

```
<html>
  <head>
    <title>My custom Web Site</title>
  </head>
```

```
    <body>
      <p>Welcome to my custom Web Site</p>
    </body>
  </html>
```

For the first test, let's time the build without using the Docker cache at all, by using the following command:

```
$ time docker image build --no-cache .
time docker image build --no-cache .
[+] Building 48.3s (9/9) FINISHED
 => [internal] load build definition from Dockerfile
 => => transferring dockerfile: 238B
 => [internal] load .dockerignore
 => => transferring context: 2B
 => [internal] load metadata for docker.io/library/fedora:latest
 => CACHED [1/4] FROM docker.io/library/fedora
 => [internal] load build context
 => => transferring context: 32B
 => [2/4] RUN dnf install -y httpd &&    dnf clean all
 => [3/4] RUN mkdir -p /var/www &&    mkdir -p /var/www/html
 => [4/4] ADD index.html /var/www/html
 => exporting to image
 => => exporting layers
 => => writing image sha256:7f94d0d6492f2d2c0b8576f0f492e03334e6a535cac85576c…

real  1m21.645s
user  0m0.428s
sys   0m0.323s
```

 Windows users should be able to run this command in a WSL2 session or use the PowerShell Measure-Command (*https://oreil.ly/ MQQY_*)[6] function to replace the Unix time command used in these examples.

The output from the time command tells us that the build without the cache took about a minute and 21 seconds and only pulled the base image from the layer cache. If you rebuild the image immediately afterward and allow Docker to use the cache, you will see that the build is very fast:

```
$ time docker image build .
[+] Building 0.1s (9/9) FINISHED
 => [internal] load build definition from Dockerfile
 => => transferring dockerfile: 37B
 => [internal] load .dockerignore
 => => transferring context: 2B
```

---

6 Full URL: *https://learn.microsoft.com/en-us/powershell/module/microsoft.powershell.utility/measure-command? view=powershell-7.3*

```
=> [internal] load metadata for docker.io/library/fedora:latest
=> [1/4] FROM docker.io/library/fedora
=> [internal] load build context
=> => transferring context: 32B
=> CACHED [2/4] RUN dnf install -y httpd &&      dnf clean all
=> CACHED [3/4] RUN mkdir -p /var/www &&      mkdir -p /var/www/html
=> CACHED [4/4] ADD index.html /var/www/html
=> exporting to image
=> => exporting layers
=> => writing image sha256:0d3aeeeeebd09606d99719e0c5197c1f3e59a843c4d7a21af…

real  0m0.416s
user  0m0.120s
sys   0m0.087s
```

Since none of the layers changed, and the cache could be fully leveraged for all four build steps, the build took only a fraction of a second to complete. Now, let's make a small improvement to the *index.html* file so that it looks like this:

```
<html>
  <head>
    <title>My custom Web Site</title>
  </head>
  <body>
    <div align="center">
      <p>Welcome to my custom Web Site!!!</p>
    </div>
  </body>
</html>
```

and then let's time the rebuild again:

```
$ time docker image build .
[+] Building 0.1s (9/9) FINISHED
 => [internal] load build definition from Dockerfile
 => => transferring dockerfile: 37B
 => [internal] load .dockerignore
 => => transferring context: 2B
 => [internal] load metadata for docker.io/library/fedora:latest
 => [internal] load build context
 => => transferring context: 214B
 => [1/4] FROM docker.io/library/fedora
 => CACHED [2/4] RUN dnf install -y httpd &&      dnf clean all
 => CACHED [3/4] RUN mkdir -p /var/www &&      mkdir -p /var/www/html
 => [4/4] ADD index.html /var/www/html
 =>  ADD index.html /var/www/html
 => exporting to image
 => => exporting layers
 => => writing image sha256:daf792da1b6a0ae7cfb2673b29f98ef2123d666b8d14e0b74…

real  0m0.456s
user  0m0.120s
sys   0m0.068s
```

If you look at the output carefully, you will see that the cache was used for most of the build. It wasn't until step 4/4, when Docker needed to copy *index.html*, that the cache was invalidated and the layers had to be re-created. Because the cache could be used for most of the build, the build still did not exceed a second.

But what would happen if you changed the order of the commands in the *Dockerfile* so that they looked like this:

```
FROM docker.io/fedora
RUN mkdir -p /var/www && \
    mkdir -p /var/www/html
ADD index.html /var/www/html
RUN dnf install -y httpd && \
    dnf clean all
CMD ["/usr/sbin/httpd", "-DFOREGROUND"]
```

Let's quickly time another test build without the cache to get a baseline:

```
$ time docker image build --no-cache .
[+] Building 51.5s (9/9) FINISHED
…
 => => writing image sha256:1cc5f2c5e4a4d1cf384f6fb3a34fd4d00e7f5e7a7308d5f1f…

real  0m51.859s
user  0m0.237s
sys   0m0.159s
```

In this case, the build took 51 seconds to complete: since we used the `--no-cache` argument, we know that nothing was pulled from the layer cache, except for the base image. The difference in time from the very first test is entirely due to fluctuating network speeds and has nothing to do with the changes that you have made to the *Dockerfile*.

Now, let's edit *index.html* again, like so:

```
<html>
  <head>
    <title>My custom Web Site</title>
  </head>
  <body>
    <div align="center" style="font-size:180%">
      <p>Welcome to my custom Web Site</p>
    </div>
  </body>
</html>
```

And now, let's time the image rebuild while using the cache:

```
$ time docker image build .
[+] Building 43.4s (9/9) FINISHED
 => [internal] load build definition from Dockerfile
 => => transferring dockerfile: 37B
 => [internal] load .dockerignore
```

```
=> => transferring context: 2B
=> [internal] load metadata for docker.io/library/fedora:latest
=> [1/4] FROM docker.io/library/fedora
=> [internal] load build context
=> => transferring context: 233B
=> CACHED [2/4] RUN mkdir -p /var/www &&     mkdir -p /var/www/html
=> [3/4] ADD index.html /var/www/html
=> [4/4] RUN dnf install -y httpd &&     dnf clean all
=> exporting to image
=> => exporting layers
=> => writing image sha256:9a05b2d01b5870649e0ad1d7ad68858e0667f402c8087f0b4…

real  0m43.695s
user  0m0.211s
sys   0m0.133s
```

The first time that you rebuilt the image, after editing the *index.html* file, it took only .456 seconds, but this time it took 43.695 seconds, almost exactly as long as it took to build the whole image without using the cache at all.

This is because you have modified the *Dockerfile* so that the *index.html* file is copied into the image very early in the process. The problem with doing it this way is that the *index.html* file changes frequently and will often invalidate the cache. The other issue is that it is unnecessarily placed before a very time-consuming step in our *Dockerfile*: installing the Apache web server.

The important lesson to take away from all of this is that order matters, and in general, you should always try to order your *Dockerfile* so that the most stable and time-consuming portions of your build process happen first and your code is added as late in the process as possible.

For projects that require you to install dependencies based on your code using tools like npm and bundle, it is also a good idea to do some research about optimizing your Docker builds for those platforms. This often includes locking down your dependency versions and storing them along with your code so that they do not need to be downloaded for each and every build.

Directory Caching

One of the many features that BuildKit adds to the image-building experience is directory caching. Directory caching is an incredibly useful tool for speeding up build times without saving a lot of files that are unnecessary for the runtime into your image. In essence, it allows you to save the contents of a directory inside your image in a special layer that can be bind-mounted at build time and then unmounted before the image snapshot is made. This is often used to handle directories where tools like Linux software installers (apt, apk, dnf, etc.), and language dependency managers (npm, bundler, pip, etc.), download their databases and archive files.

If you are unfamiliar with bind mounts and what they are, you can find a bind mount overview (*https://docs.docker.com/storage/ bind-mounts*) in the Docker documentation.

To make use of directory caching, you must have BuildKit enabled. In most circumstances, this should already be the case, but you can force it from the client side, by setting the environment variable DOCKER_BUILDKIT= to 1:

```
$ export DOCKER_BUILDKIT=1
```

Let's explore directory caching by checking out the following git repository and seeing how utilizing directory caching can significantly improve consecutive builds while still keeping the resulting image sizes smaller:

```
$ git clone https://github.com/spkane/open-mastermind.git \
  --config core.autocrlf=input

$ cd open-mastermind
$ cat Dockerfile

FROM python:3.9.15-slim-bullseye
RUN mkdir /app
WORKDIR /app
COPY . /app
RUN pip install -r requirements.txt
WORKDIR /app/mastermind
CMD ["python", "mastermind.py"]
```

This codebase has a very generic *Dockerfile* checked into the repo. Let's go ahead and see how long it takes to build this image, with and without the layer cache, and let's also examine how large the resulting image is:

```
$ time docker build --no-cache -t docker.io/spkane/open-mastermind:latest .

[+] Building 67.5s (12/12) FINISHED
…
 => => naming to docker.io/spkane/open-mastermind:latest                0.0s

real    0m28.934s
user    0m0.222s
sys     0m0.248s

$ docker image ls --format "{{ .Size }}" spkane/open-mastermind:latest
293MB

$ time docker build -t docker.io/spkane/open-mastermind:latest .

[+] Building 1.5s (12/12) FINISHED
…
 => => naming to docker.io/spkane/open-mastermind:latest                0.0s
```

```
real     0m1.083s
user     0m0.098s
sys      0m0.095s
```

From this output, we can see that this image takes just under 29 seconds to build without the layer cache and just under 2 seconds to build when it can fully utilize the layer cache. The resulting image size is 293 MB in total.

BuildKit finally has support for modifying or completely disabling the colors used for the output (*https://github.com/moby/buildkit#color-output-controls*). This is particularly nice for anyone who uses a dark background in their terminal. You can configure these colors by setting something like `export BUILDKIT_ COLORS=run=green:warning=yellow:error=red:cancel=cyan` in your environment, or you can completely disable the colors by setting `export NO_COLOR=true`.

Note that the BuildKit version used in various `docker` components and third-party tools is still being updated, so it might not work yet in every situation.

If you want to test the build, go ahead and run it:

```
$ docker container run -ti --rm docker.io/spkane/open-mastermind:latest
```

This will launch a terminal-based open source version of the Mastermind game (*https://github.com/philshem/open-mastermind*). There are on-screen directions for the game, and as a fallback, you can always exit by typing Ctrl-C.

Since this is a Python application, it uses the *requirements.txt* file to list all of the libraries that the application requires, and then the `pip` application is used in the *Dockerfile* to install these dependencies.

We are installing some unnecessary dependencies simply to make the benefits of directory caching more obvious.

Go ahead and open up the *requirements.txt* file and add a line that reads `log-symbols`, so that it looks like this:

```
colorama
# These are not required - but are used for demonstration purposes
pandas
flask
log-symbols
```

Let's rerun the build now:

```
$ time docker build -t docker.io/spkane/open-mastermind:latest \
  --progress=plain .

#1 [internal] load build definition from Dockerfile
…
#9 [5/6] RUN pip install -r requirements.txt
#9 sha256:82dbc10f1bb9fa476d93cc0d8104b76f46af8ece7991eb55393d6d72a230919e
#9 1.954 Collecting colorama
#9 2.058   Downloading colorama-0.4.5-py2.py3-none-any.whl (16 kB)
…
real    0m16.379s
user    0m0.112s
sys     0m0.082s
```

If you look at the full output for step 5/6, you will notice that all the dependencies are downloaded again, even though pip would normally have most of those dependencies cached in */root/.cache*. This inefficiency results from the builder seeing that we have made a change that impacts this layer and therefore completely re-creates the layer, so we lose that cache, even though we had it stored in the image layer.

Let's go ahead and improve this situation. To do this, we need to leverage the BuildKit directory cache (*https://github.com/moby/buildkit/blob/master/frontend/dock erfile/docs/reference.md#run---mounttypecache*), and to do that we need to make a few changes to the *Dockerfile* so that it looks like this:

```
# syntax=docker/dockerfile:1
FROM python:3.9.15-slim-bullseye
RUN mkdir /app
WORKDIR /app
COPY . /app
RUN --mount=type=cache,target=/root/.cache pip install -r requirements.txt
WORKDIR /app/mastermind
CMD ["python", "mastermind.py"]
```

There are two important changes in there. First, we added the following line:

```
# syntax=docker/dockerfile:1
```

This tells Docker that we are going to use a newer version of the *Dockerfile* frontend (*https://hub.docker.com/r/docker/dockerfile*), which provides us with access to Build-Kit's new features.

Then we edited the RUN line to look like this:

```
RUN --mount=type=cache,target=/root/.cache pip install -r requirements.txt
```

This line tells BuildKit to mount a caching layer into the container at */root/.cache* for the duration of this one build step. This will accomplish two goals for us. It will remove the contents of that directory from the resulting image, and it will also be remounted and available to pip in consecutive builds.

Let's go ahead and do a full rebuild of the image with these changes, to generate the initial cache directory contents. If you follow the output, you will see that pip downloads all the dependencies, exactly as before:

```
$ time docker build --no-cache -t docker.io/spkane/open-mastermind:latest .

[+] Building 15.2s (15/15) FINISHED
...
 => => naming to docker.io/spkane/open-mastermind:latest          0.0s
...
real    0m15.493s
user    0m0.137s
sys     0m0.096s
```

So, now let's open up the *requirements.txt* file and add a line that reads py-events:

```
colorama
# These are not required - but are used for demonstration purposes
pandas
flask
log-symbols
py-events
```

This is where the changes pay off. When we rebuild the image now, we will see that py-events and its dependencies are the only things that are downloaded; everything else uses the existing cache from our previous build, which has been mounted into the image for this build step:

```
$ time docker build -t docker.io/spkane/open-mastermind:latest \
  --progress=plain .

#1 [internal] load build definition from Dockerfile
...
#14 [stage-0 5/6] RUN --mount=type=cache,target=/root/.cache pip install …
#14 sha256:9bc72441fdf2ec5f5803d4d5df43dbe7bc6eeef88ebee98ed18d8dbb478270ba
#14 1.711 Collecting colorama
#14 1.714   Using cached colorama-0.4.5-py2.py3-none-any.whl (16 kB)
...
#14 2.236 Collecting py-events
#14 2.356   Downloading py_events-0.1.2-py3-none-any.whl (5.8 kB)
...
#16 DONE 1.4s

real    0m12.624s
user    0m0.180s
sys     0m0.112s

$ docker image ls --format "{{ .Size }}" spkane/open-mastermind:latest
261MB
```

The build time has shrunk since there is no longer a need to re-download everything each time, and the image size is also 32 MB smaller, even though we have added new dependencies to the image. This is simply because the cache directory is no longer stored directly in the image that contains the application.

BuildKit and the new *Dockerfile* frontends bring a lot of very useful features to the image-building process that you will want to be aware of. We highly recommend that you take the time to read through the reference guide (*https://github.com/moby/build kit/blob/master/frontend/dockerfile/docs/reference.md*) and become acquainted with all the available capabilities.

Troubleshooting Broken Builds

We normally expect builds to just work, especially when we've scripted them, but in the real world things go wrong. Let's spend a little bit of time discussing what you can do to troubleshoot a Docker build that is failing. In this section, we will explore two options: one that works with the pre-BuildKit approach to image building and one that works with BuildKit.

For this demonstration, we are going to reuse the `docker-hello-node` repo from earlier in the chapter. If required, you can clone it again, like this:

```
$ git clone https://github.com/spkane/docker-node-hello.git \
    --config core.autocrlf=input
Cloning into 'docker-node-hello'…
remote: Counting objects: 41, done.
remote: Total 41 (delta 0), reused 0 (delta 0), pack-reused 41
Unpacking objects: 100% (41/41), done.

$ cd docker-node-hello
```

Debugging Pre-BuildKit Images

We need a patient for the next set of exercises, so let's create a failing build. To do that, edit the *Dockerfile* so that the line that reads:

```
RUN apt-get -y update
```

now reads:

```
RUN apt-get -y update-all
```

If you are using PowerShell on Windows, you will likely need to set the environment variable that disables BuildKit before running the following `docker image build` command, and then reset it afterward:

```
PS C:\> $env:DOCKER_BUILDKIT = 0
PS C:\> docker image build `
        -t example/docker-node-hello:latest `
        --no-cache .
PS C:\> $env:DOCKER_BUILDKIT = 1
```

If you try to build the image now, you should get the following error:

```
$ DOCKER_BUILDKIT=0 docker image build -t example/docker-node-hello:latest \
  --no-cache .

Sending build context to Docker daemon  9.216kB
Step 1/14 : FROM docker.io/node:18.13.0
 ---> 9ff38e3a6d9d
...
Step 6/14 : ENV SCPATH /etc/supervisor/conf.d
 ---> Running in e903367eaeb8
Removing intermediate container e903367eaeb8
 ---> 2a236efc3f06
Step 7/14 : RUN apt-get -y update-all
 ---> Running in c7cd72f7d9bf
E: Invalid operation update-all
The command '/bin/sh -c apt-get -y update-all' returned a non-zero code: 100
```

So, how can we troubleshoot this, especially if we are not developing on a Linux system? The real trick here is to remember that almost all Docker images are layered on top of other Docker images and that you can start a container from any image. Although the meaning is not obvious on the surface, if you look at the output for `Step 6`, you will see this:

```
Step 6/14 : ENV SCPATH /etc/supervisor/conf.d
 ---> Running in e903367eaeb8
Removing intermediate container e903367eaeb8
 ---> 2a236efc3f06
```

The first line that reads `Running in e903367eaeb8` is telling you that the build process has started a new container, based on the image created in `Step 5`. The next line, which reads `Removing intermediate container e903367eaeb8`, is telling you that Docker is now removing the container after having altered it based on the instruction in `Step 6`. In this case, it was simply adding a default environment variable via `ENV SCPATH /etc/supervisor/conf.d`. The final line, which reads `--→ 2a236efc3f06`, is the one we really care about because this is giving us the image ID for the image that was generated by `Step 6`. You need this to troubleshoot the build because it is the image from the last successful step in the build.

With this information, it is possible to run an interactive container so that you can try to determine why your build is not working properly. Remember that every container image is based on the image layers below it. One of the great benefits of this is that we can just run the lower layer as a container itself, using a shell to look around!

```
$ docker container run --rm -ti 2a236efc3f06 /bin/bash
root@b83048106b0f:/#
```

From inside the container, you can now run any commands that you might need to determine what is causing your build to fail and what you need to do to fix your *Dockerfile*:

```
root@b83048106b0f:/# apt-get -y update-all
E: Invalid operation update-all

root@b83048106b0f:/# apt-get --help
apt 1.4.9 (amd64)
…

Most used commands:
  update - Retrieve new lists of packages
…

root@b83048106b0f:/# apt-get -y update
Get:1 http://security.debian.org/debian-security stretch/updates … [53.0 kB]
…
Reading package lists… Done

root@b83048106b0f:/# exit
exit
```

Once the root cause has been determined, the *Dockerfile* can be fixed, so that RUN apt-get -y update-all now reads RUN apt-get -y update, and then rebuilding the image should result in success:

```
$ DOCKER_BUILDKIT=0 docker image build -t example/docker-node-hello:latest .
Sending build context to Docker daemon  15.87kB
…
Successfully built 69f5e83bb86e
Successfully tagged example/docker-node-hello:latest
```

Debugging BuildKit Images

When using BuildKit, we have to take a slightly different approach to get access to the point where the build fails, because none of the intermediate build layers are exported from the build container to the Docker daemon.

The options for debugging BuildKit will almost certainly evolve as we move forward, but let's take a look at one approach that works now.

Assuming that the *Dockerfile* has been reverted to its original state, let's change the line that reads:

```
RUN npm install
```

so that it now reads:

```
RUN npm installer
```

and then attempt to build the image.

 Make sure that you have BuildKit enabled!

```
$ docker image build -t example/docker-node-hello:debug --no-cache .

[+] Building 51.7s (13/13) FINISHED
 => [internal] load build definition from Dockerfile                      0.0s
 …
 => [7/8] WORKDIR /data/app                                               0.0s
 => ERROR [8/8] RUN npm installer                                        0.4s
_____
 > [8/8] RUN npm installer:
#13 0.399
#13 0.399 Usage: npm <command>
 …
#13 0.402 Did you mean one of these?
#13 0.402     install
#13 0.402     install-test
#13 0.402     uninstall
_____
executor failed running [/bin/sh -c npm installer]: exit code: 1
```

We see an error as we expected, but how are we going to get access to that layer so that we can troubleshoot this?

One approach that works is to leverage multistage builds and the `--target` argument of docker image build.

Let's start by modifying the *Dockerfile* in two places. Change this line:

```
FROM docker.io/node:18.13.0
```

so that it now reads:

```
FROM docker.io/node:18.13.0 as deploy
```

and then immediately before the line that causes the error, we are going to add a new
FROM line:

```
FROM deploy
RUN npm installer
```

By doing this, we are creating a multistage build, where the first stage contains all of
the steps that we know are working and the second stage starts with our problematic
step.

If we try to rebuild this using the same command as before, it will still fail:

```
$ docker image build -t example/docker-node-hello:debug .

[+] Building 51.7s (13/13) FINISHED
…
executor failed running [/bin/sh -c npm installer]: exit code: 1
```

So, instead of doing that, let's tell Docker that we only want to build the first image in
our multistage *Dockerfile*:

```
$ docker image build -t example/docker-node-hello:debug --target deploy .

[+] Building 0.8s (12/12) FINISHED
 => [internal] load build definition from Dockerfile                 0.0s
 => => transferring dockerfile: 37B                                  0.0s
 …
 => exporting to image                                               0.1s
 => => exporting layers                                              0.1s
 => => writing image sha256:a42dfbcfc7b18ee3d30ace944ad4134ea2239a2c0  0.0s
 => => naming to docker.io/example/docker-node-hello:debug           0.0s
```

Now, we can create a container from this image and do whatever testing we require:

```
$ docker container run --rm -ti docker.io/example/docker-node-hello:debug \
  /bin/bash

root@17807997176e:/data/app# ls
index.js  package.json

root@17807997176e:/data/app# npm install
…
added 18 packages from 16 contributors and audited 18 packages in 1.248s
…

root@17807997176e:/data/app# exit
exit
```

And then once we understand what is wrong with the *Dockerfile*, we can revert our
debugging changes and fix the npm line so that the whole build works as expected.

Multiarchitecture Builds

Since the launch of Docker, the *AMD64/X86_64* architecture has been the primary platform that most containers have targeted. However, this has started to change significantly. More and more developers are using systems based on ARM64/AArch64, and cloud companies are starting to make ARM-based VMs available through their platforms, due to the lower computing costs associated with the ARM platform.

This can cause some interesting challenges for anyone who needs to build and maintain images that will target multiple architectures. How can you maintain a single, streamlined codebase and pipeline while still supporting all of these different targets?

Luckily, Docker has released a plug-in for the `docker` CLI, called `buildx`, which can help make this process pretty straightforward. In many cases, `docker-buildx` will already be installed on your system, and you can verify this like so:

```
$ docker buildx version
github.com/docker/buildx v0.9.1 ed00243a0ce2a0aee75311b06e32d33b44729689
```

 If you need to install the plug-in, you can follow the directions from the GitHub repo (*https://github.com/docker/buildx#installing*).

By default, `docker-buildx` will leverage QEMU-based virtualization (*https://www.qemu.org*) and `binfmt_misc` (*https://docs.kernel.org/admin-guide/binfmt-misc.html*) to support architectures that differ from the underlying system. This may already be set up on your Linux system, but just in case, it is a good idea to run the following command when you are first setting up a new Docker server, just to ensure that the QEMU files are properly registered and up to date:

```
$ docker container run --rm --privileged multiarch/qemu-user-static \
    --reset -p yes

Setting /usr/bin/qemu-alpha-static as binfmt interpreter for alpha
Setting /usr/bin/qemu-arm-static as binfmt interpreter for arm
Setting /usr/bin/qemu-armeb-static as binfmt interpreter for armeb
…
Setting /usr/bin/qemu-aarch64-static as binfmt interpreter for aarch64
Setting /usr/bin/qemu-aarch64_be-static as binfmt interpreter for aarch64_be
…
```

Unlike the original embedded Docker build functionality, which ran directly on the server, BuildKit can utilize a build container when it builds images, which means that there is a lot of functional flexibility that can be delivered with that build container. In the next step, we are going to create a default `buildx` container called `builder`.

If you have an existing `buildx` container by this name, you can either remove it by running `docker buildx rm builder` or you can change the name in the upcoming `docker buildx create` command.

With the next two commands, we are going to create the build container, set it as the default, and then start it up:

```
$ docker buildx create --name builder --driver docker-container --use
builder

$ docker buildx inspect --bootstrap
[+] Building 9.6s (1/1) FINISHED
 => [internal] booting buildkit                                     9.6s
 => => pulling image moby/buildkit:buildx-stable-1                  8.6s
 => => creating container buildx_buildkit_builder0                  0.9s
Name:   builder
Driver: docker-container

Nodes:
Name:      builder0
Endpoint:  unix:///var/run/docker.sock
Status:    running
Buildkit:  v0.10.5
Platforms: linux/amd64, linux/amd64/v2, linux/arm64, linux/riscv64,
           linux/ppc64le, linux/s390x, linux/386, linux/mips64le,
           linux/mips64, linux/arm/v7, linux/arm/v6
```

For this example, let's go ahead and download the wordchain Git repository, which contains a useful tool that can generate random and deterministic word sequences to help with dynamic naming needs:

```
$ git clone https://github.com/spkane/wordchain.git \
    --config core.autocrlf=input
$ cd wordchain
```

Let's go ahead and take a look at the included *Dockerfile*. You'll notice that it is a pretty normal multistage *Dockerfile* and does not have anything special in it related to the platform architecture:

```
FROM golang:1.18-alpine3.15 AS build

RUN apk --no-cache add \
    bash \
    gcc \
    musl-dev \
    openssl

ENV CGO_ENABLED=0

COPY . /build
```

```
WORKDIR /build

RUN go install github.com/markbates/pkger/cmd/pkger@latest && \
    pkger -include /data/words.json && \
    go build .

FROM alpine:3.15 AS deploy

WORKDIR /
COPY --from=build /build/wordchain /

USER 500
EXPOSE 8080

ENTRYPOINT ["/wordchain"]
CMD ["listen"]
```

In the first step, we are going to build our statically compiled Go binary, and then in the second step, we are going to package it up into a small deployment image.

The ENTRYPOINT instruction in the *Dockerfile* is an advanced instruction that allows you to separate the default process that is run by the container (ENTRYPOINT) from the command-line arguments that are passed to that process (CMD). When ENTRYPOINT is missing from the *Dockerfile*, the CMD instruction is expected to contain both the process and all the required command-line arguments.

We can go ahead and build this image and side-load it into our local Docker server by running the following command:

```
$ docker buildx build --tag wordchain:test --load .

[+] Building 2.4s (16/16) FINISHED
 => [internal] load .dockerignore                                           0.0s
 => => transferring context: 93B                                            0.0s
 => [internal] load build definition from Dockerfile                        0.0s
 => => transferring dockerfile: 461B                                        0.0s
 ...
 => exporting to oci image format                                           0.3s
 => => exporting layers                                                     0.0s
 => => exporting manifest sha256:4bd1971f2ed820b4f64ffda97707c27aac3e8eb7   0.0s
 => => exporting config sha256:ce8f8564bf53b283d486bddeb8cbb074ff9a9d4ce9   0.0s
 => => sending tarball                                                      0.2s
 => importing to docker                                                     0.0s
```

We can quickly test out the image by running the following commands:

```
$ docker container run wordchain:test random

witty-stack
```

```
$ docker container run wordchain:test random -l 3 -d .

odd.goo

$ docker container run wordchain:test --help

wordchain is an application that can generate a readable chain
    of customizable words for naming things like
    containers, clusters, and other objects.
...
```

As long as you got some random word pairs back with the first two commands, then everything is working as expected.

Now, to build this image for multiple architectures, we need to simply add the --platform argument to our build.

 Typically we would also replace --load with --push, which would push all the resulting images to the tagged repository, but in this case, we need to simply remove --load, because the Docker server cannot load images for multiple platforms at the moment, and we do not have a repository set up to push these images to. If we did have a repository and we tagged the images correctly, then we could very easily build and push all the resulting images in one step, with a command like this:

docker buildx build --platform linux/amd64,linux/arm64 --tag docker.io/spkane/wordchain:latest --push .

You can build this image for both the linux/amd64 and the linux/arm64 platforms like this:

```
$ docker buildx build --platform linux/amd64,linux/arm64 \
    --tag wordchain:test .

[+] Building 114.9s (23/23) FINISHED
...
 => [linux/arm64 internal] load metadata for docker.io/library/alpine:3.1 2.7s
 => [linux/amd64 internal] load metadata for docker.io/library/alpine:3.1 2.7s
 => [linux/arm64 internal] load metadata for docker.io/library/golang:1.1 3.0s
 => [linux/amd64 internal] load metadata for docker.io/library/golang:1.1 2.8s
...
 => CACHED [linux/amd64 build 5/5] RUN go install github.com/markbates/pk 0.0s
 => CACHED [linux/amd64 deploy 2/3] COPY --from=build /build/wordchain /  0.0s
 => [linux/arm64 build 5/5] RUN go install github.com/markbates/pkger/c 111.7s
 => [linux/arm64 deploy 2/3] COPY --from=build /build/wordchain /        0.0s
WARNING: No output specified with docker-container driver. Build result will
          only remain in the build cache. To push result image into registry
          use --push or to load image into docker use --load
```

Due to the emulation that is required when building images for nonnative architectures, you may notice that some steps take much longer than normal. This is to be expected due to the additional computational overhead from the emulation.

It is possible to set up Docker so that it will build each image on a worker with a matching architecture, which should speed things up significantly in many cases. You can find some information about this in this Docker blog article (*https://www.docker.com/blog/ speed-up-building-with-docker-buildx-and-graviton2-ec2*).

In the output for the build, you will notice lines that start with something like `=> [linux/amd64 *]` or `=> [linux/arm64 *]`. Each of these lines represents the builder working on this build step for the stated platform. Many of these steps will run in parallel, and due to caching and other considerations, each build might progress at differing speeds.

Since we did not add `--push` to our build, you will also notice that we received a warning at the end of the build. This is because the *docker-container* driver that the builder is using just left everything in the build cache, which means that we can't run the resulting images; at this point, we can only feel confident that the build is working.

There are a few `build` arguments (*https://docs.docker.com/engine/ reference/builder/#automatic-platform-args-in-the-global-scope*) that are automatically set by Docker that can be especially helpful to leverage inside your *Dockerfile* when you are doing multiarchitecture builds. As an example, `TARGETARCH` is frequently used to make sure that a given build step downloads the correct prebuilt binary for the current image's platform.

So, when we upload this image to a repository, how does Docker know which image to use for the local platform? This information is provided to the Docker server through something called an *image manifest*. We can look at the manifest for *docker.io/spkane/workdchain* by running the following:

```
$ docker manifest inspect docker.io/spkane/wordchain:latest

{
    "schemaVersion": 2,
    "mediaType": "application/vnd.docker.distribution.manifest.list.v2+json",
    "manifests": [
        {
            "mediaType": "application/vnd.docker.distribution.manifest.v2+json",
            "size": 739,
            "digest": "sha256:4bd1…bfc0",
            "platform": {
```

```
              "architecture": "amd64",
              "os": "linux"
          }
      },
      {
  ...
          "platform": {
              "architecture": "arm64",
              "os": "linux"
          }
      },
  ...
    ]
}
```

If you look through the output, you will see that there are blocks that identify the image that is required for every platform the image supports. This is accomplished via the individual digest (*https://github.com/opencontainers/image-spec/blob/ main/descriptor.md#digests*) entries that are then paired with a *platform* block. This manifest file is downloaded by the server when it requires an image, and then after referencing the manifest, the server will download the correct image for the local platform. This is why our *Dockerfile* works at all. Each FROM line lists a base image that we want to use, but it is the Docker server that utilizes this manifest file to determine exactly which image to download for each platform that the build is targeting.

Wrap-Up

At this point, you should feel pretty comfortable with image creation for Docker and should have a solid understanding of many of the core tools and functionality you can leverage to streamline your build pipeline. In the next chapter, we will start to dig into how you can use your images to create containerized processes for your projects.

## CHAPTER 5

Working with Containers

In the previous chapter, we learned how to build a Docker image and the very basic steps required for running the resulting image within a container. In this chapter, we'll first take a look at the history of container technology and then dive deeper into running containers and exploring the Docker commands that control the overall configuration, resources, and privileges that your container receives.

What Are Containers?

You might be familiar with virtualization systems like VMware or KVM that allow you to run a complete Linux kernel and operating system on top of a virtualized layer, commonly known as a *hypervisor*. This approach provides very strong isolation between workloads because each VM hosts its own operating system kernel that sits in a separate memory space on top of a hardware virtualization layer.

Containers are fundamentally different since they all share a single kernel, and isolation between workloads is implemented entirely within that one kernel. This is called *operating system virtualization*.

The `libcontainer` README (*https://github.com/opencontainers/runc/blob/main/lib container/README.md*) provides a good, short definition of a container:

> A container is a self-contained execution environment that shares the kernel of the host system and is (optionally) isolated from other containers in the system.

One of the major advantages of containers is resource efficiency, because you don't need a whole operating system instance for each isolated workload. Since you are sharing a kernel, there is one fewer layer of indirection between the isolated task and the real hardware underneath. When a process is running inside a container, there is only a little bit of code that sits inside the kernel managing the container. Contrast this with a VM, where a second layer would be running. In a VM, calls by the process to the hardware or hypervisor would require bouncing in and out of privileged mode on the processor twice, thereby noticeably slowing down many calls.

 libcontainer (*https://github.com/opencontainers/runc/tree/main/lib container*) is a Go library that is designed to provide a standard interface for managing Linux containers from applications.

But the container approach does mean that you can only run processes that are compatible with the underlying kernel. For example, unlike hardware virtualization provided by technologies like VMware or KVM, Windows applications cannot run natively inside a Linux container on a Linux host. Windows applications can, however, run inside Windows containers on a Windows host. So containers are best thought of as an OS-specific technology where you can run any of your favorite applications or daemons that are compatible with the container server's kernel. When thinking of containers, you should try very hard to throw out what you might already know about VMs and instead conceptualize a container as a wrapper around a normal process that runs on the server.

 In addition to being able to run containers inside VMs, it is completely feasible to run a VM inside a container. If you do this, then it is indeed possible to run a Windows application inside a Windows VM that is running inside a Linux container.

History of Containers

It is often the case that a revolutionary technology is an older technology that has finally arrived in the spotlight. Technology goes in waves, and some of the ideas from the 1960s are back in vogue. Similarly, Docker is a newer technology, and it has an ease of use that has made it an instant hit, but it doesn't exist in a vacuum. Much of what underpins Docker comes from work done over the last 30 years in a few different areas. We can easily trace the conceptual evolution of containers from a simple system call that was added to the Unix kernel in the late 1970s to the modern container tooling that powers many huge internet firms, like Google, Twitter, and Meta. It's worth taking some time for a quick tour through how the technology evolved and led to the creation of Docker, because understanding this helps you place it within the context of other things that you might be familiar with.

Containers are not a new idea. They are a way to isolate and encapsulate a part of the running system. The oldest technology in this area includes the very first batch processing systems. When using these early computers, the system would only run one program at a time, switching to run another program once the previous program had finished or a predefined time span had elapsed. With this design there was enforced isolation: you could make sure your program didn't step on anyone else's program because it was only possible to run one thing at a time. Although modern computers still switch tasks constantly, it is incredibly fast and completely unnoticeable to most users.

We would argue that the seeds for today's containers were planted in 1979 with the addition of the chroot system call to Version 7 Unix. chroot restricts a process's view of the underlying filesystem to a single subtree. The chroot system call is commonly used to protect the operating system from untrusted server processes like FTP, BIND, and Sendmail, which are publicly exposed and susceptible to compromise.

In the 1980s and 1990s, various Unix variants were created with mandatory access controls for security reasons.[1] This meant you had tightly controlled domains running on the same Unix kernel. Processes in each domain had an extremely limited view of the system that precluded them from interacting across domains. A popular commercial version of Unix that implemented this idea was the Sidewinder firewall built on top of BSDI Unix, but this was not possible with most mainstream Unix implementations.

That changed in 2000 when FreeBSD 4.0 was released with a new command, called jail, which was designed to allow shared-environment hosting providers to easily and securely create a separation between their processes and those that belonged to each of their customers. FreeBSD jail expanded chroot's capabilities and also restricted everything a process could do with the underlying system and other jailed processes.

In 2004, Sun released an early build of Solaris 10, which included Solaris containers, which later evolved into Solaris Zones. This was the first major commercial implementation of container technology and is still used today to support many commercial container implementations. In 2005, OpenVZ for Linux was released by the company Virtuozzo, followed in 2007 by HP's Secure Resource Partitions for HP-UX, which was later renamed HP-UX Containers.

Companies like Google, which had to deal with scaling applications for broad internet consumption and/or hosting untrusted user code, started pushing container technology in the early 2000s to facilitate reliably and securely distributing their applications across global data centers. A few companies maintained their own patched Linux kernels with container support for internal use, but as the need for these features became more evident within the Linux community, Google contributed some of its work supporting containers into the mainline Linux kernel, and in 2008,

---

1 SELinux is one current implementation.

Linux Containers (LXC) were released in version 2.6.24 of the Linux kernel. The phenomenal growth of Linux Containers across the community did not truly start to grow until 2013, with the inclusion of user namespaces in version 3.8 of the Linux kernel and the release of Docker one month later.

Nowadays, containers are used almost everywhere. Docker and OCI images provide the packaging format for a significant and growing amount of software that is delivered into production environments, and provide the basis for many production systems, including, but not limited to, Kubernetes and most "serverless" cloud technologies.

 So-called serverless technologies are not actually serverless; they simply rely on other people's servers to get work done so that the application owner does not have to worry about managing the hardware and operating system.

Creating a Container

So far we've started containers using the handy docker container run command. But docker container run is really a convenience command that wraps two separate steps into one. The first thing it does is create a container from the underlying image. We can accomplish this separately using the docker container create command. The second thing docker container run does is execute the container, which we can also do separately with the docker container start command.

The docker container create and docker container start commands both contain all the options that pertain to how a container is initially set up. In Chapter 4, we demonstrated that with the docker container run command you could map network ports in the underlying container to the host using the -p/--publish argument, and that -e/--env could be used to pass environment variables into the container.

This only just begins to touch on the array of things that you can configure when you first create a container. So let's take a look at some of the options that docker supports.

Basic Configuration

Let's start by exploring some of the ways we can tell Docker to configure our container when we create it.

Container name

When you create a container, it is built from the underlying image, but various command-line arguments can affect the final settings. Settings specified in the *Dockerfile* are always used as defaults, but you can override many of them at creation time.

By default, Docker randomly names your container (*https://github.com/moby/moby/ blob/master/pkg/namesgenerator/names-generator.go*) by combining an adjective with the name of a famous person. This results in names like *ecstatic-babbage* and *serene-albattani*. If you want to give your container a specific name, you can use the `--name` argument:

```
$ docker container create --name="awesome-service" ubuntu:latest sleep 120
```

After creating this container, you can then start it by using the `docker container start awesome-service`. It will automatically exit after 120 seconds, but you can stop it before then by running `docker container stop awesome-service`. We will dive a bit more into each of these commands a little later in the chapter.

 You can only have one container with any given name on a Docker host. If you run the preceding command twice in a row, you will get an error. You must either delete the previous container using `docker container rm` or change the name of the new container.

Labels

As mentioned in Chapter 4, labels are key/value pairs that can be applied to Docker images and containers as metadata. When new Linux containers are created, they automatically inherit all the labels from their parent image.

It is also possible to add new labels to the containers so that you can apply metadata that might be specific to that single container:

```
$ docker container run --rm -d --name has-some-labels \
  -l deployer=Ahmed -l tester=Asako \
  ubuntu:latest sleep 1000
```

You can then search for and filter containers based on this metadata, using commands like `docker container ls`:

```
$ docker container ls -a -f label=deployer=Ahmed
CONTAINER ID   IMAGE           COMMAND        … NAMES
845731631ba4   ubuntu:latest   "sleep 1000"   … has-some-labels
```

You can use the `docker container inspect` command to see all the labels that a container has:

```
$ docker container inspect has-some-labels
...

        "Labels": {
            "deployer": "Ahmed",
            "tester": "Asako"
        },

...
```

This container runs the command `sleep 1000`, so after 1,000 seconds it will stop running.

Hostname

By default, when you start a container, Docker copies certain system files on the host, including */etc/hostname*, into the container's configuration directory on the host,[2] and then uses a bind mount to link that copy of the file into the container. We can launch a default container with no special configuration, like this:

```
$ docker container run --rm -ti ubuntu:latest /bin/bash
```

This command uses the `docker container run` command, which runs `docker container create` and `docker container start` in the background. Since we want to be able to interact with the container that we are going to create for demonstration purposes, we pass in a few useful arguments. The `--rm` argument tells Docker to delete the container when it exits, the `-t` argument tells Docker to allocate a pseudo-TTY, and the `-i` argument tells Docker that this is going to be an interactive session and that we want to keep STDIN open. If there is no `ENTRYPOINT` defined in the image, then the final argument in the command is the executable and command-line arguments that we want to run within the container, which in this case is the ever-useful `/bin/bash`. If there is an `ENTRYPOINT` defined in the image, then the final argument is passed to the `ENTRYPOINT` process as a list of command-line arguments to that command.

 You might have noticed that the preceding paragraph talks about `-i` and `-t`, but the command is using the argument `-ti`. There is a lot of Unix history that explains why this is, but a quick overview (*https://nullprogram.com/blog/2020/08/01*) can be found online if you are curious.

---

2 Typically under */var/lib/docker/containers*.

If we now run the mount command from within the resulting container, we'll see something similar to this:

```
root@ebc8cf2d8523:/# mount
overlay on / type overlay (rw,relatime,lowerdir=…,upperdir=…,workdir…)
proc on /proc type proc (rw,nosuid,nodev,noexec,relatime)
tmpfs on /dev type tmpfs (rw,nosuid,mode=755)
shm on /dev/shm type tmpfs (rw,nosuid,nodev,noexec,relatime,size=65536k)
mqueue on /dev/mqueue type mqueue (rw,nosuid,nodev,noexec,relatime)
devpts on /dev/pts type devpts (rw,nosuid,noexec,relatime,…,ptmxmode=666)
sysfs on /sys type sysfs (ro,nosuid,nodev,noexec,relatime)
/dev/sda9 on /etc/resolv.conf type ext4 (rw,relatime,data=ordered)
/dev/sda9 on /etc/hostname type ext4 (rw,relatime,data=ordered)
/dev/sda9 on /etc/hosts type ext4 (rw,relatime,data=ordered)
devpts on /dev/console type devpts (rw,nosuid,noexec,relatime,…,ptmxmode=000)
proc on /proc/sys type proc (ro,nosuid,nodev,noexec,relatime)
proc on /proc/sysrq-trigger type proc (ro,nosuid,nodev,noexec,relatime)
proc on /proc/irq type proc (ro,nosuid,nodev,noexec,relatime)
proc on /proc/bus type proc (ro,nosuid,nodev,noexec,relatime)
tmpfs on /proc/kcore type tmpfs (rw,nosuid,mode=755)
root@ebc8cf2d8523:/#
```

When you see any examples with a prompt that looks something like *root@hashID*, it means that you are running a command within the container instead of on the local host.

There are occasions when a container will have been configured with a different hostname instead (e.g., using --name on the CLI), but in the default case, it's the container ID hash.

It is also possible to change the user that is used inside the container with --user, but by default, it will be *root*.

There are quite a few bind mounts in a container, but in this case, we are interested in this one:

```
/dev/sda9 on /etc/hostname type ext4 (rw,relatime,data=ordered)
```

While the device number will be different for each container, the part we care about is that the mount point is */etc/hostname*. This links the container's */etc/hostname* to the hostname file that Docker has prepared for the container, which by default contains the container's ID and is not fully qualified with a domain name.

We can check this in the container by running the following:

```
root@ebc8cf2d8523:/# hostname -f
ebc8cf2d8523
root@ebc8cf2d8523:/# exit
```

Don't forget to `exit` the container shell to return to the local host when finished.

To set the hostname specifically, we can use the `--hostname` argument to pass in a more specific value:

```
$ docker container run --rm -ti --hostname="mycontainer.example.com" \
    ubuntu:latest /bin/bash
```

Then, from within the container, we'll see that the fully qualified hostname is defined as requested:

```
root@mycontainer:/# hostname -f
mycontainer.example.com
root@mycontainer:/# exit
```

Domain Name Service

Just like */etc/hostname*, the *resolv.conf* file that configures Domain Name Service (DNS) resolution is managed via a bind mount between the host and container:

```
/dev/sda9 on /etc/resolv.conf type ext4 (rw,relatime,data=ordered)
```

Details about the *resolve.conf* file can be found online (*https://sslhow.com/understanding-etc-resolv-conf-file-in-linux*).

By default, this is an exact copy of the Docker host's *resolv.conf* file. If you didn't want this, you could use a combination of the `--dns` and `--dns-search` arguments to override this behavior in the container:

```
$ docker container run --rm -ti --dns=8.8.8.8 --dns=8.8.4.4 \
    --dns-search=example1.com --dns-search=example2.com \
    ubuntu:latest /bin/bash
```

If you want to leave the search domain completely unset, then use `--dns-search=`.

Within the container, you would still see a bind mount, but the file contents would no longer reflect the host's *resolv.conf*; instead, it would now look like this:

```
root@0f887071000a:/# more /etc/resolv.conf
nameserver 8.8.8.8
nameserver 8.8.4.4
search example1.com example2.com
root@0f887071000a:/# exit
```

MAC address

Another important piece of information that you can configure is the media access control (MAC) address for the container.

Without any configuration, a container will receive a calculated MAC address that starts with the *02:42:ac:11* prefix.

If you need to specifically set this to a value, you can do so by running something similar to this:

```
$ docker container run --rm -ti --mac-address="a2:11:aa:22:bb:33" \
    ubuntu:latest /bin/bash
```

Normally, you will not need to do that. But sometimes you want to reserve a particular set of MAC addresses for your containers to avoid conflicting with other virtualization layers that use the same private block as Docker.

Be very careful when customizing the MAC address settings. It is possible to cause ARP contention on your network if two systems advertise the same MAC address. If you have a strong need to do this, try to keep your locally administered address ranges within some of the official ranges, like *x2-xx-xx-xx-xx-xx*, *x6-xx-xx-xx-xx-xx*, *xA-xx-xx-xx-xx-xx*, and *xE-xx-xx-xx-xx-xx* (with *x* being any valid hexadecimal character).

Storage Volumes

There are times when the default disk space allocated to a container, or the container's ephemeral nature, is not appropriate for the job at hand, so you'll need storage that can persist between container deployments.

Mounting storage from the Docker host is not generally advisable because it ties your container to a particular Docker host for its persistent state. But for cases like temporary cache files or other semi-ephemeral states, it can make sense.

For times like this, you can leverage the `--mount`/`-v` command to mount directories and individual files from the host server into the container. It is important that you use fully qualified paths in the `--mount`/`-v` argument. The following example mounts */mnt/session_data* to */data* within the container:

```
$ docker container run --rm -ti \
  --mount type=bind,target=/mnt/session_data,source=/data \
  ubuntu:latest /bin/bash

root@0f887071000a:/# mount | grep data
/dev/sda9 on /data type ext4 (rw,relatime,data=ordered)
root@0f887071000a:/# exit
```

For bind mounts specifically, you can use the `-v` argument to shorten the command. When using the `-v` argument, you will notice here that the source and target files/directories are separated by a colon(:).

It is also important to note that volumes are mounted read-write by default. You can easily make `docker` mount the file or directory read-only by adding `,readonly` to end the of the `--mount` arguments, or by adding `:ro` to the end of the `-v` arguments.

```
$ docker container run --rm -ti \
  -v /mnt/session_data:/data:ro \
  ubuntu:latest /bin/bash
```

Neither the host mount point nor the mount point in the container needs to preexist for this command to work properly. If the host mount point does not exist already, then it will be created as a directory. This could cause you some issues if you were trying to point to a file instead of a directory.

In the mount options, you can see that the filesystem was mounted read-write on */data* as expected.

SELinux and Volume Mounts

If you have SELinux enabled on your Docker host, you may get a "Permission Denied" error when trying to mount a volume into your container. You can handle this by using one of the z options to the Docker command for mounting volumes:

- The lowercase z option indicates that the bind-mount content is shared among multiple containers.

- The uppercase Z option indicates that the bind-mount content is private and unshared.

If you are going to share a volume between containers, you can use the z option to the volume mount:

```
$ docker container run --rm -v /app/dhcpd/etc:/etc/dhcpd:z dhcpd
```

However, the best option is actually the Z option to the volume mount command, which will set the directory with the exact MCS label (e.g., chcon … -l s0:c1,c2) that the container will be using. This provides for the best security and will allow only a single container to mount the volume:

```
$ docker container run --rm -v /app/dhcpd/etc:/etc/dhcpd:Z dhcpd
```

 Use extreme caution with the z options. Bind-mounting a system directory such as */etc* or */var* with the Z option will very likely render your system inoperable and require you to use SELinux tools to relabel the host machine manually (*https://www.thegeekdiary.com/understanding-selinux-file-labelling-and-selinux-context*).

If the container application is designed to write into */data*, then this data will be visible on the host filesystem in */mnt/session_data* and will remain available when this container stops and a new container starts with the same volume mounted.

It is possible to tell Docker that the root volume of your container should be mounted read-only so that processes within the container cannot write anything to the root filesystem. This prevents things like logfiles, which a developer may be unaware of, from filling up the container's allocated disk in production. When it's used in conjunction with a mounted volume, you can ensure that data is written only into expected locations.

In the previous example, we could accomplish this simply by adding --read-only=true to the command:

```
$ docker container run --rm -ti --read-only=true -v /mnt/session_data:/data \
    ubuntu:latest /bin/bash

root@df542767bc17:/# mount | grep " / "
overlay on / type overlay (ro,relatime,lowerdir=…,upperdir=…,workdir=…)
root@df542767bc17:/# mount | grep data
/dev/sda9 on /data type ext4 (rw,relatime,data=ordered)
root@df542767bc17:/# exit
```

If you look closely at the mount options for the root directory, you'll notice that they are mounted with the ro option, which makes it read-only. However, the */session_data* mount is still mounted with the rw option so that our application can successfully write to the one volume to which it's designed to write.

Sometimes it is necessary to make a directory like *tmp* writable, even when the rest of the container is read-only. For this use case, you can use the --mount type=tmpfs argument with docker container run so that you can mount a *tmpfs* filesystem into the container. The *tmpfs* filesystems are completely in-memory. They will be very fast, but they are also ephemeral and will utilize additional system memory. Any data in these *tmpfs* directories will be lost when the container is stopped. The following example shows a container being launched with a 256 MB *tmpfs* filesystem mounted at */tmp*:

```
$ docker container run --rm -ti --read-only=true \
  --mount type=tmpfs,destination=/tmp,tmpfs-size=256M \
  ubuntu:latest /bin/bash

root@25b4f3632bbc:/# df -h /tmp
Filesystem      Size  Used Avail Use% Mounted on
tmpfs           256M     0  256M   0% /tmp
root@25b4f3632bbc:/# grep /tmp /etc/mtab
tmpfs /tmp tmpfs rw,nosuid,nodev,noexec,relatime,size=262144k 0 0
root@25b4f3632bbc:/# exit
```

Containers should be designed to be stateless whenever possible. Managing storage creates undesirable dependencies and can easily make deployment scenarios much more complicated.

Resource Quotas

When people discuss the types of problems they must often cope with when working in the cloud, the "noisy neighbor" is often near the top of the list. The basic problem this term refers to is that other applications running on the same physical system as yours can have a noticeable impact on your performance and resource availability.

VMs have the advantage that you can easily and very tightly control how much memory and CPU, among other resources, are allocated to the VM. When using Docker, you must instead leverage the cgroup functionality in the Linux kernel to control the resources that are available to a Linux container. The docker container create and docker container run commands directly support configuring CPU, memory, swap, and storage I/O restrictions when you create a container.

Constraints are normally applied at the time of container creation. If you need to change them, you can use the docker container update command or deploy a new container with the adjustments.

There is an important caveat here. While Docker supports various resource limits, you must have these capabilities enabled in your kernel for Docker to take advantage of them. You might need to add these as command-line parameters to your kernel on startup. To figure out if your kernel supports these limits, run `docker system info`. If you are missing any support, you will get warning messages at the bottom, like this:

```
WARNING: No swap limit support
```

 The details regarding getting cgroup support configured for your kernel are distribution specific, so you should consult the Docker documentation (*https://oreil.ly/Z70ZO*)[3] if you need help configuring things.

CPU shares

Docker has several ways to limit CPU usage by applications in containers. The original method, still commonly used, is the concept of *CPU shares*. We'll present other options as well.

The computing power of all the CPU cores in a system is considered to be the full pool of shares. Docker assigns the number 1,024 to represent the full pool. By configuring a container's CPU shares, you can dictate how much time the container gets to use the CPU. If you want the container to be able to use at most half of the computing power of the system, then you would allocate it 512 shares. These are not exclusive shares, meaning that assigning all 1,024 shares to a container does not prevent all other containers from running. Rather, it's a hint to the scheduler about how long each container should be able to run each time it's scheduled. If we have one container that is allocated 1,024 shares (the default) and two that are allocated 512, they will all get scheduled the same number of times. But if the normal amount of CPU time for each process is 100 microseconds, the containers with 512 shares will run for 50 microseconds each time, whereas the container with 1,024 shares will run for 100 microseconds.

Let's explore a little bit how this works in practice. For the following examples, we'll use a new Docker image that contains the `stress` command (*https://linux.die.net/man/1/stress*) for pushing a system to its limits.

---

3 Full URL: *https://docs.docker.com/engine/install/linux-postinstall/#your-kernel-does-not-support-cgroup-swap-limit-capabilities*

When we run stress without any cgroup constraints, it will use as many resources as we tell it to. The following command creates a load average of around five by creating two CPU-bound processes, one I/O-bound process, and two memory allocation processes. For all of the following examples, we are running on a system with two CPUs.

Note that in the following command, everything following the container image name is related to the stress command, not the docker command:

```
$ docker container run --rm -ti spkane/train-os \
    stress -v --cpu 2 --io 1 --vm 2 --vm-bytes 128M --timeout 120s
```

 This should be a reasonable command to run on any modern computer system, but be aware that it is going to stress the host system. So don't do this in a location that can't take the additional load, or even a possible failure, due to resource starvation.

If you run the top or htop command on the Docker host, near the end of the two-minute run, you can see how the system is affected by the load created by the stress program:

```
$ top -bn1 | head -n 15
top - 20:56:36 up 3 min,  2 users,  load average: 5.03, 2.02, 0.75
Tasks:  88 total,   5 running,  83 sleeping,   0 stopped,   0 zombie
%Cpu(s): 29.8 us, 35.2 sy, 0.0 ni, 32.0 id, 0.8 wa, 1.6 hi, 0.6 si, 0.0 st
KiB Mem:   1021856 total,   270148 used,   751708 free,   42716 buffers
KiB Swap:        0 total,        0 used,        0 free.   83764 cached Mem

   PID USER      PR  NI    VIRT    RES    SHR S  %CPU %MEM     TIME+ COMMAND
   810 root      20   0    7316     96      0 R  44.3  0.0   0:49.63 stress
   813 root      20   0    7316     96      0 R  44.3  0.0   0:49.18 stress
   812 root      20   0  138392  46936    996 R  31.7  4.6   0:46.42 stress
   814 root      20   0  138392  22360    996 R  31.7  2.2   0:46.89 stress
   811 root      20   0    7316     96      0 D  25.3  0.0   0:21.34 stress
     1 root      20   0  110024   4916   3632 S   0.0  0.5   0:07.32 systemd
     2 root      20   0       0      0      0 S   0.0  0.0   0:00.04 kthreadd
     3 root      20   0       0      0      0 S   0.0  0.0   0:00.11 ksoftir…
```

Docker Desktop users on non-Linux systems may discover that Docker has made the VM filesystem read-only, and it does not contain many useful tools for monitoring the VM. For these demos where you want to be able to monitor the resource usage of various processes, you can work around this by doing something like this:

```
$ docker container run --rm -it --pid=host alpine sh
/ # apk update
/ # apk add htop
/ # htop -p $(pgrep stress | tr '\n' ',')
/ # exit
```

Be aware that the preceding htop command will give you an error unless stress is actively running when you launch htop, since no processes will be returned by the pgrep command.

You will also want to exit and rerun htop each time you run a new stress instance.

If you want to run the same stress command again, with only half the amount of available CPU time, you can do so like this:

```
$ docker container run --rm -ti --cpu-shares 512 spkane/train-os \
    stress -v --cpu 2 --io 1 --vm 2 --vm-bytes 128M --timeout 120s
```

The --cpu-shares 512 is the flag that does the magic, allocating 512 CPU shares to this container. The effect of this argument might not be noticeable on a system that is not very busy. That's because the container will continue to be scheduled for the same time-slice length whenever it has work to do unless the system is constrained for resources. So in our case, the results of a top command on the host system will likely look the same, unless you run a few more containers to give the CPU something else to do.

Unlike VMs, Docker's cgroup-based constraints on CPU shares can have unexpected consequences. They are not hard limits; they are relative limits, similar to the nice command. An example is a container that is constrained to half the CPU shares but is on a system that is not very busy. Since the CPU is not busy, the limit on the CPU shares would have only a limited effect because there is no competition in the scheduler pool. When a second container that uses a lot of CPU is deployed to the same system, suddenly the effect of the constraint on the first container will be noticeable. Consider this carefully when constraining containers and allocating resources.

CPU pinning

It is also possible to pin a container to one or more CPU cores. This means that work for this container will be scheduled only on the cores that have been assigned to this container. That is useful if you want to hard-shard CPUs between applications or if you have applications that need to be pinned to a particular CPU for things like cache efficiency.

In the following example, we are running a stress container pinned to the first of two CPUs, with 512 CPU shares:

```
$ docker container run --rm -ti \
  --cpu-shares 512 --cpuset-cpus=0 spkane/train-os \
  stress -v --cpu 2 --io 1 --vm 2 --vm-bytes 128M --timeout 120s
```

> The --cpuset-cpus argument is zero-indexed, so your first CPU core is 0. If you tell Docker to use a CPU core that does not exist on the host system, you will get a Cannot start container error. On a two-CPU example host, you could test this by using --cpuset-cpus=0-2.

If you run top again, you should notice that the percentage of CPU time spent in user space (us) is lower than it previously was, since we have restricted two CPU-bound processes to a single CPU:

```
%Cpu(s): 18.5 us, 22.0 sy, 0.0 ni, 57.6 id, 0.5 wa, 1.0 hi, 0.3 si, 0.0 st
```

> When you use CPU pinning, additional CPU sharing restrictions on the container only take into account other containers running on the same set of cores.

Using the CPU Completely Fair Scheduler (CFS) within the Linux kernel, you can alter the CPU quota for a given container by setting the --cpu-quota flag to a valid value when launching the container with docker container run.

Simplifying CPU quotas

While CPU shares were the original mechanism in Docker for managing CPU limits, Docker has evolved a great deal since, and one of the ways that it now makes users' lives easier is by greatly simplifying how CPU quotas can be set. Instead of trying to set correct CPU shares and quotas yourself, you can now simply tell Docker how much CPU you would like to be available to your container, and it will do the math required to set the underlying cgroups correctly.

The `--cpus` command can be set to a floating-point number between 0.01 and the number of CPU cores on the Docker server:

```
$ docker container run --rm -ti --cpus=".25" spkane/train-os \
    stress -v --cpu 2 --io 1 --vm 2 --vm-bytes 128M --timeout 60s
```

If you try to set the value too high, you'll get an error message from Docker (not the `stress` application) that will give you the correct range of CPU cores that you have to work with:

```
$ docker container run --rm -ti --cpus="40.25" spkane/train-os \
    stress -v --cpu 2 --io 1 --vm 2 --vm-bytes 128M --timeout 60s
docker: Error response from daemon: Range of CPUs is from
    0.01 to 4.00, as there are only 4 CPUs available.
See 'docker container run --help'.
```

The `docker container update` command can be used to dynamically adjust the resource limits of one or more containers. You could adjust the CPU allocation on two containers simultaneously, for example, like so:

```
$ docker container update --cpus="1.5" 092c5dc85044 92b797f12af1
```

 Docker sees CPUs the same way that Linux sees them. Hyperthreading and cores are interpreted by Linux and exposed via the special file */proc/cpuinfo*. When you use the `--cpus` command in Docker, you are referring to how many of the entries in this file you want the container to have access to, whether they refer to a standard core or a hyper-threaded core.

Memory

We can control how much memory a container can access in a manner similar to constraining the CPU. There is, however, one fundamental difference: while constraining the CPU only impacts the application's priority for CPU time, the memory limit is a *hard* limit. Even on an unconstrained system with 96 GB of free memory, if we tell a container that it may have access only to 24 GB, then it will only ever get to use 24 GB regardless of the free memory on the system. Because of the way the virtual memory system works on Linux, it's possible to allocate more memory to a container than the system has actual RAM. In this case, the container will resort to using swap, just like a normal Linux process.

Let's start a container with a memory constraint by passing the `--memory` option to the `docker container run` command:

```
$ docker container run --rm -ti --memory 512m spkane/train-os \
    stress -v --cpu 2 --io 1 --vm 2 --vm-bytes 128M --timeout 10s
```

When you use the `--memory` option alone, you are setting both the amount of RAM and the amount of swap that the container will have access to. So by using

--memory 512m here, we've constrained the container to 512 MB of RAM and 512 MB of additional swap space. Docker supports b, k, m, or g, representing bytes, kilobytes, megabytes, or gigabytes, respectively. If your system somehow runs Linux and Docker and has multiple terabytes of memory, then unfortunately you're going to have to specify it in gigabytes.

If you would like to set the swap separately or disable it altogether, you need to also use the --memory-swap option. This defines the total amount of memory and swap available to the container. If we rerun our previous command, like so:

```
$ docker container run --rm -ti --memory 512m --memory-swap=768m \
    spkane/train-os stress -v --cpu 2 --io 1 --vm 2 --vm-bytes 128M \
    --timeout 10s
```

then we're telling the kernel that this container can have access to 512 MB of memory and 256 MB of additional swap space. Setting the --memory-swap option to -1 will disable the swap completely within the container.

 Again, unlike CPU shares, memory is a hard limit! This is good because the constraint doesn't suddenly have a noticeable effect on the container when another container is deployed to the system. But it does mean that you need to be careful that the limit closely matches your container's needs because there is no wiggle room. An out-of-memory container causes the kernel to behave just like it would if the system were out of memory. It will try to find a process to kill so that it can free up space. This is a common failure case where containers have their memory limits set too low. The telltale sign of this issue is a container exit code of 137 and kernel out-of-memory (OOM) messages in the Docker server's dmesg output.

So, what happens if a container reaches its memory limit? Well, let's give it a try by modifying one of our previous commands and lowering the memory significantly:

```
$ docker container run --rm -ti --memory 100m spkane/train-os \
    stress -v --cpu 2 --io 1 --vm 2 --vm-bytes 128M --timeout 10s
```

While all of our other runs of the stress container ended with a line like this:

```
stress: info: [17] successful run completed in 10s
```

we see that this run quickly fails with a line similar to this:

```
stress: FAIL: [1] (451) failed run completed in 0s
```

This is because the container tries to allocate more memory than it is allowed, and the Linux OOM killer is invoked and starts killing processes within the cgroup to reclaim memory. In this case, our container has a single-parent process that has spawned a few children processes, and when the OOM killer kills one of the children processes, the parent process cleans everything up and exits with an error.

 Docker has features that allow you to tune and disable the Linux OOM killer by using the --oom-kill-disable and the --oom-score-adj arguments to docker container run, but they are not recommended for almost any use cases.

If you access your Docker server, you can see the kernel message related to this event by running dmesg. The output will look something like this:

```
[ 4210.403984] stress invoked oom-killer: gfp_mask=0x24000c0 …
[ 4210.404899] stress cpuset=5bfa65084931efabda59d9a70fa8e88 …
[ 4210.405951] CPU: 3 PID: 3429 Comm: stress Not tainted 4.9 …
[ 4210.406624] Hardware name:   BHYVE, BIOS 1.00 03/14/2014
…
[ 4210.408978] Call Trace:
[ 4210.409182]  [<ffffffff94438115>] ? dump_stack+0x5a/0x6f
….
[ 4210.414139]  [<ffffffff947f9cf8>] ? page_fault+0x28/0x30
[ 4210.414619] Task in /docker-ce/docker/5…3
killed as a result of limit of /docker-ce/docker/5…3
[ 4210.416640] memory: usage 102380kB, limit 102400kB, failc …
[ 4210.417236] memory+swap: usage 204800kB, limit 204800kB,  …
[ 4210.417855] kmem: usage 1180kB, limit 9007199254740988kB, …
[ 4210.418485] Memory cgroup stats for /docker-ce/docker/5…3:
cache:0KB rss:101200KB rss_huge:0KB mapped_file:0KB dirty:0KB
writeback:11472KB swap:102420KB inactive_anon:50728KB
active_anon:50472KB inactive_file:0KB active_file:0KB unevictable:0KB
…
[ 4210.426783] Memory cgroup out of memory: Kill process 3429…
[ 4210.427544] Killed process 3429 (stress) total-vm:138388kB,
anon-rss:44028kB, file-rss:900kB, shmem-rss:0kB
[ 4210.442492] oom_reaper: reaped process 3429 (stress), now
anon-rss:0kB, file-rss:0kB, shmem-rss:0kB
```

This OOM event will also be recorded by Docker and viewable via docker system events:

```
$ docker system events
2018-01-28T15:56:19.972142371-08:00 container oom \
    d0d803ce32c4e86d0aa6453512a9084a156e96860e916ffc2856fc63ad9cf88b \
    (image=spkane/train-os, name=loving_franklin)
```

Block I/O

Many containers are just stateless applications and won't need block I/O restrictions. But Docker also supports limiting block I/O in a few different ways via the cgroups mechanism.

The first way is applying some prioritization to a container's use of block device I/O. You enable this by manipulating the default setting of the blkio.weight cgroup attribute. This attribute can have a value of 0 (disabled) or a number between 10 and 1,000, the default being 500. This limit acts a bit like CPU shares, in that the system will divide all of the available I/O between every process within a cgroup slice by 1,000, with the assigned weights impacting how much available I/O is available to each process.

To set this weight on a container, you need to pass the --blkio-weight to your docker container run command with a valid value. You can also target a specific device using the --blkio-weight-device option.

As with CPU shares, tuning the weights is hard to get right in practice, but we can make it vastly simpler by limiting the maximum number of bytes or operations per second that are available to a container via its cgroup. The following settings let us control that:

```
--device-read-bps    Limit read rate (bytes per second) from a device
--device-read-iops   Limit read rate (IO per second) from a device
--device-write-bps   Limit write rate (bytes per second) to a device
--device-write-iops  Limit write rate (IO per second) to a device
```

You can test how these impact the performance of a container by running some of the following commands, which use the Linux I/O tester bonnie (*https://www.coker.com.au/bonnie*):

```
$ time docker container run --rm -ti spkane/train-os:latest bonnie++ \
    -u 500:500 -d /tmp -r 1024 -s 2048 -x 1
…
real  0m27.715s
user  0m0.027s
sys   0m0.030s

$ time docker container run -ti --rm --device-write-iops /dev/vda:256 \
    spkane/train-os:latest bonnie++ -u 500:500 -d /tmp -r 1024 -s 2048 -x 1
…
real  0m58.765s
user  0m0.028s
sys   0m0.029s

$ time docker container run -ti --rm --device-write-bps /dev/vda:5mb \
    spkane/train-os:latest bonnie++ -u 500:500 -d /tmp -r 1024 -s 2048 -x 1
…
```

PowerShell users should be able to use the Measure-Command (*https://learn.microsoft.com/en-us/powershell/module/microsoft.powershell.utility/measure-command?view=powershell-7.3*) function to replace the Unix time command used in these examples.

In our experience, the `--device-read-iops` and `--device-write-iops` arguments are the most effective way to set block I/O limits and are the ones we recommend.

ulimits

Before Linux cgroups, there was another way to place a limit on the resources available to a process: the application of user limits via the `ulimit` command. That mechanism is still available and still useful for all of the use cases (*https://www.linux howtos.org/Tips%20and%20Tricks/ulimit.htm*) where it was traditionally used.

The following code is a list of the types of system resources that you can usually constrain by setting soft and hard limits via the `ulimit` command:

```
$ ulimit -a
core file size          (blocks, -c) 0
data seg size           (kbytes, -d) unlimited
scheduling priority             (-e) 0
file size               (blocks, -f) unlimited
pending signals                 (-i) 5835
max locked memory       (kbytes, -l) 64
max memory size         (kbytes, -m) unlimited
open files                      (-n) 1024
pipe size            (512 bytes, -p) 8
POSIX message queues     (bytes, -q) 819200
real-time priority              (-r) 0
stack size              (kbytes, -s) 10240
cpu time               (seconds, -t) unlimited
max user processes              (-u) 1024
virtual memory          (kbytes, -v) unlimited
file locks                      (-x) unlimited
```

It is possible to configure the Docker daemon with the default user limits that you want to apply to every container. The following command tells the Docker daemon to start all containers with a soft limit of 50 open files and a hard limit of 150 open files:

```
$ sudo dockerd --default-ulimit nofile=50:150
```

You can then override these ulimits on a specific container by passing in values using the `--ulimit` argument:

```
$ docker container run --rm -d --ulimit nofile=150:300 nginx
```

There are some additional advanced commands that you can use when creating containers, but this covers many of the more common use cases. The Docker client documentation (*https://dockr.ly/2ME0ygi*) lists all the available options and is updated with each Docker release.

Starting a Container

Before we got into the details of containers and constraints, we created our container using the docker container create command. That container is just sitting there without doing anything. There is a configuration but no running process. When we're ready to start the container, we can do so using the docker container start command.

Let's say that we needed to run a copy of Redis, a common key/value store. We won't do anything with this Redis container, but it's a lightweight, long-lived process and serves as an example of something we might do in a real environment. We could first create the container:

```
$ docker container create -p 6379:6379 redis:2.8
Unable to find image 'redis:7.0' locally
7.0: Pulling from library/redis
3f4ca61aafcd: Pull complete
…
20bf15ad3c24: Pull complete
Digest: sha256:8184cfe57f205ab34c62bd0e9552dffeb885d2a7f82ce4295c0df344cb6f0007
Status: Downloaded newer image for redis:7.0
092c5dc850446324e4387485df7b76258fdf9ed0aedcd53a37299d35fc67a042
```

The result of the command is some output, the last line of which is the full hash that was generated for the container. We could use that long hash to start it, but if we failed to note it down, we could also list all the containers on the system, whether they are running or not, using the following:

```
$ docker container ls -a --filter ancestor=redis:2.8
CONTAINER ID IMAGE      COMMAND              CREATED       … NAMES
092c5dc85044 redis:7.0 "docker-entrypoint.s…" 46 seconds ago elegant_wright
```

We can confirm the identity of our container by filtering the output by the image that we used and examining the container's creation time. We can then start the container with the following command:

```
$ docker container start 092c5dc85044
```

 Most Docker commands will work with the container name, the full hash, the short hash, or even just enough of the hash to make it unique. In the previous example, the full hash for the container is 092c5dc850446324e…a37299d35fc67a042, but the short hash that is shown in most command output is 092c5dc85044. This short hash consists of the first 12 characters of the full hash. In the previous example, running docker container start 6b7 would have worked just fine.

That *should* have started the container, but with it running in the background we won't necessarily know if something went wrong. To verify that it's running, we can run the following:

```
$ docker container ls
CONTAINER ID  IMAGE      COMMAND                …  STATUS         …
092c5dc85044  redis:7.0  "docker-entrypoint.s…" …  Up 2 minutes …
```

And, there it is: running as expected. We can tell because the status says Up and shows how long the container has been running.

Auto-Restarting a Container

In many cases, we want our containers to restart if they exit. Some containers are very short-lived and come and go quickly. But for production applications, for instance, you expect them to be up and running at all times after you've told them to run. If you are running a more complex system, a scheduler may do this for you.

In the simple case, we can tell Docker to manage restarts on our behalf by passing the --restart argument to the docker container run command. It takes four values: no, always, on-failure, or unless-stopped. If restart is set to no, the container will never restart if it exits. If it is set to always, the container will restart whenever it exits, with no regard to the exit code. If restart is set to on-failure, whenever the container exits with a nonzero exit code, Docker will try to restart the container. If we set restart to on-failure:3, Docker will try and restart the container three times before giving up. unless-stopped is the most common choice and will restart the container unless it is intentionally stopped with something like docker container stop.

We can see this in action by rerunning our last memory-constrained stress container without the --rm argument but with the --restart argument:

```
$ docker container run -ti --restart=on-failure:3 --memory 100m \
    spkane/train-os stress -v --cpu 2 --io 1 --vm 2 --vm-bytes 128M \
    --timeout 120s
```

In this example, we'll see the output from the first run appear on the console before it dies. If we run a docker container ls immediately after the container dies, we'll likely see that Docker has restarted the container:

```
$ docker container ls
…  IMAGE            …  STATUS                 …
…  spkane/train-os  …  Up Less than a second …
```

It will continue to fail because we haven't given it enough memory to function properly. After three attempts, Docker will give up, and we'll see the container disappear from the output of docker container ls.

Stopping a Container

Containers can be stopped and started at will. You might think that starting and stopping a container is analogous to pausing and resuming a normal process, but it's not quite the same in reality. When stopped, the process is not paused; it exits. And when a container is stopped, it no longer shows up in the normal `docker container ls` output. On reboot, Docker will attempt to start all of the containers that were running at shutdown. If you need to prevent a container from doing any additional work, without actually stopping the process, then you can pause the Linux container with `docker container pause` and `unpause`, which will be discussed in more detail later. For now, go ahead and stop the Redis container that we started a little earlier:

```
$ docker container stop 092c5dc85044
$ docker container ls
CONTAINER ID IMAGE COMMAND CREATED STATUS PORTS NAMES
```

Now that we have stopped the container, nothing is in the running container list! We can start it back up with the container ID, but it would be inconvenient to have to remember that. So `docker container ls` has an additional option (`-a`) to show all containers, not just the running ones:

```
$ docker container ls -a
CONTAINER ID   IMAGE      STATUS                ...
092c5dc85044   redis:7.0 Exited (0) 2 minutes ago …
...
```

That `STATUS` field now shows that our container exited with a status code of 0 (no errors). We can start it back up with the same configuration it had before:

```
$ docker container start 092c5dc85044
092c5dc85044

$ docker container ls -a
CONTAINER ID   IMAGE      STATUS           ...
092c5dc85044   redis:7.0 Up 14 seconds …
...
```

Voilà, our container is back up and running and configured just as it was before.

 Remember that containers exist as a blob of configuration in the Docker system even when they are not started. This means that as long as the container has not been deleted, you can restart it without needing to re-create it. Although memory and temporary file system (tmpfs) contents will have been lost, all of the container's other filesystem contents and metadata, including environment variables and port bindings, are saved and will still be in place when you restart the container.

By now we've probably thumped on enough about the idea that containers are just a tree of processes that interact with the system in essentially the same way as any other process on the server. But it's important to point it out here again because it means that we can send Unix signals to our process in the containers that they can then respond to. In the previous docker container stop example, we're sending the container a SIGTERM signal and waiting for the container to exit gracefully. Containers follow the same process group signal propagation that any other process group would receive on Linux.

A normal docker container stop sends a SIGTERM to the process. If you want to force a container to be killed if it hasn't stopped after a certain amount of time, you can use the -t argument, like this:

```
$ docker container stop -t 25 092c5dc85044
```

This tells Docker to initially send a SIGTERM signal as before, but if the container has not stopped within 25 seconds (the default is 10), it tells Docker to send a SIGKILL signal to forcefully kill it.

Although stop is the best way to shut down your containers, there are times when it doesn't work and you'll need to forcefully kill a container, just as you might have to do with any process outside of a container.

Killing a Container

When a process is misbehaving, docker container stop might not cut it. You might just want the container to exit immediately.

In these circumstances, you can use docker container kill. As you'd expect, it looks a lot like docker container stop:

```
$ docker container start 092c5dc85044
092c5dc85044

$ docker container kill 092c5dc85044
092c5dc85044
```

A docker container ls command now shows that the container is no longer running, as expected:

```
$ docker container ls
CONTAINER ID IMAGE COMMAND CREATED STATUS PORTS NAMES
```

Just because it was killed rather than stopped does not mean you can't start it again, though. You can just issue a docker container start like you would for a nicely stopped container. Sometimes you might want to send another signal to a container, one that is not stop or kill. Like the Linux kill command, docker container kill supports sending any Unix signal. Let's say we wanted to send a USR1 signal to our container to tell it to do something like reconnect a remote logging session. We could do the following:

```
$ docker container start 092c5dc85044
092c5dc85044

$ docker container kill --signal=USR1 092c5dc85044
092c5dc85044
```

If our container process was designed to do something with the USR1 signal, it would now do it. Any standard Unix signal can be sent to a container using this method.

Pausing and Unpausing a Container

There are a few reasons why we might not want to completely stop our container. We might want to pause it, leave its resources allocated, and leave its entries in the process table. That could be because we're taking a snapshot of its filesystem to create a new image or just because we need some CPU on the host for a while. If you are used to normal Unix process handling, you might wonder how this works since containerized processes are just processes.

Pausing leverages the cgroup freezer (*https://www.kernel.org/doc/Documenta tion/cgroup-v1/freezer-subsystem.txt*), which essentially just prevents your process from being scheduled until you unfreeze it. This will prevent the container from doing anything while maintaining its overall state, including memory contents. Unlike stopping a container, where the processes are made aware that they are stopping via the SIGSTOP signal, pausing a container doesn't send any information to the container about its state change. That's an important distinction. Several Docker commands use pausing and unpausing internally as well. Here is how we pause a container:

```
$ docker container start 092c5dc85044
092c5dc85044

$ docker container pause 092c5dc85044
092c5dc85044
```

To pause and unpause containers in Windows, you must be using Hyper-V or WSL2 as the underlying virtualization technology.

If we look at the list of running containers, we will now see that the Redis container status is listed as (Paused):

```
$ docker container ls
CONTAINER ID  IMAGE      … STATUS                  …
092c5dc85044  redis:7.0 … Up 25 seconds (Paused)  …
```

Attempting to use the container in this paused state would fail. It's present, but nothing is running. We can now resume the container by using the docker container unpause command:

```
$ docker container unpause 092c5dc85044
092c5dc85044

$ docker container ls
CONTAINER ID  IMAGE      … STATUS          …
092c5dc85044  redis:7.0 … Up 55 seconds …
```

It's back to running, and docker container ls correctly reflects the new state. It shows Up 55 seconds now because Docker still considers the container to be running even when it is paused.

Cleaning Up Containers and Images

After running all these commands to build images, create containers, and run them, we have accumulated a lot of image layers and container folders on our system.

We can list all the containers on our system using the docker container ls -a command and then delete any of the containers in the list. We must stop all containers that are using an image before removing the image itself. Assuming we've done that, we can remove it as follows, using the docker container rm command:

```
$ docker container stop 092c5dc85044
092c5dc85044ls

$ docker container rm 092c5dc85044
092c5dc85044
```

> It is possible to remove a running container if you use the -f or --force flag with docker container rm.

We can then list all the images on our system using the following:

```
$ docker image ls
REPOSITORY       TAG     IMAGE ID      CREATED       SIZE
ubuntu           latest  5ba9dab47459  3 weeks ago   188.3MB
redis            7.0     0256c63af7db  2 weeks ago   117MB
spkane/train-os  latest  78fb082a4d65  4 months ago  254MB
```

We can then delete an image and all associated filesystem layers by running the following:

```
$ docker image rm 0256c63af7db
```

 If you try to delete an image that is in use by a container, you will get a Conflict, cannot delete error. You should stop and delete the container(s) first.

There are times, especially during development cycles when it makes sense to completely purge all the images or containers from your system. The easiest way to do this is by running the docker system prune command:

```
$ docker system prune
WARNING! This will remove:
        - all stopped containers
        - all networks not used by at least one container
        - all dangling images
        - all build cache
Are you sure you want to continue? [y/N] y
Deleted Containers:
cbbc42acfe6cc7c2d5e6c3361003e077478c58bb062dd57a230d31bcd01f6190
…
Deleted Images:
deleted: sha256:bec6ec29e16a409af1c556bf9e6b2ec584c7fb5ffbfd7c46ec00b30bf …
untagged: spkane/squid@sha256:64fbc44666405fd1a02f0ec731e35881465fac395e7 …
…
Total reclaimed space: 1.385GB
```

 To remove all unused images, instead of only dangling images, try docker system prune -a.

It is also possible to craft more specific commands to accomplish similar goals.

To delete all of the containers on your Docker hosts, use the following command:

```
$ docker container rm $(docker container ls -a -q)
```

And to delete all the images on your Docker host, this command will get the job done:

```
$ docker image rm $(docker images -q)
```

The `docker container ls` and `docker images` commands both support a `filter` argument that can make it easy to fine-tune your delete commands for certain circumstances.

To remove all containers that exited with a nonzero state, you can use this filter:

```
$ docker container rm $(docker container ls -a -q --filter 'exited!=0')
```

And to remove all untagged images, you can type this:

```
$ docker image rm $(docker images -q -f "dangling=true")
```

 You can read the official Docker documentation (*https://docs.docker.com/engine/reference/commandline/ps/#filtering*) to explore the filtering options. At the moment, there are very few filters to choose from, but more will likely be added over time.

You can also make your own very creative filters by stringing together commands using pipes (|) and other similar techniques.

In production systems that see a lot of deployments, you can sometimes end up with old containers or unused images lying around and filling up disk space. It can be useful to script the `docker system prune` command to run on a schedule (e.g., running under `cron` or via a `systemd` timer).

Windows Containers

Up to now we have focused entirely on Docker commands for Linux containers, since this is the most common use case and works on all Docker platforms. However, since 2016, the Microsoft Windows platform has supported running Windows containers that include native Windows applications and can be managed with the usual set of Docker commands.

Windows containers are not the focus of this book, since they still only make up a small portion of production containers and aren't 100% compatible with the rest of the Docker ecosystem because they require Windows-specific container images. However, they're a growing and important part of the Docker world, so we'll take a brief look at how they work. In fact, except for the actual contents of the containers, almost everything else works the same as Linux containers. In this section, we'll run through a quick example of how you can run a Windows container on Windows 10+ with Hyper-V and Docker.

 For this to work, you must be using Docker Desktop on a compatible 64-bit edition of Windows 10 or later.

The first thing you'll need to do is switch Docker from Linux containers to Windows containers. To do this, right-click on the Docker whale icon in your taskbar, select "Switch to Windows Containers…," and then confirm the switch (Figures 5-1 and 5-2).

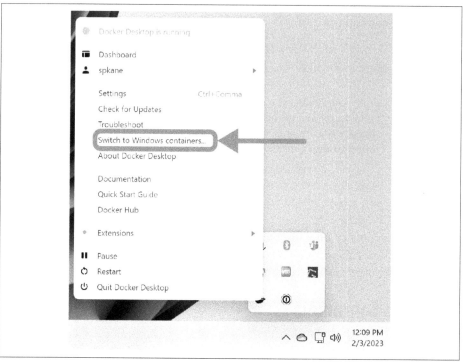

Figure 5-1. Switch to Windows containers

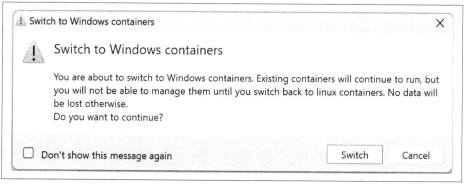

Figure 5-2. Switch to Windows containers confirmation

This process might take some time, although it usually happens almost immediately. Unfortunately, there is no notification that the switch has completed. If you right-click on the Docker icon again, you should now see "Switch to Linux Containers…" in place of the original option.

If the first time you right-click on the Docker icon, it reads "Switch to Linux Containers…," then you are already configured for Windows containers.

We can test a simple Windows container by opening up PowerShell (*https://oreil.ly/SiTXP*)[4] and trying to run the following command:

```
PS C:\> docker container run --rm -it mcr.microsoft.com/powershell `
        pwsh -command `
        'Write-Host "Hello World from Windows `($IsWindows`)"'

Hello World from Windows (True)
```

This will download and launch a base container for PowerShell (*https://hub.docker.com/_/microsoft-powershell*) and then use scripting to print Hello World from Windows (True) to the screen.

If the output from the preceding command prints Hello World from Windows (false), then you have not switched over to Windows Container mode, or you are running this command on a non-Windows platform.

If you want to build a Windows container image that accomplishes roughly the same task, you can create the following *Dockerfile*:

```
# escape=`
FROM mcr.microsoft.com/powershell
SHELL ["pwsh", "-command"]

RUN Add-Content C:\helloworld.ps1 `
    'Write-Host "Hello World from Windows"'

CMD ["pwsh", "C:\\helloworld.ps1"]
```

When you build this *Dockerfile*, it will base the image on mcr.microsoft.com/powershell, create a small PowerShell script, and then configure the image to run that script when this image is used to launch a container.

---

4 Full URL: *https://learn.microsoft.com/en-us/powershell/scripting/overview?view=powershell-7.3&viewFallbackFrom=powershell-6*

You may have noticed that we had to escape the backslash (\) with an additional backslash in the preceding *Dockerfile*'s CMD line. This is because Docker has its roots in Unix, and the backslash has a special meaning in Unix shells. So, even though we changed the escape character (*https://docs.docker.com/ engine/reference/builder/#escape*) for the *Dockerfile* to match what is used in PowerShell by default (which we set via the SHELL directive (*https://docs.docker.com/engine/reference/builder/ #shell-form-entrypoint-example*)), we still need to escape some backslashes to ensure that Docker does not misinterpret them.

If you build this *Dockerfile* now, you'll see something similar to this:

```
PS C:\> docker image build -t windows-helloworld:latest .

Sending build context to Docker daemon  2.048kB
Step 1/4 : FROM mcr.microsoft.com/powershell
 ---> 7d8f821c04eb
Step 2/4 : SHELL ["pwsh", "-command"]
 ---> Using cache
 ---> 1987fb489a3d
Step 3/4 : RUN Add-Content C:\helloworld.ps1
               'Write-Host "Hello World from Windows"'
 ---> Using cache
 ---> 37df47d57bf1
Step 4/4 : CMD ["pwsh", "C:\\helloworld.ps1"]
 ---> Using cache
 ---> 03046ff628e4
Successfully built 03046ff628e4
Successfully tagged windows-helloworld:latest
```

And now if you run the resulting image, you'll see this:

```
PS C:\> docker container run --rm -ti windows-helloworld:latest

Hello World from Windows
```

Microsoft maintains good documentation about Windows containers (*https://oreil.ly/ fYMHl*)[5] that also includes an example of building a container that launches a .NET application (*https://oreil.ly/WG2W2*).[6]

---

5 Full URL: *https://learn.microsoft.com/en-us/virtualization/windowscontainers/about*

6 Full URL: *https://learn.microsoft.com/en-us/virtualization/windowscontainers/quick-start/building-sample-app*

On the Windows platform, it is also useful to know that you can get improved isolation for your container by launching it inside a dedicated and very lightweight Hyper-V VM. You can do this very easily by simply adding the `--isolation=hyperv` option to your `docker container create` and `docker container run` commands. There is a small performance and resource penalty for this, but it significantly improves the isolation of your container. You can read more about this in the documentation (*https://learn.microsoft.com/en-us/virtualization/windowscon tainers/manage-containers/hyperv-container*).

Even if you plan to mostly work with Windows containers, for the rest of the book you should switch back to Linux containers so that all the examples work as expected. When you are done reading and are ready to dive into building your containers, you can always switch back.

Remember that you can re-enable Linux containers by right-clicking on the Docker icon and selecting "Switch to Linux Containers…."

Wrap-Up

In the next chapter, we'll continue our exploration of what Docker brings to the table. For now, it's probably worth doing a little experimentation on your own. We suggest exercising some of the container control commands we covered here so that you're familiar with the command-line options and the overall syntax. Now would even be a great time to try to design and build a small image and then launch it as a new container. When you are ready to continue, head on to Chapter 6!

CHAPTER 6

Exploring Docker

Now that you have some experience working with containers and images, we can explore some of Docker's other capabilities. In this chapter, we'll continue to use the `docker` command-line tool to talk to the running `dockerd` server that you've configured while visiting some of the other fundamental commands.

Docker provides commands to do several additional things easily:

- Printing the Docker version
- Viewing the server information
- Downloading image updates
- Inspecting containers
- Entering a running container
- Returning a result
- Viewing logs
- Monitoring statistics
- And much more…

Let's take a look at these as well as some of the additional community tooling that augments Docker's native capabilities.

Printing the Docker Version

If you completed the last chapter, you have a working Docker daemon on a Linux server or VM, and you've started a base container to make sure it's all working. If you haven't set that up already and you want to try out the steps in the rest of the book, you'll want to follow the installation steps in Chapter 3 before you move on with this section.

The absolute simplest thing you can do with Docker is print the versions of the various components. It might not sound like much, but this is a useful tool to have because Docker is built from a multitude of components whose versions will directly dictate what functionality is available to you. Knowing how to show the version will also help you troubleshoot certain types of connection issues between the client and server. For example, the Docker client might give you a cryptic message about mismatched API versions, and it's nice to be able to translate that into Docker versions so you know which component needs updating. This command talks to the remote Docker server, so if the client can't connect to the server for any reason, the client will report an error and then only print out the client version information. If you find that you are having connectivity problems, you should probably revisit the steps in the last chapter.

 You can always directly log in to the Docker server and run docker commands from a shell on the server if you are troubleshooting issues or simply do not want to use the docker client to connect to a remote system. On most Docker servers, this will require either root privileges or membership in the docker group to connect to the Unix domain socket that Docker is listening on.

Since we just installed all of the Docker components at the same time, when we run docker version, we should see that all of our versions match:

```
$ docker version
Client:
 Cloud integration: v1.0.24
 Version:           20.10.17
 API version:       1.41
 Go version:        go1.17.11
 Git commit:        100c701
 Built:             Mon Jun  6 23:04:45 2022
 OS/Arch:           darwin/amd64
 Context:           default
 Experimental:      true

Server: Docker Desktop 4.10.1 (82475)
 Engine:
  Version:          20.10.17
```

```
API version:       1.41 (minimum version 1.12)
Go version:        go1.17.11
Git commit:        a89b842
Built:             Mon Jun  6 23:01:23 2022
OS/Arch:           linux/amd64
Experimental:      false
containerd:
 Version:          1.6.6
 GitCommit:        10c12954828e7c7c9b6e0ea9b0c02b01407d3ae1
runc:
 Version:          1.1.2
 GitCommit:        v1.1.2-0-ga916309
docker-init:
 Version:          0.19.0
 GitCommit:        de40ad0
```

Notice how we have different sections representing the client and server. In this case, we have a matching client and server since we just installed them together. But it's important to note that this won't always be the case. Hopefully, in your production systems, you can manage to keep the same version running on most systems. But it's not uncommon for development environments and build systems to have slightly different versions.

API clients and libraries will usually work across a large number of Docker versions, depending on which API version they require. In the Server section, we can see that the current API version is 1.41 and the minimum API it will serve is 1.12. This is useful information when you're working with third-party clients, and now you know how to verify this information.

Server Information

We can also find out a lot about the Docker server via the Docker client. Later we'll talk more about what all of this means, but you can find out which filesystem backend the Docker server is running, which kernel version it is on, which operating system it is running on, which plug-ins are installed, which runtime is being used, and how many containers and images are currently stored there. docker system info will present you with something similar to this, which has been shortened for brevity:

```
$ docker system info
Client:
 …
 Plugins:
  buildx: Docker Buildx (Docker Inc., v0.8.2)
  compose: Docker Compose (Docker Inc., v2.6.1)
  extension: Manages Docker extensions (Docker Inc., v0.2.7)
  sbom: View the packaged-based Software Bill Of Materials (SBOM) …
  scan: Docker Scan (Docker Inc., v0.17.0)
```

```
Server:
 Containers: 11
 …
 Images: 6
 Server Version: 20.10.17
 Storage Driver: overlay2
 …
 Plugins:
  Volume: local
  Network: bridge host ipvlan macvlan null overlay
  Log: awslogs fluentd gcplogs gelf journald json-file local logentries …
 …
 Runtimes: io.containerd.runc.v2 io.containerd.runtime.v1.linux runc
 Default Runtime: runc
 …
 Kernel Version: 5.10.104-linuxkit
 Operating System: Docker Desktop
 OSType: linux
 Architecture: x86_64
 …
```

Depending on how your Docker daemon is set up, this might look somewhat different. Don't be concerned about that; this is just to give you an example. Here we can see that our server is a Docker Desktop release running the 5.10.104 Linux kernel and backed with the overlay2 filesystem driver. We also have a few images and containers on the server. With a fresh install, this number should be zero.

The information about plug-ins is worth pointing out here. It's telling us about all the things this installation of Docker supports. On a fresh install, things will look more or less like this, depending on which new plug-ins are distributed with Docker. Docker itself is made up of many different plug-ins all working together. This is powerful because it means it's also possible to install several other plug-ins contributed by members of the community. It's useful to be able to see which are installed even if you just want to make sure Docker has recognized one that you recently added.

In most installations, */var/lib/docker* will be the default root directory used to store images and containers. If you need to change this, you can edit your Docker startup scripts to launch the daemon, with the --data-root argument pointing to a new storage location. To test this by hand, you could run something like this:

```
$ sudo dockerd \
    -H unix:///var/run/docker.sock \
    --data-root="/data/docker"
```

By default, the configuration file for the Docker server (*https://oreil.ly/jp7iK*)[1] can be found in */etc/docker/daemon.json*. Most of the arguments that we discuss passing directly to dockerd can be permanently set in this file. If you are using Docker Desktop, you are advised to modify this file in the Docker Desktop UI.

We will talk more about runtimes later, but here you can see that we have three runtimes installed. The runc runtime is the default Docker runtime. If you think of Linux containers, you are usually thinking about the type of container that runc builds. On this server, we also have the io.containerd.runc.v2 and io.containerd.runtime.v1.linux runtimes installed. We'll talk more about some other runtimes in Chapter 11.

Downloading Image Updates

We're going to use an Ubuntu base image for the following examples. Even if you already grabbed the ubuntu:latest base image once, you can pull it again and it will automatically pick up any updates that have been published since you last ran it.

This is because latest is a tag that, by convention, is supposed to represent the latest build of the container. However, the latest tag is controversial, since it is not permanently pinned to a specific image and can have different meanings across different projects. Some people use it to point to the most recent stable release, some use it to point to the last build produced by their CI/CD system, and others simply refuse to tag any of their images with latest. That being said, it is still in wide use and can be useful in preproduction environments where the convenience of using it outweighs the lack of assurances that a real version provides:

Invoking docker image pull will look like this:

```
$ docker image pull ubuntu:latest

latest: Pulling from library/ubuntu
405f018f9d1d: Pull complete
Digest: sha256:b6b83d3c331794420340093eb706a6f152d9c1fa51b262d9bf34594887c2c7ac
Status: Downloaded newer image for ubuntu:latest
docker.io/library/ubuntu:latest
```

That command pulled down only the layers that have changed since we last ran the command. You might see a longer or shorter list, or even an empty list, depending on when you last pulled the image, what changes have been pushed to the registry since then, and how many layers the target image contains.

---

1 Full URL: *https://docs.docker.com/engine/reference/commandline/dockerd/#daemon-configuration-file*

It's good to remember that even though you pulled latest, Docker won't automatically keep the local image up to date for you. You'll be responsible for doing that yourself. However, if you deploy an image based on a newer copy of ubuntu:latest, the Docker client will download the missing layers during the deployment just like you would expect. Keep in mind that this is the behavior of the Docker client, and other libraries or API tools may not behave this way. It's highly recommended that you always deploy production code using a fixed version tag rather than the latest tag. This helps guarantee that you get the version you expect and there are no unexpected surprises.

In addition to referring to items in the registry by the latest tag or another version number tag, you can refer to them by their content-addressable tag, which looks like this:

```
sha256:b6b83d3c331794420340093eb706a6f152d9c1fa51b262d9bf34594887c2c7ac
```

These are generated as a hashed sum of the contents of the image and are a very precise identifier. This is by far the safest way to refer to Docker images when you need to make sure you are getting the exact version you expect because these can't be moved like a version tag. The syntax for pulling them from the registry is very similar, but note the @ in the tag:

```
$ docker image pull ubuntu@sha256:b6b83d3c331794420340093eb706a6f152d…
```

Unlike most Docker commands where you may shorten the hash, you cannot do that with SHA-256 hashes. You must use the full hash here.

Inspecting a Container

Once you have a container created, running or not, you can now use docker to see how it was configured. This is often useful in debugging and also has some other information that can be useful for identifying a container.

For this example, go ahead and start up a container:

```
$ docker container run --rm -d -t ubuntu /bin/bash
3c4f916619a5dfc420396d823b42e8bd30a2f94ab5b0f42f052357a68a67309b
```

We can list all our running containers with docker container ls to ensure everything is running as expected, and to copy the container ID:

```
$ docker container ls
CONTAINER ID  IMAGE          COMMAND     … STATUS         … NAMES
3c4f916619a5  ubuntu:latest  "/bin/bash" … Up 31 seconds … angry_mestorf
```

In this case, our ID is 3c4f916619a5. We could also use angry_mestorf, which is the dynamic name assigned to our container. Many underlying tools need the unique container ID though, so it's useful to get into the habit of looking at that first. As we mentioned earlier, the ID as shown is the truncated (or short) version, but Docker treats these interchangeably with the long versions. As is the case in many version control systems, this hash is just the prefix of a much longer hash. Internally, the kernel uses a 64-byte hash to identify the container. But that's painful for humans to use, so Docker supports the shortened hash.

The output to docker container inspect is pretty verbose, so we'll cut it down in the following code block to a few values worth pointing out. You should look at the full output to see what else you think is interesting:

```
$ docker container inspect 3c4f916619a5

[{
    "Id": "3c4f916619a5dfc420396d823b42e8bd30a2f94ab5b0f42f052357a68a67309b",
    "Created": "2022-07-17T17:26:53.6117625412",
    ...
    "Args": [],
    ...
    "Image": "sha256:27941809078cc9b2802deb2b0bb6feed6c...7f200e24653533701ee",
    ...
    "Config": {
        "Hostname": "3c4f916619a5",
        ...
        "Env": [
          "PATH=/usr/local/sbin:/usr/local/bin:/usr/sbin:/usr/bin:/sbin:/bin"
        ],
        "Cmd": [
            "/bin/bash"
        ],
        ...
        "Image": "ubuntu",
        ...
    },
    ...
}]
```

Note that long "Id" string. That's the full unique identifier of this container. Luckily we can use the short version, even if that's still not especially convenient. We can also see that the exact time when the container was created is much more precise than what docker container ls gives us.

Some other interesting things are shown here as well: the top-level command in the container, the environment that was passed to it at creation time, the image on which it's based, and the hostname inside the container. All of these are configurable at container creation time if you need to do so. The usual method for passing configuration to containers, for example, is via environment variables, so being able to see how a container was configured via `docker container inspect` can reveal a lot when you're debugging.

You can go ahead and stop the current container by running something like `docker container stop 3c4f916619a5`.

Exploring the Shell

Let's get a container running with just an interactive `bash` shell so we can take a look around. We'll do that, as we did before, by running something like this:

```
$ docker container run --rm -it ubuntu:22.04 /bin/bash
```

That will run an Ubuntu 22.04 LTS container with the bash shell as the top-level process. By specifying the `22.04` tag, we can be sure to get a particular version of the image. So, when we start that container, what processes are running?

```
root@35fd1ad27228:/# ps -ef
UID        PID  PPID  C STIME TTY          TIME CMD
root         1     0  0 17:45 pts/0    00:00:00 /bin/bash
root         9     1  0 17:47 pts/0    00:00:00 ps -ef
```

Wow, that's not much, is it? It turns out that when we told `docker` to start `bash`, we didn't get anything but that. We're inside a whole Linux distribution image, but no other processes started for us automatically. We only got what we asked for. It's good to keep that in mind going forward.

> Linux containers don't, by default, start anything in the background as a full VM would. They're a lot lighter weight than that and therefore don't start an `init` system. You can, of course, run a whole `init` system if you need to, or the `tini` init system (*https://github.com/krallin/tini*) that is built into Docker, but you have to ask for it. We'll talk about that more in Chapter 7.

That's how we get a shell running in a container. Feel free to poke around and see what else looks interesting inside the container. You might have a pretty limited set of commands available. You're in a base Ubuntu distribution, though, so you can fix that by using `apt-get update`, followed by `apt-get install…` to download more packages. However, these applications are only going to be around for the life of this container. You're modifying the top layer of the container, not the base image! Containers are by nature ephemeral, so anything you do inside this container won't outlast it.

When you are done in the container, make sure to `exit` the shell, which will then naturally stop the container:

```
root@35fd1ad27228:/# exit
```

Returning a Result

How inefficient would it be to spin up a whole VM to run one command and get the results? You usually wouldn't want to do this because it would be very time-consuming and would require booting a whole operating system to simply execute one command. But Docker and Linux containers do not work the same way as VMs do: containers are very lightweight and don't have to boot up like an operating system does. Running something like a quick background job and waiting for the exit code is a normal use case for a Linux container. You can think of it as a way to get remote access to a containerized system and have access to any of the individual commands inside that container with the ability to pipe data to and from them and return exit codes.

This can be useful in lots of scenarios: you might, for instance, have system health checks run this way remotely or have a series of machines with processes that you spin up via Docker to process a workload and then return. The docker command-line tools proxy the results to the local machine. If you run the remote command in foreground mode and don't specify doing otherwise, docker will redirect its stdin to the remote process, and the remote process's stdout and stderr to your terminal. The only things we have to do to get this functionality are to run the command in the foreground and not allocate a TTY on the remote. This is also the default configuration! No command-line options are required.

When we run these commands, Docker creates a new container, executes the command that we requested inside the container's namespaces and cgroups, removes the container, and then exits so that nothing is left running or taking up unnecessary disk space between invocations. The following code should give you an idea of the types of things that you can do:

```
$ docker container run --rm ubuntu:22.04 /bin/false
$ echo $?
1

$ docker container run --rm ubuntu:22.04 /bin/true
$ echo $?
0

$ docker container run --rm ubuntu:22.04 /bin/cat /etc/passwd

root:x:0:0:root:/root:/bin/bash
daemon:x:1:1:daemon:/usr/sbin:/usr/sbin/nologin
…
nobody:x:65534:65534:nobody:/nonexistent:/usr/sbin/nologin
_apt:x:100:65534::/nonexistent:/usr/sbin/nologin

$ docker container run --rm ubuntu:22.04 /bin/cat /etc/passwd | wc -l

19
```

Here we executed /bin/false on the remote server, which will always exit with a status of 1. Notice how docker proxied that result to us in the local terminal. Just to prove that it returns other results, we also run /bin/true, which will always return a 0. And there it is.

Then we actually ask docker to run cat /etc/passwd on the remote container. What we get is a printout of the */etc/passwd* file contained inside that container's filesystem. Because that's just regular output on *stdout*, we can pipe it into local commands just like we would anything else.

 The previous code pipes the output into the local wc command, not a wc command in the container. The pipe itself is not passed to the container. If you want to pass the whole command, including the pipes, to the server, you need to invoke a complete shell on the remote side and pass a quoted command, like bash -c "<your command> | <something else>". In the previous code, that would be docker container run ubuntu:22.04 /bin/bash -c "/bin/cat /etc/passwd | wc -l".

Getting Inside a Running Container

You can pretty easily get a shell running in a new container, based on almost any image, as we demonstrated earlier with docker container run. But it's not the same as getting a new shell inside an existing container that is actively running your application. Every time you use docker container run, you get a new container. But if you have an existing container that is running an application and you need to debug it from inside the container, you need something else.

Using docker container exec is the Docker-native way to get a new interactive process in a container, but there is also a more Linux-native way to do it, called nsenter. We will take a look at docker container exec in this section and cover nsenter later in "nsenter" on page 334.

 You may be wondering why you would ever want to do this. In development, this can be very useful when you are actively building and testing your application. This is the mechanism that development containers (*https://containers.dev*) use in IDEs like Visual Studio Code (*https://code.visualstudio.com/docs/devcontainers/containers*).

In production, it isn't considered good practice to SSH into your production servers, and this is roughly the same thing; but there are times when it's very important to see what's going on inside the actual environment, and this can help you out in those situations.

docker container exec

First, let's take a look at the easiest and best way to get inside a running container. The dockerd server and docker command-line tool support remotely executing a new process in a running container via the docker container exec command. So let's start up a container in background mode and then enter it using docker container exec and invoking a shell.

The command you invoke doesn't have to be a shell: it's possible to run individual commands inside the container and see their results outside it using docker container exec. But if you want to get inside the container to look around, a shell is the easiest way to do that.

To run docker container exec, we'll need our container's ID. For this demo, let's create a container that will just run the sleep command for 600 seconds:

```
$ docker container run -d --rm  ubuntu:22.04 sleep 600
9f09ac4bcaa0f201e31895b15b479d2c82c30387cf2c8a46e487908d9c285eff
```

The short ID for this container is 9f09ac4bcaa0. We can now use that to get inside the container with docker container exec. The command line for that, unsurprisingly, looks a lot like the command line for docker container run. We request an interactive session and a pseudo-TTY with the -i and -t flags:

```
$ docker container exec -it 9f09ac4bcaa0 /bin/bash
root@9f09ac4bcaa0:/#
```

Note that we got a command line back that tells us the ID of the container we're running inside. That's pretty useful for keeping track of where we are. We can now run a normal Linux ps to see what else is running inside our container. We should see the sleep process that was created when the container was originally started:

```
root@9f09ac4bcaa0:/# ps -ef
UID        PID  PPID  C STIME TTY          TIME CMD
root         1     0  0 20:22 ?        00:00:00 sleep 600
root         7     0  0 20:23 pts/0    00:00:00 /bin/bash
root        15     7  0 20:23 pts/0    00:00:00 ps -ef
```

Type exit to get out of the container when you are done.

You can also run additional processes in the background via docker container exec. You use the -d option just like with docker container run. But you should think hard about doing that for anything but debugging because you lose the repeatability of the image deployment if you depend on this mechanism. Other people would then have to know what to pass to docker container exec to get the desired functionality. If you're tempted to do this, you would probably reap bigger gains from rebuilding your container image to launch both processes in a repeatable way. If you need to signal to the software inside the container to take some action like rotating logs or reloading a configuration, it is cleaner to leverage docker container kill -s <SIGNAL> with the standard Unix signal name to pass information to the process inside the container.

docker volume

Docker supports a volume subcommand that makes it possible to list all of the volumes stored in your root directory and then discover additional information about them, including where they are physically stored on the server.

These volumes are not bind-mounted; instead, they are special data containers that provide a useful method for persisting data.

If we run a normal docker command that bind-mounts a directory, we'll notice that it does not create any Docker volumes:

```
$ docker volume ls
DRIVER              VOLUME NAME

$ docker container run --rm -d -v /tmp:/tmp ubuntu:latest sleep 120
6fc97c50fb888054e2d01f0a93ab3b3db172b2cd402fc1cd616858b2b5138857

$ docker volume ls
DRIVER              VOLUME NAME
```

However, you can easily create a new volume with a command like this:

```
$ docker volume create my-data
```

If you then list all your volumes, you should see something like this:

```
$ docker volume ls

DRIVER              VOLUME NAME
local               my-data

$ docker volume inspect my-data

[
    {
        "CreatedAt": "2022-07-31T16:19:42Z",
        "Driver": "local",
        "Labels": {},
        "Mountpoint": "/var/lib/docker/volumes/my-data/_data",
        "Name": "my-data",
        "Options": {},
        "Scope": "local"
    }
]
```

Now you can start a container with this data volume attached to it by running the following:

```
$ docker container run --rm \
    --mount source=my-data,target=/app \
    ubuntu:latest touch /app/my-persistent-data
```

That container created a file in the data volume and then immediately exited.

If we now mount that data volume to a different container, we will see that our data is still there:

```
$ docker container run --rm \
    --mount source=my-data,target=/app \
    fedora:latest ls -lFa /app/my-persistent-data

-rw-r--r-- 1 root root 0 Jul 31 16:24 /app/my-persistent-data
```

And finally, you can delete the data volume when you are done with it by running the following:

```
$ docker volume rm my-data

my-data
```

If you try to delete a volume that is in use by a container (whether it is running or not), you'll get an error like this:

```
Error response from daemon: unable to remove volume:
    remove my-data: volume is in use - [
    d0763e6e8d79e55850a1d3ab21e9d…,
    4b40d52978ea5e784e66ddca8bc22…]
```

These commands should help you explore your containers in great detail. Once we've explained namespaces more in Chapter 11, you'll get a better understanding of exactly how all these pieces interact and combine to create a container.

Logging

Logging is a critical part of any production application. When things go wrong, logs can be a critical tool in restoring service, so they need to be done well. There are some common ways in which we expect to interact with application logs on Linux systems, some better than others. If you're running an application process on a box, you might expect the output to go to a local logfile that you could read through. Or perhaps you might expect the output to simply be logged to the kernel buffer where it can be read from dmesg. Or, as on many modern Linux distributions with systemd, you might expect logs to be available from journalctl. Because of the container's restrictions and how Docker is constructed, none of these will work without at least some configuration on your part. But that's OK because logging has first-class support in Docker.

Docker makes logging easier in a few critical ways. First, it captures all of the normal text output from applications in the containers it manages. Anything sent to stdout or stderr in the container is captured by the Docker daemon and streamed into a configurable logging backend. Secondly, like many other parts of Docker, this system is pluggable, and there are lots of powerful options available to you as plug-ins. But let's not dive into the deep end just yet.

docker container logs

We'll start with the simplest Docker use case: the default logging mechanism. There are limitations to this mechanism, which we'll explain in a minute, but for the most common use cases, it works well, and it's very convenient. If you are running Docker in development, this is probably the only logging strategy you'll use there. This logging method has been there from the very beginning and is well understood and supported. The mechanism is the json-file method. The docker container logs command exposes most users to this.

As implied by the name, when you run the default json-file logging plug-in, your application's logs are streamed by the Docker daemon into a JSON file for each container. This lets us retrieve logs for any container at any time.

We can display some logs by starting an nginx container:

```
$ docker container run --rm -d --name nginx-test --rm nginx:latest
```

and then:

```
$ docker container logs nginx-test
...
2022/07/31 16:36:05 [notice] 1#1: using the "epoll" event method
2022/07/31 16:36:05 [notice] 1#1: nginx/1.23.1
2022/07/31 16:36:05 [notice] 1#1: built by gcc 10.2.1 20210110 (Debian 10.2.1-6)
2022/07/31 16:36:05 [notice] 1#1: OS: Linux 5.10.104-linuxkit
...
```

This is nice because Docker allows you to get the logs remotely, right from the command line, on demand. That's very useful for low-volume logging.

 To limit the log output to more recent logs, you can use the --since option to display logs only after a specified RFC 3339 date (e.g., 2002-10-02T10:00:00-05:00), Unix timestamp (e.g., 1450071961), standard timestamp (e.g., 20220731), or Go duration string (e.g., 5m45s). You can also use --tail followed by the number of lines you would like to tail.

The actual files backing this logging are on the Docker server itself, by default in */var/lib/docker/containers/<container_id>/* where the *<container_id>* is replaced by the actual container ID. If you take a look at the file named *<container_id>*-json.log, you'll see that it's a file with each line representing a JSON object. It will look something like this:

```
{"log":"2022/07/31 16:36:05 [notice] 1#1: using the \"epoll\" event method\n",
  "stream":"stderr","time":"2022-07-31T16:36:05.189234362Z"}
```

That log field is exactly what was sent to stdout on the process in question; the stream field tells us that this was stdout and not stderr, and the precise time that the Docker daemon received it is provided in the time field. It's an uncommon format for logging, but it's structured rather than just a raw stream, which is beneficial if you want to do anything with the logs later.

Like a logfile, you can also tail the Docker logs live with docker container logs -f:

```
$ docker container logs -f nginx-test
...
2022/07/31 16:36:05 [notice] 1#1: start worker process 35
2022/07/31 16:36:05 [notice] 1#1: start worker process 36
2022/07/31 16:36:05 [notice] 1#1: start worker process 37
2022/07/31 16:36:05 [notice] 1#1: start worker process 38
```

This looks identical to the usual docker container logs, but the client will continue to wait for, and then display, new messages as they are received from the server, much like the Linux command line tail -f. You can type Ctrl-C to exit the logs stream at any time:

```
---
$ docker container stop nginx-test
---
```

 By configuring the tag log option similar to --log-opt tag="{{.ImageName}}/{{.ID}}", it is possible to change the default log tag (which every log line will start with) to something more useful. By default, Docker logs will be tagged with the first 12 characters of the container ID.

For single-host logging, this mechanism is pretty good. Its shortcomings are around log rotation, remote access to the logs once they've been rotated, and disk space usage for high-volume logging. Despite being backed by a JSON file, this mechanism performs well enough that most production applications can log this way if that's the solution that works for you. But if you have a more complex environment, you're going to want something more robust and with centralized logging capabilities.

 The default settings for dockerd do not currently enable log rotation. You'll want to make sure you specify the --log-opt max-size and --log-opt max-file settings via the command line or the *daemon.json* configuration file if you are running in production. Those settings limit the largest file size before rotation and the maximum number of logfiles to keep, respectively. max-file does not do anything unless you've also set max-size to tell Docker when to rotate the logs. When this is enabled, the docker container logs mechanism will return data only from the current logfile.

More Advanced Logging

For those times when the default mechanism isn't enough—and at scale, it's probably not—Docker also supports configurable logging backends. This list of plug-ins is constantly growing. Currently supported are the json-file we described earlier, as well as syslog, fluentd, journald, gelf, awslogs, splunk, gcplogs, local, and logentries, which are used for sending logs to various popular logging frameworks and services.

That's a big list of plug-ins we just threw out there. The supported option that currently is the simplest for running Docker at scale is sending your container logs to syslog directly from Docker. You can specify this on the Docker command line with the --log-driver=syslog option or set it as the default in the *daemon.json* file for all containers.

The *daemon.json* file is the configuration for the dockerd server. It can usually be found in the */etc/docker/* directory on the server. For Docker Desktop, this file can be edited in Preferences → Docker Engine from the UI. If you change this file, you will need to restart Docker Desktop or the dockerd daemon.

There are also several third-party plug-ins available. We've seen mixed results from third-party plug-ins, primarily because they complicate installing and maintaining Docker. However, you may find that there is a third-party implementation that's perfect for your system, and it might be worth the installation and maintenance hassle.

Some caveats apply to all of the logging drivers. For example, Docker supports only one at a time. This means that you can use the syslog or gelf logging driver, but not along with the json-file driver. Unless you run json-file or journald, you will lose the ability to use the docker container logs command! This may not be expected and is a big consideration when you are changing the driver.

Some plug-ins are designed to send the logs to a remote endpoint and keep a local JSON copy for the docker container logs command, but you will need to determine if the plug-in that you want to use supports this. There are too many gotchas to go through for each driver, but you should keep in mind the trade-off between guaranteed delivery of logs and the potential for breaking your Docker deployment. UDP-based solutions or other nonblocking options are recommended.

Traditionally, most Linux systems have some kind of syslog receiver, whether it be syslog, rsyslog, or any of the many other options. This protocol in its various forms has been around for a long time and is fairly well supported by most deployments. When migrating to Docker from a traditional Linux or Unix environment, many companies already have syslog infrastructure in place, which means this is often the easiest migration path as well.

Many newer Linux distributions are based on the `systemd` init system and therefore use `journald` for logging by default, which is different from `syslog`.

While syslog is a traditional solution, it has its problems. The Docker syslog driver supports TLS, TCP, and UDP connection options, which sounds great, but you should be cautious about streaming logs from Docker to a remote log server over TCP or TLS. The problem with this is that they are both run on top of connection-oriented TCP sessions, and Docker tries to connect to the remote logging server at the time of container startup. If it fails to make the connection, it will block trying to start the container. If you are running this as your default logging mechanism, this can strike at any time on any deployment.

This is not a particularly usable state for production systems, and thus it is recommended that you use the UDP option for syslog logging if you intend to use the `syslog` driver. This does mean your logs are not encrypted and do not have guaranteed delivery. There are various philosophies around logging, and you'll need to balance your need for logs against the reliability of your system. We tend to recommend erring on the side of reliability, but if you run in a secure audit environment, you may have different priorities.

 You can log directly to a remote syslog-compatible server from a single container by setting the log option `syslog-address` similar to this: `--log-opt syslog-address=udp://192.168.42.42:123`.

One final caveat to be aware of regarding most of the logging plug-ins: they are blocking by default, which means that logging back-pressure can cause issues with your application. You can change this behavior by setting `--log-opt mode=non-blocking` and then setting the maximum buffer size for logs to something like `--log-opt max-buffer-size=4m`. Once these are set, the application will no longer block when that buffer fills up. Instead, the oldest loglines in memory will be dropped. Again, reliability needs to be weighed here against your business's need to receive all the logs.

Some third-party libraries and programs write to the filesystem for various (and sometimes unexpected) reasons. If you are trying to design clean containers that do not write directly into the container filesystem, you should consider utilizing the `--read-only` and `--mount type=tmpfs` options to `docker container run` that we discussed in Chapter 4. Writing logs *inside* the container is not recommended. It makes them hard to get to, prevents them from being preserved beyond the container life span, and can wreak havoc with the Docker filesystem backend.

Monitoring Docker

Among the most important requirements for production systems is that they are observable and measurable. A production system where you are blind to how it's behaving won't serve you well. In modern operations environments, we want to monitor everything meaningful and report as many useful statistics as we can. Docker supports container health checks and some basic reporting capabilities via `docker container stats` and `docker system events`. We'll show you those and then look at a community offering from Google that does some nice graphing output, and then we'll take a look at a—currently experimental—feature of Docker that exports container metrics to the Prometheus monitoring system.

Container Statistics

Let's start with the CLI tools that ship with Docker itself. The `docker` CLI has an endpoint for viewing important statistics of running containers. The command-line tool can stream from this endpoint and every few seconds report back on one or more listed containers, giving basic statistics information about what's happening. `docker container stats`, like the Linux `top` command, takes over the current terminal and updates the same lines on the screen with the current information. It's hard to show that in print so we'll just give an example, but this updates every few seconds by default.

Command-line statistics

Start an active container:

```
$ docker container run --rm -d --name stress \
    docker.io/spkane/train-os:latest \
    stress -v --cpu 2 --io 1 --vm 2 --vm-bytes 128M --timeout 60s
```

Then run the `stats` command to look at the new container:

```
$ docker container stats stress
CONTAINER ID NAME    CPU %    MEM USAGE/LIMIT    MEM % NET I/O    BLOCK I/O PIDS
1a9f52f0855f stress 476.50% 36.09MiB/7.773GiB 0.45% 1.05kB/0B 0B/0B      6
```

You can type Ctrl-C to exit the `stats` stream at any time.

 You can use the `--no-stream` option to get a single-point-in-time set of statistics that will not update and will return you back to the command line after the command completes.

Let's break that rather dense output down into some manageable chunks. We have the following:

- The container ID (but not the name).
- The amount of CPU it's currently consuming. One hundred percent is equivalent to one whole CPU core.
- The amount of memory it has in use, followed by the maximum amount it's allowed to use.
- Network and block I/O statistics.
- The number of active processes inside the container.

Some of these will be more useful than others for debugging, so let's take a look at what you can do with them.

One of the more helpful pieces of output here is the percentage of memory used versus the limit that was set for the container. One common problem with running production containers is that overly aggressive memory limits can cause the Linux kernel's OOM killer to stop the container over and over again. The `stats` command can help you identify and troubleshoot these types of issues.

Concerning I/O statistics, if you run all of your applications in containers, then this summary can make it very clear where your I/O is going from the system. Before containers, this was much harder to figure out!

The number of active processes inside the container helps debug as well. If you have an application that is spawning children without reaping them, this can expose it pretty quickly.

One great feature of `docker container stats` is that it can show not just one container but all of them in a single summary. That can be pretty revealing, even on boxes where you think you know what they are doing.

That is all useful and easy to digest because it's human formatted and available on the command line. But there is an additional endpoint on the Docker API that provides a *lot* more information than is shown in the client. We've steered away from directly utilizing the API in this book so far, but in this case, the data provided by the API is so much richer than the client that we'll go ahead and use curl to make an API request and see what our container is doing. It's nowhere near as nice to read, but there is a lot more detail.

 Remember that basically everything that the docker client can do can be done directly through the Docker APIs. This means that you can programmatically do very similar things in your applications if there is a need.

The example in "stats API endpoint" on page 157 is a good intro to calling the API directly.

stats API endpoint

The /stats/ endpoint that we'll hit on the API will continue to stream statistics to us as long as we keep the connection open. Since as humans we can't easily parse the JSON, we'll just ask for one line and then use the tool jq to "pretty-print" it. For this command to work, you'll need to have jq installed (version 2.6 or later). If you don't and you still want to see the JSON output, you can skip the pipe to jq, but you'll get plain, ugly JSON back. If you already have a favorite JSON pretty printer, feel free to use that instead.

Most Docker daemons will be installed with the API available only on the Unix domain socket and not published on TCP. So we'll use curl from the Docker server host itself to call the API. If you plan to monitor this endpoint in production, you would need to expose the Docker API on a TCP port. This is not something that we recommend, but the Docker documentation (*https://dockr.ly/2Lzuox2*) will walk you through this.

 If you are not on the Docker server or using Docker Desktop locally, you may need to inspect the contents of the DOCKER_HOST environment variable, using something like echo $DOCKER_HOST, to discover the hostname or IP address of the Docker server that you are using.

First, start up a container that you can read statistics from:

```
$ docker container run --rm -d --name stress \
    docker.io/spkane/train-os:latest \
    stress -v --cpu 2 --io 1 --vm 2 --vm-bytes 128M --timeout 60s
```

Now that the container is running, you can get an ongoing stream of statistics about the container in JSON format by running something like curl with your container's name or hash.

 In the following examples, we are running curl against the Docker socket, but you could just as easily run it against the Docker port if it is available.

```
$ curl --no-buffer -XGET --unix-socket /var/run/docker.sock \
    http://docker/containers/stress/stats
```

 This JSON stream of statistics will not stop on its own. So for now, we can use the Ctrl-C key combination to stop it.

To get a single group of statistics, we can run something similar to this:

```
$ curl -s -XGET --unix-socket /var/run/docker.sock \
    http://docker/containers/stress/stats | head -n 1 | jq
```

And finally, if we have jq (*https://stedolan.github.io/jq*) or another tool capable of pretty-printing JSON, we can make this output human readable, as shown here:

```
$ curl -s -XGET --unix-socket /var/run/docker.sock \
    http://docker/containers/stress/stats | head -n 1 | jq
{
  "read": "2022-07-31T17:41:59.1059483Z",
  "preread": "0001-01-01T00:00:00Z",
  "pids_stats": {
    "current": 6,
    "limit": 18446744073709552000
  },
  "blkio_stats": {
    "io_service_bytes_recursive": [
      {
        "major": 254,
        "minor": 0,
        "op": "read",
        "value": 0
      },
      ...
    ]
  },
  "num_procs": 0,
  "storage_stats": {},
  "cpu_stats": {
```

```
      "cpu_usage": {
        "total_usage": 101883204000,
        "usage_in_kernelmode": 43818021000,
        "usage_in_usermode": 58065183000
  …
      },
    },
    "memory_stats": {
      "usage": 183717888,
      "stats": {
        "active_anon": 0,
        "active_file": 0,
  …
      },
      "limit": 8346021888
    },
    "name": "/stress",
    "id": "9be7c9de26864ac97e07fc3d8e3ffb5bb52cc2ba49f569d4ba8d407f8747851f",
    "networks": {
      "eth0": {
        "rx_bytes": 1046,
        "rx_packets": 9,
  …
      }
    }
  }
```

There is *a lot* of information in there. We've cut it down to prevent wasting any more trees or electrons than necessary, but even so, there is a lot to digest. The main idea is to let you see how much data is available from the API about each container. We won't spend much time going into the details, but you can get quite detailed memory usage information, as well as block I/O and CPU usage information.

If you are doing your own monitoring, this is a great endpoint to hit as well. A drawback, however, is that it's one endpoint per container, so you can't get the statistics about all containers from a single call.

Container Health Checks

As with any other application, when you launch a container it is possible that it will start and run but never actually enter a healthy state where it could receive traffic. Production systems also fail, and your application may become unhealthy at some point during its life, so you need to be able to deal with that.

Many production environments have standardized ways to health-check applications. Unfortunately, there's no clear standard for how to do that across organizations, and it's unlikely that many companies do it in the same way. For this reason, monitoring systems have been built to handle that complexity so that they can work in a lot of different production systems. It's a clear place where a standard would be a big win.

To help remove this complexity and standardize on a universal interface, Docker has added a health-check mechanism. Following the shipping container metaphor, Linux containers should really look the same to the outside world no matter what is inside the container, so Docker's health-check mechanism not only standardizes health checking for containers but also maintains the isolation between what is inside the container and what it looks like on the outside. This means that containers from Docker Hub or other shared repositories can implement a standardized health-checking mechanism, and it will work in any other Docker environment designed to run production containers.

Health checks are a build-time configuration item and are created with a HEALTHCHECK definition in the *Dockerfile*. This directive tells the Docker daemon what command it can run inside the container to ensure the container is in a healthy state. As long as the command exits with a code of zero (0), Docker will consider the container to be healthy. Any other exit code will indicate to Docker that the container is not in a healthy state, at which point appropriate action can be taken by a scheduler or monitoring system.

We will be using the following project to explore Docker Compose in a few chapters. But, for the moment, it includes a useful example of Docker health checks. Go ahead and pull down a copy of the code, and then navigate into the *rocketchat-hubot-demo/mongodb/docker/* directory:

```
$ git clone https://github.com/spkane/rocketchat-hubot-demo.git \
    --config core.autocrlf=input
$ cd rocketchat-hubot-demo/mongodb/docker
```

In this directory, you will see a *Dockerfile* and a script called docker-healthcheck. If you view the *Dockerfile*, this is all that you will see:

```
FROM docker.io/bitnami/mongodb:4.4
# Newer Upstream Dockerfile:
# https://github.com/bitnami/containers/blob/
# f9fb3f8a6323fb768fd488c77d4f111b1330bd0e/bitnami/mongodb
# /5.0/debian-11/Dockerfile

COPY docker-healthcheck /usr/local/bin/

# Useful Information:
# https://docs.docker.com/engine/reference/builder/#healthcheck
# https://docs.docker.com/compose/compose-file/#healthcheck
HEALTHCHECK CMD ["docker-healthcheck"]
```

It is very short because we are basing this on the upstream Mongo image (*https://oreil.ly/Is1yt*),[2] and our image inherits a lot of things from that, including the entry point, default command, and port to expose.

 Bitnami significantly refactored their container repositories in early 2023, so this link points to a slightly newer version of the *Dockerfile* that targets MongoDB 5.0. We are using MongoDB 4.4 in this example, but the link should still get the point across.

```
EXPOSE 27017
ENTRYPOINT [ "/opt/bitnami/scripts/mongodb/entrypoint.sh" ]
CMD [ "/opt/bitnami/scripts/mongodb/run.sh" ]
```

 Be aware that Docker will forward traffic to a container's ports even when the container and underlying processes are still spinning up.

So, in our *Dockerfile* we are only adding a single script that can health-check our container, and defining a health-check command that runs that script.

You can build the container like this:

```
$ docker image build -t mongo-with-check:4.4 .
 => [internal] load build definition from Dockerfile              0.0s
 => => transferring dockerfile: 37B                               0.0s
 => [internal] load .dockerignore                                 0.0s
 => => transferring context: 2B                                   0.0s
 => [internal] load metadata for docker.io/bitnami/mongodb:4.4    0.5s
 => [internal] load build context                                 0.0s
 => => transferring context: 40B                                  0.0s
 => CACHED [1/2] FROM docker.io/bitnami/mongodb:4.4@sha256:9162…ae209  0.0s
 => [2/2] COPY docker-healthcheck /usr/local/bin/                 0.0s
 => exporting to image                                            0.0s
 => => exporting layers                                           0.0s
 => => writing image sha256:a6ef…da808                            0.0s
 => => naming to docker.io/library/mongo-with-check:4.4           0.0s
```

And then run the container and look at the docker container ls output:

```
$ docker container run -d --rm --name mongo-hc mongo-with-check:4.4
5a807c892428ab0641232c82bd477fc8d1142c9e15c27d5946b8bfe7056e2695

$ docker container ls
```

---

2 Full URL: *https://github.com/bitnami/containers/blob/f9fb3f8a6323fb768fd488c77d4f111b1330bd0e/bit nami/mongodb/5.0/debian-11/Dockerfile*

```
... IMAGE                 ... STATUS                PORTS    ...
... mongo-with-check:4.4 … Up 1 second (health: starting) 27017/tcp …
```

You should notice that the STATUS column now has a health section in parentheses. Initially, this will display health: starting as the container is starting up. You can change the amount of time that Docker waits for the container to initialize using the --health-start-period argument to docker container run. The status will change to healthy once the container is up and the health check is successful. It might take this container 40+ seconds to transition into a healthy state:

```
$ docker container ls
... IMAGE                 ... STATUS                PORTS        ...
... mongo-with-check:4.4 … Up 32 seconds (healthy) 27017/tcp …
```

You can query this status directly, using the docker container inspect command:

```
$ docker container inspect --format='{{.State.Health.Status}}' mongo-hc
healthy

$ docker container inspect --format='{{json .State.Health}}' mongo-hc | jq
{
  "Status": "healthy",
  "FailingStreak": 0,
  "Log": [
    …
  ]
}
```

If your container begins failing its health check, the status will change to unhealthy, and you can then determine how to handle the situation:

```
$ docker container ls
... IMAGE                 ... STATUS                PORTS        ...
... mongo-with-check:4.4 … Up 9 minutes (unhealthy) 27017/tcp …
```

At this point, you can stop the container by simply running docker container stop mongo-hc.

 As with most systems, you can configure a lot of details about your health checks, including how often Docker checks the health (--health-interval), how many failures are required to cause the container to be marked unhealthy (--health-retries), and more. You can even disable the health check completely (--no-healthcheck) if needed.

This feature is very useful, and you should strongly consider using it in all of your containers. This will help you improve both the reliability of your environment and the visibility you have into how things are running in it. It is also supported by many production schedulers and monitoring systems, so it should be easy to implement.

As always, the usefulness of a health check is largely determined by how well written it is and how accurately it determines the state of the service.

docker system events

The dockerd daemon internally generates an events stream around the container lifecycle. This is how various parts of the system find out what is going on in other parts. You can also tap into this stream to see what lifecycle events are happening for containers on your Docker server. This, as you probably expect by now, is implemented in the docker CLI tool as another command-line argument. When you run this command, it will block and continually stream messages to you. Behind the scenes, this is a long-lived HTTP request to the Docker API that returns messages in JSON blobs as they occur. The docker CLI tool decodes them and prints some data to the terminal.

This events stream is useful in monitoring scenarios or triggering additional actions, like wanting to be alerted when a job completes. For debugging purposes, it allows you to see when a container died even if Docker restarts it later. Down the road, this is a place where you might also find yourself directly implementing some tooling against the API.

In one terminal, go ahead and run the events command:

```
$ docker system events
```

You will notice that nothing happens.

In another terminal, go ahead and launch the following short-lived container:

```
$ docker container run --rm --name sleeper debian:latest sleep 5
```

In the original terminal that is running the events command, you should now see something like this:

```
…09:59.606… container create d6… (image=debian:latest, name=sleeper)
…09:59.610… container attach d6… (image=debian:latest, name=sleeper)
…09:59.631… network connect ea… (container=d60b…, name=bridge, type=bridge)
…09:59.827… container start d6… (image=debian:latest, name=sleeper)
…10:04.854… container die d6… (exitCode=0, image=debian:latest, name=sleeper)
…10:04.907… network disconnect ea… (container=d60b…, name=bridge, type=bridge)
…10:04.922… container destroy d6… (image=debian:latest, name=sleeper)
```

You can type Ctrl-C to exit the events stream at any time.

As with the Docker statistics, you can access the Docker system events via `curl` using a command like `curl --no-buffer -XGET --unix-socket /var/run/docker.sock` *http://docker/events.*

In this example, we ran a short-lived container that simply counted 5 seconds and then exited.

The `container create`, `container attach`, `network connect`, and `container start` events are all the steps required to get the container into a running state. When the container exits, the events stream logs a `container die`, `network disconnect`, and `container destroy` message. Each one of these marks a step in completely tearing down the container. Docker also helpfully tells us the ID of the image that the container is running on. This can be useful for tying deployments to events, for example, because a deployment usually involves a new image.

If you have a server where containers are not staying up, the `docker system events` stream is pretty helpful in seeing what's going on and when. But if you're not watching it at the time, Docker very helpfully caches some of the events, and you can still get at them for some time afterward. You can ask it to display events after a time with the `--since` option, or before with the `--until` option. You can also use both to limit the window to a narrow scope of time when an issue you are investigating may have occurred. Both options take ISO time formats like those in the previous example (e.g., 2018-02-18T14:03:31-08:00).

There are a few specific event types that you should go out of your way to monitor:

`container oom`
    Appears when a container runs out of memory

`container exec_create`
`container exec_start`
`container exec_die`
    Appear when someone has used `docker container exec` to
    enter a container, which could signal a security incident

cAdvisor

`docker container stats` and `docker system events` are useful but don't get us graphs to look at yet. And graphs are pretty helpful when we're trying to see trends. Of course, other people have filled some of this gap. When you begin to explore the options for monitoring Docker, you will find that many of the major monitoring tools now provide some functionality to help you improve the visibility into your containers' performance and ongoing state.

In addition to the commercial tooling provided by companies like Datadog, Ground-Work, and New Relic, there are plenty of options for free, open source tools like Prometheus or even Nagios. We'll talk about Prometheus in "Prometheus Monitoring" on page 167. Soon after Docker was introduced, Google released its internal container monitoring tool as a well-maintained open source project on GitHub, called cAdvisor (*https://github.com/google/cadvisor*). Although cAdvisor can be run outside of Docker, by now you're probably not surprised to hear that the easiest implementation of cAdvisor is to simply run it as a Linux container.

To install cAdvisor on most Linux systems, all you need to do is run this code.

 This command is intended to be run directly on a Linux Docker server. It will not work properly when run from a Windows or macOS system.

```
$ docker container run \
  --volume=/:/rootfs:ro \
  --volume=/var/run:/var/run:ro \
  --volume=/sys:/sys:ro \
  --volume=/var/lib/docker/:/var/lib/docker:ro \
  --volume=/dev/disk/:/dev/disk:ro \
  --publish=8080:8080 \
  --detach=true \
  --name=cadvisor \
  --privileged \
  --rm \
  --device=/dev/kmsg \
  gcr.io/cadvisor/cadvisor:latest

Unable to find image 'cadvisor/cadvisor:latest' locally
Pulling repository cadvisor/cadvisor
f0643dafd7f5: Download complete
...
ba9b663a8908: Download complete
Status: Downloaded newer image for cadvisor/cadvisor:latest
f54e6bc0469f60fd74ddf30770039f1a7aa36a5eda6ef5100cddd9ad5fda350b
```

 On Red Hat Enterprise Linux (RHEL)-based systems, you may need to add the following line to the docker container run command shown here: --volume=/cgroup:/cgroup \.

Once you have done this, you will be able to navigate to your Docker host on port 8080 to see the cAdvisor web interface (e.g., *http://172.17.42.10:8080/*) and the various detailed charts it has for the host and individual containers (see Figure 6-1).

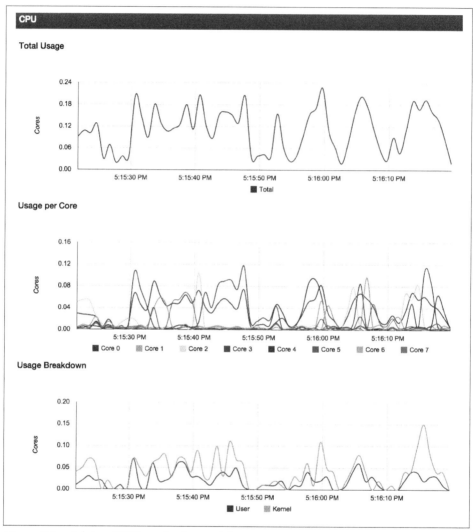

Figure 6-1. cAdvisor CPU graphs (example)

cAdvisor provides a REST API endpoint, which can easily be queried for detailed information by your monitoring systems:

```
$ curl http://172.17.42.10:8080/api/v2.1/machine/
```

You can find details about the cAdvisor API in the official documentation (*https://github.com/google/cadvisor/blob/master/docs/api_v2.md*).

The amount of detail provided by cAdvisor should be sufficient for many of your graphing and monitoring needs.

Prometheus Monitoring

The Prometheus (*https://prometheus.io*) monitoring system has become a popular solution for monitoring distributed systems. It works largely on a pull model, where it reaches out and gathers statistics from endpoints on a timed basis. Docker has an endpoint that was built for Prometheus and makes it easy to integrate your container stats into a Prometheus monitoring system. At the time of this writing, the endpoint is currently experimental and not enabled in the dockerd server by default. Our brief experience with it shows that it seems to work well, and it's a pretty slick solution, as we'll show you. We should point out that this solution is for monitoring the dockerd server, in contrast to the other solutions, which exposed information about the containers.

To export metrics to Prometheus, we need to reconfigure the dockerd server to enable the experimental features and to expose the metrics listener on a port of our choice. This is nice because we don't have to expose the whole Docker API on a TCP listener to get metrics out of the system—a security win at the expense of a little more configuration. To do that, we can either provide the --experimental and --metrics-addr= options on the command line, or we can put them into the *daemon.json* file that the daemon uses to configure itself. Because many current distributions run systemd, and changing configurations there is highly dependent on your installation, we'll use the *daemon.json* option since it's more portable. We'll demonstrate this on Ubuntu Linux 22.04 LTS. On this distribution, the file is usually not present to begin with. So let's put one there using your favorite editor.

 As previously mentioned, the *daemon.json* file for Docker Desktop can be edited in Preferences → Docker Engine from the UI. If you change this file, you will need to restart Docker Desktop or the dockerd daemon.

Adjust or add the following lines to the *daemon.json* file:

```
{
  "experimental": true,
  "metrics-addr": "0.0.0.0:9323"
}
```

You should now have a file that contains only what you just pasted and nothing else.

Any time you make a service available on the network, you need to consider what security risks you might introduce. We believe the benefit of making metrics available is worth the trade-off, but you should think through the repercussions in your scenario. For example, making metrics available on the public internet is probably not a good idea in almost all cases.

When we restart Docker, we'll now have a listener on all addresses on port 9323. That's where Prometheus will connect to get the metrics. But first, we need to restart the dockerd server. Docker Desktop automatically takes care of the restart for you, but if you are on the Linux Docker server, then you can run something like `sudo systemctl restart docker` to restart the daemon. You should not get any errors returned from the restart. If you do, you likely have something set incorrectly in the *daemon.json* file.

Now you can test the metrics endpoint with `curl`:

```
$ curl -s http://localhost:9323/metrics | head -15

# HELP builder_builds_failed_total Number of failed image builds
# TYPE builder_builds_failed_total counter
builder_builds_failed_total{reason="build_canceled"} 0
builder_builds_failed_total{reason="build_target_not_reachable_error"} 0
builder_builds_failed_total{reason="command_not_supported_error"} 0
builder_builds_failed_total{reason="dockerfile_empty_error"} 0
builder_builds_failed_total{reason="dockerfile_syntax_error"} 0
builder_builds_failed_total{reason="error_processing_commands_error"} 0
builder_builds_failed_total{reason="missing_onbuild_arguments_error"} 0
builder_builds_failed_total{reason="unknown_instruction_error"} 0
# HELP builder_builds_triggered_total Number of triggered image builds
# TYPE builder_builds_triggered_total counter
builder_builds_triggered_total 0
# HELP engine_daemon_container_actions_seconds The number of seconds it
# takes to process each container action
# TYPE engine_daemon_container_actions_seconds histogram
```

If you run this locally, you should get very similar output. It might not be identical, and that's OK as long as you get something that is not an error message.

So now we have a place where Prometheus can get to our statistics. But we need to have Prometheus running somewhere, right? We can easily do that by spinning up a container. But first, we need to write a simple config. We'll put it in */tmp/prometheus/prometheus.yaml*. You can use your favorite editor to put the following into the file:

```
# Scrape metrics every 5 seconds and name the monitor 'stats-monitor'
global:
  scrape_interval: 5s
  external_labels:
```

```
        monitor: 'stats-monitor'

    # We're going to name our job 'DockerStats' and we'll connect to the docker0
    # bridge address to get the stats. If your docker0 has a different IP address
    # then use that instead. 127.0.0.1 and localhost will not work.
    scrape_configs:
      - job_name: 'DockerStats'
        static_configs:
        - targets: ['172.17.0.1:9323']
```

 For Docker Desktop, you can also use `host.docker.inter`
`nal:9323` or `gateway.docker.internal:9323` in place of the
`172.17.0.1:9323` shown here. Both of these hostnames will point
to the container's IP address.

As noted in the file, you should use the IP address of your `docker0` bridge here, or
the IP address of your `ens3` or `eth0` interface since `localhost` and `127.0.0.1` are
not routable from the container. The address we used here is the usual default for
`docker0`, so it's probably the right one for you.

Now that we've written that out, we need to start up the container using this config:

```
$ docker container run --rm -d -p 9090:9090 \
    -v /tmp/prometheus/prometheus.yaml:/etc/prometheus.yaml \
    prom/prometheus --config.file=/etc/prometheus.yaml
```

That will run the container and volume-mount the config file we made into the
container so that it will find the settings it needs to monitor our Docker endpoint.
If it starts up cleanly, you should now be able to open your browser and navigate
to port 9090 on your host. There you will get a Prometheus window, something like
Figure 6-2.

In the following figure, you'll see that we've selected one of the metrics, the
`engine_daemon_events_total`, and graphed it over a short period. You can easily
query any of the other metrics in the drop-down. Further work and exploration
with Prometheus would allow you to define alerts and alerting policies based on
these metrics as well. And it is easy to monitor so much more than just the `dockerd`
server. You can also expose metrics for Prometheus from your applications. If you're
intrigued and want to look at something more advanced, you might take a look
at dockprom (*https://github.com/stefanprodan/dockprom*), which leverages Grafana to
make nice dashboards and also queries your container metrics like those in the
Docker API `/stats` endpoint.

Figure 6-2. Prometheus event graph (example)

Exploration

This should give you all the basics you need to start running containers. It's probably worth downloading a container or two from the Docker Hub registry and exploring a bit on your own to get used to the commands we just learned. There are many other things you can do with Docker, including but not limited to the following:

- Copying files in and out of the container with `docker container cp`
- Saving an image to a tarball with `docker image save`
- Loading an image from a tarball with `docker image import`

Docker has a huge feature set that you will likely grow into over time. Each new release adds more functionality as well. We'll get into a lot more detail later on about many of the other commands and features, but keep in mind that Docker's whole feature set is very large.

Wrap-Up

In the next chapter, we'll dive into more technical details about how Docker works and how you can use this knowledge to debug your containerized applications.

## CHAPTER 7

Debugging Containers

Once you've shipped an application to production, there will come a day when it's not working as expected. It's always nice to know ahead of time what to expect when that day comes. It's also important to have a good understanding of debugging containers before moving on to more complex deployments. Without debugging skills, it will be difficult to see where orchestration systems have gone wrong. So let's take a look at debugging containers.

In the end, debugging a containerized application is not all that different from debugging a normal process on a system except that the tools are somewhat different. Docker provides some pretty nice tooling to help you out! Some of these map to regular system tools, and some go further.

It is also critical to understand that your application is not running in a separate system from the other Docker processes. They share a kernel, and depending on your container configuration, they may share other things like a storage subsystem and network interfaces. This means that you can get a lot of information about what your container is doing from the system.

If you're used to debugging applications in a VM environment, you might think you would need to enter the container to inspect an application's memory or CPU use, or to debug its system calls. However, this is not so! Despite feeling in many ways like a virtualization layer, processes in containers are just processes on the Linux host itself. If you want to see a process list across all of the Linux containers on a machine, you could log in to the server and run ps with your favorite command-line options. However, you can use the docker container top command from anywhere to see the list of processes running in your container from the viewpoint of the underlying Linux kernel. Let's take a more detailed look at some of the things that you can do when debugging a containerized application that do not require the use of either docker container exec or nsenter.

Process Output

One of the first things you'll want to know when debugging a container is what is running inside it. As we mentioned previously, Docker has a built-in command for doing just that: docker container top. This is not the only way to see what's going on inside a container, but it is by far the easiest to use. Let's see how that works:

```
$ docker container run --rm -d --name nginx-debug --rm nginx:latest
796b282bfed33a4ec864a32804ccf5cbbee688b5305f094c6fbaf20009ac2364

$ docker container top nginx-debug

UID    PID  PPID C STIME TTY TIME  CMD
root   2027 2002 0 12:35 ?   00:00 nginx: master process nginx -g daemon off;
uuidd  2085 2027 0 12:35 ?   00:00 nginx: worker process
uuidd  2086 2027 0 12:35 ?   00:00 nginx: worker process
uuidd  2087 2027 0 12:35 ?   00:00 nginx: worker process
uuidd  2088 2027 0 12:35 ?   00:00 nginx: worker process
uuidd  2089 2027 0 12:35 ?   00:00 nginx: worker process
uuidd  2090 2027 0 12:35 ?   00:00 nginx: worker process
uuidd  2091 2027 0 12:35 ?   00:00 nginx: worker process
uuidd  2092 2027 0 12:35 ?   00:00 nginx: worker process

$ docker container stop nginx-debug
```

To run docker container top, we need to pass it the name or ID of our container, and then we receive a nice listing of what is running inside our container, ordered by PID just as we'd expect from Linux ps output.

There are some oddities here, though. The primary one is the name-spacing of user IDs and filesystems.

It is important to understand that the username for a particular user ID (UID) can be completely different between each container and the host system. It is even possible that a specific UID has no named user in the container or host's /etc/passwd file associated with it at all. This is because Unix does not require a UID to have a named user associated with it, and Linux namespaces, which we discuss much more in "Namespaces" on page 299, provide some isolation between the container's concept of valid users and those on the underlying host.

Let's look at a more concrete example of this. Let's consider a production Docker server running Ubuntu 22.04 and a container running on it that has an Ubuntu distribution inside. If you run the following commands on the Ubuntu host, you would see that UID 7 is named lp:

```
$ id 7

uid=7(lp) gid=7(lp) groups=7(lp)
```

There is nothing special about the UID number we are using here. You don't need to take any particular note of it. It was chosen simply because it is used by default on both platforms but represents a different username.

If we then enter the standard Fedora container on that Docker host, you will see that UID 7 is set to halt in */etc/passwd*. By running the following commands, you can see that the container has a completely different perspective of who UID 7 is:

```
$ docker container run --rm -it fedora:latest /bin/bash

root@c399cb807eb7:/# id 7
uid=7(halt) gid=0(root) groups=0(root)

root@c399cb807eb7:/# grep x:7: /etc/passwd
halt:x:7:0:halt:/sbin:/sbin/halt

root@409c2a8216b1:/# exit
```

If we then run `ps aux` on the theoretical Ubuntu Docker server while that container is running as UID 7 (`-u 7`), we see that the Docker host shows the container process as being run by `lp` instead of `halt`:

```
$ docker container run --rm -d -u 7 fedora:latest sleep 120

55…c6

$ ps aux | grep sleep

lp         2388  0.2  0.0   2204   784 ?     … 0:00 sleep 120
vagrant    2419  0.0  0.0   5892  1980 pts/0 … 0:00 grep --color=auto sleep
```

This could be particularly confusing if a well-known user like `nagios` or `postgres` were configured on the host system but not in the container, yet the container ran its process with the same ID. This namespacing can make the `ps` output look quite strange. It might, for example, look like the `nagios` user on your Docker host is running the `postgresql` daemon that was launched inside a container, if you don't pay close attention.

One solution to this is to dedicate a nonzero UID to your containers. On your Docker servers, you can create a `container` user as UID 5000 and then create the same user in your base container images. If you then run all your containers as UID 5000 (`-u 5000`), not only will you improve the security of your system by not running container processes as UID 0, but you will also make the `ps` output on the Docker host easier to decipher by displaying the `container` user for all of your running container processes. Some systems use the `nobody` or `daemon` user for the same purpose, but we prefer `container` for clarity. There is a little more detail about how this works in "Namespaces" on page 299.

Likewise, because the process has a different view of the filesystem, paths that are shown in the `ps` output are relative to the container and not the host. In these cases, knowing it is in a container is a big win.

So that's how you use the Docker tooling to look at what's running in a container. But that's not the only way, and in a debugging situation, it might not be the best way. If you hop onto a Docker server and run a normal Linux `ps` to see what's running, you get a full list of everything containerized and not containerized just as if they were all equivalent processes. There are some ways to look at the process output to make things a lot clearer. For example, you can facilitate debugging by looking at the Linux `ps` output in tree form so that you can see all of the processes descended from Docker. Here's what that might look like when you use the BSD command-line flags to look at a system that is currently running two containers; we'll chop the output to just the part we care about.

Docker Desktop's VM contains minimal versions of most Linux tools, and some of these commands may not produce the same output that you will get if you use a standard Linux server as the Docker daemon host.

```
$ ps axlfww

… /usr/bin/containerd
…
… /usr/bin/dockerd -H fd:// --containerd=/run/containerd/containerd.sock
… \_ /usr/bin/docker-proxy -proto tcp -host-ip 0.0.0.0 -host-port 8080 \
      -container-ip 172.17.0.2 -container-port 8080
… \_ /usr/bin/docker-proxy -proto tcp -host-ip :: -host-port 8080 \
      -container-ip 172.17.0.2 -container-port 8080
…
… /usr/bin/containerd-shim-runc-v2 -namespace moby -id 97…3d -address /run/…
… \_ sleep 120
```

```
…
… /usr/bin/containerd-shim-runc-v2 -namespace moby -id 69…7c -address /run/…
```

 Many of the ps commands in this example work only on Linux distributions with the full ps command. Some stripped-down versions of Linux, like Alpine, run the BusyBox shell, which does not have full ps support and won't show some of this output. We recommend running a full distribution on your host systems like Ubuntu or Fedora CoreOS.

Here you can see that we're running one instance of containerd, which is the main container runtime used by the Docker daemon. dockerd has two docker-proxy subprocesses running at the moment, which we will discuss in more detail in "Network Inspection" on page 182.

Each process that is using containerd-shim-runc-v2 represents a single container and all of the processes that are running inside that container. In this example, we have two containers. They show up as containerd-shim-runc-v2, followed by some additional information about the process, including the container ID. In this case, we are running one instance of Google's cadvisor and one instance of sleep in another container. Each container that has ports mapped will have at least one docker-proxy process that is used to map the required network ports between the container and the host Docker server. In this example, both docker-proxy processes are related to cadvisor. One is mapping the ports for IPv4 addresses, and the other is mapping ports for IPv6 addresses.

Because of the tree output from ps, it's pretty clear which processes are running in which containers. If you're a bigger fan of Unix SysV command-line flags, you can get a similar, but not as nice-looking, tree output with ps -ejH:

```
$ ps -ejH

… containerd
…
… dockerd
…   docker-proxy
…   docker-proxy
…
… containerd-shim
…   cadvisor
…
… containerd-shim
…   sleep
```

You can get a more concise view of the `docker` process tree by using the `pstree` command. Here, we'll use `pidof` to scope it to the tree belonging to `docker`:

```
$ pstree `pidof dockerd`

dockerd─┬─docker-proxy───7*[{docker-proxy}]
        ├─docker-proxy───6*[{docker-proxy}]
        └─10*[{dockerd}]
```

This doesn't show us PIDs and therefore is useful only for getting a sense of how things are connected. But this is conceptually clear output when there are a lot of processes running on a host. It's far more concise and provides a nice high-level map of how things connect. Here we can see the same containers that were shown in the previous `ps` output, but the tree is collapsed so we get multipliers like 7* when there are seven duplicate processes.

We can get a full tree with PIDs if we run `pstree`, as shown here:

```
$ pstree -p `pidof dockerd`

dockerd(866)─┬─docker-proxy(3050)─┬─{docker-proxy}(3051)
             │                    ├─{docker-proxy}(3052)
             │                    ├─{docker-proxy}(3053)
             │                    ├─{docker-proxy}(3054)
             │                    ├─{docker-proxy}(3056)
             │                    ├─{docker-proxy}(3057)
             │                    └─{docker-proxy}(3058)
             ├─docker-proxy(3055)─┬─{docker-proxy}(3059)
             │                    ├─{docker-proxy}(3060)
             │                    ├─{docker-proxy}(3061)
             │                    ├─{docker-proxy}(3062)
             │                    ├─{docker-proxy}(3063)
             │                    └─{docker-proxy}(3064)
             ├─{dockerd}(904)
             ├─{dockerd}(912)
             ├─{dockerd}(913)
             ├─{dockerd}(914)
             ├─{dockerd}(990)
             ├─{dockerd}(1014)
             ├─{dockerd}(1066)
             ├─{dockerd}(1605)
             ├─{dockerd}(1611)
             └─{dockerd}(2228)
```

This output provides us with a very good look at all the processes attached to Docker and what they are running.

If you wanted to inspect a single container and its processes, you could determine the container's main process ID and then use `pstree` to see all the related subprocesses:

```
$ ps aux | grep containerd-shim-runc-v2
root     3072  … /usr/bin/containerd-shim-runc-v2 -namespace moby -id 69…7c …
```

```
root    4489  … /usr/bin/containerd-shim-runc-v2 -namespace moby -id f1…46 …
vagrant 4651  … grep --color=auto shim

$ pstree -p 3072
containerd-shim(3072)─┬─cadvisor(3092)─┬─{cadvisor}(3123)
                      │                 ├─{cadvisor}(3124)
                      │                 ├─{cadvisor}(3125)
                      │                 ├─{cadvisor}(3126)
                      │                 ├─{cadvisor}(3127)
                      │                 ├─{cadvisor}(3128)
                      │                 ├─{cadvisor}(3180)
                      │                 ├─{cadvisor}(3181)
                      │                 └─{cadvisor}(3182)
                      ├─{containerd-shim}(3073)
                      ├─{containerd-shim}(3074)
                      ├─{containerd-shim}(3075)
                      ├─{containerd-shim}(3076)
                      ├─{containerd-shim}(3077)
                      ├─{containerd-shim}(3078)
                      ├─{containerd-shim}(3079)
                      ├─{containerd-shim}(3080)
                      ├─{containerd-shim}(3121)
                      └─{containerd-shim}(3267)
```

Process Inspection

If you're logged in to the Docker server, you can inspect running processes using all of the standard debugging tools. Common debugging tools like strace work as expected. In the following code, we'll inspect an nginx process running inside a container:

```
$ docker container run --rm -d --name nginx-debug --rm nginx:latest

$ docker container top nginx-debug

UID      PID   PPID … CMD
root     22983 22954 … nginx: master process nginx -g daemon off;
systemd+ 23032 22983 … nginx: worker process
systemd+ 23033 22983 … nginx: worker process

$ sudo strace -p 23032

strace: Process 23032 attached
epoll_pwait(10,
```

 If you run strace, you will need to type Ctrl-C to exit the strace process.

You can see that we get the same output that we would from noncontainerized processes on the host. Likewise, an `lsof` shows us that the files and sockets open in a process work as expected:

```
$ sudo lsof -p 22983
COMMAND    PID USER … NAME
nginx    22983 root … /
nginx    22983 root … /
nginx    22983 root … /usr/sbin/nginx
nginx    22983 root … /usr/sbin/nginx (stat: No such file or directory)
nginx    22983 root … /lib/aarch64-linux-gnu/libnss_files-2.31.so (stat: …
nginx    22983 root … /lib/aarch64-linux-gnu/libc-2.31.so (stat: …
nginx    22983 root … /lib/aarch64-linux-gnu/libz.so.1.2.11 (path inode=…)
nginx    22983 root … /usr/lib/aarch64-linux-gnu/libcrypto.so.1.1 (stat: …
nginx    22983 root … /usr/lib/aarch64-linux-gnu/libssl.so.1.1 (stat: …
nginx    22983 root … /usr/lib/aarch64-linux-gnu/libpcre2-8.so.0.10.1 (stat: …
nginx    22983 root … /lib/aarch64-linux-gnu/libcrypt.so.1.1.0 (path …
nginx    22983 root … /lib/aarch64-linux-gnu/libpthread-2.31.so (stat: …
nginx    22983 root … /lib/aarch64-linux-gnu/libdl-2.31.so (stat: …
nginx    22983 root … /lib/aarch64-linux-gnu/ld-2.31.so (stat: …
nginx    22983 root … /dev/zero
nginx    22983 root … /dev/null
nginx    22983 root … pipe
nginx    22983 root … pipe
nginx    22983 root … pipe
nginx    22983 root … protocol: UNIX-STREAM
nginx    22983 root … pipe
nginx    22983 root … pipe
nginx    22983 root … protocol: TCP
nginx    22983 root … protocol: TCPv6
nginx    22983 root … protocol: UNIX-STREAM
nginx    22983 root … protocol: UNIX-STREAM
nginx    22983 root … protocol: UNIX-STREAM
```

Note that the paths to the files are all relative to the container's view of the backing filesystem, which is not the same as the host view. Due to this, if you are on the host system, you may not be able to easily find a specific file from one of your running containers. In most cases, it's probably best to enter the container using `docker container exec` to look at the files with the same view that the processes inside it have.

It's possible to run the GNU debugger (`gdb`) and other process inspection tools in the same manner as long as you're `root` and have proper permissions to do so.

It is worth mentioning here that it is also possible to run a new debugging container that can see the processes of an existing container and therefore provide additional tools to debug issues. We will discuss the underlying details of this command later, in "Namespaces" on page 299 and "Security" on page 303:

```
$ docker container run -ti --rm --cap-add=SYS_PTRACE \
    --pid=container:nginx-debug spkane/train-os:latest bash
```

```
[root@e4b5d2f3a3a7 /]# ps aux
USER PID %CPU %MEM … TIME COMMAND
root   1  0.0  0.2 … 0:00 nginx: master process nginx -g daemon off;
101   30  0.0  0.1 … 0:00 nginx: worker process
101   31  0.0  0.1 … 0:00 nginx: worker process
root 136  0.0  0.1 … 0:00 bash
root 152  0.0  0.2 … 0:00 ps aux

[root@e4b5d2f3a3a7 /]# strace -p 1
strace: Process 1 attached
rt_sigsuspend([], 8

[Control-C]
strace: Process 1 detached
<detached …>

[root@e4b5d2f3a3a7 /]# exit

$ docker container stop nginx-debug
```

You will need to type Ctrl-C to exit the strace process.

Controlling Processes

When you have a shell directly on the Docker server, you can, in many ways, treat containerized processes just like any other process running on the system. If you're remote, you might send signals with docker container kill because it's expedient. But if you're already logged in to a Docker server for a debugging session or because the Docker daemon is not responding, you can just kill the process like you would any other.

Unless you kill the top-level process in the container (PID 1 inside the container), killing a process will not terminate the container itself. That *might* be desirable if you were killing a runaway process, but it might leave the container in an unexpected state. Developers probably expect that all the processes are running if they can see their container in docker container ls. It could also confuse a scheduler like Mesos or Kubernetes or any other system that is health-checking your application. Keep in mind that containers are supposed like a single bundle to the outside world. If you need to kill off something inside the container, it's best to replace the whole container. Containers offer an abstraction that tools interoperate with. They expect the internals of the container to be predictable and remain consistent.

Terminating processes is not the only reason to send signals. And since containerized processes are just normal processes in many respects, they can be passed the whole array of Unix signals listed in the manpage for the Linux `kill` command. Many Unix programs will perform special actions when they receive certain predefined signals. For example, `nginx` will reopen its logs when receiving a `SIGUSR1` signal. Using the Linux `kill` command, you can send any Unix signal to a container process on the local server.

Process Control in Containers

Unless you run an orchestrator like Kubernetes that can handle multiple containers in a larger abstraction like a pod, we consider it a best practice to run some kind of process control in your production containers. Whether it be `tini` (*https://github.com/krallin/tini*), `upstart` (*https://upstart.ubuntu.com*), `runit` (*http://smarden.org/runit*), `s6` (*https://skarnet.org/software/s6*), or something else, this approach allows you to treat containers atomically even when they contain more than one process. You should, however, try very hard not to run more than one thing inside your container, to ensure that your container is scoped to handle one well-defined task and does not grow into a monolithic container.

In either case, you will want `docker container ls` to reflect the presence of the whole container so that you don't need to worry about whether an individual process inside it has died. If you can assume that the presence of a container and absence of error logs means that things are working, you can treat `docker container ls` output as the truth about what's happening on your Docker systems. It also means any orchestration system you use can do the same.

It is also a good idea to ensure that you understand the complete behavior of your preferred process control service, including memory or disk utilization, Unix single handling, and so on, since this can impact your container's performance and behavior. Generally, the lightest-weight systems are the best.

Because containers work just like any other process, it's important to understand how they can interact with your application in less than helpful ways. There are some special needs in a container for processes that spawn background children—that is, anything that forks and daemonizes so the parent no longer manages the child process lifecycle. Jenkins build containers are one common example where people see this go wrong. When daemons fork into the background, they become children of PID 1 on Unix systems. Process 1 is special and is usually an `init` process of some kind.

PID 1 is responsible for making sure that children are reaped. In your container, by default, your main process will be PID 1. Since you probably won't be handling the reaping of children from your application, you can end up with zombie processes in your container. There are a few solutions to this problem. The first is to run an init system in the container of your own choosing—one that is capable of handling PID 1 responsibilities. s6, runit, and others described in the preceding note can be easily used inside the container.

But Docker itself provides an even simpler option that solves just this one case without taking on all the capabilities of a full init system. If you provide the --init flag to docker container run, Docker will launch a very small init process based on the tini project (*https://github.com/krallin/tini*) that will act as PID 1 inside the container on startup. Whatever you specify in your *Dockerfile* as the CMD is passed to tini and otherwise works in the same way you would expect. It does, however, replace anything you might have in the ENTRYPOINT section of your *Dockerfile*.

When you launch a Linux container without the --init flag, you get something like this in your process list:

```
$ docker container run --rm -it alpine:3.16 sh
/ # ps -ef

PID   USER     TIME   COMMAND
   1 root      0:00 sh
   5 root      0:00 ps -ef

/ # exit
```

Notice that in this case, the CMD we launched is PID 1. That means it is responsible for child reaping. If we are launching a container where that is important, we can pass --init to make sure that when the parent process exits, children are reaped:

```
$ docker container run --rm -it --init alpine:3.16 sh
/ # ps -ef

PID   USER     TIME   COMMAND
   1 root      0:00 /sbin/docker-init -- sh
   5 root      0:00 sh
   6 root      0:00 ps -ef

/ # exit
```

Here, you can see that the PID 1 process is /sbin/docker-init. That has in turn launched the shell binary for us as specified on the command line. Because we now have an init system inside the container, the PID 1 responsibilities fall to it rather than the command we used to invoke the container. In most cases, this is what you want. You may not need an init system, but it's small enough that you should consider having at least tini inside your containers in production.

In general, you probably only need an init process inside your container if you are running multiple parent processes or you have processes that do not respond to Unix signals properly.

Network Inspection

Compared to process inspection, debugging containerized applications at the network level can be more complicated. Unlike traditional processes running on the host, Linux containers can be connected to the network in multiple ways. If you are running the default setup, as the vast majority of people are, then your containers are all connected to the network via the default bridge network that Docker creates. This is a virtual network where the host is the gateway to the rest of the world. We can inspect these virtual networks with the tooling that ships with Docker. You can get it to show you which networks exist by calling the `docker network ls` command:

```
$ docker network ls

NETWORK ID      NAME      DRIVER    SCOPE
f9685b50d57c    bridge    bridge    local
8acae1680cbd    host      host      local
fb70d67499d3    none      null      local
```

Here we can see the default bridge network, the host network, which is for any containers running in `host` network mode (see "Host networking" on page 325), and the none network, which disables network access entirely for the container. If you use `docker compose` or other orchestration tools, they may create additional networks here with different names.

But seeing which networks exist doesn't make it any easier to see what's on those networks. So, you can see which containers are attached to any particular named network with the `docker network inspect` command. This produces a fair amount of output. It shows you all of the containers that are attached to the specified network and a number of details about the network itself. Let's take a look at the default bridge network:

```
$ docker network inspect bridge
[
    {
        "Name": "bridge",
        …
        "Driver": "bridge",
        "EnableIPv6": false,
        …
        "Containers": {
            "69e9…c87c": {
                "Name": "cadvisor",
                …
                "IPv4Address": "172.17.0.2/16",
                "IPv6Address": ""
            },
            "a2a8…e163": {
                "Name": "nginx-debug",
```

```
            …
            "IPv4Address": "172.17.0.3/16",
            "IPv6Address": ""
        }
    },
    "Options": {
        "com.docker.network.bridge.default_bridge": "true",
        …
        "com.docker.network.bridge.host_binding_ipv4": "0.0.0.0",
        "com.docker.network.bridge.name": "docker0",
        …
    },
    "Labels": {}
    }
]
```

We've excluded some of the details here to shrink the output a bit. But what we can see is that there are two containers on the bridge network, and they are attached to the docker0 bridge on the host. We can also see the IP addresses of each container (IPv4Address and IPv6Address) and the host network address they are bound to (host_binding_ipv4). This is useful when you are trying to understand the internal structure of the bridged network. If you have containers on different networks, they may not have connectivity to one another, depending on how the networks were configured.

In general, we recommend leaving your containers on the default bridge network until you have a good reason not to or are running docker compose or a scheduler that manages container networks on its own. In addition, naming your containers in some identifiable way helps here because we can't see the image information. The name and ID are the only references we have in this output that can tie us back to a docker container ls listing. Some schedulers don't do a good job of naming containers, which is too bad because it can be really helpful for debugging.

As we've seen, containers will normally have their own network stack and their own IP address, unless they are running in host networking mode, which we will discuss further in "Networking" on page 323. But what about when we look at them from the host machine itself? Because containers have their own network and addresses, they won't show up in all netstat output on the host. But we know that the ports you map to your containers are bound to the host.

Running `netstat -an` on the Docker server works as expected, as shown here:

```
$ sudo netstat -an

Active Internet connections (servers and established)
Proto Recv-Q Send-Q Local Address           Foreign Address         State
tcp        0      0 0.0.0.0:8080            0.0.0.0:*               LISTEN
tcp        0      0 127.0.0.53:53           0.0.0.0:*               LISTEN
tcp        0      0 0.0.0.0:22              0.0.0.0:*               LISTEN
tcp        0      0 192.168.15.158:22       192.168.15.120:63920    ESTABLISHED
tcp6       0      0 :::8080                 :::*                    LISTEN
tcp6       0      0 :::22                   :::*                    LISTEN
udp        0      0 127.0.0.53:53           0.0.0.0:*
udp        0      0 192.168.15.158:68       0.0.0.0:*
raw6       0      0 :::58                   :::*                    7
...
```

Here we can see all of the interfaces that we're listening on. Our container is bound to port 8080 on IP address 0.0.0.0. That shows up. But what happens when we ask `netstat` to show us the process name that's bound to the port?

```
$ sudo netstat -anp

Active Internet connections (servers and established)
Proto  … Local Address       Foreign Address         … PID/Program name
tcp    … 0.0.0.0:8080        0.0.0.0:*               … 1516/docker-proxy
tcp    … 127.0.0.53:53       0.0.0.0:*               … 692/systemd-resolve
tcp    … 0.0.0.0:22          0.0.0.0:*               … 780/sshd: /usr/sbin
tcp    … 192.168.15.158:22   192.168.15.120:63920    … 1348/sshd: vagrant
tcp6   … :::8080             :::*                    … 1522/docker-proxy
tcp6   … :::22               :::*                    … 780/sshd: /usr/sbin
udp    … 127.0.0.53:53       0.0.0.0:*               … 692/systemd-resolve
udp    … 192.168.15.158:68   0.0.0.0:*               … 690/systemd-network
raw6   … :::58               :::*                    … 690/systemd-network
```

We see the same output, but notice what is bound to the port: docker-proxy. That's because, in its default configuration, Docker has a proxy written in Go that sits between all of the containers and the outside world. That means that when we look at this output, all containers running via Docker will be associated with docker-proxy. Notice that there is no clue here about which specific container docker-proxy is handling. Fortunately, `docker container ls` shows us which containers are bound to which ports, so this isn't a big deal. But it's not obvious, and you probably want to be aware of it before you're debugging a production failure. Still, passing the p flag to `netstat` is helpful in identifying which ports are tied to containers.

 If you're using host networking in your container, then this layer is skipped. There is no docker-proxy, and the process in the container can bind to the port directly. It also shows up as a normal process in `netstat -anp` output.

Other network inspection commands work largely as expected, including `tcpdump`, but it's important to remember that `docker-proxy` is there, in between the host's network interface and the container, and that the containers have their own network interfaces on a virtual network.

Image History

When you're building and deploying a single container, it's easy to keep track of where it came from and what images it's sitting on top of. But this rapidly becomes unmanageable when you're shipping many containers with images that are built and maintained by different teams. How can you tell what layers are actually underneath the one your container is running on? Your container's image tag hopefully makes it clear which build of your application you're running, but the image tag doesn't reveal anything about the image layers that your application is built on. `docker image history` does just that. You can see each layer that exists in the inspected image, the sizes of each layer, and the commands that were used to build it:

```
$ docker image history redis:latest

IMAGE          … CREATED BY                                         SIZE     COMMENT
e800a8da9469 … /bin/sh -c #(nop)  CMD ["redis-server"]              0B
<missing>      … /bin/sh -c #(nop)  EXPOSE 6379                      0B
<missing>      … /bin/sh -c #(nop)  ENTRYPOINT ["docker-entry…      0B
<missing>      … /bin/sh -c #(nop) COPY file:e873a0e3c13001b5…      661B
<missing>      … /bin/sh -c #(nop) WORKDIR /data                    0B
<missing>      … /bin/sh -c #(nop)  VOLUME [/data]                  0B
<missing>      … /bin/sh -c mkdir /data && chown redis:redis …      0B
<missing>      … /bin/sh -c set -eux;   savedAptMark="$(apt-m…      32.4MB
<missing>      … /bin/sh -c #(nop)  ENV REDIS_DOWNLOAD_SHA=f0…      0B
<missing>      … /bin/sh -c #(nop)  ENV REDIS_DOWNLOAD_URL=ht…      0B
<missing>      … /bin/sh -c #(nop)  ENV REDIS_VERSION=7.0.4         0B
<missing>      … /bin/sh -c set -eux;   savedAptMark="$(apt-ma…     4.06MB
<missing>      … /bin/sh -c #(nop)  ENV GOSU_VERSION=1.14           0B
<missing>      … /bin/sh -c groupadd -r -g 999 redis && usera…      331kB
<missing>      … /bin/sh -c #(nop)  CMD ["bash"]                    0B
<missing>      … /bin/sh -c #(nop) ADD file:6039adfbca55ed34a…      74.3MB
```

Using `docker image history` can be useful, for example, when you are trying to determine why the size of the final image is much larger than expected. The layers are listed in order, with the first one at the bottom of the list and the last one at the top.

Here we can see that the command output has been truncated in a few cases. For long commands, adding the `--no-trunc` option to the `docker image history` command will let you see the complete command that was used to build each layer. Just be aware that `--no-trunc` will make the output much larger and more difficult to visually scan in most cases.

Inspecting a Container

In Chapter 4, we showed you how to read the `docker container inspect` output to see how a container is configured. But underneath that is a directory on the host's disk that is dedicated to the container. Usually this is */var/lib/docker/containers*. If you look at that directory, it contains very long SHA hashes, as shown here:

```
$ sudo ls /var/lib/docker/containers

106ead0d55af55bd803334090664e4bc821c76dadf231e1aab7798d1baa19121
28970c706db0f69716af43527ed926acbd82581e1cef5e4e6ff152fce1b79972
3c4f916619a5dfc420396d823b42e8bd30a2f94ab5b0f42f052357a68a67309b
589f2ad301381b7704c9cade7da6b34046ef69ebe3d6929b9bc24785d7488287
959db1611d632dc27a86efcb66f1c6268d948d6f22e81e2a22a57610b5070b4d
a1e15f197ea0996d31f69c332f2b14e18b727e53735133a230d54657ac6aa5dd
bad35aac3f503121abf0e543e697fcade78f0d30124778915764d85fb10303a7
bc8c72c965ebca7db9a2b816188773a5864aa381b81c3073b9d3e52e977c55ba
daa75fb108a33793a3f8fcef7ba65589e124af66bc52c4a070f645fffbbc498e
e2ac800b58c4c72e240b90068402b7d4734a7dd03402ee2bce3248cc6f44d676
e8085ebc102b5f51c13cc5c257acb2274e7f8d1645af7baad0cb6fe8eef36e24
f8e46faa3303d93fc424e289d09b4ffba1fc7782b9878456e0fe11f1f6814e4b
```

That's a bit daunting. But those are just the container IDs in long form. If you want to look at the configuration for a particular container, you just need to use `docker container ls` to find its short ID, and then find the directory that matches:

```
$ docker container ls

CONTAINER ID    IMAGE                                    COMMAND             ...
c58bfeffb9e6    gcr.io/cadvisor/cadvisor:v0.44.1-test    "/usr/bin/cadvisor…" ...
```

You can view the short ID from `docker container ls`, then match it to the `ls /var/lib/docker/containers` output to see that you want the directory beginning with `c58bfeffb9e6`. Command-line tab completion is helpful here. If you need exact matching, you can do a `docker container inspect c58bfeffb9e6` and grab the long ID from the output. This directory contains some pretty interesting files related to the container:

```
$ cd /var/lib/docker/containers/\
c58bfeffb9e6e607f3aacb4a06ca473535bf9588450f08be46baa230ab43f1d6

$ ls -la

total 48
drwx--x---   4 root root 4096 Aug 20 10:38 .
drwx--x--- 30 root root 4096 Aug 20 10:25 ..
-rw-r-----   1 root root  635 Aug 20 10:34 c58bf…f1d6-json.log
drwx------   2 root root 4096 Aug 20 10:24 checkpoints
-rw-------   1 root root 4897 Aug 20 10:38 config.v2.json
-rw-r--r--   1 root root 1498 Aug 20 10:38 hostconfig.json
```

```
-rw-r--r--  1 root root   13 Aug 20 10:24 hostname
-rw-r--r--  1 root root  174 Aug 20 10:24 hosts
drwx--x---  2 root root 4096 Aug 20 10:24 mounts
-rw-r--r--  1 root root  882 Aug 20 10:24 resolv.conf
-rw-r--r--  1 root root   71 Aug 20 10:24 resolv.conf.hash
```

As we discussed in Chapter 5, this directory contains some files that are bind-mounted directly into your container, like *hosts*, *resolv.conf*, and *hostname*. If you are running the default logging mechanism, then this directory is also where Docker stores the JSON file containing the log that is shown with the `docker container logs` command, the JSON configuration that backs the `docker container inspect` output (*config.v2.json*), and the networking configuration for the container (*hostconfig.json*). The *resolv.conf.hash* file is used by Docker to determine when the container's file has diverged from the current one on the host so it can be updated.

This directory can also be really helpful in the event of severe failure. Even if we're not able to enter the container, or if `docker` is not responding, we can look at how the container was configured. It's also pretty useful to understand where those files are mounted from inside the container. Keep in mind that it's not a good idea to modify these files. Docker expects them to contain reality, and if you alter that reality, you're asking for trouble. But it's another avenue for information on what's happening in your container.

Filesystem Inspection

Docker, regardless of the backend actually in use, has a layered filesystem that allows it to track the changes in any given container. This is how the images are assembled when you do a build, but it is also useful when you're trying to figure out if a Linux container has changed anything and, if so, what. A common problem with containerized applications is that they may continue to write things into the container's filesystem. Normally, you don't want your containers to do that, to the extent possible, and it can help debugging to figure out if your processes have been writing into the container. Sometimes this is helpful in turning up stray logfiles that exist in the container as well. As with most of the core tools, this kind of inspection is built into the `docker` command-line tooling and is also exposed via the API. Let's take a look at what this shows us. Let's launch a quick container and use its name to explore this:

```
$ docker container run --rm -d --name nginx-fs nginx:latest
1272b950202db25ee030703515f482e9ed576f8e64c926e4e535ba11f7536cc4

$ docker container diff nginx-fs
C /run
A /run/nginx.pid
C /var
C /var/cache
C /var/cache/nginx
A /var/cache/nginx/scgi_temp
```

```
A /var/cache/nginx/uwsgi_temp
A /var/cache/nginx/client_temp
A /var/cache/nginx/fastcgi_temp
A /var/cache/nginx/proxy_temp
C /etc
C /etc/nginx
C /etc/nginx/conf.d
C /etc/nginx/conf.d/default.conf

$ docker container stop nginx-fs
nginx-fs
```

Each line begins with either A or C, which is shorthand for *added* or *changed*, respectively. We can see that this container is running nginx, that the nginx configuration file has been written to, and that some temporary files have been created in a new directory named /var/cache/nginx. Being able to find out how the container filesystem is being used can be very useful when you are trying to optimize and harden your container's filesystem usage.

Further detailed inspection requires exploring the container with docker container export, docker container exec, or nsenter and the like, to see exactly what is in the filesystem. But docker container diff gives you a good place to start.

Wrap-Up

At this point, you should have a good idea of how to deploy and debug individual containers in development and production, but how do you start to scale this for larger application ecosystems? In the next chapter, we'll take a look at one of the simpler Docker orchestration tools: Docker Compose. This tool is a nice bridge between a single Linux container and a production orchestration system. It delivers a lot of value in development environments and throughout the DevOps pipeline.

## CHAPTER 8

Exploring Docker Compose

At this point, you should have a good feel for the docker command and how to use it to build, launch, monitor, and debug your applications. Once you are comfortable working with individual containers, it won't be long before you'll want to share your projects and start building more complex projects that require multiple containers to function properly. This is particularly the case in development environments, where running a whole stack of containers can easily simulate many production environments on your local machine.

If you're running a whole stack of containers, however, every container needs to be run with the proper setup to ensure that the underlying application is configured correctly and will run as expected. Getting these settings correct every time can be challenging, especially when you are not the person who originally wrote the application. To help with this during development, people often resort to trying to write shell scripts that can build and run multiple containers consistently. Although this works, it can become difficult to understand for a newcomer and hard to maintain as the project changes over time. It's also not necessarily repeatable between projects.

To help address this problem, Docker, Inc., released a tool primarily aimed at developers called Docker Compose. This tool is included with Docker Desktop, but you can also install it by following the online installation directions (*https://docs.docker.com/compose/install*).

Docker Compose was originally a separate application written in Python that was run using the command `docker-compose`. This command is referred to as Docker Compose version 1 and has recently been replaced with Docker Compose version 2. Docker Compose v2 was completely rewritten in Go, as a Docker client plug-in. If `docker compose version` returns a result, then you have the plug-in installed. If not, we highly recommend that you take a little time to install it now.

Docker Compose is an incredibly useful tool that can streamline all sorts of development tasks that have traditionally been very cumbersome and error prone. It can easily be leveraged to help developers quickly spin up complicated application stacks, compile applications without the need for setting up complex local development environments, and much more.

In this chapter, we'll do a run-through of how to use Compose to its best advantage. We'll be using a GitHub repository in all of the following examples. If you want to run the examples as we go through them, you should run the following command to download the code, if you didn't already do that in Chapter 6:

```
$ git clone https://github.com/spkane/rocketchat-hubot-demo.git \
    --config core.autocrlf=input
```

 In the example, shell script and *docker-compose.yaml* files below some lines have been truncated to fit in the margins. Make sure that you use the files from this Git repository if you plan to try these examples yourself.

This repository contains the configuration we'll need to launch a complete web service that includes a MongoDB datastore, the open source Rocket.Chat communications server, a Hubot ChatOps (*https://goo.gl/hKT3QW*) bot, and a `zmachine-api` instance for a little surprise entertainment value.

Configuring Docker Compose

Before we dive into using the `docker compose` command, it is useful to see the kind of ad hoc tooling it replaces. So let's take a moment to look at a shell script that could be used to build and deploy a local copy of our service for development and local testing via Docker. This output is long and detailed, but it's important to prove the point about why Docker Compose is a huge leap over shell scripting.

We do not recommend running this shell script. It is simply an example, and in your environment, it may not work or may leave things in an odd state.

```bash
#!/bin/bash

# This is here just to keep people from really running this.
exit 1

# The actual script
#
# Note: This has not been updated to directly mirror the docker-compose file
#       since it is just intended to make a point.

set -e
set -u

if [ $# -ne 0 ] && [ ${1} == "down" ]; then
  docker rm -f hubot || true
  docker rm -f zmachine || true
  docker rm -f rocketchat || true
  docker rm -f mongo-init-replica || true
  docker rm -f mongo || true
  docker network rm botnet || true
  echo "Environment torn down..."
  exit 0
fi

# Global Settings
export PORT="3000"
export ROOT_URL="http://127.0.0.1:3000"
export MONGO_URL="mongodb://mongo:27017/rocketchat"
export MONGO_OPLOG_URL="mongodb://mongo:27017/local"
export MAIL_URL="smtp://smtp.email"
export RESPOND_TO_DM="true"
export HUBOT_ALIAS=". "
export LISTEN_ON_ALL_PUBLIC="true"
export ROCKETCHAT_AUTH="password"
export ROCKETCHAT_URL="rocketchat:3000"
export ROCKETCHAT_ROOM=""
export ROCKETCHAT_USER="hubot"
export ROCKETCHAT_PASSWORD="bot-pw!"
export BOT_NAME="bot"
export EXTERNAL_SCRIPTS="hubot-help,hubot-diagnostics,hubot-zmachine"
export HUBOT_ZMACHINE_SERVER="http://zmachine:80"
export HUBOT_ZMACHINE_ROOMS="zmachine"
export HUBOT_ZMACHINE_OT_PREFIX="ot"

docker build -t spkane/mongo:4.4 ./mongodb/docker
```

```
docker push spkane/mongo:4.4
docker pull spkane/zmachine-api:latest
docker pull rocketchat/rocket.chat:5.0.4
docker pull rocketchat/hubot-rocketchat:latest

docker rm -f hubot || true
docker rm -f zmachine || true
docker rm -f rocketchat || true
docker rm -f mongo-init-replica || true
docker rm -f mongo || true

docker network rm botnet || true

docker network create -d bridge botnet

docker container run-d \
  --name=mongo \
  --network=botnet \
  --restart unless-stopped \
  -v $(pwd)/mongodb/data/db:/data/db \
  spkane/mongo:4.4 \
  mongod --oplogSize 128 --replSet rs0
sleep 5
docker container run-d \
  --name=mongo-init-replica \
  --network=botnet \
  spkane/mongo:4.4 \
  'mongo mongo/rocketchat --eval "rs.initiate({ _id: ''rs0'', members: [ { … '
sleep 5
docker container run-d \
  --name=rocketchat \
  --network=botnet \
  --restart unless-stopped  \
  -v $(pwd)/rocketchat/data/uploads:/app/uploads \
  -p 3000:3000 \
  -e PORT=${PORT} \
  -e ROOT_URL=${ROOT_URL} \
  -e MONGO_URL=${MONGO_URL} \
  -e MONGO_OPLOG_URL=${MONGO_OPLOG_URL} \
  -e MAIL_URL=${MAIL_URL} \
  rocketchat/rocket.chat:5.0.4
docker container run-d \
  --name=zmachine \
  --network=botnet \
  --restart unless-stopped  \
  -v $(pwd)/zmachine/saves:/root/saves \
  -v $(pwd)/zmachine/zcode:/root/zcode \
  -p 3002:80 \
  spkane/zmachine-api:latest
docker container run-d \
  --name=hubot \
  --network=botnet \
```

```
  --restart unless-stopped  \
  -v $(pwd)/hubot/scripts:/home/hubot/scripts \
  -p 3001:8080 \
  -e RESPOND_TO_DM="true" \
  -e HUBOT_ALIAS=". " \
  -e LISTEN_ON_ALL_PUBLIC="true" \
  -e ROCKETCHAT_AUTH="password" \
  -e ROCKETCHAT_URL="rocketchat:3000" \
  -e ROCKETCHAT_ROOM="" \
  -e ROCKETCHAT_USER="hubot" \
  -e ROCKETCHAT_PASSWORD="bot-pw!" \
  -e BOT_NAME="bot" \
  -e EXTERNAL_SCRIPTS="hubot-help,hubot-diagnostics,hubot-zmachine" \
  -e HUBOT_ZMACHINE_SERVER="http://zmachine:80" \
  -e HUBOT_ZMACHINE_ROOMS="zmachine" \
  -e HUBOT_ZMACHINE_OT_PREFIX="ot" \
  rocketchat/hubot-rocketchat:latest
echo "Environment setup…"
exit 0
```

At this point, you can probably follow most of this script pretty easily. As you may already have noticed, this is a hassle to read, is not very flexible, will be a pain to edit, and might fail unexpectedly in several places. If we were to follow shell script best practices and handle all the possible errors here in an effort to guarantee that it was repeatable, it would also be two to three times as long as it already is. Without a lot of work extracting common functionality for error handling, you'd also have to rewrite much of that logic every time you have a new project like this. This is not a very good way to approach a process that you need to work every time you use it. This is where good tooling comes in. You can accomplish the same thing with Docker Compose while also making it significantly more repeatable and easier to read, understand, and maintain.

In contrast to this messy shell script, which is very repetitive and prone to breaking, Docker Compose is typically configured with a single, declarative YAML (*https://yaml.org*) file for each project, named *docker-compose.yaml*. This configuration file is very easy to read and will work in a very repeatable fashion so that each user has the same experience when they run it. Here you can see an example *docker-compose.yaml* file that could be used to replace the preceding brittle shell script:

```
version: '3'
services:
  mongo:
    build:
      context: ../mongodb/docker
    image: spkane/mongo:4.4
    restart: unless-stopped
    environment:
      MONGODB_REPLICA_SET_MODE: primary
      MONGODB_REPLICA_SET_NAME: rs0
      MONGODB_PORT_NUMBER: 27017
```

```
      MONGODB_INITIAL_PRIMARY_HOST: mongodb
      MONGODB_INITIAL_PRIMARY_PORT_NUMBER: 27017
      MONGODB_ADVERTISED_HOSTNAME: mongo
      MONGODB_ENABLE_JOURNAL: "true"
      ALLOW_EMPTY_PASSWORD: "yes"
    # Port 27017 already exposed by upstream
    # See the newer upstream Dockerfile:
    # https://github.com/bitnami/containers/blob/
    # f9fb3f8a6323fb768fd488c77d4f111b1330bd0e/bitnami/
    # mongodb/5.0/debian-11/Dockerfile#L52
    networks:
      - botnet
  rocketchat:
    image: rocketchat/rocket.chat:5.0.4
    restart: unless-stopped
    labels:
      traefik.enable: "true"
      traefik.http.routers.rocketchat.rule: Host(`127.0.0.1`)
      traefik.http.routers.rocketchat.tls: "false"
      traefik.http.routers.rocketchat.entrypoints: http
    volumes:
      - "../rocketchat/data/uploads:/app/uploads"
    environment:
      ROOT_URL: http://127.0.0.1:3000
      PORT: 3000
      MONGO_URL: "mongodb://mongo:27017/rocketchat?replicaSet=rs0"
      MONGO_OPLOG_URL: "mongodb://mongo:27017/local?replicaSet=rs0"
      DEPLOY_METHOD: docker
    depends_on:
      mongo:
        condition: service_healthy
    ports:
      - 3000:3000
    networks:
      - botnet
  zmachine:
    image: spkane/zmachine-api:latest
    restart: unless-stopped
    volumes:
      - "../zmachine/saves:/root/saves"
      - "../zmachine/zcode:/root/zcode"
    depends_on:
      - rocketchat
    expose:
      - "80"
    networks:
      - botnet
  hubot:
    image: rocketchat/hubot-rocketchat:latest
    restart: unless-stopped
    volumes:
      - "../hubot/scripts:/home/hubot/scripts"
```

```
  environment:
    RESPOND_TO_DM: "true"
    HUBOT_ALIAS: ". "
    LISTEN_ON_ALL_PUBLIC: "true"
    ROCKETCHAT_AUTH: "password"
    ROCKETCHAT_URL: "rocketchat:3000"
    ROCKETCHAT_ROOM: ""
    ROCKETCHAT_USER: "hubot"
    ROCKETCHAT_PASSWORD: "bot-pw!"
    BOT_NAME: "bot"
    EXTERNAL_SCRIPTS: "hubot-help,hubot-diagnostics,hubot-zmachine"
    HUBOT_ZMACHINE_SERVER: "http://zmachine:80"
    HUBOT_ZMACHINE_ROOMS: "zmachine"
    HUBOT_ZMACHINE_OT_PREFIX: "ot"
  depends_on:
    - zmachine
  ports:
    - 3001:8080
  networks:
    - botnet
networks:
  botnet:
    driver: bridge
```

The *docker-compose.yaml* file makes it easy to describe all the important requirements for each of your services and how they need to communicate with one another. And we get a lot of validation and logic checking for free that we didn't even have time to write into our shell script and that we'd probably get wrong on occasion, no matter how careful we are.

So, what did we tell Compose to do in that YAML file? The first line of our file simply tells Docker Compose what version of the Compose configuration language (*https://docs.docker.com/compose/compose-file*) this file was designed for:

```
version: '3'
```

The rest of our document is divided into two sections: services and networks.

For starters, let's take a quick look at the networks section. In this *docker-compose.yaml* file, we are defining a single, named Docker network:

```
networks:
  botnet:
    driver: bridge
```

This is a very simple configuration that tells Docker Compose to create a single network, named botnet, using the (default) bridge driver, which will bridge the Docker network with the host's networking stack.

The services section is the most important part of the configuration and tells Docker Compose what applications you want to launch. Here, the services section defines five services: mongo, mongo-init-replica, rocketchat, zmachine, and hubot. Each named service then contains sections that tell Docker how to build, configure, and launch that service.

If you take a look at the mongo service, you will see that the first subsection is called build and contains a context key. This informs Docker Compose that it can build this image and that the files required for the build are located in the *../../mongodb/docker* directory, which is two levels above the directory containing the *docker-compose.yaml* file:

```
build:
    context: ../../mongodb/docker
```

If you look at the *Dockerfile* in the *mongodb/docker* directory, you will see this:

```
FROM mongo:4.4

COPY docker-healthcheck /usr/local/bin/

# Useful Information:
# https://docs.docker.com/engine/reference/builder/#healthcheck
# https://docs.docker.com/compose/compose-file/#healthcheck
HEALTHCHECK CMD ["docker-healthcheck"]
```

Take a moment to look at the HEALTHCHECK line. This tells Docker what command should be run to check the health of the container. Docker will not take action based on this health check, but it will report the health so that other things can make use of this information. If you are curious, feel free to take a look at the docker-healthcheck script in the *mongodb/docker* directory.

The next setting, image, defines the image tag that you want either to apply to your build or to download (if you're not building an image) and then run:

```
image: spkane/mongo:4.4
```

With the restart option, you tell Docker when you want it to restart your containers. In most cases, you'll want Docker to restart your containers any time that you have not specifically stopped them:

```
restart: unless-stopped
```

Next, you will see an environment section. This is where you can define any environment variables that you want to pass into your container:

```
environment:
    MONGODB_REPLICA_SET_MODE: primary
    MONGODB_REPLICA_SET_NAME: rs0
    MONGODB_PORT_NUMBER: 27017
    MONGODB_INITIAL_PRIMARY_HOST: mongodb
    MONGODB_INITIAL_PRIMARY_PORT_NUMBER: 27017
    MONGODB_ADVERTISED_HOSTNAME: mongo
```

```
MONGODB_ENABLE_JOURNAL: "true"
ALLOW_EMPTY_PASSWORD: "yes"
```

The final subsection for the mongo service, networks, tells Docker Compose which network this container should be attached to:

```
networks:
  - botnet
```

At this point, let's jump down to the rocketchat service. This service does not have a build subsection; instead, it only defines an image tag that tells Docker Compose that it cannot build this image and must instead try to pull and launch a preexisting Docker image with the defined tag.

The first new subsection that you will notice in this service is called volumes.

A lot of services have at least some data that should be persisted during development, despite the ephemeral nature of containers. To accomplish this, it is easiest to mount a local directory into the containers. The volumes section allows you to list all the local directories that you would like to have mounted into a container, and define where they go. This command will bind-mount *../rocketchat/data/uploads* into */app/ uploads* inside the container:

```
volumes:
  - "../rocketchat/data/uploads:/app/uploads"
```

You may have noticed that we do not define a volume for Mon-goDB, which might seem a bit counterintuitive. Although a bind-mounted volume would be useful to store the database files in, MongoDB will fail to write to the native Windows filesystem, so we leave this out to achieve the broadest compatibility and instead let the database write into the container for this development use case.

The primary result of this is that when you delete the container using a command like docker compose down, all of the data in the MongoDB instance will be lost.

We could easily solve this MongoDB storage problem by using a data volume container (*https://docs.docker.com/storage/volumes/ #create-and-manage-volumes*), but this example is specifically using bind mounts for the volumes.

In almost all cases, you should not use host-based local storage for containers in production. This can be very convenient in development since you are using a single host, but in production, your containers will often be deployed to whatever node has space and resources, and will lose access to files stored on a single host's filesystem. In production, if you need stateful storage, you have to leverage things like network-based storage, Kubernetes Persistent Volumes, etc.

In the `environment` section for the `rocketchat` service, you will see that the value for the `MONGO_URL` does not use an IP address or fully qualified domain name. This is because all of these services are running on the same Docker network, and Docker Compose configures each container so that it can find the others via their service names. This means that we can easily configure URLs like this to simply point at the service name and internal port for the container we need to connect to. And, if we rearrange things, these names will continue to point to the right container in our stack. They are also nice because they make it quite explicit to the reader what the dependency is for that container:

```
environment:
    ...
    MONGO_URL: "mongodb://mongo:27017/rocketchat?replicaSet=rs0"
    ...
```

 The *docker-compose.yaml* file can also refer to environment variables using the `${VARIABLE_NAME}` format, which makes it possible to pull in secrets without actually storing them in this file. Docker Compose also supports an *.env* (*https://docs.docker.com/ compose/env-file*) file, which can be very useful for handling secrets and environment variables that change between developers, for example.

The `depends_on` section defines a container that must be running before this container can be started. By default, `docker compose` only ensures that the container is running, not that it is healthy; however, you can leverage the HEALTHCHECK functionality in Docker, and the condition statement in Docker Compose, to require that the dependent service be healthy before Docker Compose brings the new service up. It is important to remember that this only impacts startup. Docker will report services that become unhealthy later on, but it does not take any action to correct the situation unless the container exits, in which case, Docker will restart the container if it is configured to do so:

```
depends_on:
    mongo:
        condition: service_healthy
```

We discuss Docker's health-check functionality in more detail in "Container Health Checks" on page 159. You can also find more information in the documentation for Docker (*https://dockr.ly/ 2MYnLZL*) and Docker Compose (*https://dockr.ly/2wt366J*).

The `ports` subsection allows you to define all the ports that you want to be mapped from the container to the host:

```
ports:
  - 3000:3000
```

The `zmachine` service uses only one new subsection, called `expose`. This section allows us to tell Docker that we want to expose this port to the other containers on the Docker network but not to the underlying host. This is why you do not provide a host port to map this port to:

```
expose:
  - "80"
```

You might notice at this point that, while we expose a port for `zmachine`, we didn't expose a port in the `mongo` service. It wouldn't have hurt anything to expose the `mongo` port, but we didn't need to because it is already exposed by the upstream `mongo` *Dockerfile* (*https://github.com/docker-library/mongo/blob/ 58bdba62b65b1d1e1ea5cbde54c1682f120e0676/3.2/Dockerfile#L95*). This is sometimes a little opaque. `docker image history` on the built image can be helpful here.

Here we've used an example that is complex enough to expose you to some of the power of Docker Compose, but it is by no means exhaustive. There is a great deal else that you can configure in a *docker-compose.yaml* file, including security settings, resource quotas, and much more. You can find a lot of detailed information about configuration for Compose in the official Docker Compose documentation (*https:// docs.docker.com/compose/compose-file*).

Launching Services

We configured a set of services for our application in the YAML file. That tells Compose what we're going to launch and how to configure it. So, let's get it up and running! To run our first Docker Compose command, we need to be sure that we are in the same directory as the *docker-compose.yaml* file:

```
$ cd rocketchat-hubot-demo/compose
```

Once you are in the correct directory, you can confirm that the configuration is correct by running the following:

```
$ docker compose config
```

If everything is fine, the command will print out your configuration file. If there is a problem, the command will print an error with details about the problem, like so:

```
services.mongo Additional property builder is not allowed
```

You can build any containers that you need by using the `build` option. Any services that use images will be skipped:

```
$ docker compose build

=> [internal] load build definition from Dockerfile                   0.0s
=> => transferring dockerfile: 32B                                    0.0s
=> [internal] load .dockerignore                                      0.0s
=> => transferring context: 2B                                        0.0s
=> [internal] load metadata for docker.io/bitnami/mongodb:4.4         1.2s
=> [auth] bitnami/mongodb:pull token for registry-1.docker.io         0.0s
=> [internal] load build context                                      0.0s
=> => transferring context: 40B                                       0.0s
=> [1/2] FROM docker.io/bitnami/mongodb:4.4@sha256:9162…ae209         0.0s
=> CACHED [2/2] COPY docker-healthcheck /usr/local/bin/               0.0s
=> exporting to image                                                 0.0s
=> => exporting layers                                                0.0s
=> => writing image sha256:a6ef…da808                                 0.0s
=> => naming to docker.io/spkane/mongo:4.4                            0.0s
```

You can start up your web service in the background by running the following command:

```
$ docker compose up -d

[+] Running 5/5
 ⠿ Network compose_botnet            Created      0.0s
 ⠿ Container compose-mongo-1         Healthy     62.0s
 ⠿ Container compose-rocketchat-1    Started     62.3s
 ⠿ Container compose-zmachine-1      Started     62.5s
 ⠿ Container compose-hubot-1         Started     62.6s
```

Docker Compose prefixes the network and container names with a project name. By default, this is the name of the directory that contains your *docker-compose.yaml* file. Since this command was run in a directory named *compose*, you can see that everything starts with `compose` as the project name.

 Windows users: when you first bring up the services, Windows may prompt you to authorize *vpnkit*, and Docker Desktop for Windows may also prompt you to share your disk. You must click both the "Allow access" and the "Share it" buttons for the network and volume shares to work and everything to come up properly.

Once everything comes up, we can take a quick look at the logs for all of the services (Figure 8-1):

```
$ docker compose logs
```

```
compose-rocketchat-1 | |             Commit Hash: 29fb34babc        |
compose-rocketchat-1 | |             Commit Branch: HEAD            |
compose-rocketchat-1 | |                                           |
compose-rocketchat-1 | +-----------------------------------------+
compose-mongo-1      | {"t":{"$date":"2023-03-31T20:48:04.893+00:00"},"s":"I",  "c":"REPL",      "id":21300,
   "ctx":"ReplCoord-0","msg":"Starting replication applier thread"}
compose-mongo-1      | {"t":{"$date":"2023-03-31T20:48:04.893+00:00"},"s":"I",  "c":"REPL",      "id":21301,
   "ctx":"ReplCoord-0","msg":"Starting replication reporter thread"}
compose-hubot-1      | hubot-zmachine@0.1.0 node_modules/hubot-zmachine
compose-hubot-1      | npm info ok
```

Figure 8-1. docker compose logs output

You can't see it well in print here, but if you're following along, note that all of the logs are color coded by service and interlaced by the time Docker received the log lines. This makes it a lot easier to follow what's happening, even though several services are logging messages at once.

It can take Rocket.Chat a little while to set up the database and be ready to accept connections. Once the Rocket.Chat logs print a line that contains SERVER RUNNING, things should be ready to go:

```
$ docker compose logs rocketchat | grep "SERVER RUNNING"

compose-rocketchat-1  | |                SERVER RUNNING                |
```

At this point, we have successfully launched a reasonably complex application that makes up a stack of containers. We'll take a look at this simple application now so that you can see what we built and get a more complete understanding of the Compose tooling. While this next section does not strictly have anything to do with Docker itself, it is intended to show you how easy it is to use Docker Compose to set up complex and fully functioning web services.

Exploring Rocket.Chat

 In this section, we're going to diverge from Docker for a moment and take a look at Rocket.Chat. We'll spend a few pages on it so that you know enough about it that you can hopefully start to appreciate how much easier it is to set up a complex environment using Docker Compose. Feel free to skip down to "Exercising Docker Compose" on page 211, if you would like.

We'll shortly dig further into what's happening behind the scenes of our setup. But to do that effectively, we should now take a brief moment to explore the application stack we built. Rocket.Chat (*https://rocket.chat*), the primary application we launched with Docker Compose, is an open source chat client/server application. To see how it works, let's launch a web browser and navigate to *http://127.0.0.1:3000*.

When you get there, you see the Admin Info screen for Rocket.Chat (Figure 8-2).

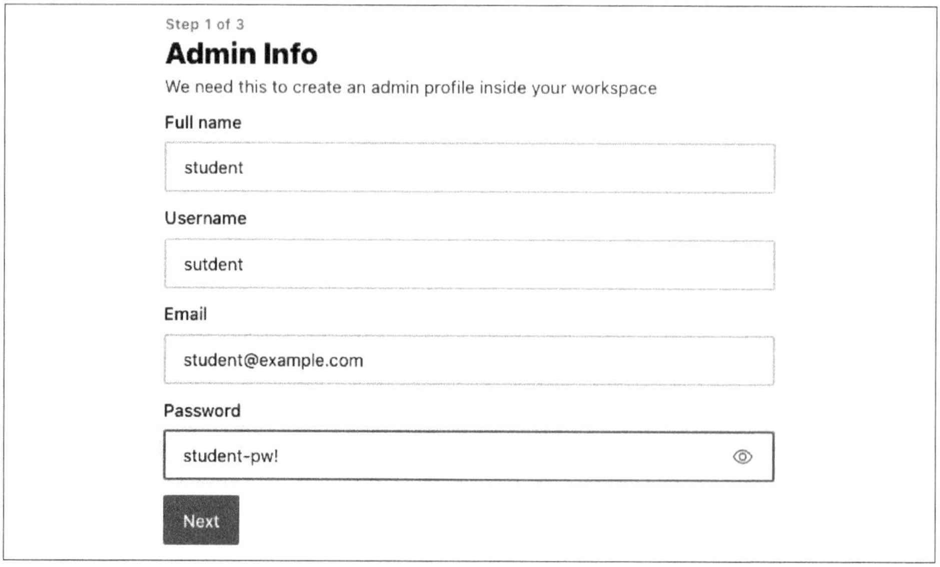

Figure 8-2. Rocket.Chat Admin Info screen

Fill out the form like this:

- Full name: **student**
- Username: **student**
- Email: **student@example.com**
- Password: **student-pw!**

Then click the blue Next button.

You then see the Organization Info screen (Figure 8-3).

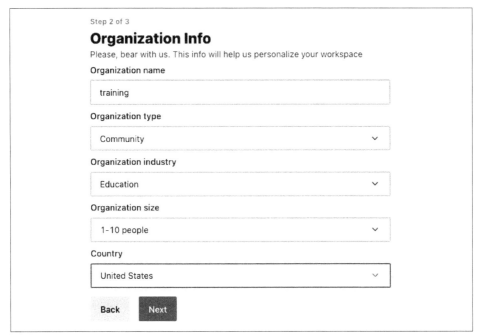

Figure 8-3. Rocket.Chat Organization Info screen

The specifics of this form are not critical, but you can fill it in something like this:

- Organization name: **training**
- Organization type: **Community**
- Organization industry: **Education**
- Organization size: **1-10 people**
- Country: **United States**

Then click the blue Next button.

At this point, you see the Register Your Server screen (Figure 8-4).

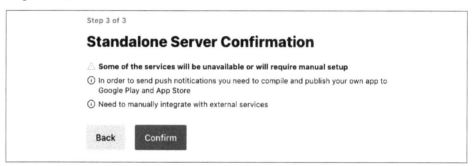

Figure 8-4. Rocket.Chat Register Your Server screen

You can simply delete and uncheck everything and then click the small blue "Continue as standalone" link. You then see the Standalone Server Configuration screen (Figure 8-5).

Figure 8-5. Rocket.Chat Standalone Server Confirmation screen

Click the blue Confirm button.

 If you are using `localhost` or something other than 127.0.0.1 to reach Rocket.Chat in your browser, you may get a pop-up window asking if you would like to update the `SITE_URL`. In most cases, go ahead and let it update that value so that it matches what you are using.

Congratulations—you are now logged in to a fully functional chat client, but you aren't done yet. The Docker Compose configuration launched an instance of a Hubot (*https://hubot.github.com*) chat assistant and the mysterious zmachine, so let's take a look at those.

Since the Rocket.Chat server is brand new, it doesn't yet have a user that our bot can use. Let's remedy that.

Start by clicking the top of the left sidebar, where you see a purple box with the letter S in it. Click Administration in the pop-up menu (Figure 8-6).

Figure 8-6. Rocket.Chat Administration sidebar

In the Administration panel, click Users (Figure 8-7).

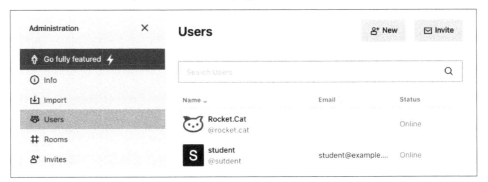

Figure 8-7. Rocket.Chat User screen

On the top-far-right side of the screen, click the New button to display the Add User screen (Figure 8-8).

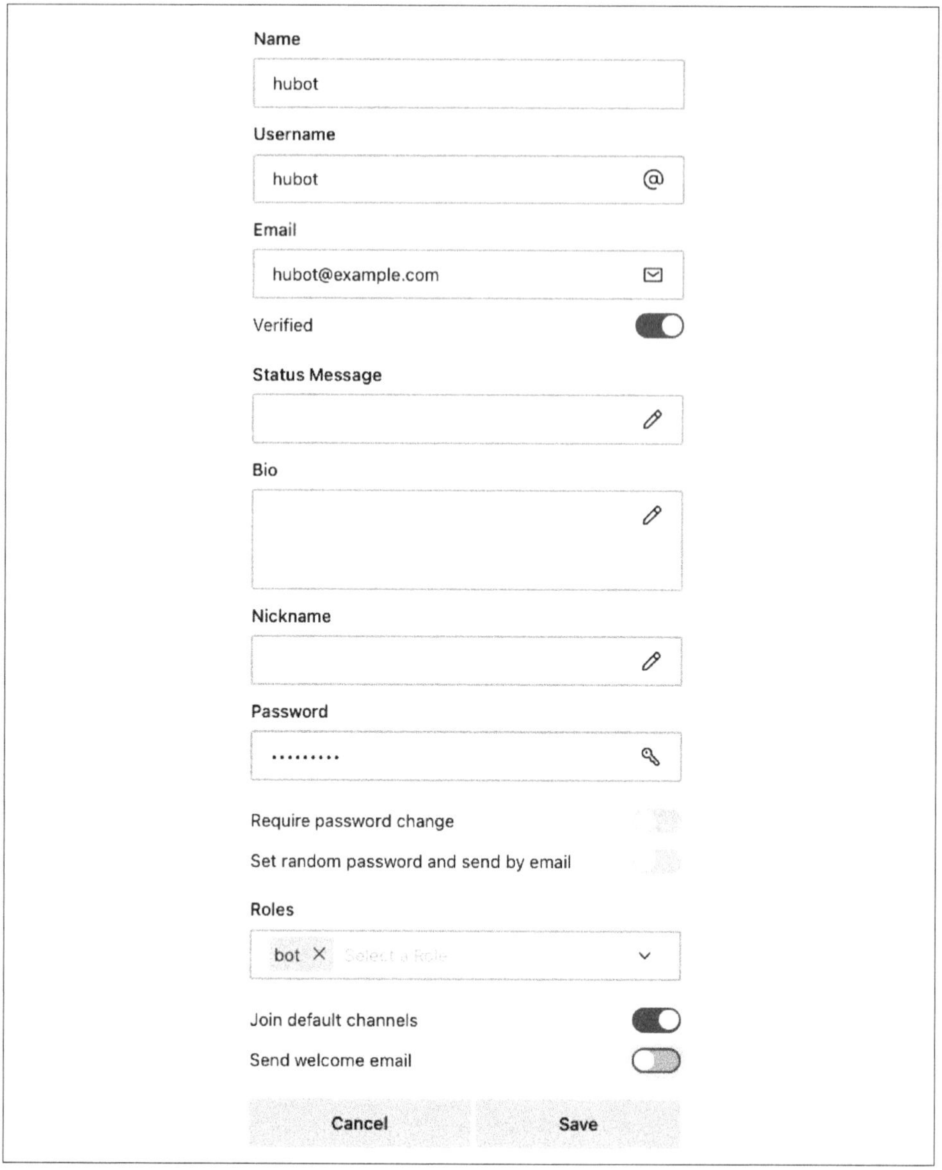

Figure 8-8. Rocket.Chat Add User screen

Fill out the form as follows:

- Name: **hubot**
- Username: **hubot**
- Email: **hubot@example.com**

- Click: **Verified** (**Blue**)
- Password: **bot-pw!**
- Roles: **bot**
- Disable: **Send welcome email** (**Gray**)

Click Save to create the user.

To ensure that the bot can log in, we also need to disable two-factor authentication, which is enabled by default. To do this, click Settings at the bottom of the Administration sidebar on the left side of your browser (Figure 8-9).

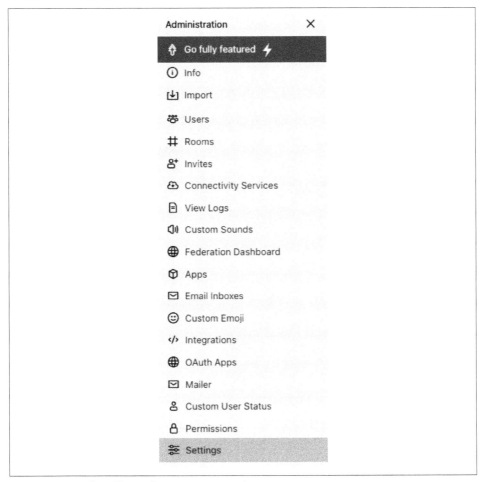

Figure 8-9. Rocket.Chat Administration settings

The Settings screen is displayed (Figure 8-10).

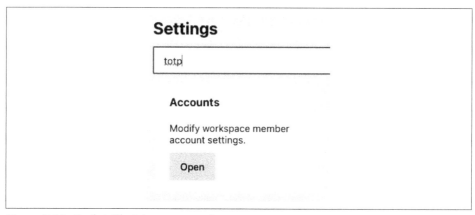

Figure 8-10. Rocket.Chat Accounts settings

In the new text search bar, type **totp**, then click the Open button under Accounts.

You should now see a long list of settings (Figure 8-11).

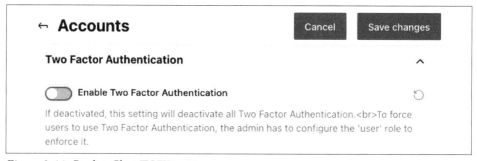

Figure 8-11. Rocket.Chat TOTP settings

Scroll down to the Two Factor Authentication section, expand it, and then deselect the Enable Two Factor Authentication option.

Once you have done this, click "Save changes."

At the top of the left side of the Administration panel, click the X to close the panel (Figure 8-12).

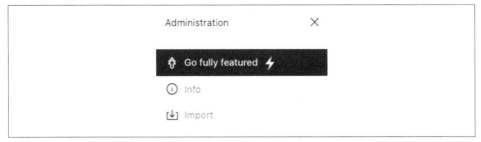

Figure 8-12. Rocket.Chat close Administration panel

In the left side panel under Channels, click "general" (Figure 8-13).

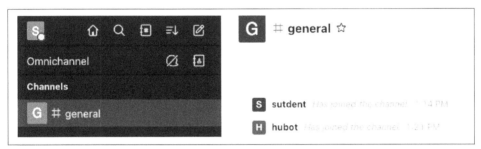

Figure 8-13. Rocket.Chat general channel

And finally, if you don't already see a message in the channel that "Hubot has joined the channel," go ahead and tell Docker Compose to restart the Hubot container. This will force Hubot to try and log into the chat server again, now that there is a user for the service to use:

```
$ docker compose restart hubot
Restarting unix_hubot_1 … done
```

If everything went according to plan, you should now be able to navigate back to your web browser and send commands to Hubot in the chat window.

Hubot should auto-join the General channel when it logs into the server, but just in case, you can send the following message in the General channel to explicitly invite Hubot:

```
/invite @hubot
```

You may get a message from the internal admin `rocket.cat` that says "@hubot is already in here." This is perfectly fine.

The environment variables used to configure Hubot defined its alias as a period. So you can now try typing . `help` to test that the bot is responding. If everything is working, you should get a list of commands that the bot understands and will respond to:

```
> . help
. adapter - Reply with the adapter
. echo <text> - Reply back with <text>
. help - Displays all of the help commands that this bot knows about.
. help <query> - Displays all help commands that match <query>.
. ping - Reply with pong
. time - Reply with current time
…
```

Finally, try typing the following:

```
. ping
```

Hubot should respond with PONG.

If you type:

```
. time
```

then Hubot will tell you what the time is set to on the server.

So, for one last diversion, try creating a new chat channel by typing /create zmachine in the chat window. You should now be able to click on the new zmachine channel in the left sidebar and invite Hubot with the chat command /invite @hubot.

 When you do this, Hubot might say:

```
There's no game for zmachine!
```
This is nothing to be concerned about.

Next, try typing the following commands into the chat window to play a chat-based version of the famous game *Colossal Cave Adventure* (*https://en.wikipedia.org/wiki/ Interactive_fiction#Adventure*):

```
. z start adventure

more
look
go east
examine keys
get keys

. z save firstgame
. z stop
. z start adventure
. z restore firstgame

inventory
```

Interactive fiction can be addictive and a huge time sink. You have been warned. That being said, if you aren't already familiar with it and are interested in learning more, take a look at some of these resources:

- Definition of interactive fiction (*https://en.wikipedia.org/wiki/Interactive_fiction*)
- Emulator (*https://davidgriffith.gitlab.io/frotz*)
- Development (*https://ganelson.github.io/inform-website*)
- Games (*https://oreil.ly/IrOLh*)[1]
- Competition (*https://ifcomp.org*)

You've now seen how easy it can be to configure, launch, and manage complex web services that require multiple components to accomplish their jobs using Docker Compose. In the next section, we will explore a few more of the features that Docker Compose includes.

You could avoid much of the Rocket.Chat setup by providing MongoDB with a preconfigured Rocket.Chat database, but it felt important to remove any magic from this example to make it clearer how everything fits together.

Exercising Docker Compose

Now that you have the full Rocket.Chat stack running and understand what the application is doing, we can dig in to get a little more insight into how the services are running. Some of the common Docker commands are also exposed as Compose commands, but for a specific stack rather than a single container or all of the containers on a host. You can run `docker compose top` to see an overview of your containers and the processes that are running in them:

```
$ docker compose top

compose-hubot-1
UID    PID    … CMD
1001   73342  … /usr/bin/qemu-x86_64 /bin/sh /bin/sh -c node -e "console.l…"
1001   73459  … /usr/bin/qemu-x86_64 /usr/local/bin/node node node_modules/…

compose-mongo-1
UID    PID    … CMD
1001   71243  … /usr/bin/qemu-x86_64 /opt/bitnami/mongodb/bin/mongod /opt/…
```

---

1 Full URL: *https://ifarchive.org/indexes/if-archiveXgamesXzcode.html*

```
compose-rocketchat-1
UID   PID   … CMD
65533 71903 … /usr/bin/qemu-x86_64 /usr/local/bin/node node main.js

compose-zmachine-1
UID  PID   … CMD
root 71999 … /usr/bin/qemu-x86_64 /usr/local/bin/node node /root/src/server.js
root 75078 … /usr/bin/qemu-x86_64 /root/src/../frotz/dfrotz /root/src/…
```

Similar to how you would normally enter a running Linux container using the
docker container exec command, you can run commands inside containers via the
Docker Compose tooling using the docker compose exec command. Because docker
compose is a newer tool, it provides some convenient shortcuts over the standard
docker commands. In the case of docker compose exec, you do not need to pass
in -i -t, and you can use the Docker Compose service name instead of trying to
remember the container ID or name:

```
$ docker compose exec mongo bash

I have no name!@0078134f9370:/$ mongo
MongoDB shell version v4.4.15
connecting to: mongodb://127.0.0.1:27017/?compressors=disabled&…
Implicit session: session { "id" : UUID("daec9543-bb9c-4e8c-ba6b…") }
MongoDB server version: 4.4.15
…
rs0:PRIMARY> exit
bye
I have no name!@0078134f9370:/$ exit
exit
```

docker compose logs and docker compose exec are probably the
most useful commands for troubleshooting. If Docker Compose
cannot build your image or start your container at all, you will
need to fall back to the standard docker commands to debug your
image and container, as we discussed in "Troubleshooting Broken
Builds" on page 92 and "Getting Inside a Running Container" on
page 146.

You can also use Docker Compose to start and stop and, in most environments,
pause and unpause either a single container or all of your containers, depending on
what you need:

```
$ docker compose stop zmachine
[+] Running 1/1
 ⠿ Container compose-zmachine-1  Stopped                                  0.3s
$ docker compose start zmachine
[+] Running 2/2
 ⠿ Container compose-mongo-1      Healthy                                 0.5s
 ⠿ Container compose-zmachine-1  Started                                  0.4s
```

```
$ docker compose pause
[+] Running 4/0
 ⠿ Container compose-mongo-1       Paused                          0.0s
 ⠿ Container compose-zmachine-1    Paused                          0.0s
 ⠿ Container compose-rocketchat-1  Paused                          0.0s
 ⠿ Container compose-hubot-1       Paused                          0.0s
$ docker compose unpause
[+] Running 4/0
 ⠿ Container compose-zmachine-1    Unpaused                        0.0s
 ⠿ Container compose-hubot-1       Unpaused                        0.0s
 ⠿ Container compose-rocketchat-1  Unpaused                        0.0s
 ⠿ Container compose-mongo-1       Unpaused                        0.0s
```

Finally, when you want to tear everything down and delete all the containers created by Docker Compose, you can run the following command:

```
$ docker compose down
[+] Running 5/5
 ⠿ Container compose-hubot-1       Removed                        10.4s
 ⠿ Container compose-zmachine-1    Removed                         0.1s
 ⠿ Container compose-rocketchat-1  Removed                         0.6s
 ⠿ Container compose-mongo-1       Removed                         0.9s
 ⠿ Network compose_botnet          Removed                         0.1s
```

 When you delete the MongoDB container using the docker com pose down command, all data in the MongoDB instance will be lost.

Managing Configuration

Docker Compose offers a few important capabilities that can help you significantly improve the flexibility of your *docker-compose.yaml* files. In this section, we will explore how you can avoid hardcoding many configuration values into your *docker-compose.yaml* files while still making them easy to use by default.

Default Values

If we take a look at the *services:rocketchat:environment* section of the *docker-compose.yaml* file, we will see something like this:

```
environment:
  RESPOND_TO_DM: "true"
  HUBOT_ALIAS: ". "
  LISTEN_ON_ALL_PUBLIC: "true"
  ROCKETCHAT_AUTH: "password"
  ROCKETCHAT_URL: "rocketchat:3000"
  ROCKETCHAT_ROOM: ""
  ROCKETCHAT_USER: "hubot"
```

```
ROCKETCHAT_PASSWORD: "bot-pw!"
BOT_NAME: "bot"
EXTERNAL_SCRIPTS: "hubot-help,hubot-diagnostics,hubot-zmachine"
HUBOT_ZMACHINE_SERVER: "http://zmachine:80"
HUBOT_ZMACHINE_ROOMS: "zmachine"
HUBOT_ZMACHINE_OT_PREFIX: "ot"
```

Now, if we look at *docker-compose-defaults.yaml* inside the same directory, we will see that this same section looks like this:

```
environment:
  RESPOND_TO_DM: ${HUBOT_RESPOND_TO_DM:-true}
  HUBOT_ALIAS: ${HUBOT_ALIAS:-. }
  LISTEN_ON_ALL_PUBLIC: ${HUBOT_LISTEN_ON_ALL_PUBLIC:-true}
  ROCKETCHAT_AUTH: ${HUBOT_ROCKETCHAT_AUTH:-password}
  ROCKETCHAT_URL: ${HUBOT_ROCKETCHAT_URL:-rocketchat:3000}
  ROCKETCHAT_ROOM: ${HUBOT_ROCKETCHAT_ROOM:-}
  ROCKETCHAT_USER: ${HUBOT_ROCKETCHAT_USER:-hubot}
  ROCKETCHAT_PASSWORD: ${HUBOT_ROCKETCHAT_PASSWORD:-bot-pw!}
  BOT_NAME: ${HUBOT_BOT_NAME:-bot}
  EXTERNAL_SCRIPTS: ${HUBOT_EXTERNAL_SCRIPTS:-hubot-help,
                     hubot-diagnostics,hubot-zmachine}
  HUBOT_ZMACHINE_SERVER: ${HUBOT_ZMACHINE_SERVER:-http://zmachine:80}
  HUBOT_ZMACHINE_ROOMS: ${HUBOT_ZMACHINE_ROOMS:-zmachine}
  HUBOT_ZMACHINE_OT_PREFIX: ${HUBOT_ZMACHINE_OT_PREFIX:-ot}
```

This is using a technique called *variable interpolation (https://docs.docker.com/compose/compose-file/#interpolation)* that Docker Compose has borrowed directly from many common Unix shells, like bash.

In the original file, the environment variable ROCKETCHAT_PASSWORD is hardcoded to the value "bot-pw!":

```
ROCKETCHAT_PASSWORD: "bot-pw!"
```

By using this new approach, we are stating that we want ROCKETCHAT_PASSWORD to be set to the value of the HUBOT_ROCKETCHAT_PASSWORD variable if it is set in the user's environment, and if it is not, then ROCKETCHAT_PASSWORD should be set to the default value of bot-pw!:

```
ROCKETCHAT_PASSWORD: ${HUBOT_ROCKETCHAT_PASSWORD:-bot-pw!}
```

This provides us with a great deal of flexibility since we can now make almost everything configurable while still providing reasonable defaults for the most common use case. We can easily test this out by running docker compose up with the new file:

```
$ docker compose -f docker-compose-defaults.yaml up -d

[+] Running 5/5
 ⠿ Network compose_botnet            Created                    0.0s
 ⠿ Container compose-mongo-1         Healthy                   31.0s
 ⠿ Container compose-rocketchat-1    Started                   31.2s
```

```
⠿ Container compose-zmachine-1      Started                              31.5s
⠿ Container compose-hubot-1         Started                              31.8s
```

By default, this will result in the exact same stack that we spun up earlier. However, we could easily make changes to it now by simply setting one or more environment variables in our terminal before running our docker compose commands:

```
$ docker compose -f docker-compose-defaults.yaml down
…

$ docker compose -f docker-compose-defaults.yaml config | \
    grep ROCKETCHAT_PASSWORD

    ROCKETCHAT_PASSWORD: bot-pw!

$ HUBOT_ROCKETCHAT_PASSWORD="my-unique-pw" docker compose \
    -f docker-compose-defaults.yaml config | \
    grep ROCKETCHAT_PASSWORD

    ROCKETCHAT_PASSWORD: my-unique-pw
```

In the examples here, Docker Compose will treat an empty environment variable exactly the same as one that is set to an empty string. If an empty string is a valid value in your use case, then you will want to modify the format of the variable substitution line so that it looks like this: ${VARIABLE_NAME-default-value}. We recommend reading through the documentation for this feature (*https://docs.docker.com/compose/compose-file/#interpolation*) so that you understand all the possibilities.

This is pretty nice, but what if we don't want to provide a default value at all and instead want to force the user to set something? We can do this pretty easily as well.

Some readers might be uncomfortable with the fact that we are passing in the password as part of the command line, since those passwords might be viewable in the system process list, etc., but don't worry—we will address that in just a few minutes.

Mandatory Values

To set a mandatory value, we simply need to alter the variable substitution line a bit. It seems like a bad idea to pass in a default password, so let's go ahead and make that value required.

In the *docker-compose-defaults.yaml* file, ROCKETCHAT_PASSWORD is defined like this:

```
ROCKETCHAT_PASSWORD: ${HUBOT_ROCKETCHAT_PASSWORD:-bot-pw!}
```

In the newer *docker-compose-env.yaml* file, we can see that it is defined like this:

```
ROCKETCHAT_PASSWORD:
    ${HUBOT_ROCKETCHAT_PASSWORD:?HUBOT_ROCKETCHAT_PASSWORD must be set!}
```

Instead of containing a default value, this approach defines an error string if the variable is not set to a nonempty string in the environment. If we try to simply spin up these services now, we will get an error message:

```
$ docker compose -f docker-compose-env.yaml up -d

invalid interpolation format for
  services.hubot.environment.ROCKETCHAT_PASSWORD.
You may need to escape any $ with another $.
required variable HUBOT_ROCKETCHAT_PASSWORD is missing a value:
  HUBOT_ROCKETCHAT_PASSWORD must be set!
```

The output gives us a few hints about what might be wrong, but the last two lines are pretty clear, and the final message is the exact error message that we defined, so it can be set to whatever makes the most sense in the situation.

If we go ahead and pass in our own password, then everything spins up just fine:

```
$ HUBOT_ROCKETCHAT_PASSWORD="a-b3tt3r-pw" docker compose \
    -f docker-compose-env.yaml up -d

[+] Running 5/5
 ⠿ Network compose_botnet          Created       0.0s
 ⠿ Container compose-mongo-1       Healthy      31.0s
 ⠿ Container compose-rocketchat-1  Started      31.3s
 ⠿ Container compose-zmachine-1    Started      31.5s
 ⠿ Container compose-hubot-1       Started      31.8s

$ docker compose -f docker-compose-env.yaml down
…
```

The dotenv File

Passing in a single environment variable is not that difficult, but if you need to pass in a lot of custom values, or even one real secret, then setting them in the local terminal isn't ideal. This is where the *.env* (*dotenv*) file can be very useful.

The *.env* file is a special file standard (*https://www.dotenv.org/docs/security/env*) that is intended to be parsed by programs that need additional configuration information that is specific to the local environment.

In the preceding use case, we must set a password to spin up our Docker Compose environment. We can pass in the environment every time, but this isn't ideal for at least a few reasons. It would be nice if we could set it in a way that is reasonably secure for a single-user environment and that will also make our lives a bit easier and less error prone.

In essence, a *.env* file is simply a list of key/value pairs. Since this file is intended to be unique to the local environment and will often contain at least one secret, we should start by ensuring that we will never accidentally commit these files into our revision control system. To do this with git, we can simply make sure that our *.gitignore* file includes *.env*, which, in this case, it already does:

```
$ grep .env ../.gitignore
.env
```

Assuming that we are on a single-user system, we can now safely create a *.env* file in the same directory that contains our *docker-compose.yaml* file(s).

For this example, let's go ahead and make the contents of our *.env* file look like this:

```
HUBOT_ROCKETCHAT_PASSWORD=th2l@stPW!
```

We could add many more key/value pairs to this file, but to keep things simple, we are only focusing on this one password. If you run git status after creating this file, you should notice that git is completely ignoring the new file, which is exactly what we want:

```
$ git status
On branch main
Your branch is up to date with 'origin/main'.

nothing to commit, working tree clean
```

 A *.env* file is not a Unix shell script. There are subtle but important differences between this format and how you might define variables in a standard shell script. The most important one is that, in most circumstances, you should not surround values with quotation marks.

In the previous section, when we ran docker compose -f docker-compose-env.yaml up -d without setting the HUBOT_ROCKETCHAT_PASSWORD, we got an error, but if we try this again after creating the *.env* file, things should work just fine:

```
$ docker compose -f docker-compose-env.yaml up -d

[+] Running 5/5
 ⋮ Network compose_botnet          Created           0.0s
 ⋮ Container compose-mongo-1        Healthy          31.1s
 ⋮ Container compose-rocketchat-1   Started          31.3s
 ⋮ Container compose-zmachine-1     Started          31.5s
 ⋮ Container compose-hubot-1        Started          31.8s
```

Let's confirm that the value that has been assigned to `ROCKETCHAT_PASSWORD` is what we set it to in the *.env* file:

```
$ docker compose \
    -f docker-compose-env.yaml config | \
    grep ROCKETCHAT_PASSWORD

  ROCKETCHAT_PASSWORD: th2l@stPW!
```

We can see that the value is indeed set to what we defined in the *.env* file. This is because Docker Compose will always read in the key/value pairs that are defined in a *.env* file that lives in the same directory as the *docker-compose.yaml* file that we are using.

It is important to understand the precedence that is in effect here. The very first thing that Docker Compose does is read all the defaults that are set in the *docker-compose.yaml* file. It then reads the *.env* file and overrides any of the defaults, which are values defined in the file. Then it finally looks at any environment variables that are set in the local environment and overwrites values previously defined with these.

This means that the defaults in the file should be the most common settings, then each user can define their common changes in the local *.env* file, and finally, they can rely on local environment variables when they need to make an unusual change for a specific use case. Using these features with Docker Compose helps ensure that you can build a very repeatable process that still contains enough flexibility to cover most common workflows.

 There are additional features of Docker Compose that we do not cover, like override files (*https://docs.docker.com/compose/extends*). As you start to use Docker Compose more, it is worth your time to review the documentation (*https://docs.docker.com/compose*) so that you are aware of any additional features that might be useful for your projects.

Wrap-Up

You should now have a very good feel for the types of things you can accomplish with Docker Compose and how you can use this tool to decrease the toil and increase the repeatability of your development environments.

In the next chapter, we will explore some of the tools that are available to help you scale Docker inside your data center and in the cloud.

## CHAPTER 9

The Path to Production Containers

Now that we've explored tooling for bringing up a stack of containers on a single host, we need to look at how we'd do this in a large-scale production environment. In this chapter, our goal is to show you how you might take containers to production based on our own experiences. There are myriad ways in which you will probably need to tailor this to your applications and environments, but this should provide you with a solid starting point to help you understand the Docker philosophy in practical terms.

Getting to Production

Getting an application from the point where it is built and configurable to the point where it is running on production systems is one of the most mine-ridden steps in going from zero to production. This has traditionally been complicated but is vastly simplified by the shipping container model. If you can imagine what it was like to load goods into a ship to take across the ocean before shipping containers existed, you have a sense of what most traditional deployment systems look like. In that old shipping model, randomly sized boxes, crates, barrels, and all manner of other packages were loaded by hand onto ships. They then had to be manually unloaded by someone who could tell which pieces needed to be unloaded first so that the whole pile wouldn't collapse like a Jenga (*https://en.wikipedia.org/wiki/Jenga*) puzzle.

Shipping containers changed all that: we now have a standardized box with well-known dimensions. These containers can be packed and unloaded in a logical order, and whole groups of items arrive together when expected. The shipping industry built machinery to manage them very efficiently. The Docker deployment model is very similar. All Linux containers support the same external interface, and the tooling just drops them on the servers they are supposed to be on without any concern for what's inside.

In the new model, when we have a running build of our application, we don't have to write much custom tooling to kick off deployment. If we only want to ship it to one server, the docker command-line tooling will handle most of that for us. If we want to send it to more servers, then we will have to look at some of the more advanced tooling from the broader container ecosystem. In either case, there are things your application will need to be aware of and concerns you will need to consider before taking your containerized application to production.

There is a progression you will follow while getting your applications to production with Docker:

1. Locally build and test a Docker image on your development box.
2. Build your official image for testing and deployment, usually from a continuous integration (CI) or build system.
3. Push the image to a registry.
4. Deploy your Docker image to your server, then configure and start the container.

As your workflow evolves, you will eventually collapse all of those steps into a single fluid workflow:

1. Orchestrate the building, testing, and storage of images and the deployment of containers to production servers.

But there is a lot more to the story than that. At the most basic level, a production story must encompass three things:

- It must be a repeatable process. Each time you invoke it, it needs to do the same thing. Ideally, it will do the same thing for all your applications.
- It needs to handle configuration for you. You must be able to define your application's configuration in a particular environment and then guarantee that it will ship that configuration on each deployment.
- It must deliver an executable artifact that can be started.

To accomplish that, there are several things you need to think about. We'll try to help with that by presenting a framework you can use to think about your application in its environment.

Docker's Role in Production Environments

We've covered a lot of capabilities that Docker brings to the table, and we've talked about some general production strategies. Before we dive deeper into production containers, let's look at how Docker fits into both a traditional and more modern production environment. If you are moving to Docker from a more traditional system, you can pick and choose which pieces you will delegate to Docker, to a deployment tool, or to a larger platform like Kubernetes or a cloud-based container system, or perhaps you'll even decide to leave it on your more traditional infrastructure. We have successfully transitioned multiple systems from traditional deployments to containerized systems, and there is a wide spectrum of good solutions. But understanding the required components and what makes up the modern and more traditional variants will put you on the right path to making good choices.

In Figure 9-1 we describe several concerns that need to be considered in a production system, the modern components that address them, and the systems they might replace in a more traditional environment. We divide these up into concerns that are addressed by Docker itself and those we ascribe to what we call the *platform*. The platform is a system that usually wraps around a cluster of servers and presents a common interface for Linux container management. This might be a unified system like Kubernetes or Docker Swarm, or it might consist of separate components that combine to form a platform. During the transition to a fully containerized system with a scheduler, the platform might be more than one thing at a time. So let's take a look at each of these concerns and see how they fit together.

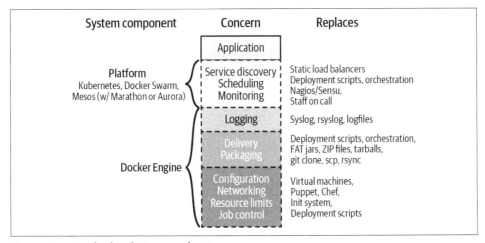

Figure 9-1. Docker's role in a production system

In Figure 9-1, you can see that the application is sitting on the top of the stack. It relies on all of the concerns below it in a production system. In some cases, your environment may call these concerns out specifically, and in others, they may be addressed by something you don't necessarily think of as filling that concern. But your production applications will rely on most of these in one way or another, and they will need to be addressed in your production environment. If you want to transition from an existing environment to a Linux Container-based environment, you'll want to think about how you are providing these today and how they might be addressed in the new system.

We'll start with familiar territory and then go from the bottom to the top. That familiar territory is your application. Your application is on the top! Everything else is there to deliver functionality to your application. After all, it's the application that delivers business value, and everything else is there to make that possible, to facilitate doing it at scale and reliably, and to standardize how it works across applications. While the order of the items underneath your application is intentional, it's not the case that each layer provides functionality to the one above. They are all providing that functionality to the application itself.

Because Linux containers and Docker can facilitate a lot of this functionality, containerizing your system will make many of these choices easier. As we get closer to the platform part of the stack, we'll have more to think about, but understanding everything that lies below it will make that much more manageable.

Let's start with application job control.

Job Control

Job control is a fundamental requirement for a modern deployment. This is part of the blue block in the drawing of concerns. You basically can't have a system of any kind without job control. It's something we have more traditionally left to the operating system, or one of the Linux init systems (systemd, System V init, runit, BSD rc scripts, etc.) more specifically. We tell the operating system about a process we want to have running, and then we configure what the behavior should be when restarting it, reloading its configuration, and managing the lifecycle of the application.

When we want to start or stop the application, we rely on these systems to handle that. We also rely on them in some cases to keep the application running more robustly by, for example, restarting it when it fails. Different applications require different job control. In a traditional Linux system, you might use cron to start and stop jobs on a timed basis. systemd might be responsible for restarting your application if it crashes. But, how the system does so is up to the specifics of that system, and there are many different implementations to deal with, which is not great.

If we're moving to the shipping container model, we want to be able to treat all jobs more or less the same way from the outside. We might need a little more metadata about them to get them to do the right thing, but we don't want to look inside the container. The Docker engine provides a strong set of primitives around job control—for example, docker container start, docker container stop, docker container run, and docker container kill—which map to most of the critical steps in the lifecycle of an application. All of the platforms that are built around Docker containers, including Kubernetes, follow these lifecycle behaviors as well. We've placed this at the bottom of the stack of concerns because it's fundamentally the lowest abstraction that Docker provides for your application. Even if we didn't use any other part of Docker, this would be a big win because it's the same for all applications and for all the platforms that run Docker containers.

Resource Limits

Sitting above job control are resource limits. In Linux systems, it is possible to use Linux control groups (cgroups) (*https://www.kernel.org/doc/html/latest/admin-guide/cgroup-v2.html*) directly to manage resource limits if we want to, and some production environments have done exactly that. But more traditionally we have relied on things like ulimit (*https://linuxconfig.org/limit-user-environment-with-ulimit-linux-command*) and the different settings of application runtime environments like the Java, Ruby, or Python VMs. In cloud systems, one of the early wins was that we could spin up individual virtual servers to limit the resources around a single business application. This was a nice innovation: no more noisy neighbor applications. Compared to containers, however, that is a pretty coarse-grained control.

With Linux containers, you can easily apply a wide set of resource controls to your containers via cgroups. It's up to you to decide whether or not you'll restrict your application's access to things like memory, disk space, or I/O when running in production. However, we highly recommend that you take the time to do this once you're comfortable with the needs of your application. If you don't, you won't be able to take advantage of one of the core features of containerized applications: running multiple applications on the same machine, largely without interference. As we've discussed, Docker gives this to you for free, and it's a core part of what makes a container valuable. You can review the specific arguments that Docker uses to manage these resources in Chapter 5.

Networking

There is a lot of detail about Docker networking in Chapter 11, so we won't touch on it too heavily here, but your containerized system will need to manage connecting your applications on the network. Docker provides a rich set of configuration options for networking. You should decide on one mechanism to use in your production environment and standardize that across containers. Trying to mix them is not an easy path to success. If you are running a platform like Kubernetes, then some of these decisions will be made for you. But the good part is that generally, the complexity of how the network is constructed is outside the concern of the application in the container. Consider that Docker or your bigger platform will provide this to you, and your application can work the same way inside the container on a local machine as it would in production as long as you follow a few rules:

1. Rely on Docker or your platform to map your ports dynamically and tell your application what they are mapped to. This is often provided to the application in the form of an environment variable.

2. Avoid protocols like FTP or RTSP that map random ports for return traffic. This is very difficult to support in a containerized platform.

3. Rely on the DNS provided to your container by Docker or your production runtime.

If you follow these rules, then generally your application can be quite agnostic about where it is deployed. Most production environments will provide you the ability to define the actual configuration and apply them at runtime. Docker Compose, Docker Swarm mode, Kubernetes, and cloud provider runtimes, like ECS, all do this for you.

Configuration

All applications need to somehow have access to their configuration. There are two levels of configuration for an application. The lowest level is how it expects the Linux environment around it to be configured. Containers handle this by providing a *Dockerfile* that we can use to build the same environment repeatably. In a more traditional system, we might have used a configuration management system like Chef, Puppet, or Ansible to do this. You may still use those systems in a containerized world, but you are usually not using them to provide dependencies to applications. That job belongs to Docker and the *Dockerfile*. Even if the contents of the *Dockerfile* are different for different applications, the mechanism and tooling are all the same—and that's a huge win.

The next level of configuration is the configuration directly applied to the application. We talked earlier about this in detail. Docker's native mechanism is to use environment variables, and this works across all modern platforms. Some systems, notably, make it easier to rely on more traditional configuration files. Kubernetes, in particular, makes it relatively easy to rely on files, but we recommend against it if you truly want a portable, container-native application. We find that this can significantly impact the observability of the application and discourage you from relying on that crutch. There is more about the reasoning behind environment variables in Chapter 13.

Packaging and Delivery

We'll lump packaging and delivery together in our discussion here. This is an area where a containerized system has major advantages over a traditional one. Here we don't have to stretch our imaginations to see the parallels to the shipping container model: we have a consistent package, the container image, and a standardized way to get them places—Docker's registry and the `image pull` and `image push` facilities. In more traditional systems, we would have built handcrafted deployment tooling, some of which we hopefully standardized across our applications. But if we needed to have a multilanguage environment, this would have been trouble. In your containerized environment, you'll need to consider how you handle packaging your applications into images and how you store those images.

The easiest path for the latter is a paid subscription to a hosted, commercial image registry. If that's acceptable to your company, then you should consider it. Several cloud providers, including Amazon, have image-hosting services that you can deploy inside your environment, which is another good option. You can, of course, also build and maintain an internal private registry, as we talked about in "Running a Private Registry" on page 68. There is a broad ecosystem of providers available to you, and you should survey your options.

Logging

Logging sits on the boundary of concerns that you can rely on Docker to provide in your containerized environment and concerns that the platform needs to manage. That's because, as we detailed in Chapter 6, Docker can collect all the logs from your containers and ship them somewhere. But by default, that somewhere is not even off of the local system. That might be great for a limited-size environment, and you could stop considering it there if local host storage is good enough for you. But your platform will be responsible for handling logs from lots of applications on lots of systems, so you'll probably want to centralize these logs into a system that significantly improves visibility and simplifies troubleshooting. When designing this, refer back to Chapter 6 for more details on logging. Some systems, like Kubernetes, are opinionated about the collecting of logs. But from the application's standpoint, you only need to make sure it sends them to `stdout` or `stderr` and let Docker or the platform handle the rest.

Monitoring

The first part of the system not neatly tied up in a bow by Docker or Linux containers in general is still improved by the standardization that Docker brings to the table. The ability to health-check applications in a standardized way, as discussed in Chapter 6, means that the process for monitoring application health is simplified. In many systems, the platform itself handles monitoring, and the scheduler will dynamically shut down unhealthy containers and potentially move the workload to a different server or restart the workload on the same system. In older systems, containers are often monitored by existing systems like Nagios, Zabbix, or other traditional monitoring systems. As we showed in Chapter 6, there are also newer options, including systems like Prometheus. The Application Performance Monitoring (APM) vendors, like New Relic, Datadog, or Honeycomb, all have first-class support for Linux containers and the applications that they contain as well. So if your application is already monitored by one of them, chances are that you don't need to change much.

In older systems, it is generally engineers who are paged and respond to issues and make decisions about how to handle failed applications. In dynamic systems, this work generally moves into more automated processes that belong inside the platform. In a transitional period, your system may have both while moving to an automated system where engineers are paged only when the platform really can't intervene. In any case, a human will still need to be the final line of defense. But the containerized system is much easier to handle when things do go wrong because the mechanisms are standardized across applications.

Scheduling

How do you decide which services run on which servers? Containers are easy to move around because Docker provides such good mechanisms for doing so. And that opens up lots of possibilities for better resource usage, better reliability, self-healing services, and dynamic scaling. But something has to make those decisions.

In older systems, this was often handled with dedicated servers per service. You often configured a list of servers into the deployment scripts, and the same set of servers would receive the new application on each deployment. One-service-per-server models drove early virtualization in private data centers. Cloud systems encouraged the one-service-per-server model by making it easy to slice and dice servers into commodity virtual servers. Autoscaling in systems like AWS handled part of this dynamic behavior. But if you move to containers, where many services may be running on the same virtual server, scaling and dynamic behaviors at the server level don't help you.

Distributed schedulers

Distributed schedulers leverage Docker to let you reason about your entire network of servers almost as if it were a single computer. The idea here is that you define some policies about how you want your application to run, and you let the system figure out where to run it and how many instances of it to run. If something goes wrong on a server or with the application, you let the scheduler start it up again on any available healthy resource that meets the application's requirements. This fits more into Docker, Inc., founder Solomon Hykes's (*https://www.linkedin.com/in/solomonhykes*) original vision for Docker: a way to run your application anywhere without worrying about how it gets there. Generally, zero downtime deployment in this model is done in the blue-green style (*https://martinfowler.com/bliki/BlueGreenDe ployment.html*), where you launch the new generation of an application alongside the old generation and then slowly migrate work from the old stack to the new one.

Using the metaphor now made famous by Kelsey Hightower (*https://youtu.be/ HlAXp0-M6SY?t=10m23s*), the scheduler is the system that plays Tetris for you, placing services on servers for the best fit, on the fly.

While it was not the first—that honor goes to platforms like Mesos and Cloud Foundry—today Kubernetes (*https://kubernetes.io*), which came out of Google in 2014, is the undoubted leader when it comes to container-based schedulers. The early releases of Kubernetes took the lessons that Google learned from its own internal Borg (*https://kubernetes.io/blog/2015/04/borg-predecessor-to-kubernetes*) system and brought those to the open source community. It was built on Docker and Linux containers from the beginning and supports not only Docker's `containerd` but also a few of the other container runtimes—all of which use Docker containers. Kubernetes is a big system with a lot of moving pieces. There are many different commercial and cloud-based distributions of Kubernetes. The Cloud Native Computing Foundation (*https://landscape.cncf.io/members?cat egory=certified-kubernetes-distribution,certified-kubernetes-hosted,certified-kubernetes- installer&grouping=category*) provides certifications to ensure that each distribution meets certain standards within the broader Kubernetes community. This space continues to change rapidly, and while Kubernetes is really powerful, it's an actively evolving target that can be hard to stay on top of. If you are building a brand-new system from scratch, you will probably want to strongly consider Kubernetes. In the absence of other experience, if you are running on a cloud, your provider's implementation will likely be the easiest path to follow. While we encourage you to consider it for any complex system, Kubernetes is not the only option.

Docker Swarm mode came out of Docker, Inc., in 2015 and is built as a Docker-native system from the ground up. It might be an attractive option if you are looking for a very simple orchestration tool that stays completely within the Docker platform and is supported by a single vendor. Docker Swarm mode has not seen much adoption in the market, and since Docker is integrating Kubernetes so heavily into its tooling, this is probably not as clear a path as it once was.

Orchestration

When we talk about schedulers, we often talk about not just their ability to match jobs to resources but their orchestration capabilities as well. By that, we mean the ability to command and organize applications and deployments across a whole system. Your scheduler might move jobs for you on the fly or allow you to run tasks on each server specifically. This was more commonly handled in older systems by specific orchestration tools.

In most modern container systems, all the orchestration tasks, including scheduling, are handled by the core cluster software, whether it be Kubernetes, Swarm, a cloud provider's bespoke container-management system, or something else.

Of all the features delivered by the platform, scheduling is undoubtedly the most powerful. It also has the most impact on applications when moving them into containers. Many traditional applications are not designed to have service discovery and resource allocation change underneath them and require a significant number of changes to work well in a truly dynamic environment. For this reason, your move to a containerized system may not necessarily encompass moving to a scheduled platform initially. Often the best path to production containers lies in containerizing your applications while running inside the traditional system and then moving on to a more dynamic, scheduled system. This might mean initially running your applications as containers on the same servers they are currently deployed to, and then once that is working well, you can introduce a scheduler to the mix.

Service Discovery

You can think of service discovery as the mechanism by which the application finds all the other services and resources it needs on the network. Rare is the application that has no dependency on anything else. Stateless, static websites are perhaps one of the only systems that may not need any service discovery. Nearly everything else needs to know something about the surrounding system and requires a way to discover that information. Most of the time this involves more than one system, but they are usually tightly coupled.

You might not think of them this way, but in traditional systems, load balancers are one of the primary means for service discovery. Load balancers are used for reliability and scaling, but they also keep track of all of the endpoints associated with a particular service. This is sometimes manually configured and sometimes more dynamic, but the way other systems find endpoints for a service is by using a known address or name for the load balancer. That's a form of service discovery, and load balancers are a common way to do this in older systems. They often are used for this in modern environments, too, even if they don't look much like traditional load balancers. Other means for service discovery in older systems are static database configurations or application configuration files.

As you saw back in Figure 9-1, Docker does not address service discovery in your environment, except when using Docker Swarm mode. For the vast majority of systems, service discovery is left to the platform. This means it's one of the first things you'll need to resolve in a more dynamic system. Containers are by nature easily moved, and that can break traditional systems if they were built around more statically deployed applications. Each platform handles this differently, and you'll want to understand what works best with your system.

 Docker Swarm (classic Swarm) (*https://github.com/docker-archive/ classicswarm*) and Docker Swarm mode (*https://docs.docker.com/ engine/swarm*) are not the same things. We will discuss Docker Swarm mode in more detail in Chapter 10.

Some examples of service discovery mechanisms you might be familiar with include the following:

- Load balancers with well-known addresses
- Round-robin DNS
- DNS SRV records
- Dynamic DNS systems
- Multicast DNS
- Overlay networks with well-known addresses
- Gossip protocols
- Apple's Bonjour protocol (*https://en.wikipedia.org/wiki/Bonjour_(software)*)
- Apache ZooKeeper (*https://zookeeper.apache.org*)
- HashiCorp's Consul (*https://www.consul.io*)
- etcd (*https://etcd.io*)

That's a big list, and there are a lot more options than that. Some of these systems also do a lot more than just service discovery, which can confuse the issue. An example of service discovery that may be closer to hand while you're trying to understand this concept is the linking mechanism used by Docker Compose in Chapter 8. This mechanism relies on a DNS system that the dockerd server supplies, which allows one service in Docker Compose to reference another peer service's name and return the correct container IP address. Kubernetes, at its simplest, also has a system that works like this, with injected environment variables. But these are the simplest forms of discovery on modern systems.

Often you find that the interface to these systems relies on having well-known names and/or ports for a service. You might call out to *http://service-a.example.com* to reach service A on a well-known name. Or you might call out to *http://services.example.com:service-a-port* to reach the same service on a well-known name and port. Modern environments often handle this differently. Usually, within a new system, this process will be managed and fairly seamless. And it's frequently easy for new applications to call out of the platform to more traditional systems, but sometimes it's not as easy going the other way. Often, the best initial system (though not necessarily longer term) is one in which you present dynamically configured load balancers that are easily reachable by systems in your older environment. Kubernetes provides for this in the form of Ingress routes and might be one path to consider if you are using that platform.

Examples of this include the following:

- Kubernetes's Ingress controllers (*https://oreil.ly/7ucPN*),[1] including Traefik (*https://oreil.ly/RbuvY*)[2] or Contour (*https://projectcontour.io*), among others
- Linkerd (*https://linkerd.io*) service mesh
- Standalone Sidecar service discovery (*https://github.com/NinesStack/sidecar*) with Lyft's Envoy (*https://github.com/envoyproxy/envoy*) proxy
- Istio (*https://istio.io*) service mesh and Lyft's Envoy

If you are running a blended modern and traditional system, getting traffic into the newer containerized system is generally the harder problem to solve and the one you should think through first.

Production Wrap-Up

Many people will start by using simple Docker orchestration tools. However, as the number of containers and frequency with which you deploy containers grows, the appeal of distributed schedulers will quickly become apparent. Tools like Kubernetes allow you to abstract individual servers and whole data centers into large pools of resources in which to run container-based tasks.

There are undoubtedly many other worthy projects out there in the deployment space. But these are the most commonly cited and have the most publicly available information at the time of this writing. It's a fast-evolving space, so it's worth taking a look around to see what new tools are being shipped.

In any case, you should start by getting a Linux container infrastructure up and running and then look at outside tooling. Docker's built-in tooling might be good enough for you. We suggest using the lightest-weight tool for the job, but having

---

1 Full URL: *https://kubernetes.io/docs/concepts/services-networking/ingress*

2 Full URL: *https://doc.traefik.io/traefik/providers/kubernetes-ingress*

flexibility is a great place to be, and Linux containers are increasingly supported by more and more powerful tooling.

Docker and the DevOps Pipeline

So once we have considered and implemented all of that functionality, we should have our production environment in robust shape. But how do we know it works? One of Docker's key promises is the ability to test your application and all of its dependencies in exactly the operating environment it would have in production. It can't guarantee that you have properly tested external dependencies like databases, nor does it provide any magical test framework, but it can make sure that your libraries and other code dependencies are all tested together. Changing underlying dependencies is a critical place where things go wrong, even for organizations with strong testing discipline. With Docker, you can build your image, run it on your development box, and then test the same image in your continuous-integration pipeline before shipping it to production servers.

Testing your containerized application is not much more complicated than testing your application itself, as long as your test environment is designed to manage Linux container workloads. Next, let's cover one example of how you might do this.

Quick Overview

Let's draw up an example production environment for a fictional company. We'll try to describe something similar to the environment at a lot of companies, with Docker thrown into the mix for illustration purposes.

Our fictional company's environment has a pool of production servers that run Docker daemons and an assortment of applications deployed there. There are multiple build and test workers that are tied to the pipeline coordination server. We'll ignore deployment for now and talk about it once our fictional application has been tested and is ready to ship.

Figure 9-2 shows what a common workflow looks like for testing containerized applications, including the following steps:

1. A build is triggered by some outside means—for example, from a webhook call from a source code repository or a manual trigger by a developer.
2. The build server kicks off a container image build.
3. The image is created on the local server.
4. The image is tagged with a build or version number or a commit hash.
5. A new container, based on the newly built image, is configured to run the test suite.

6. The test suite is run against the container, and the result is captured by the build server.

7. The build is marked as passing or failing.

8. Passed builds are shipped to an image registry or other storage mechanism.

You'll notice that this isn't too different from common patterns for testing applications. At a minimum, you need to have a job that can kick off a test suite. The steps we're adding here are just to create a container image first and invoke the test suite inside of the container.

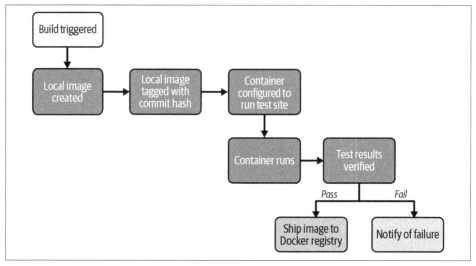

Figure 9-2. Docker testing workflow chart

Let's look at how this works for the application we're deploying at our fictional company. We just updated our application and pushed the latest code to our Git repository. We have a post-commit hook that triggers a build on each commit, so that job is kicked off on the build server, which is also running the dockerd daemon. The job on the build server assigns the task to a test worker. The worker doesn't have dockerd running, but it has the docker command-line tool installed. So we run our docker image build against the remote dockerd daemon, generating a new image on the remote Docker server.

> You should build your container image exactly as you'll ship it to production. If you need to make concessions for testing, they should be externally provided switches, either via environment variables or through command-line arguments. The whole idea is to test the exact build that you'll ship, so this is a critical point.

Once the image has been built, our test job will create and run a new container based on our new production image. Our image is configured to run the application in production, but we need to run a different command for testing. That's OK! Docker lets us do that simply by providing the command at the end of the docker container run command. In production, our imaginary container would start supervisor, which in turn would start up an nginx instance and some Ruby unicorn web server instances behind that. But for testing, we don't need that nginx, and we don't need to run our web application. Instead, our build job invokes the container like this:

```
$ docker container run -e ENVIRONMENT=testing -e API_KEY=12345 \
    -it awesome_app:version1 /opt/awesome_app/test.sh
```

We called docker container run, but we did a couple of extra things here, too. We passed a couple of environment variables into the container: ENVIRONMENT and API_KEY. These can either be new or overrides for the ones Docker already exports for us. We also asked for a particular tag—in this case, version1. That will make sure we build on top of the correct image even if another build is running simultaneously. Then we override the command that our container was configured to start in the *Dockerfile*'s CMD line. Instead, we call our test script, */opt/awesome_app/test.sh*. Although it is not necessary in this example, you should note that in some cases you will need to override the *Dockerfile*'s ENTRYPOINT (--entrypoint) to run something other than the default command for that container.

 Always pass the precise Docker tag (usually a version or commit hash) for your image into the test job. If you always use latest, then you won't be able to guarantee that another job has not moved that tag just after your build was kicked off. If you use the most precise tag possible, then you can be sure you're testing the right build of the application.

A critical point to make here is that docker container run will exit with the exit status of the command that was invoked in the container. That means we can just look at the exit status to see if our tests were successful. If your test suite is properly designed, this is probably all you need. If you need to run multiple steps, or the exit code can't be relied on, one way to handle this is to capture all of the output of the test run into a file and then sift through the output to look for status messages. Our fictional build system does just that. We write out the output from the test suite, and our *test.sh* echoes either Result: SUCCESS! or Result: FAILURE! on the last line to signify if our tests passed. If you need to rely on this mechanism, be sure to look for some output string that won't appear by happenstance in your normal test suite output. If we need to look for "success," for example, we should limit it to looking at the last line of the file, and maybe also ensure that the whole line matched the exact output we would normally expect. In this case, we look at just the last line of the file and find our success string, so we mark the build as passed.

There is one more container-specific step. We want to take our passed build and push that image to our registry. The registry is the interchange point between builds and deployments. It also allows us to share the image with our peers and other builds that might be built on top of it. But for now, let's just think of it as the place where we put and tag successful builds. Our build script will now do a `docker image tag` to give the image the right build tag(s), potentially including `latest`, and then perform a `docker image push` to push the build to the registry.

That's it! As you can see, there is not much to this compared with testing a normal application. We took advantage of Docker's client/server model to invoke the test on a different server from our primary test server, and we wrapped up our tests into a consolidated shell script to generate our output status. Overall it is very similar to most other modern build system approaches.

The most critical takeaway is that our fictional company's system makes sure that they only ship applications whose test suites have passed on the same Linux distribution, with the same libraries and the same build settings. That container might then also be tested against any outside dependencies like databases or caches without having to mock them. None of this guarantees success, but it gets us a lot closer to that than the dependency roulette often experienced by production deployment systems that are not built on container technology.

 If you use Jenkins for continuous integration or are looking for a good way to test scaling Docker, there are many plug-ins (*https://plugins.jenkins.io*) for Docker, Mesos, and Kubernetes that are worth investigating. Many hosted, commercial platforms now provide containerized CI environments as well, including CircleCI (*https://circleci.com*) and GitHub Actions (*https://github.blog/ 2022-02-02-build-ci-cd-pipeline-github-actions-four-steps*).

Outside Dependencies

But what about those external dependencies that we glossed over? Things like the database, or Memcached or Redis instances that we need to run our tests against our container? If our fictional company's application needs a database to run, or a Memcached or Redis instance, we need to solve that external dependency to have a clean test environment. It would be nice to use the container model to support that dependency. With some work, you can do this with tools like Docker Compose (*https://github.com/docker/compose*), which we described in detail in Chapter 8. In Docker Compose, our build job could express some dependencies between containers, and then Compose will connect them seamlessly.

Being able to test your application in an environment that looks like where it will live is a huge win. Compose makes this pretty easy to set up. You'll still need to rely on your own language's testing framework for the tests, but the environment is really easy to orchestrate.

Wrap-Up

Now that we've surveyed how a containerized application interacts with the outside environment, and where the boundaries lie in each of those areas, we're ready to explore how Docker clusters can be built to support the global, always-on, on-demand nature of many modern technology operations.

## CHAPTER 10

Containers at Scale

A major strength of containers is their ability to abstract away the underlying hardware and operating system so that your application is not constrained to any particular host or environment. It facilitates scaling a stateless application not just horizontally within your data center but also across cloud providers without many of the traditional barriers you would encounter. True to the shipping container metaphor, a container on one cloud looks like a container on another.

Many organizations find turnkey cloud deployments of Linux containers appealing because they can gain many of the immediate benefits of a scalable container-based platform without needing to completely build something in-house. Even though this is true, the barrier is actually pretty low for building your own platform in the cloud or in your own data center, and we'll cover some options for doing that shortly.

The major public cloud providers have all worked to support Linux containers natively in their offerings. Some of the largest efforts to support Linux containers in the public cloud include the following:

- Amazon Elastic Container Service (*https://aws.amazon.com/ecs*)
- Google Cloud Run (*https://cloud.google.com/run*)
- Azure Container Apps (*https://azure.microsoft.com/en-us/services/container-apps*)

Many of the same companies also have robust hosted Kubernetes offerings like these:

- Amazon Elastic Kubernetes Service (*https://aws.amazon.com/eks*)
- Google Kubernetes Engine (*https://cloud.google.com/kubernetes-engine*)
- Azure Kubernetes Service (*https://azure.microsoft.com/en-us/services/kubernetes-service*)

It's trivial to install Docker on a Linux instance in one of the public clouds. But getting Docker onto the server is usually just one step in creating a full production environment. You could do this completely on your own, or you could use the many tools available from the major cloud providers, Docker, Inc., and the broader container community. Much of the tooling will work equally well in either a public cloud or your own data center.

In the realm of schedulers and more complex tooling systems, we have plenty of choices for systems that replicate much of the functionality you would get from a public cloud provider. Even if you run in a public cloud, there are some compelling reasons why you might choose to run your own Linux container environment rather than use one of the off-the-shelf offerings.

In this chapter, we'll cover some options for running Linux containers at scale, first going through the much simpler Docker Swarm mode and then diving into some more advanced tools like Kubernetes and some of the larger cloud offerings. All of these examples should give you a view of how you can leverage Docker to provide an incredibly flexible platform for your application workloads.

Docker Swarm Mode

After building the container runtime in the form of the Docker engine, the engineers at Docker turned to the problems of orchestrating a fleet of individual Docker hosts and effectively packing those hosts full of containers. The first tool that evolved from this work was called Docker Swarm. As we explained early on, and rather confusingly, there are now two things called "Swarm," both of which come from Docker, Inc.

The original standalone Docker Swarm is now commonly referred to as Docker Swarm (classic) (*https://github.com/docker-archive/classicswarm*), but there is a second "Swarm" implementation that is more specifically called Swarm mode (*https://docs.docker.com/engine/swarm*). Instead of being a separate product, this is built into the Docker client. The built-in Swarm mode is a lot more capable than the original Docker Swarm and is intended to replace it entirely. Swarm mode has the major advantage of not requiring you to install anything separately. You already have this clustering capability on any of your systems that are running Docker! This is the Docker Swarm implementation that we'll focus on here. Hopefully, now that you know that there have been two different Docker Swarm implementations, you won't get confused by contradictory information on the internet.

The idea behind Docker Swarm mode is to present a single interface to the docker client tool but have that interface be backed by a whole cluster rather than a single Docker daemon. Swarm is primarily aimed at managing clustered computing resources via the Docker tools. It has grown a lot since its first release and now contains several scheduler plug-ins with different strategies for assigning containers to hosts, and it comes with some basic service discovery built in. But it remains only one building block of a more complex solution.

Swarm clusters can contain one or more managers that act as the central management hub for your Docker cluster. It is best to set up an odd number of managers. Only one manager will act as the cluster leader at a time. As you add more nodes to Swarm, you are merging them into a single, cohesive cluster that can be easily controlled with the Docker tooling.

Let's get a Swarm cluster up and running. To start, you will need three or more Linux servers that can talk to each other over the network. Each of these servers should be running recent releases of Docker Community Edition from the official Docker software repositories.

Refer to Chapter 3 for details on installing the docker-ce packages on Linux.

For this example, we will use three Ubuntu servers running docker-ce. The very first thing you'll need to do is ssh to the server that you want to use as the Swarm manager, and then run the swarm init command using the IP address for your Swarm manager:

```
$ ssh 172.17.4.1
…

ubuntu@172.17.4.1:$ sudo docker swarm init --advertise-addr 172.17.4.1

Swarm initialized: current node (hypysglii5syybd2zew6ovuwq) is now a manager.

To add a worker to this swarm, run the following command:

    docker swarm join --token SWMTKN-1-14……a4o55z01zq 172.17.4.1:2377

To add a manager to this swarm, run 'docker swarm join-token manager'
and follow the instructions.
```

There are steps that you must take to secure a Docker Swarm mode cluster, which we are not covering here. Before you run Docker Swarm mode on any long-lived systems, make sure that you understand the options and have taken proper steps to secure the environment.

In many of this chapter's examples, you must use the correct IP addresses for your manager and worker nodes.

This step will initialize the Swarm manager and give you the token that is required for nodes that want to join the cluster. Make note of this token somewhere safe, like a password manager. Don't worry too much if you lose this token; you can always get it again by running the following command on the manager:

```
sudo docker swarm join-token --quiet worker
```

You can inspect your progress so far by running your local docker client pointed at the new manager node's IP address:

```
$ docker -H 172.17.4.1 system info

…
Swarm: active
  NodeID: l9gfcj7xwii5deveu3raf4782
  Is Manager: true
  ClusterID: mvdaf2xsqwjwrb94kgtn2mzsm
  Managers: 1
  Nodes: 1
  Default Address Pool: 10.0.0.0/8
  SubnetSize: 24
  Data Path Port: 4789
  Orchestration:
   Task History Retention Limit: 5
  Raft:
   Snapshot Interval: 10000
   Number of Old Snapshots to Retain: 0
   Heartbeat Tick: 1
   Election Tick: 10
  Dispatcher:
   Heartbeat Period: 5 seconds
  CA Configuration:
   Expiry Duration: 3 months
   Force Rotate: 0
  Autolock Managers: false
  Root Rotation In Progress: false
  Node Address: 172.17.4.1
  Manager Addresses:
   172.17.4.1:2377
…
```

You can also list all of the nodes that are currently in the cluster with the following command:

```
$ docker -H 172.17.4.1 node ls

ID       HOSTNAME      STATUS AVAILABILITY MANAGER STATUS ENGINE VERSION
l9…82 * ip-172-17-4-1 Ready  Active       Leader         20.10.7
```

At this point, you can add the two additional servers as workers to the Swarm cluster. This is what you'd do in production if you were going to scale up, and Swarm makes this pretty easy:

```
$ ssh 172.17.4.2 \
    "sudo docker swarm join --token SWMTKN-1-14……a4o55z01zq 172.17.4.1:2377"

This node joined a swarm as a worker.

$ ssh 172.17.4.3 \
    "sudo docker swarm join --token SWMTKN-1-14……a4o55z01zq 172.17.4.1:2377"

This node joined a swarm as a worker.
```

 Adding additional managers is important and can be done as easily as adding the workers. You just need to pass in the manager join token instead of the worker join token. You can get this token by running docker swarm join-token manager on any of the active nodes.

If you rerun docker node ls, you should now see that you have a total of three nodes in your cluster, and only one of them is marked as the Leader:

```
$ docker -H 172.17.4.1 node ls

ID       HOSTNAME      STATUS AVAILABILITY MANAGER STATUS ENGINE VERSION
l9…82 * ip-172-17-4-1 Ready  Active       Leader         20.10.7
3d…7b   ip-172-17-4-2 Ready  Active                      20.10.7
ip…qe   ip-172-17-4-3 Ready  Active                      20.10.7
```

This is all that's required to get a Swarm cluster up and running in Swarm mode (Figure 10-1)!

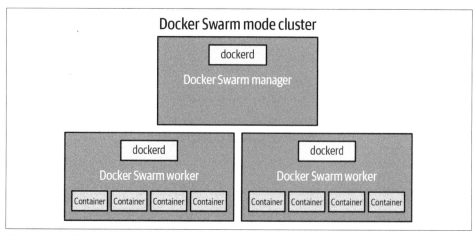

Figure 10-1. Simple Docker Swarm mode cluster

The next thing you should do is create a network for your services to use. There is a default network called `ingress` in Swarm, but it is very easy to create additional ones for better isolation:

```
$ docker -H 172.17.4.1 network create --driver=overlay default-net

ckwh5ph4ksthvx6843ytrl5ik

$ docker -H 172.17.4.1 network ls

NETWORK ID      NAME              DRIVER    SCOPE
494e1a1bf8f3    bridge            bridge    local
xqgshg0nurzu    default-net       overlay   swarm
2e7d2d7aaf0f    docker_gwbridge   bridge    local
df0376841891    host              host      local
n8kjd6oa44fr    ingress           overlay   swarm
b4720ea133d6    none              null      local
```

Up to this point, we've just been getting the underlying pieces running, and so far we haven't deployed any real business logic. So let's launch your first service into the cluster. You can do that with a command like this:

```
$ docker -H 172.17.4.1 service create --detach=true --name quantum \
    --replicas 2 --publish published=80,target=8080 --network default-net \
    spkane/quantum-game:latest

tiwtsbf270mh83032kuhwv07c
```

The service we're launching with starts containers that host the *Quantum game* (*https://github.com/stared/quantum-game*). This is a browser-based puzzle game that uses real quantum mechanics. We hope that this is a more interesting example than another Hello World!

Although we're using the latest tag in many of these examples, you shouldn't ever use this tag in production. It is convenient for this book since we can easily push out updates to the code, but this tag floats and cannot be pinned to a specific release over a long period. That means if you use latest, then your deployments are not repeatable! It can also easily lead to a situation where you don't have the same version of an application running on all the servers.

Let's see where those containers ended up by running docker service ps against the service name you created:

```
$ docker -H 172.17.4.1 service ps quantum

ID      NAME       IMAGE        NODE           DESIRED… CURRENT… ERROR PORTS
rk…13 quantum.1 spkane/qua… ip-172-17-4-1 Running   Running…
lz…t3 quantum.2 spkane/qua… ip-172-17-4-2 Running   Running…
```

Swarm mode uses a routing mesh between the nodes to automatically route traffic to a container that can serve the request. When you specify a published port in the docker service create command, the mesh makes it possible to hit this port on any of your three nodes and will route you to the web application. Notice that we said any of the *three* nodes even though you only have two instances running. Traditionally, you would have also had to set up a separate reverse proxy layer to accomplish this, but its batteries are included with Swarm mode.

To prove it, you can test the service now by pointing a web browser to the IP address of any of your nodes:

```
http://172.17.4.1/
```

If everything is working as expected, you should see the first puzzle board for the *Quantum Game* (*https://quantumgame.io*):

```
To get a list of all the services, we can use +service ls+:

$ docker -H 172.17.4.1 service ls

ID     NAME     MODE        REPLICAS IMAGE                     PORTS
iu…9f quantum replicated 2/2        spkane/quantum-game:latest *:80->8080/tcp
```

This gives us a summary view of the most commonly needed information, but sometimes that's not enough. Docker maintains a lot of other metadata about services, just like it does for containers. We can get detailed information about a service with service inspect:

```
$ docker -H 172.17.4.1 service inspect --pretty quantum

ID:      iuoh6oxrec9fk67ybwuikutqa
Name:    quantum
Service Mode:  Replicated
 Replicas:  2
```

```
Placement:
UpdateConfig:
 Parallelism:  1
 On failure:  pause
 Monitoring Period: 5s
 Max failure ratio: 0
 Update order:      stop-first
RollbackConfig:
 Parallelism:  1
 On failure:  pause
 Monitoring Period: 5s
 Max failure ratio: 0
 Rollback order:    stop-first
ContainerSpec:
 Image:     spkane/quantum-game:latest@sha256:1f57…4a8c
 Init:    false
Resources:
Networks: default-net
Endpoint Mode:  vip
Ports:
  PublishedPort = 80
  Protocol = tcp
  TargetPort = 8080
  PublishMode = ingress
```

There is a lot of info here, so let's point out some of the more important things. First, we can see that this is a replicated service with two replicas, just like we saw in the `service ls` command. We can also see that Docker is health-checking the service at 5-second intervals. Running an update to the service will use the `stop-first` method, which means it will take our service first to $N-1$ and then spin up a new instance to take us back to N. You might want to always run in $N+1$ mode so that you are never down a node during updates in production. You can change that with the `--update-order=start-first` option to the `service update` command. It will exhibit the same behavior in a rollback scenario, and we can likewise change that with `--rollback-order=start-first`.

In a real-world scenario, we not only need to be able to launch our service, but we also need to be able to scale it up and down. It would be a shame if we had to redeploy it to do that, not to mention it could introduce any number of additional issues. Luckily, Swarm mode makes it easy to scale our services with a single command. To double the number of instances you have running from two to four, you can simply run this:

```
$ docker -H 172.17.4.1 service scale --detach=false quantum=4

quantum scaled to 4
overall progress: 4 out of 4 tasks
1/4: running   [==================================================>]
2/4: running   [==================================================>]
3/4: running   [==================================================>]
```

```
4/4: running   [==================================================>]
verify: Service converged
```

 We used --detach=false in the previous command so that it was easier to see what was happening.

We can now use `service ps` to show us that Swarm did what we asked. This is the same command we ran earlier, but now we should have more copies running! But wait, didn't we ask for more copies than we have nodes?

```
$ docker -H 172.17.4.1 service ps quantum

ID     NAME       IMAGE          NODE           DESIRED... CURRENT... ERROR PORTS
rk...13 quantum.1 spkane/quan... ip-172-17-4-1  Running    Running...
lz...t3 quantum.2 spkane/quan... ip-172-17-4-2  Running    Running...
mh...g8 quantum.3 spkane/quan... ip-172-17-4-3  Running    Running...
cn...xb quantum.4 spkane/quan... ip-172-17-4-1  Running    Running...
```

You'll notice that you have two services running on the same host. Did you expect that? This may not be ideal for host resiliency, but by default Swarm will prioritize ensuring that you have the number of instances that you requested over spreading individual containers across hosts when possible. If you don't have enough nodes, you will get multiple copies on each node. In a real-world scenario, you need to think carefully about placement and scaling. You might not be able to get away with running multiple copies on the same host when you lose a whole node. Would your application still serve users at that reduced scale?

When you need to deploy a new release of your software, you will want to use the `docker service update` command. There are a lot of options for this command, but here's one example:

```
$ docker -H 172.17.4.1 service update --update-delay 10s \
    --update-failure-action rollback --update-monitor 5s \
    --update-order start-first --update-parallelism 1 \
    --detach=false \
    --image spkane/quantum-game:latest-plus quantum

quantum
overall progress: 4 out of 4 tasks
1/4: running   [==================================================>]
2/4: running   [==================================================>]
3/4: running   [==================================================>]
4/4: running   [==================================================>]
verify: Service converged
```

Running this command will cause Swarm to update your service one container at a time, pausing in between each update. Once this is done, you should be able to open up the service's URL in a new private or incognito browsing session (to sidestep the browser's local cache) and see that the game background is now green instead of blue.

Great, you have now successfully applied an update, but what if something were to go wrong? We might need to deploy a previous release to get back to working order. You could now roll back to the previous version, with the correct blue background, by using the `service rollback` command, which we discussed in passing a little bit earlier:

```
$ docker -H 172.17.4.1 service rollback quantum

quantum
rollback: manually requested rollback
overall progress: rolling back update: 4 out of 4 tasks
1/4: running    [>                                                 ]
2/4: running    [>                                                 ]
3/4: running    [>                                                 ]
4/4: running    [>                                                 ]
verify: Service converged
```

That's about as nice a rollback mechanism as you could ask for a stateless service. You don't have to keep track of the previous version; Docker does that for you. All you need to do is tell it to roll back and it pulls the previous metadata out of its internal storage and performs the rollback. Just like during deployment, Docker can health-check your containers to make sure the rollback is working correctly.

 This rollback mechanism will always go back to the last deployed version, so if you run it multiple times in a row, it will just flip between two versions.

Building on `docker service` is a command called `docker stack`, which enables you to deploy a specially designed *docker-compose.yaml* file to a Docker Swarm mode or Kubernetes cluster. If you go back and check out the Git repo that we used in Chapter 8, we can deploy a modified version of that container stack into our current Swarm mode cluster:

```
$ git clone https://github.com/spkane/rocketchat-hubot-demo.git \
    --config core.autocrlf=input
```

Inside that repository is a directory called *stack* that contains a modified version of the *docker-compose.yaml* file that we used earlier:

```
$ cd rocketchat-hubot-demo/stack
```

If you wanted to spin up this setup in the Swarm mode cluster, you could run the following command:

```
$ docker -H 172.17.4.1 stack deploy --compose-file docker-compose-stack.yaml \
    rocketchat

Creating network rocketchat_default
Creating service rocketchat_hubot
Creating service rocketchat_mongo
Creating service rocketchat_rocketchat
Creating service rocketchat_zmachine
```

Now you can list what stacks are in the cluster and see what services were added by the stack:

```
$ docker -H 172.17.4.1 stack ls

NAME          SERVICES   ORCHESTRATOR
rocketchat    4          Swarm

$ docker -H 172.17.4.1 service ls

ID       NAME          ... ... IMAGE                                   PORTS
iu...9f quantum       ... 2/2 spkane/quantum-game:latest            *:80->8080/tcp
nh...jd ..._hubot      ... 1/1 rocketchat/hubot-rocketchat:latest *:3001->8080/tcp
gw...qv ..._mongo      ... 1/1 spkane/mongo:4.4
m3...vd ..._rocketchat ... 1/1 rocketchat/rocket.chat:5.0.4         *:3000->3000/tcp
lb...91 ..._zmachine   ... 1/1 spkane/zmachine-api:latest
```

 This stack is for basic demonstration purposes and has not been well tested for this use case; however, it should give you an idea of how you could assemble something similar.

You may notice that it takes a while for all the containers to come up and that Hubot will continue to restart. This is expected since Rocket.Chat has not been configured yet. The Rocket.Chat setup is covered in Chapter 8.

At this point, you could point your web browser at port 3000 on one of the Swarm nodes (e.g., *http://172.17.4.1:3000/* in these examples), and you should see the initial setup page for Rocket.Chat.

You can see all the containers that are managed by the stack, with docker stack ps:

```
$ docker -H 172.17.4.1 stack ps -f "desired-state=running" rocketchat

ID       NAME            IMAGE                   NODE ... CURRENT STATE            ...
b5...1h ..._hubot.1     rocketchat/hubot-rocket... ...-1 ... Running 14 seconds ago
eq...88 ..._mongo.1     spkane/mongo:4.4           ...-2 ... Running 11 minutes ago
5x...8u ..._rocketchat.1 rocketchat/rocket.chat:... ...-3 ... Running 11 minutes ago
r5...x4 ..._zmachine.1  spkane/zmachine-api:lat... ...-4 ... Running 12 minutes ago
```

When you are done, you can go ahead and tear down the stack like this:

```
$ docker -H 172.17.4.1 stack rm rocketchat

Removing service rocketchat_hubot
Removing service rocketchat_mongo
Removing service rocketchat_rocketchat
Removing service rocketchat_zmachine
Removing network rocketchat_default
```

 If you try to immediately spin everything back up, you might get some unexpected errors. Just waiting a few moments should fix things while the cluster finishes tearing down the old network for the stack, etc.

So, what happens if one of your servers is experiencing an issue and you need to take it offline? In this case, you can easily drain all the services off of a single node by using the --availability option to the docker node update command.

Let's take a look at the nodes that you have in the cluster again:

```
docker -H 172.17.4.1 node ls

ID       HOSTNAME      STATUS AVAILABILITY MANAGER STATUS ENGINE VERSION
l9…82 * ip-172-17-4-1 Ready  Active       Leader         20.10.7
3d…7b   ip-172-17-4-2 Ready  Active                      20.10.7
ip…qe   ip-172-17-4-3 Ready  Active                      20.10.7
```

Let's also check where our containers are currently running:

```
$ docker -H 172.17.4.1 service ps -f "desired-state=running" quantum

ID      NAME       IMAGE       NODE          DESIRED… CURRENT… ERROR  PORTS
sc…1h quantum.1 spkane/qua… ip-172-17-4-1 Running  Running…
ax…om quantum.2 spkane/qua… ip-172-17-4-2 Running  Running…
p4…8h quantum.3 spkane/qua… ip-172-17-4-3 Running  Running…
g8…tw quantum.4 spkane/qua… ip-172-17-4-1 Running  Running…
```

 In the previous command, we used a filter so that the output showed only the currently running processes. By default, Docker will also show you the previous containers that were running in a tree format so that you can see things like updates and rollbacks in the output.

If you have determined that the server at 172.17.4.3 needs downtime, you could drain the tasks of that node and move them to another host by modifying the availability state to drain in Swarm:

```
$ docker -H 172.17.4.1 node update --availability drain ip-172-17-4-3

ip-172-17-4-3
```

If we inspect the node, we can see that the availability is now set to drain:

```
$ docker -H 172.17.4.1 node inspect --pretty ip-172-17-4-3

ID:             ipohyw73hvf70td9licnls9qe
Hostname:                 ip-172-17-4-3
Joined at:                2022-09-04 16:59:52.922451346 +0000 utc
Status:
 State:        Ready
 Availability:             Drain
 Address:      172.17.4.3
Platform:
 Operating System:  linux
 Architecture:      x86_64
Resources:
 CPUs:         2
 Memory:       7.795GiB
Plugins:
 Log:      awslogs, fluentd, gcplogs, gelf, journald, json-file, local,
           logentries, splunk, syslog
 Network:      bridge, host, ipvlan, macvlan, null, overlay
 Volume:       local
Engine Version:    20.10.7
TLS Info:
 TrustRoot:
 …

 Issuer Subject:   …
 Issuer Public Key:   …
```

You might be wondering what effect that has on the service. We told one of the nodes to stop running copies of the service, and they either have to go away or migrate somewhere else. What did it do? We can look at the details of our service again and see that all the running containers on that host have been moved to a different node:

```
$ docker -H 172.17.4.1 service ps -f "desired-state=running" quantum

ID       NAME       IMAGE        NODE           DESIRED… CURRENT… ERROR    PORTS
sc…1h quantum.1  spkane/qua… ip-172-17-4-1 Running   Running…
ax…om quantum.2  spkane/qua… ip-172-17-4-2 Running   Running…
p4…8h quantum.3  spkane/qua… ip-172-17-4-2 Running   Running…
g8…tw quantum.4  spkane/qua… ip-172-17-4-1 Running   Running…
```

At this point, it is safe to bring down the node and do whatever work is required to make it healthy again. When you are ready to add the node back into the Swarm cluster, you can do so by running the following:

```
$ docker -H 172.17.4.1 node update --availability active ip-172-17-4-3

ip-172-17-4-3
```

We'll spare you from reinspecting the node at the moment, but you can always rerun the `node inspect` command if you want to see what this looks like.

 When you add a node back to the cluster, containers will not automatically balance! However, a new deployment or update should result in the containers being evenly spread across the nodes.

Once you are done, you can remove your service and network with the following commands:

```
$ docker -H 172.17.4.1 service rm quantum

quantum

$ docker -H 172.17.4.1 network rm default-net

default-net
```

And then verify that they are both indeed completely gone:

```
$ docker -H 172.17.4.1 service ps quantum

no such service: quantum

$ docker -H 172.17.4.1 network ls

NETWORK ID      NAME              DRIVER    SCOPE
494e1a1bf8f3    bridge            bridge    local
2e7d2d7aaf0f    docker_gwbridge   bridge    local
df0376841891    host              host      local
n8kjd6oa44fr    ingress           overlay   swarm
b4720ea133d6    none              null      local
```

That's all for now! At this point, you can safely tear down all of the servers that were a part of your Swarm cluster if you no longer need them.

That was kind of a whirlwind tour, but it covers the basics of using Swarm mode in Docker Engine and should help get you started building your own Docker clusters wherever you might decide to use them.

Kubernetes

Now let's take some time to look at Kubernetes. Since its release to the public during DockerCon (*https://events.docker.com/events/dockercon*) 2014, Kubernetes has grown rapidly and is now probably the most widely adopted of the container platforms. It is not the oldest or most mature product today—that distinction goes to Mesos, which first launched in 2009 before containers were in widespread use—but Kubernetes was purpose-built for containerized workloads, has a great mix of functionality that is ever evolving, and also enjoys a very strong community that includes many early Docker and Linux container adopters. This mix has helped significantly increase its popularity over the years. At DockerCon EU 2017, Docker, Inc., announced that Kubernetes support will be coming to the Docker Engine tooling itself. Docker Desktop is capable of spinning up a single-node Kubernetes cluster, and the client can deploy container stacks for development purposes. This provides a nice bridge for developers who use Docker locally but deploy to Kubernetes.

Like Linux itself, Kubernetes is available in several distributions, both free and commercial. There is a wide variety of distributions that are available and supported to varying degrees. Kubernetes widespread adoption means that it now has some pretty nice tooling for local development installations.

 The Kubernetes coverage in this book is intended to provide some basic guidance on how you can integrate your Linux container workflow with Kubernetes, but we do not go into a lot of detail about the Kubernetes ecosystem here. We highly recommend reading *Kubernetes: Up & Running*, by Brendan Burns et al. (O'Reilly) (*https://www.oreilly.com/library/view/kubernetes-up-and/9781098110192*), or any of the other great materials out there to familiarize yourself with all the relevant concepts and terminology.

Minikube

Minikube was one of the original tools for managing a local Kubernetes installation and is the first one that we will be focusing on here. Most of the concepts that you'll learn while working with Minikube can be applied to any Kubernetes implementation, including the options that we'll discuss after Minikube, so it's a great place to start.

There are many other options for running a local Kubernetes cluster. We are starting with minikube because the container or VM that it spins up is a pretty standard single-node Kubernetes install. In addition to the tools that we will be discussing in this section, we highly recommend exploring k3s (*https://k3s.io*), k3d (*https://k3d.io*), k0s (*https://k0sproject.io*), and microk8s (*https://microk8s.io*) as well.

What Is Minikube?

Minikube is a whole distribution of Kubernetes for a single instance. It manages a container or VM on your computer that presents a working Kubernetes installation and allows you to use all the same tooling that you would use in a production system. In scope, it's a little bit like Docker Compose: it will let you stand up a whole stack locally. It goes one step further than Compose, though, in that it has all the production APIs. As a result, if you run Kubernetes in production, you can have an environment on your desktop that is reasonably close in function, if not in scale, to what you are running in production.

Minikube is fairly unique in that all of the distribution is controlled from a single binary you download and run locally. It will automatically detect which containerization or VM manager you have locally and will set up and run a container or VM with all of the necessary Kubernetes services in it. That means getting started with it is pretty simple.

So let's install it!

Installing Minikube

Most of the installation is the same across all platforms because once you have the tools installed, they will be your gateway to the VM running your Kubernetes installation. To get started, just skip to the section that applies to your operating system. Once you have the tool up and running, you can follow the shared documentation.

We need two tools to use Minikube effectively: minikube and kubectl. For our simple installation, we're going to leverage the fact that both of these commands are static binaries with no outside dependencies, which makes them easy to install.

There are several other ways to install Minikube. We're going to show you what we think is the simplest path on each platform. If you have strong preferences about how to install these applications, feel free to use your preferred approach. On Windows, for example, you might prefer to use the Chocolatey package manager (*https://chocolatey.org*), or the Snap package system (*https://snapcraft.io*) on Linux.

macOS. Just as in Chapter 3, you will need to have Homebrew installed on your system. If you don't, go back to Chapter 3 and make sure you have it set up. Once you do, it's trivial to install the `minikube` client:

```
$ brew install minikube
```

This will cause Homebrew to download and install Minikube. It will look something like this depending, on your configuration:

```
==> Downloading https://ghcr.io/v2/homebrew/core/kubernetes-cli/…/1.25.0
Already downloaded: …/Homebrew/downloads/…kubernetes-cli…manifest.json
==> Downloading https://ghcr.io/v2/homebrew/core/kubernetes-cli/blobs/sha256…
Already downloaded: …/Homebrew/downloads/…kubernetes-cli--1.25…bottle.tar.gz
==> Downloading https://ghcr.io/v2/homebrew/core/minikube/manifests/1.26.1
Already downloaded: …/Homebrew/downloads/…minikube-1.26.1.…_manifest.json
==> Downloading https://ghcr.io/v2/homebrew/core/minikube/blobs/sha256:…
Already downloaded: …/Homebrew/downloads/…minikube--1.26.1…bottle.tar.gz
==> Installing dependencies for minikube: kubernetes-cli
==> Installing minikube dependency: kubernetes-cli
==> Pouring kubernetes-cli--1.25.0.arm64_monterey.bottle.tar.gz
🍺  /opt/homebrew/Cellar/kubernetes-cli/1.25.0: 228 files, 52.8MB
==> Installing minikube
==> Pouring minikube--1.26.1.arm64_monterey.bottle.tar.gz
==> Caveats
Bash completion has been installed to:
  /opt/homebrew/etc/bash_completion.d
==> Summary
🍺  /opt/homebrew/Cellar/minikube/1.26.1: 9 files, 70.6MB
==> Running `brew cleanup minikube`…
Disable this behavior by setting HOMEBREW_NO_INSTALL_CLEANUP.
Hide these hints with HOMEBREW_NO_ENV_HINTS (see `man brew`).
==> Caveats
==> minikube
Bash completion has been installed to:
  /opt/homebrew/etc/bash_completion.d
```

That's it! Let's test to make sure it's in your path:

```
$ which minikube
/opt/homebrew/bin/minikube
```

Homebrew on *arm64* systems install into */opt/homebrew/bin* instead of */usr/local/bin*.

If you don't get a response, you will need to make sure you have */usr/local/bin* and */opt/homebrew/bin* in your PATH environment variable. Assuming that passes, you now have the `minikube` tool installed.

kubectl should have been automatically installed since it is a dependency of mini kube, but you can also do it explicitly with brew as well. Generally, the version of kubectl in Homebrew will match the current release of minikube, so using brew install should help prevent mismatches:

```
$ brew install kubernetes-cli
```

We'll test that the same way we tested minikube:

```
$ which kubectl
/opt/homebrew/bin/kubectl
```

We're good to go!

Windows.   As with installing Docker Desktop on Windows, you may want to install Hyper-V or another supported virtualization platform to run a Kubernetes VM. To install minikube, you simply download the binary and put it in a place you have in your PATH so that you can execute it on the command line. You can download the most recent release of minikube from GitHub (*https://github.com/kubernetes/min ikube/releases/latest*). You'll want to rename the Windows executable that you download to *minikube.exe*; otherwise, you'll be doing a lot more typing than you probably want!

 You can find more details about the Windows install process and that binary executable from the Minikube install documentaton (*https://minikube.sigs.k8s.io/docs/start*).

You then need to get the latest Kubernetes CLI tool, kubectl, to interact with your distribution. Unfortunately, there is not a */latest* path for downloading that. So, to make sure you have the latest version, you need to get the latest version (*https:// storage.googleapis.com/kubernetes-release/release/stable.txt*) from the website and then plug it into a URL, like this:

https://storage.googleapis.com/kubernetes-release/release/<VERSION>/bin/windows/ amd64/kubectl.exe.

Once you've downloaded that, you again need to make sure it's accessible from your PATH to make the rest of our exploration easier.

Linux.   On Linux, you will want to have Docker installed and should consider installing either KVM (Linux's Kernel-based Virtual Machine) or VirtualBox so that minikube can create and manage a Kubernetes VM for you. Because minikube is just a single binary, once you have it installed, there is no need to install any additional packages. And, because minikube is a statically linked binary, it should pretty much work on any distribution you want to run it on. Although we could do all the installation in a one-liner, we are going to break it up into a few steps to make it easier to understand and troubleshoot. Note that at the time of this writing, the binary is hosted on *googleapis*, which usually maintains very stable URLs. So, here we go:

```
# Download the file, save as 'minikube'
$ curl -Lo minikube \
    https://storage.googleapis.com/minikube/releases/latest/minikube-linux-amd64

# Make it executable
$ chmod +x minikube

# Move it to /usr/local/bin
$ sudo mv minikube /usr/local/bin/
```

You'll need to make sure that */usr/local/bin* is in your path. Now that we have minikube, we also need to fetch kubectl, which we can do like this:

```
# Get the latest version number
$ KUBE_VERSION=$(curl -s \
    https://storage.googleapis.com/kubernetes-release/release/stable.txt)

# Fetch the executable
$ curl -LO \
    https://storage.googleapis.com/kubernetes-release/\
release/$(KUBE_VERSION)/bin/linux/amd64/kubectl

# Make it executable
$ chmod +x kubectl

# Move it to /usr/local/bin
$ sudo mv kubectl /usr/local/bin/
```

 One of the URLs in the example has been continued on the following line so that it fits in the margins. You may find that you need to reassemble the URL and remove the backslashes for the command to work properly in your environment.

That's it for installation—we're ready to go.

Running Kubernetes

Now that we have the minikube tool, we can use it to bootstrap our Kubernetes cluster. This is normally pretty straightforward. You usually don't need to do any configuration beforehand. In this example, you will see that minikube decided to use the *docker driver*, although there are others that could be selected.

To start minikube, go ahead and run the following:

```
$ minikube start

🙂 minikube v1.26.1 on Darwin 12.5.1 (arm64)
   Automatically selected the docker driver. Other choices: parallels, ssh, …
🏃 Using Docker Desktop driver with root privileges
   Starting control plane node minikube in cluster minikube
🚜 Pulling base image …
💾 Downloading Kubernetes v1.24.3 preload …
   > preloaded-images-k8s-v18-v1…: 342.82 MiB / 342.82 MiB  100.00% 28.22 M
   > gcr.io/k8s-minikube/kicbase: 348.00 MiB / 348.00 MiB  100.00% 18.13 MiB
   > gcr.io/k8s-minikube/kicbase: 0 B [_____] ?% ? p/s 16s
🔥 Creating docker container (CPUs=2, Memory=4000MB) …
🐳 Preparing Kubernetes v1.24.3 on Docker 20.10.17 …
   • Generating certificates and keys …
   • Booting up control plane …
   • Configuring RBAC rules …
🔎 Verifying Kubernetes components…
   • Using image gcr.io/k8s-minikube/storage-provisioner:v5
   Enabled addons: storage-provisioner, default-storageclass
🏄 Done! kubectl is now configured to use "minikube" cluster and
   "default" namespace by default
```

So what did we just do? Minikube packs a lot into that one command. In this case, we launched a single Linux container that is providing us a functioning Kubernetes installation on our local system. If we had used one of the virtualization drivers with minikube, then we would have created a complete VM running Kubernetes instead on a single container.

It then runs all of the necessary components of Kubernetes inside Linux containers on the host. You can easily explore the minikube container or VM to see what you got:

```
$ minikube ssh

docker@minikube:~$
```

On your Kubernetes cluster, you probably won't be using SSH to get into the command line that often. But we want to see what's installed and get a handle on the fact that when we run minikube, we're controlling an environment that is running many processes. Let's take a look at what is running on the Docker instance on our Kubernetes cluster:

```
docker@minikube:~$ docker container ls

…ID   IMAGE       COMMAND                    …  NAMES
48…cf ba…57       "/storage-provisioner" …  k8s_storage-provisioner_storage-…
4e…8d ed…e8       "/coredns -conf /etc…" …  k8s_coredns_coredns-6d4b75cb6d-…
1d…3d …pause:3.6 "/pause"                   … k8s_POD_coredns-6d4b75cb6d-…
82…d3 7a…dc       "/usr/local/bin/kube…" …  k8s_kube-proxy_kube-proxy-…
```

```
27…10 …pause:3.6 "/pause"              … k8s_POD_kube-proxy-zb6w2_kube-…
15…ce …pause:3.6 "/pause"              … k8s_POD_storage-provisioner_kube-…
ff…3d f9…55      "kube-controller-man…" … k8s_kube-controller-manager_kube-…
33…c5 …pause:3.6 "/pause"              … k8s_POD_kube-controller-manager-…
30…97 a9…df      "etcd --advertise-cl…" … k8s_etcd_etcd-minikube_kube-…
f5…41 53…a6      "kube-apiserver --ad…" … k8s_kube-apiserver_kube-apiserver-…
5b…08 8f…73      "kube-scheduler --au…" … k8s_kube-scheduler_kube-scheduler-…
87…cc …pause:3.6 "/pause"              … k8s_POD_kube-apiserver-…
5a…14 …pause:3.6 "/pause"              … k8s_POD_etcd-minikube_kube-…
6f…0c …pause:3.6 "/pause"              … k8s_POD_kube-scheduler-…
```

We won't dive too much into what each component is, but by now you should hopefully see how the mechanism works. Also, it's pretty easy to upgrade the components since they are just containers, are versioned, and can be pulled from an upstream container repository.

Go ahead and exit the shell that you have on the Minikube system:

```
docker@minikube:~$ exit
```

minikube commands. In the interest of space and time, we won't go through all of the commands for minikube. We encourage you to run it without any options, take a look at the output, and play around with what's available. That being said, let's take a quick look at some of the most interesting commands. We'll cover a few more later in the course of installing an application stack, but here's a quick survey.

To see what was going on inside the system, earlier we used minikube ssh, which is great for debugging or inspecting the system directly. Without directly accessing the Minikube system, we can always check on the cluster status using another minikube command:

```
$ minikube status

minikube
type: Control Plane
host: Running
kubelet: Running
apiserver: Running
kubeconfig: Configured
```

This shows us that everything is looking good. Two other useful commands include:

Command	Action
minikube ip	Retrieve the IP address of the Minikube VM.
minikube update-check	Check your version of Minikube against the most recent release.

To apply an upgrade, you can simply use the same mechanism you used to install it originally.

Critically, the `minikube status` command also shows us that the `kubeconfig` is properly configured. We will need this so that `kubectl` knows how to connect to our cluster.

We started the Kubernetes cluster with `minikube start`. As you might expect, following the style of Docker CLI arguments, `minikube stop` will stop all the Kubernetes components and the Linux container or VM. To completely clean up your environment, you can also delete the cluster by running `minikube delete`.

Kubernetes Dashboard

Now that we have Minikube up and running, we don't just have the command-line tools to interact with; we have a whole Kubernetes Dashboard installed that we can explore. We can reach it via the `minikube dashboard` command. Go ahead and run that—it should launch your web browser pointed to the correct IP address and port of the Kubernetes Dashboard! There is a lot of stuff on the dashboard, and we're not able to cover it all, but feel free to click around and explore. Depending on your previous exposure to Kubernetes, some of the terms in the dashboard's sidebar will be familiar to you, but many of them may be completely foreign. If you don't have a computer in front of you, Figure 10-2 shows a screenshot of what an empty Minikube installation looks like from the Service link in the dashboard sideboard.

Figure 10-2. Kubernetes Dashboard (example)

If you explore the Nodes link under Cluster in the left sidebar, you should see a single node in the cluster, named `minikube`. This is the container or VM that we started, and the dashboard, like the other components, is hosted in one of the containers we saw when we connected to the Minikube system earlier. We'll take another look at the dashboard when we've deployed something into our cluster.

Kubernetes exposes almost everything that you see on the dashboard with the `kubectl` command as well, which makes it very scriptable with shell scripts.

For example, running `kubectl get services` or `kubectl get nodes` should show you the same information that you can see on the dashboard.

While clicking around, you may notice that Kubernetes itself shows up as a component inside the system, just like your applications will.

You will need to type Ctrl-C to exit the `minikube dashboard` process and return to your terminal prompt.

Kubernetes containers and pods

Now that we have a Kubernetes cluster up and running, and you've seen how easy that is to do locally, we need to pause to talk about a concept that Kubernetes adds on top of the container abstraction. Kubernetes came out of the experiences that Google had running its massive platform. Google encountered most of the situations you might see in a production platform and had to work out concepts to make it easier to understand and solve the kinds of problems you run into when managing a large installation. In doing so, Google created a complex set of new abstractions. Kubernetes embraces many of these and thus has a whole vocabulary unto itself. We won't try to get into all of these, but it's important to understand the most central of these new abstractions—a concept that sits a layer above the container and is known as a *pod*.

The term *pod* came about because the Docker mascot is Moby, the whale, and a group of whales is called a *pod*.

In Kubernetes parlance, a pod is one or more containers sharing the same cgroups and namespaces. You can also isolate the containers themselves from one another inside the same pod using cgroups and namespaces. A pod is intended to encapsulate all of the processes or applications that need to be deployed together to create a functioning unit, which the scheduler can then manage. All of the containers in the pod can talk to one another on `localhost`, which eliminates any need to discover one another. So why not just deploy a big container with all the applications inside it? The advantage of a pod over a massive container is that you can still resource-limit the individual application separately and leverage the large library of public Linux containers to construct your application.

Additionally, Kubernetes administrators often leverage the pod abstraction to have a container run on pod startup to make sure things are configured properly for the others, to maintain a shared resource, or to announce the application to others, for example. This allows you to make finer-grained containers than you might if you have to group things into the same container. Another nice part of the pod abstraction is the ability to share mounted volumes.

Pods have a life span much like a Linux container. They are essentially ephemeral and can be redeployed to new hosts according to the lifecycle of the application or the host it runs on. Containers in a pod even share the same IP address when facing the outside world, which means they look like a single entity from the network level. Just as you would run only one instance of an application per container, you generally run one instance of a given container inside a pod. The easiest way to think about pods is that they are a group of Linux containers that work together as if they were one container, for most purposes. If you need only one container, then you still get a pod deployed by Kubernetes, but that pod contains only one container. The nice thing about this is that there is only one abstraction as far as the Kubernetes scheduler is concerned: the pod. Containers are managed by some of the runtime pieces that construct the pod and also by the configuration that you use to define them.

One critical difference between a pod and a container is that you don't construct pods in a build step. They are a runtime abstraction that is defined in a JSON or YAML manifest and lives only inside Kubernetes. So you build your Linux containers and send them to a registry, then define and deploy your pods using Kubernetes. In reality, you don't usually directly describe a pod either; the tools generate it for you through the concept of a deployment. But the pod is the unit of execution and scheduling in a Kubernetes cluster. There is a lot more to it, but that's the basic concept, and it's probably easiest to understand with a simple example. The pod abstraction is more complicated than thinking of your system in terms of individual containers, but it can be pretty powerful.

Let's deploy something

When working with pods in Kubernetes, we usually manage them through the abstraction of a *deployment*. A deployment is just a pod definition with some additional information, including health monitoring and replication configuration. It contains the definition of the pod and a little metadata about it. So let's look at a basic deployment and get it running.

The simplest thing we can deploy on Kubernetes is a pod that contains just one container. We are going to use the `httpbin` (*https://httpbin.org*) application to explore the basics of deployment on Kubernetes, and we'll call our deployment `hello-minikube`.

We've used the `minikube` command, but to get things done on Kubernetes itself, we now need to leverage the `kubectl` command we installed earlier:

```
$ kubectl create deployment hello-minikube \
    --image=kennethreitz/httpbin:latest --port=80

deployment.apps/hello-minikube created
```

To see what that did for us, we can use the `kubectl get all` command to list the most important objects that are now in our cluster:

```
$ kubectl get all

NAME                                READY   STATUS    RESTARTS   AGE
pod/hello-minikube-ff49df9b8-svl68  1/1     Running   0          2m39s

NAME                 TYPE        CLUSTER-IP   EXTERNAL-IP   PORT(S)   AGE
service/kubernetes   ClusterIP   10.96.0.1    <none>        443/TCP   98m

NAME                             READY   UP-TO-DATE   AVAILABLE   AGE
deployment.apps/hello-minikube   1/1     1            1           2m39s

NAME                                        DESIRED   CURRENT   READY   AGE
replicaset.apps/hello-minikube-ff49df9b8    1         1         1       2m39s
```

With that one command, Kubernetes created a deployment, a ReplicaSet to manage scaling, and a pod. We want to ensure that our pod shows a STATUS of Running. If yours isn't, just wait and run the command a couple more times until you see the status change. The `service/kubernetes` entry is a running service that represents Kubernetes itself. But where is our service? We can't get to it yet. It's essentially in the same state a Linux container would be if you didn't tell it to expose any ports. So we need to tell Kubernetes to do that for us:

```
$ kubectl expose deployment hello-minikube --type=NodePort
service/hello-minikube exposed
```

This has now created a service we can reach and interact with. A *service* is a wrapper for one or more deployments of an application and can tell us how to contact the application. In this case, we get a `NodePort`, which exposes a port on every node in the cluster that will be routed to the underlying pods. Let's get Kubernetes to tell us how to get to it:

```
$ kubectl get services

NAME            TYPE        CLUSTER-IP       EXTERNAL-IP   PORT(S)         AGE
hello-minikube  NodePort    10.105.184.177   <none>        80:32557/TCP    8s
kubernetes      ClusterIP   10.96.0.1        <none>        443/TCP         107m
```

You might think you could now connect to *http://10.105.184.177:8080* to get to our service. But those addresses are not reachable from your host system because of the container or VM in which Minikube is running. So we need to get minikube to tell us where to find the service:

```
$ minikube service hello-minikube --url
http://192.168.99.100:30616
```

In some configurations, you may see a message like this:

```
! Because you are using a Docker driver on darwin,
    the terminal needs to be open to run it.
```

This indicates that transparently wiring the networking from your host to the Kubernetes services is not possible at the moment, and you will need to leave the command running while you explore your application. You can use a local web browser or open up another terminal to run commands like curl.

When you are done, you can type Ctrl-C in the original terminal session to kill the minikube service command.

The nice thing about this command, like many of the other Kubernetes commands, is that it is scriptable and command-line friendly under normal circumstances. If we want to open it with curl on the command line, we can often just include the minikube command call in our request:

```
$ curl -H foo:bar $(minikube service hello-minikube --url)/get

{
  "args": {},
  "headers": {
    "Accept": "*/*",
    "Foo": "bar",
    "Host": "127.0.0.1:56695",
    "User-Agent": "curl/7.85.0"
  },
  "origin": "172.17.0.1",
  "url": "http://127.0.0.1:56695/get"
}
```

httpbin is a simple HTTP request and response API that can be used to test and confirm HTTP services. Not the world's most exciting application, but you can see that we are able to contact our service and get a response back from it via curl.

This is the simplest use case. We didn't configure much and relied on Kubernetes to do the right thing using its defaults. In the next step, we'll take a look at something more complicated. But first, let's shut down our new service and deployment. It takes two commands to do that: one to remove the service and the other to delete it:

```
$ kubectl delete service hello-minikube
service "hello-minikube" deleted
```

```
$ kubectl delete deployment hello-minikube
deployment.apps "hello-minikube" deleted

$ kubectl get all

NAME                 TYPE        CLUSTER-IP   EXTERNAL-IP   PORT(S)    AGE
service/kubernetes   ClusterIP   10.96.0.1    <none>        443/TCP    138m
```

Deploying a realistic stack

Let's now deploy something that looks more like a production stack. We'll deploy an application that can fetch PDF documents from an S3 bucket, cache them on disk locally, and rasterize individual pages to PNG images on request, using the cached document. To run this application, we'll want to write our cache files somewhere other than inside the container. We want to have them go somewhere a little more permanent and stable. And this time we want to make things repeatable so that we're not deploying our application through a series of CLI commands that we need to remember and hopefully get right each time. Kubernetes, much like Docker Compose, lets us define our stack in one or more YAML files that contain all of the definitions we care about in one place. This is what you want in a production environment and is similar to what you've seen for the other production tools.

The service we'll now create will be called lazyraster (as in "rasterize on demand"), and each time you see that in the YAML definition, you'll know we're referring to our application. Our persistent volume will be called cache-data. Again, Kubernetes has a huge vocabulary that we can't entirely address here, but to make it clear what we're looking at, we need to introduce two more concepts: PersistentVolume and PersistentVolumeClaim. A PersistentVolume is a physical resource that we provision inside the cluster. Kubernetes has support for many kinds of volumes, from local storage on a node to Amazon Elastic Block Store (Amazon EBS) volumes (*https://docs.aws.amazon.com/AWSEC2/latest/UserGuide/AmazonEBS.html*) on AWS and similar on other cloud providers. It also supports Network File System (NFS) (*https://en.wikipedia.org/wiki/Network_File_System*) and other more modern network filesystems. A PersistentVolume stores data with a lifecycle that is independent of our application or deployments. This lets us store data that persists between application deployments. For our cache, that's what we'll use. A PersistentVolumeClaim is a link between the physical resource of the PersistentVolume and the application that needs to consume it. We can set a policy on the claim that allows either a single read/write claim or many read claims. For our application we just want a single read/write claim to our cache-data PersistentVolume.

If you want more detail about some of the concepts we've talked about here, the Kubernetes project maintains a glossary (*https:// kubernetes.io/docs/reference/glossary/?fundamental=true*) of all the terms involved in operating Kubernetes. This can be very helpful. Each entry in the glossary is also linked to much more in-depth detail on other pages.

You can check out the file we will be using in this section by running the following:

```
$ git clone \
    https://github.com/bluewhalebook/\
docker-up-and-running-3rd-edition.git --config core.autocrlf=input

Cloning into 'docker-up-and-running-3rd-edition'…
…

$ cd docker-up-and-running-3rd-edition/chapter_10/kubernetes
```

The URL in the example has been continued on the following line so that it fits in the margins. You may find that you need to reassemble the URL and remove the backslashes for the command to work properly.

We will start by looking at the manifest YAML file, called *lazyraster-service.yaml*. The full manifest contains multiple YAML documents separated by `---`. We will discuss each section individually here.

Service definition

```
apiVersion: v1
kind: Service
metadata:
  name: lazyraster
  labels:
    app: lazyraster
spec:
  type: NodePort
  ports:
    - port: 8000
      targetPort: 8000
      protocol: TCP
  selector:
    app: lazyraster
```

The first section defines our `Service`. The second and third sections, which we'll see in a moment, respectively define our `PersistentVolumeClaim` and then our actual `Deployment`. We've told Kubernetes that our service will be called `lazyraster` and that it will be exposed on port 8000, which maps to the actual 8000 in our container.

We've exposed that with the NodePort mechanism, which simply makes sure that our application is exposed on the same port on each host, much like the --publish flag to docker container run. This is helpful with minikube since we'll run only one instance, and the NodePort type makes it easy for us to access it from our computer just like we did earlier. As with many parts of Kubernetes, there are several options other than NodePort, and you can probably find a mechanism that's ideal for your production environment. NodePort is good for minikube, but it might work well for more statically configured load balancers as well.

So, back to our Service definition. The Service is going to be connected to the Deployment via the selector, which we apply in the spec section. Kubernetes widely uses labels as a way to reason about similar components and to help tie them all together. Labels are key/value pairs that are arbitrarily defined and that can then be queried to identify pieces of your system. Here the selector tells Kubernetes to look for Deployments with the label app: lazyraster. Notice that we also apply the same label to the Service itself. That's helpful if we want to identify all the components together later, but it's the selector section that ties the Deployment to our Service. So we now have a Service, but it doesn't do anything yet. We need more definitions to make Kubernetes do what we want.

PersistentVolumeClaim definition

```
apiVersion: v1
kind: PersistentVolumeClaim
metadata:
  name: cache-data-claim
  labels:
    app: lazyraster
spec:
  accessModes:
    - ReadWriteOnce
  resources:
    requests:
      storage: 100Mi
```

The next section defines our PersistentVolumeClaim and likewise the Persistent Volume that backs it. A PersistentVolumeClaim is a way to name a volume and claim that you have a token to access that particular volume in a particular way. Notice, though, that we didn't define the PersistentVolume here. That's because Kubernetes is doing that work for us using what it calls *Dynamic Volume Provisioning*. In our case, the use is pretty simple: we want a read/write claim to a volume, and we'll let Kubernetes put that in a volume container for us. But you can imagine a scenario where an application is going to be deployed into a cloud provider and where dynamic provisioning would truly come into its own. In that scenario, we don't want to have to make separate calls to have our volume created in the cloud for us. We want Kubernetes to handle that. That's what Dynamic Volume Provisioning is all about. Here, it will just create a container for us to hold our persistent data, and mount it into our pod when we stake our claim. We don't do a lot in this section except name it, ask for 100 MB of data, and tell Kubernetes it's a read/write mount-once-only volume.

 There's a large number of possible volume providers in Kubernetes. Which ones are available to you is in part determined by which provider or cloud service you are running on. You should take a look and see which ones make the most sense for you when you are preparing to head into production.

Deployment definition

```yaml
apiVersion: apps/v1
kind: Deployment
metadata:
  name: lazyraster
  labels:
    app: lazyraster
spec:
  selector:
    matchLabels:
      app: lazyraster
  strategy:
    type: RollingUpdate
  template:
    metadata:
      labels:
        app: lazyraster
    spec:
      containers:
      - image: relistan/lazyraster:demo
        name: lazyraster
        env:
        - name: RASTER_RING_TYPE
          value: memberlist
        - name: RASTER_BASE_DIR
          value: /data
        ports:
        - containerPort: 8000
          name: lazyraster
        volumeMounts:
        - name: cache-data
          mountPath: /data
      volumes:
      - name: cache-data
        persistentVolumeClaim:
          claimName: cache-data-claim
```

The Deployment creates the pods for us and uses the Linux container for our application. We define some metadata about the application, including its name and one label, just like we did for the other definitions. We also apply another selector here to find the other resources we're tied to. In the strategy section, we say we want to have a RollingUpdate, which is a strategy that causes our pods to be cycled through one by one during deployment. We could also pick Recreate, which would simply destroy all existing pods and then create new ones afterward.

In the template section, we define how to stamp out copies of this deployment. The container definition includes the Docker image name, the ports to map, volumes to mount, and some environment variables that the lazyraster application needs. The very last part of the spec asks to have our PersistentVolumeClaim named cache-data-claim.

And that's it for the application definition. Now let's stand it up!

 There are many more options and a rich set of directives you can specify here to tell Kubernetes how to handle your application. We've walked through a couple of simple options, but we encourage you to explore the Kubernetes documentation to learn more.

Deploying the application

Before we continue, let's see what's in our Kubernetes cluster by using the kubectl command:

```
$ kubectl get all

NAME                 TYPE        CLUSTER-IP   EXTERNAL-IP   PORT(S)   AGE
service/kubernetes   ClusterIP   10.96.0.1    <none>        443/TCP   160m
```

We have only one thing defined at the moment, a service called service/kubernetes. A naming convention used widely in Kubernetes is to preface the type of object with the object Kind, which is sometimes shortened to a two- or three-letter abbreviation. Sometimes you will see service represented as svc. If you are curious, you can see all of the resources and their short names by running the command kubectl api-resources. So let's go ahead and get our service, deployment, and volume into the cluster!

```
$ kubectl apply -f ./lazyraster-service.yaml

service/lazyraster created
persistentvolumeclaim/cache-data-claim created
deployment.apps/lazyraster created
```

That output looks like what we expected: we have a service, a persistent volume claim, and a deployment. So let's see what's in the cluster now:

```
$ kubectl get all

NAME                               READY   STATUS    RESTARTS   AGE
pod/lazyraster-644cb5c66c-zsjxd    1/1     Running   0          17s


NAME                 TYPE        CLUSTER-IP      EXTERNAL-IP  PORT(S)          AGE
service/kubernetes   ClusterIP   10.96.0.1       <none>       443/TCP          161m
service/lazyraster   NodePort    10.109.116.225  <none>       8000:32544/TCP   17s


NAME                           READY   UP-TO-DATE   AVAILABLE   AGE
deployment.apps/lazyraster     1/1     1            1           17s


NAME                                       DESIRED   CURRENT   READY   AGE
replicaset.apps/lazyraster-644cb5c66c      1         1         1       17s
```

You can see that a bunch more happened behind the scenes. And also, where is our volume or persistent volume claim? We have to ask for that separately:

```
$ kubectl get pvc

NAME              STATUS  VOLUME     CAPACITY  ACCESS MODES  STORAGECLASS  AGE
cache-data-claim  Bound   pvc-1a…41  100Mi     RWO           standard      65s
```

 `kubectl get all` does nothing of the sort. It would be more aptly named `get all-of-the-most-common-resources`, but there are several other resources you can fetch. The Kubernetes project hosts a handy cheat sheet (*https://kubernetes.io/docs/reference/kubectl/ cheatsheet*) to make this more discoverable.

So what about that `replicaset.apps` that appeared in the `get all` output? That is a ReplicaSet. A ReplicaSet is a piece of Kubernetes that is responsible for making sure that our application is running the right number of instances all the time and that they are healthy. We don't normally have to worry about what happens inside the ReplicaSet because the deployment we created manages it for us. You can manage the ReplicaSet yourself if need be, but most of the time you won't need to or want to.

We didn't tell `kubectl` any specific number of instances, so we got one. And we can see that both the desired and current states match. We'll take a look at that in a moment. But first, let's connect to our application and see what we've got:

```
$ minikube service --url lazyraster
http://192.168.99.100:32185
```

You will probably get a different IP address and port back. That's fine! This is very dynamic stuff. And that's why we use the `minikube` command to manage it for us.

Also, remember that `minikube` will warn you if you need to keep the `service` command running while you explore the `lazyraster` service. So grab the address that came back, open your web browser, and paste it into the

---

URL bar like this: *http://<192.168.99.100:32185>/documents/docker-up-and-running-public/sample.pdf?page=1*. You'll need to substitute the IP and port into the URL to make it work for you.

You'll need to be connected to the internet because the `lazyraster` application is going to go out to the internet, fetch a PDF from a public S3 bucket, and then render the first page from the document as a PNG in a process called *rasterization*. If everything worked, you should see a copy of the front cover of an earlier edition of this book! This particular PDF has two pages, so feel free to try changing the argument to `?page=2`. If you do that, you may notice it renders *much* faster than the first page. That's because the application is using our persistent volume to cache the data. You can also specify `width=2048` or ask for a JPEG instead of a PNG with `imageType=image/jpeg`. You could rasterize the front page as a very large JPEG, like this:

http://<192.168.99.100:32185>/documents/docker-up-and-running-public/sample.pdf?page=1&imageType=image/jpeg&width=2048

If you have a public S3 bucket with other PDFs in it, you can simply substitute the bucket name for `docker-up-and-running-public` in the URL to hit your bucket instead. If you want to play with the application some more, check out the *Nitro/lazyraster* repo on GitHub (*https://github.com/Nitro/lazyraster*).

Scaling up

In real life you don't just deploy applications; you operate them as well. One of the huge advantages of scheduled workloads is the ability to scale them up and down at will, within the resource constraints available to the system. In our case, we only have one Minikube node, but we can still scale up our service to better handle load and provide more reliability during deployments. Kubernetes, as you might imagine, allows scaling up and down quite easily. For our service, we will need only one command to do it. Then we'll take another look at the `kubectl` output and also at the Kubernetes Dashboard we introduced earlier so we can prove that the service scaled.

In Kubernetes, the thing we will scale is not the service; it's the deployment. Here's what that looks like:

```
$ kubectl scale --replicas=2 deploy/lazyraster
deployment.apps/lazyraster scaled
```

Great, that did something! But what did we get?

```
$ kubectl get deployment/lazyraster

NAME         READY   UP-TO-DATE   AVAILABLE   AGE
lazyraster   2/2     2            2           16m
```

We now have two instances of our application running. Let's see what we got in the logs:

```
$ kubectl logs deployment/lazyraster

Found 2 pods, using pod/lazyraster-644cb5c66c-zsjxd
Trying to clear existing Lazyraster cached files (if any) in the background…
Launching Lazyraster service…
time="2022-09-10T21:14:16Z" level=info msg="Settings ----------------…
time="2022-09-10T21:14:16Z" level=info msg="  * BaseDir: /data"
time="2022-09-10T21:14:16Z" level=info msg="  * HttpPort: 8000"
…
time="2022-09-10T21:14:16Z" level=info msg="  * LoggingLevel: info"
time="2022-09-10T21:14:16Z" level=info msg="-------------------------…
…
time="2022-09-10T21:14:16Z" level=info msg="Listening on tcp://:6379"
…
```

We asked for logs for the deployment, but Kubernetes tells us two pods are running, so it simply picked one of them to show us the logs from. We can see the replica starting up. If we want to specify a particular instance to look at, we can ask for the logs for that pod with something like `kubectl logs pod/lazyraster-644cb5c66c-zsjxd`, using the output from `kubectl get pods` to find the pod in question.

We now have a couple of copies of our application running. What does that look like on the Kubernetes Dashboard? Let's navigate there with `minikube dashboard`. Once we're there, we'll select "Workloads - Deployments" from the left sidebar and then click on the `lazyraster` deployment, which should display a screen that looks like Figure 10-3.

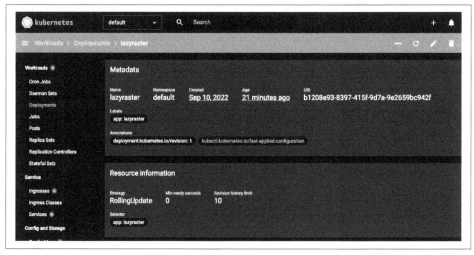

Figure 10-3. `lazyraster` service dashboard (example)

We encourage you to click around some more in the Kubernetes Dashboard to see what else is presented. With the concepts you've picked up here, a lot should be clearer now, and you can probably figure out some more on your own. Likewise, kubectl has a lot of other options available as well, many of which you'll need in a real production system. The cheat sheet we discussed earlier (*https://kuber netes.io/docs/reference/kubectl/cheatsheet*) is a real lifesaver here!

As always, you can type Ctrl-C at any time to exit the running minikube dashboard command.

kubectl API

We haven't shown you an API yet, and, as we've discussed with Docker, it can be really useful to have a simple API to interact with for scripting, programming, and other general operational needs. You can write programs to talk directly to the Kubernetes API, but for local development and other simple use cases, you can use kubectl as a nice proxy to Kubernetes, and it presents a clean API that is accessible with curl and JSON command-line tools. Here's an example of what you can do:

```
$ kubectl proxy
Starting to serve on 127.0.0.1:8001
```

We've now got kubectl itself serving up a web API on the local system! You'll need to read more about what's possible, but let's get it to show us the individual instances of the lazyraster application. We can do that by opening the following URL in a browser or by using curl in another terminal window: *http://localhost:8001/api/v1/ namespaces/default/endpoints/lazyraster*.

There is a lot of output here, but the part we care about is the subsets section:

```
{
...
  "subsets": [
    {
      "addresses": [
        {
          "ip": "172.17.0.5",
          "nodeName": "minikube",
          "targetRef": {
            "kind": "Pod",
            "namespace": "default",
            "name": "lazyraster-644cb5c66c-zsjxd",
            "uid": "9631395d-7e68-47fa-bb9f-9641d724d8f7"
          }
        },
        {
          "ip": "172.17.0.6",
          "nodeName": "minikube",
          "targetRef": {
```

```
            "kind": "Pod",
            "namespace": "default",
            "name": "lazyraster-644cb5c66c-pvcmj",
            "uid": "e909d424-7a91-4a74-aed3-69562b74b422"
          }
        }
      ],
      "ports": [
        {
          "port": 8000,
          "protocol": "TCP"
        }
      ]
    }
  ]
}
```

What's interesting here is that we can see that both instances are running on the Minikube host and that they have different IP addresses. If we were building a cloud-native application that needed to know where the other instances of the application were running, this would be a good way to do that.

You can type Ctrl-C at any time to exit the running `kubectl proxy` processes, and then you can remove the deployment and all of its components by running the following command. It may take Kubernetes a minute or so to delete everything and return you to the terminal prompt:

```
$ kubectl delete -f ./lazyraster-service.yaml

service "lazyraster" deleted
persistentvolumeclaim "cache-data-claim" deleted
deployment.apps "lazyraster" deleted
```

And then finally, you can go ahead and remove your Minikube cluster if you are done with everything in it for now:

```
$ minikube delete

🔥  Deleting "minikube" in docker …
🔥  Deleting container "minikube" …
🔥  Removing /Users/spkane/.minikube/machines/minikube …
💀  Removed all traces of the "minikube" cluster.
```

 Kubernetes is a really big system, with great community involvement. We've just shown you the tip of the iceberg with Minikube, but if you are interested, there are many other Kubernetes distributions and tools to explore.

Docker Desktop-Integrated Kubernetes

Docker Desktop comes with support for an integrated single-node Kubernetes cluster that can be run by simply enabling an option in the application preferences.

The integrated Kubernetes cluster is not easily configurable, but it does provide a very accessible option for those who simply need to verify some basic functionality against a current Kubernetes installation.

To enable Docker Desktop's built-in Kubernetes functionality, launch Docker Desktop and then open up Preferences from the Docker whale icon in your task/menu bar. Then select the Kubernetes tab, click Enable Kubernetes, and finally click the "Apply & Restart" button to make the required changes to the VM. The first time you do this, Docker will utilize the kubeadm (*https://kubernetes.io/docs/reference/setup-tools/kubeadm*) command to set up the Kubernetes cluster.

 If you are interested in a bit more information about how the Docker Desktop-integrated Kubernetes is set up, Docker has a good blog post (*https://www.docker.com/blog/how-kubernetes-works-under-the-hood-with-docker-desktop*) that covers some of these details.

This will create a new kubectl context called docker-desktop and should automatically switch you to this context.

You can confirm which context you are currently set to by running the following:

```
$ kubectl config current-context

docker-desktop
```

If you need to change the current context, you can do so like this:

```
$ kubectl config use-context docker-desktop --namespace=default

Switched to context "docker-desktop".
```

And finally, if you want to completely unset the current context, you can use this command:

```
$ kubectl config unset current-context

Property "current-context" unset.
```

Once this cluster is running, you can interact with it just like any other Kubernetes cluster via the kubectl command. Whenever you shut down Docker Desktop, this will also shut down the Kubernetes cluster.

If you want to completely disable this Kubernetes cluster, go back into the Preferences panel, select the Kubernetes tab, and un-check Enable Kubernetes.

Kind

The final option that we are going to discuss here is kind, a very simple but useful tool that allows you to manage a Kubernetes cluster made up of one or more Linux containers running in Docker. The tool name, kind, is an acronym that means "Kubernetes in Docker" but also refers to the fact that object types in Kubernetes are identified in the API by a field called Kind.

 You will find that searching for this tool on the web can be a bit difficult, but you can always find the tool and documentation on its primary website (*https://kind.sigs.k8s.io*).

kind provides a nice middle ground between the simplistic Kubernetes cluster that is embedded into the Docker VM and the minikube VM, which can be overly complex at times. kind is distributed as a single binary and can be installed with your favorite package manager or by simply navigating to the kind project releases page (*https:// github.com/kubernetes-sigs/kind/releases*) and downloading the most recent release for your system. If you manually download the binary, make sure that you rename the binary to kind, copy it to a directory in your path, and then ensure that it has the correct permissions so that users can run it.

Once kind is installed, you can try to create your first cluster with it by running the following:

```
$ kind create cluster --name test

Creating cluster "test" …
 ✓ Ensuring node image (kindest/node:v1.25.3)
 ✓ Preparing nodes
 ✓ Writing configuration
 ✓ Starting control-plane
 ✓ Installing CNI
 ✓ Installing StorageClass
Set kubectl context to "kind-test"
You can now use your cluster with:

kubectl cluster-info --context kind-test

Thanks for using kind!
```

By default, this command will spin up a single Docker container that represents a one-node Kubernetes cluster, using the most current stable Kubernetes release that kind currently supports.

kind has already set the Kubernetes current context to point at the cluster, so we can start running kubectl commands immediately:

```
$ kubectl cluster-info

Kubernetes control plane is running at https://127.0.0.1:56499
CoreDNS is running at
https://127.0.0.1:56499/api/v1/namespaces/kube-system/services/kube-dns:dns/proxy

To further debug and diagnose cluster problems, use 'kubectl cluster-info dump'.
```

You can see a redacted version of the information used by kubectl to connect to the Kubernetes server by running the following:

```
$ kubectl config view --minify

apiVersion: v1
clusters:
- cluster:
    certificate-authority-data: DATA+OMITTED
    server: https://127.0.0.1:56499
  name: kind-test
contexts:
- context:
    cluster: kind-test
    user: kind-test
  name: kind-test
current-context: kind-test
kind: Config
preferences: {}
users:
- name: kind-test
  user:
    client-certificate-data: REDACTED
    client-key-data: REDACTED
```

kind has some advanced features (*https://kind.sigs.k8s.io/docs/user/quick-start/#advanced*) that can generally be controlled by passing in a configuration file with the --config argument when spinning up the cluster.

You may find some of the follwing features useful:

- Changing the version of Kubernetes that is used
- Spinning up multiple worker nodes
- Spinning up multiple control plane nodes for HA testing
- Mapping ports between Docker and the local host system

- Enabling and disabling Kubernetes feature gates (*https://kubernetes.io/docs/reference/command-line-tools-reference/feature-gates*)
- Exporting control plane component logs with `kind export logs`
- And more

 One thing to remember when using `kind` is that Kubernetes is running inside one or more containers, which are potentially running inside a Linux VM when you are using something like Docker Desktop. This may mean that you need to set up some additional port forwarding when you spin up the cluster. This can be done using the `extraPortMappings` setting in the `kind` config.

At this point, you can go ahead and delete the cluster by running the following command:

```
$ kind delete cluster --name test

Deleting cluster "test" …
```

Amazon ECS and Fargate

One of the most popular cloud providers is Amazon via their AWS offerings. Support for running containers natively has existed in AWS Elastic Beanstalk (*https://amzn.to/2wNa1rL*) since mid-2014. But that service assigns only a single container to an Amazon instance, which means that it's not ideal for short-lived or lightweight containers. Amazon Elastic Compute Cloud (Amazon EC2) itself is a great platform for hosting your own Docker environment, though, and because Docker is powerful, you don't necessarily need much on top of your instances to make this a productive environment to work in. But Amazon has spent a lot of engineering time building a service that treats containers as first-class citizens: the Amazon Elastic Container Service (Amazon ECS). In the last few years, Amazon has built upon this support with products like the Elastic Kubernetes Services (EKS) and AWS Fargate.

 Fargate is simply a marketing label Amazon uses for the feature of ECS that makes it possible for AWS to automatically manage all the nodes in your container cluster so that you can focus on deploying your service.

The ECS is a set of tools that coordinates several AWS components. With ECS, you have a choice of whether or not you will run the Fargate tooling on top. If you do, then you don't need to handle as much of the work. If you don't, then in addition to the cluster nodes to handle your workload, you will also need to add one or more

EC2 instances to the cluster running Docker and Amazon's special ECS agent. If you run Fargate, then the cluster is automatically managed for you. In either case, you spin up the cluster and then push your containers into it.

The Amazon ECS agent (*https://github.com/aws/amazon-ecs-agent*) we just mentioned works with the ECS service to coordinate your cluster and schedule containers to your hosts. You will only be directly exposed to this when you manage a traditional non-Fargate ECS cluster.

Core AWS Setup

The rest of this section assumes that you have access to an AWS account and some familiarity with the service. You can learn about pricing and create a new account at *https://aws.amazon.com/free*. Amazon offers a free service tier, which may be enough for you to experiment with if you don't already have a paid account. After you have your AWS account set up, you will need at least one administrative user, a key pair, an Amazon virtual private cloud (AWS VPC), and a default security group in your environment. If you do not already have these set up, follow the directions in the Amazon documentation (*https://amzn.to/2FcPDSL*).

IAM Role Setup

Amazon's Identity and Access Management (Amazon IAM) roles are used to control what actions a user can take within your cloud environment. We need to make sure we can grant access to the right actions before moving on with the ECS. To work with the ECS, you must create a role called `ecsInstanceRole` that has the `AmazonEC2ContainerServiceRole` managed role attached to it. The easiest way to do this is by logging in to the AWS console (*https://console.aws.amazon.com*) and navigating to Identity and Access Management (*https://console.aws.amazon.com/iam/home*):

 Check to ensure that you don't already have the proper role. If it already exists, then you should double-check that it is set up properly, as these directions have changed a bit over the years.

1. In the left sidebar, click Roles.
2. Then, click the "Create role" button.
3. Under AWS Service, select Elastic Container Service.
4. Under "Select your use case," select Elastic Container Service.
5. Click Next: Permissions.

6. Click Next: Review.

7. In Role Name, type `ecsInstanceRole`.

8. Click "Create role."

If you are interested in storing container configuration in an S3 object storage bucket, take a look at the Amazon ECS container agent configuration documentation (*https://amzn.to/2PNapOL*).

AWS CLI Setup

Amazon supplies command-line tools that make it easy to work with their API-driven infrastructure. You will need to install a very recent version of the AWS CLI tools. Amazon has detailed documentation (*https://amzn.to/1PCpPNA*) that covers the installation of their tools, but the basic steps are as follows.

Installation

Here we'll cover the native installation on a few different OSes, but be aware that you can also run the AWS CLI via a Docker container (*https://docs.aws.amazon.com/cli/latest/userguide/getting-started-docker.html#cliv2-docker-install*)! You can feel free to skip to the one you care about. If you're curious or just like installation instructions, by all means, read them all!

macOS

In Chapter 3, we discussed installing Homebrew. If you previously did this, you can install the AWS CLI using the following commands:

```
$ brew update
$ brew install awscli
```

Windows

Amazon provides a standard MSI installer for Windows, which can be downloaded from Amazon S3 for your architecture:

- 32-bit Windows (*https://s3.amazonaws.com/aws-cli/AWSCLI32.msi*)

- 64-bit Windows (*https://s3.amazonaws.com/aws-cli/AWSCLI64.msi*)

Other

The Amazon CLI tools are written in Python. So on most platforms, you can install the tools with the Python `pip` package manager by running the following from a shell:

```
$ pip install awscli --upgrade --user
```

Some platforms won't have `pip` installed by default. In that case, you can use the `easy_install` package manager, like this:

```
$ easy_install awscli
```

Configuration

Quickly verify that your AWS CLI version is at least 1.7.0 with the following command:

```
$ aws --version
```

```
aws-cli/1.14.50 Python/3.6.4 Darwin/17.3.0 botocore/1.9.3
```

To configure the AWS CLI tool, ensure that you have access to your AWS access key ID and AWS secret access key, and then run the `configure` command. You will be prompted for your authentication information and some preferred defaults:

```
$ aws configure
```

```
AWS Access Key ID [None]: EXAMPLEEXAMPLEEXAMPLE
AWS Secret Access Key [None]: ExaMPleKEy/7EXAMPL3/EXaMPLeEXAMPLEKEY
Default region name [None]: us-east-1
Default output format [None]: json
```

At this point, it's a really good idea to test that the CLI tools are working correctly before proceeding. You can easily do that by running the following command to list the IAM users in your account:

```
$ aws iam list-users
```

Assuming everything went according to plan and you chose JSON as your default output format, you should get something like this:

```
{
    "Users": [
        {
            "Path": "/",
            "UserName": "administrator",
            "UserId": "ExmaPL3ExmaPL3ExmaPL3Ex",
            "Arn": "arn:aws:iam::936262807352:user/myuser",
            "CreateDate": "2021-04-08T17:22:23+00:00",
            "PasswordLastUsed": "2022-09-05T15:56:21+00:00"
        }
    ]
}
```

Container Instances

The first thing you need to do after installing the required tools is to create at least a single cluster that your Docker hosts will register with when they are brought online.

 The default cluster is imaginatively named *default*. If you keep this name, you do not need to specify --cluster-name in many of the commands that follow.

The first thing you need to do is create a cluster in the container service. You will then launch your tasks in the cluster once it's up and running. For these examples, you should start by creating a cluster called fargate-testing:

```
$ aws ecs create-cluster --cluster-name fargate-testing

{
    "cluster": {
        "clusterArn": "arn:aws:ecs:us-east-1:1…2:cluster/fargate-testing",
"clusterName": "fargate-testing",
        "status": "ACTIVE",
        "registeredContainerInstancesCount": 0,
        "runningTasksCount": 0,
        "pendingTasksCount": 0,
        "activeServicesCount": 0,
        "statistics": [],
        "tags": [],
        "settings": [
            {
                "name": "containerInsights",
                "value": "disabled"
            }
        ],
        "capacityProviders": [],
        "defaultCapacityProviderStrategy": []
    }
}
```

Before AWS Fargate was released, you were required to create AWS EC2 instances running docker and the ecs-agent, and add them to your cluster. You can still use this approach if you want (EC2 launch type), but Fargate makes it much easier to run a dynamic cluster that can scale fluidly with your workload.

Tasks

Now that our container cluster is set up, we need to start putting it to work. To do this, we need to create at least one task definition. The Amazon ECS defines the term *task definition* as a list of containers grouped together.

To create your first task definition, open up your favorite editor, copy in the following JSON, and then save it as *webgame-task.json* in your current directory, as shown here:

```
{
  "containerDefinitions": [
    {
      "name": "web-game",
      "image": "spkane/quantum-game",
      "cpu": 0,
      "portMappings": [
        {
          "containerPort": 8080,
          "hostPort": 8080,
          "protocol": "tcp"
        }
      ],
      "essential": true,
      "environment": [],
      "mountPoints": [],
      "volumesFrom": []
    }
  ],
  "family": "fargate-game",
  "networkMode": "awsvpc",
  "volumes": [],
  "placementConstraints": [],
  "requiresCompatibilities": [
    "FARGATE"
  ],
  "cpu": "256",
  "memory": "512"
}
```

You can also check out these files and a few others by running the following:

```
git clone \
  https://github.com/bluewhalebook/\
docker-up-and-running-3rd-edition.git \
  --config core.autocrlf=input
```

The URL has been continued on the following line so that it fits in the margins. You may find that you need to reassemble the URL and remove the backslashes for the command to work properly.

In this task definition, we are saying that we want to create a task family called fargate-game running a single container called web-game that is based on the *Quantum* web game (*https://github.com/stared/quantum-game*). As you may have seen in an earlier chapter, this Docker image launches a browser-based puzzle game that uses real quantum mechanics.

Fargate limits some of the options that you can set in this config-uration, including `networkMode` and the `cpu` and `memory` settings. You can find out more about the options in the task definition from the official AWS documentation (*https://amzn.to/2PkliGR*).

In this task definition, we define some constraints on memory and CPU usage for the container, in addition to telling Amazon whether this container is essential to the task. The `essential` flag is useful when you have multiple containers defined in a task, and not all of them are required for the task to be successful. If `essential` is true and the container fails to start, then all the containers defined in the task will be killed and the task will be marked as failed. We can also use the task definition to define almost all of the typical variables and settings that would be included in a *Dockerfile* or on the `docker container run` command line.

To upload this task definition to Amazon, you will need to run a command similar to what is shown here:

```
$ aws ecs register-task-definition --cli-input-json file://./webgame-task.json
{
    "taskDefinition": {
        "taskDefinitionArn": "arn:aws:ecs:…:task-definition/fargate-game:1",
        "containerDefinitions": [
            {
                "name": "web-game",
                "image": "spkane/quantum-game",
                "cpu": 0,
                "portMappings": [
                    {
                        "containerPort": 8080,
                        "hostPort": 8080,
                        "protocol": "tcp"
                    }
                ],
                "essential": true,
                "environment": [],
                "mountPoints": [],
                "volumesFrom": []
            }
        ],
        "family": "fargate-game",
        "networkMode": "awsvpc",
        "revision": 1,
        "volumes": [],
        "status": "ACTIVE",
        "requiresAttributes": [
            {
                "name": "com.amazonaws.ecs.capability.docker-remote-api.1.18"
            },
            {
```

```
        "name": "ecs.capability.task-eni"
        }
    ],
    "placementConstraints": [],
    "compatibilities": [
        "EC2",
        "FARGATE"
    ],
    "requiresCompatibilities": [
        "FARGATE"
    ],
    "cpu": "256",
    "memory": "512",
    "registeredAt": "2022-09-05T09:10:18.184000-07:00",
    "registeredBy": "arn:aws:iam::…:user/me"
    }
}
```

We can then list all of our task definitions by running the following:

```
$ aws ecs list-task-definitions
{
    "taskDefinitionArns": [
        "arn:aws:ecs:us-east-1:…:task-definition/fargate-game:1",
    ]
}
```

Now you are ready to create your first task in your cluster. You do so by running a command like the one shown next. The count argument in the command allows you to define how many copies of this task you want to be deployed into your cluster. For this job, one is enough.

You will need to modify the following command to reference a valid subnet ID and security-group ID from your AWS VPC. You should be able to find these in the AWS console (*https://console.aws.amazon.com/vpc/home*) or by using the AWS CLI commands aws ec2 describe-subnets and aws ec2 describe-security-groups. You can also tell AWS to assign your tasks a public IP address by using a network configuration similar to this:

```
awsvpcConfiguration={subnets=[subnet-abcd1234],
                    securityGroups=[sg-abcd1234],
                    assignPublicIp=ENABLED}
```

Assigning a public IP address may be required if you are using public subnets:

```
$ aws ecs create-service --cluster fargate-testing --service-name \
    fargate-game-service --task-definition fargate-game:1 --desired-count 1 \
    --launch-type "FARGATE" --network-configuration \
    "awsvpcConfiguration={subnets=[subnet-abcd1234],\
    securityGroups=[sg-abcd1234]}"
```

```json
{
    "service": {
        "serviceArn": "arn:aws:ecs:…:service/fargate-game-service",
        "serviceName": "fargate-game-service",
        "clusterArn": "arn:aws:ecs:…:cluster/fargate-testing",
        "loadBalancers": [],
        "serviceRegistries": [],
        "status": "ACTIVE",
        "desiredCount": 1,
        "runningCount": 0,
        "pendingCount": 0,
        "launchType": "FARGATE",
        "platformVersion": "LATEST",
        "platformFamily": "Linux",
        "taskDefinition": "arn:aws:ecs:…:task-definition/fargate-game:1",
        "deploymentConfiguration": {
            "deploymentCircuitBreaker": {
                "enable": false,
                "rollback": false
            },
            "maximumPercent": 200,
            "minimumHealthyPercent": 100
        },
        "deployments": [
            {
                "id": "ecs-svc/…",
                "status": "PRIMARY",
                "taskDefinition": "arn:aws:ecs:…definition/fargate-game:1",
                "desiredCount": 1,
                "pendingCount": 0,
                "runningCount": 0,
                "failedTasks": 0,
                "createdAt": "2022-09-05T09:14:51.653000-07:00",
                "updatedAt": "2022-09-05T09:14:51.653000-07:00",
                "launchType": "FARGATE",
                "platformVersion": "1.4.0",
                "platformFamily": "Linux",
                "networkConfiguration": {
…
                },
                "rolloutState": "IN_PROGRESS",
                "rolloutStateReason": "ECS deployment ecs-svc/… in progress."
            }
        ],
        "roleArn": "…aws-service-role/ecs.amazonaws.com/AWSServiceRoleForECS",
        "events": [],
        "createdAt": "2022-09-05T09:14:51.653000-07:00",
        "placementConstraints": [],
        "placementStrategy": [],
        "networkConfiguration": {
…
        },
```

```
            "schedulingStrategy": "REPLICA",
            "createdBy": "arn:aws:iam::…:user/me",
            "enableECSManagedTags": false,
            "propagateTags": "NONE",
            "enableExecuteCommand": false
        }
    }
```

 Fargate and the awsvpc network require that you have a service-linked role for ECS. In the preceding output, you should see a line that ends like this:

```
"role/aws-service-role/ecs.amazonaws.com/
AWSServiceRoleForECS"
```

Most of the time this will be autogenerated for you, but you can create it manually using the following command:

```
$ aws iam create-service-linked-role \
    --aws-service-name ecs.amazonaws.com
```

You can now list all of the services in your cluster with the following command:

```
$ aws ecs list-services --cluster fargate-testing
{
    "serviceArns": [
        "arn:aws:ecs:us-west-2:…:service/fargate-testing/fargate-game-service"
    ]
}
```

To retrieve all the details about your service, run the following:

```
$ aws ecs describe-services --cluster fargate-testing \
    --services fargate-game-service

{
    "services": [
        {
…
            "deployments": [
                {
                    "id": "ecs-svc/…",
                    "status": "PRIMARY",
                    "taskDefinition": "arn:…:task-definition/fargate-game:1",
                    "desiredCount": 1,
                    "pendingCount": 1,
                    "runningCount": 0,
                    "createdAt": "2022-09-05T09:14:51.653000-07:00",
                    "updatedAt": "2022-09-05T09:14:51.653000-07:00",
                    "launchType": "FARGATE",
                    "platformVersion": "1.4.0",
                    "platformFamily": "Linux",
                    "networkConfiguration": {
```

```
            },
            "rolloutState": "IN_PROGRESS",
            "rolloutStateReason": "ECS deployment ecs-svc/…progress."
          }
        ],
        "roleArn": "…role/ecs.amazonaws.com/AWSServiceRoleForECS",
        "events": [
          {
            "id": "83bd5c2eed5d4866bb7ec8c3c938666c",
            "createdAt": "2022-09-05T09:14:54.950000-07:00",
            "message": "(…game-service) has started 1 tasks: (…)."
          }
        ],
...
      }
    ],
    "failures": []
}
```

This output will tell you a lot about all the tasks in your service. In this case, we have a single task running at the moment.

> The task-definition value is a name followed by a number (fargate-game:1). The number is the revision. If you edit your task and re-register it with the aws ecs register-task-definition command, you will get a new revision, which means that you will want to reference that new revision in various commands, like aws ecs update-service. If you don't change that number, you will continue to launch containers using the older JSON. This versioning makes it very easy to roll back changes and test new revisions without impacting all future instances.

If you want to see what individual tasks are running in your cluster, you can run the following:

```
$ aws ecs list-tasks --cluster fargate-testing
{
    "taskArns": [
        "arn:aws:ecs:…:task/fargate-testing/83bd5c2eed5d4866bb7ec8c3c938666c"
    ]
}
```

Since you only have a single task in your cluster at the moment, this list is very small.

To get more details about the individual task, you can run the following command after substituting the task ID with the correct one from your cluster:

```
$ aws ecs describe-tasks --cluster fargate-testing \
  --task 83bd5c2eed5d4866bb7ec8c3c938666c
```

```
{
    "tasks": [
        {
            "attachments": [
                {
                    "details": [
…
…
                        {
                            "name": "networkInterfaceId",
                            "value": "eni-00a40225208c9411a"
                        },
…
                        {
                            "name": "privateIPv4Address",
                            "value": "172.31.42.184"
                        }
                    ]
                }
            ],
            "attributes": [
…
            ],
            "availabilityZone": "us-west-2b",
            "clusterArn": "arn:aws:ecs:us-west-2:…:cluster/fargate-testing",
            "connectivity": "CONNECTED",
            "connectivityAt": "2022-09-05T09:23:46.929000-07:00",
            "containers": [
                {
                    "containerArn": "arn:…:container/fargate-testing/…",
                    "taskArn": "arn:…:task/fargate-testing/…",
                    "name": "web-game",
                    "image": "spkane/quantum-game",
                    "runtimeId": "83bd…998",
                    "lastStatus": "RUNNING",
                    "networkInterfaces": [
                        {
                            "attachmentId": "ddab…373a",
                            "privateIpv4Address": "172.31.42.184"
                        }
                    ],
                    "healthStatus": "UNKNOWN",
                    "cpu": "0"
                }
            ],
            "cpu": "256",
            "createdAt": "2022-09-05T09:23:42.700000-07:00",
            "desiredStatus": "RUNNING",
            "enableExecuteCommand": false,
            "group": "service:fargate-game-service",
            "healthStatus": "UNKNOWN",
            "lastStatus": "RUNNING",
```

```
            "launchType": "FARGATE",
            "memory": "512",
            "overrides": {
                "containerOverrides": [
                    {
                        "name": "web-game"
                    }
                ],
                "inferenceAcceleratorOverrides": []
            },
            "platformVersion": "1.4.0",
            "platformFamily": "Linux",
            "pullStartedAt": "2022-09-05T09:59:36.554000-07:00",
            "pullStoppedAt": "2022-09-05T09:59:46.361000-07:00",
            "startedAt": "2022-09-05T09:59:48.546000-07:00",
            "startedBy": "ecs-svc/…",
            "tags": [],
            "taskArn": "arn:aws:…:task/fargate-testing/83bd…666c",
            "taskDefinitionArn": "arn:aws:…:task-definition/fargate-game:1",
            "version": 4,
            "ephemeralStorage": {
                "sizeInGiB": 20
            }
        }
    ],
    "failures": []
}
```

If you notice that the lastStatus key is displaying a value of PENDING, this most likely means that your service is still starting up. You can describe the task again to ensure that it has completed transitioning into a RUNNING state. After verifying that the lastStatus key is set to RUNNING, you should be able to test your container.

Depending on the network setup, your task may not be able to download the image. If you see an error like this:

"stoppedReason":   "CannotPullContainerError: inspect image has been retried 5 time(s): failed to resolve ref \"docker.io/spkane/quantum-game:latest\": failed to do request: Head *https://registry-1.docker.io/v2/spkane/quantum-game/manifests/latest*: dial tcp 54.83.42.45:443: i/o timeout"

then you should read through this troubleshooting guide (*https://oreil.ly/FYo9Z*).[1]

---

1 Full URL: *https://docs.aws.amazon.com/AmazonECS/latest/developerguide/task_cannot_pull_image.html*

Testing the Task

You will need a modern web browser installed on your system to connect to the container and test the web game.

In the previous output, you'll notice that the `privateIPv4Address` for the example task was listed as `172.31.42.184`. Yours will be different.

 If you need more information about the network setup for your task and the EC2 instance that it is running on, you can grab the `networkInterfaceId` from the `aws ecs describe-tasks` output and then append that to the `aws ec2 describe-network-interfaces --network-interface-ids` command to get everything you should need, including the `PublicIp` value if you configured your service for that.

Ensure that you are connected to a network that can reach either the public or private IP address of your host, then launch your web browser and navigate to port 8080 on that IP address.

In the example, this private URL would look like this:

```
http://172.31.42.184:8080/
```

If everything is working as expected, you should be greeted by the *Quantum Game* puzzle board.

The official version of the game can be found at *https://quantumgame.io*.

 We completely understand if you get distracted at this point and stop reading for a few hours to try to solve some puzzles and learn a little bit of quantum mechanics at the same time. The book won't notice! Put it down, play the puzzles, and pick it back up later.

Stopping the Task

Right, so we have a running task. Now let's take a look at stopping it. To do that, you need to know the task ID. One way to obtain this is by relisting all the tasks running in your cluster:

```
$ aws ecs list-tasks --cluster fargate-testing
{
    "taskArns": [
        "arn:aws:ecs:…:task/fargate-testing/83bd5c2eed5d4866bb7ec8c3c938666c"
    ]
}
```

You can also obtain it from the service information:

```
$ aws ecs describe-services --cluster fargate-testing \
    --services fargate-game-service
{
...
                  {
                      "id": "6b7f…0384",
                      "createdAt": "2022-09-05T09:59:23.917000-07:00",
                      "message": "…: (task 83bd5c2eed5d4866bb7ec8c3c938666c)."
                  }
    ...
}
```

Finally, we can stop the task by running the following command with the correct task ID:

```
$ aws ecs stop-task --cluster fargate-testing \
    --task 83bd5c2eed5d4866bb7ec8c3c938666c
{
        "desiredStatus": "STOPPED",
    ...
        "lastStatus": "RUNNING",
    ...
        "stopCode": "UserInitiated",
        "stoppedReason": "Task stopped by user",
        "stoppingAt": "2022-09-05T10:29:05.110000-07:00",
    ...
}
```

If you describe the task again using the same task ID, you should now see that the lastStatus key is set to STOPPED:

```
$ aws ecs describe-tasks --cluster fargate-testing \
    --task 83bd5c2eed5d4866bb7ec8c3c938666c
{
...
            "desiredStatus": "STOPPED",
    ...
            "lastStatus": "STOPPED",
    ...
}
```

Listing all the tasks in our cluster should return an empty set:

```
$ aws ecs list-tasks --cluster fargate-testing
{
    "taskArns": []
}
```

At this point, you could start creating more complicated tasks that tie multiple containers together and rely on the ECS and Fargate tooling to spin up hosts and deploy the tasks into your cluster as needed.

If you want to tear down the rest of the ECS environment, you can run the following commands:

```
$ aws ecs delete-service --cluster fargate-testing \
  --service fargate-game-service  --force
…

$ aws ecs delete-cluster --cluster fargate-testing
…
```

Wrap-Up

In this chapter, we've certainly presented you with a lot of options! It's unlikely that you'll ever need to use all of these, since many of them overlap. However, each one has a unique perspective on exactly what a production system should look like and what problems are the most important to solve. After exploring all of these tools, you should have a pretty good idea of the wide range of options you can choose from to build your production Linux container environment.

Underlying all of these tools is Docker's highly portable image format for Linux containers and its ability to abstract away so much of the underlying Linux system, which makes it easy to move your applications fluidly between your data center and as many cloud providers as you want. Now you just have to choose which approach will work best for you and your organization and then implement it.

In the meantime, let's jump into the next chapter and explore some of the most technical topics in the Docker ecosystem, including security, networking, and storage.

## CHAPTER 11

Advanced Topics

In this chapter, we'll do a quick pass through some of the more advanced topics. We're going to assume that you have a pretty good hold on Docker by now and that you've already got it in production or you're at least a regular user. We'll talk about how containers work in detail and about some of the aspects of Docker security, Docker networking, Docker plug-ins, swappable runtimes, and other advanced configurations.

Some of this chapter covers configurable changes you can make to your Docker installation. These can be useful, but Docker has good defaults, so as with most software, you should stick to the defaults on your operating system unless you have a good reason to change them and have educated yourself on what those changes mean to you. Getting your installation right for your environment will likely involve some trial and error, tuning, and adjustment over time. However, changing settings from their defaults before understanding them well is not recommended.

Containers in Detail

Though we usually talk about Linux containers as a single entity, they are actually implemented through several separate mechanisms built into the Linux kernel that all work together: control groups (cgroups), namespaces, Secure Computing Mode (seccomp), and SELinux or AppArmor, all of which serve to *contain* the process. cgroups provide for resource limits, namespaces allow for processes to use identically named resources and isolate them from one another's view of the system, Secure Computing Mode limits which system calls a process can use, and SELinux or AppArmor provides additional strong security isolation for processes. So, to start, what do cgroups and namespaces do for you?

Before we launch into detail, an analogy might help you understand how each of these subsystems plays into the way that containers work. Imagine that the typical computer is like a large open warehouse, full of workers (processes). The warehouse is full of space and resources, but it is very easy for the workers to get in one another's way, and most of the resources are simply used by whomever gets them first.

When you are running Docker and using Linux containers for your workloads, it is like that warehouse has been converted into an office building, where each worker now has their own individual office. Each office has all the normal things that the workers need to accomplish their jobs, and in general, they can now work without worrying much about what other people (processes) are doing.

Namespaces make up the walls of the office and ensure that processes cannot interact with neighboring processes in any way that they are not specifically allowed to. Control groups are a bit like paying rent to receive utilities. When the process is first spun up, it is assigned time on the CPU and storage subsystem that it will be allowed each cycle, in addition to the amount of memory that it will be allowed to use at any moment. This helps ensure that the workers (processes) have the resources they need, without allowing them to use resources or space reserved for others. Imagine the worst kind of noisy neighbors, and you can suddenly truly appreciate good, solid barriers between offices. Finally, Secure Computing Mode, SELinux, and AppArmor are a bit like office security, ensuring that even if something unexpected or untoward happens, it is unlikely to cause much more than the headache of filling out paperwork and filing an incident report.

cgroups

Traditional distributed system design dictates running each intensive task on its own virtual server. So, for example, you don't run your applications on the database server because they have competing resource demands, and their resource usage could grow unbounded and begin to dominate the server, starving the database of performance.

On real hardware systems, this could be quite expensive, so solutions like virtual servers are very appealing, in part because you can share expensive hardware between competing applications, and the virtualization layer will handle your resource partitioning. But while it saves money, this is still a fairly expensive approach if you don't need all the other separation provided by virtualization, because running multiple kernels introduces a reasonable overhead on the applications. Maintaining VMs is also not the cheapest solution. All the same, cloud computing has shown that it's immensely powerful and, with the right tooling, incredibly effective.

But if the only kind of isolation you needed was resource partitioning, wouldn't it be great if you could get that on the same kernel without running another operating system instance? For many years, you could assign a "niceness" value to a process, and it would give the scheduler hints about how you wanted this process to be treated in relation to the others. But it wasn't possible to impose hard limits like those that you get with VMs. And niceness is not at all fine-grained: you can't give something more I/O and less CPU than other processes. This fine-grained control, of course, is one of the promises of Linux containers, and the mechanism that they use to provide that functionality is cgroups, which predate Docker and were invented to solve just this problem.

Control groups allow you to set limits on resources for processes and their children. This is the mechanism that the Linux kernel uses to control limits on memory, swap, CPU, storage, and network I/O resources. cgroups are built into the kernel and originally shipped in 2007 in Linux 2.6.24. The official kernel documentation (*https:// www.kernel.org/doc/Documentation/cgroup-v2.txt*) defines them as "a mechanism to organize processes hierarchically and distribute system resources along the hierarchy in a controlled and configurable manner." It's important to note that this setting applies to a process and all of the children that descend from it. That's exactly how containers are structured.

> It is worth mentioning that there have been at least two major releases of Linux control groups: v1 (*https://www.ker nel.org/doc/Documentation/cgroup-v1/cgroups.txt*) and v2 (*https:// www.kernel.org/doc/Documentation/cgroup-v2.txt*). Make sure that you know which version is being used in production so that you can leverage all the abilities that it provides.

Every Linux container is assigned a cgroup that is unique to that container. All of the processes in the container will be in the same group. This means that it's easy to control resources for each container as a whole without worrying about what might be running. If a container is redeployed with new processes added, you can have Docker assign the same policy and it will apply to the whole container and all the process containers within it.

We talked previously about the cgroups hooks exposed by Docker via its API. That interface allows you to control memory, swap, and disk usage. But there are lots of other things that you can manage with cgroups, including tagging network packets from a container so that you can use those tags to prioritize traffic. You might find that in your environment you need to use some of these levers to keep your containers under control, and there are a few ways you can go about doing that. By their very nature, cgroups need to do a lot of accounting of resources used by each group. That means that when you're using them, the kernel has a lot of interesting statistics about how much CPU, RAM, disk I/O, and so on your processes are using. So Docker uses cgroups not just to limit resources but also to report on them. These are many of the metrics you see, for example, in the output of docker container stats.

The /sys filesystem

The primary way to control cgroups in a fine-grained manner, even if you configured them with Docker, is to manage them yourself. This is the most powerful method because changes don't just happen at container creation time—they can be done on the fly.

On systems with `systemd`, there are command-line tools like `systemctl` that you can use to do this. But since cgroups are built into the kernel, the method that works everywhere is to talk to the kernel directly via the /sys filesystem. If you're not familiar with /sys, it's a filesystem that directly exposes several kernel settings and outputs. You can use it with simple command-line tools to tell the kernel how you would like it to behave.

This method of configuring cgroups controls for containers only works directly on the Docker server, so it is not available remotely via any API. If you use this method, you'll need to figure out how to script this for your environment.

Changing cgroups values yourself, outside of any Docker configuration, breaks some of the repeatability of a Docker deployment. Unless you implement changes in your deployment process, settings will revert to their defaults when containers are replaced. Some schedulers take care of this for you, so if you run one in production, you might check the documentation to see how to best apply these changes repeatably.

Let's use an example of changing the CPU cgroups settings for a container we have just started up. We need to get the long ID of the container, and then we need to find it in the /sys filesystem. Here's what that looks like:

```
$ docker container run -d spkane/train-os \
    stress -v --cpu 2 --io 1 --vm 2 --vm-bytes 128M --timeout 360s

dcbb…8e86f1dc0a91e7675d3c93895cb6a6d83371e25b7f0bd62803ed8e86
```

Here, we've had `docker container run` give us the long ID in the output, and the ID we want is `dcbb…8e86f1dc0a91e7675d3c93895cb6a6d83371e25b7f0bd62803ed8e86`. You can see why Docker normally truncates this.

In the examples, we may need to truncate the ID to make it fit into the constraints of a standard page. But remember that you will need to use the long ID!

Now that we have the ID, we can find our container's cgroup in the */sys* filesystem. */sys* is laid out so that each type of setting is grouped into a module, and that module might be exposed at a different place in the */sys* filesystem. So when we look at CPU settings, we won't see `blkio` settings, for example. You might take a look around in */sys* to see what else is there. But for now we're interested in the CPU controller, so let's inspect what that gives us. You need `root` access on the system to do this because you're manipulating kernel settings.

Remember our `nsenter` trick we originally discussed in Chapter 3. You can run `docker container run --rm -it --privileged --pid=host debian nsenter -t 1 -m -u -n -i sh` to get access to the Docker host, even if you can't SSH into the server.

```
$ ls /sys/fs/cgroup/docker/dcbb...8e86
```

cgroup.controllers	cpuset.cpus.partition	memory.high
cgroup.events	cpuset.mems	memory.low
cgroup.freeze	cpuset.mems.effective	memory.max
cgroup.max.depth	hugetlb.2MB.current	memory.min
cgroup.max.descendants	hugetlb.2MB.events	memory.oom.group
cgroup.procs	hugetlb.2MB.events.local	memory.stat
cgroup.stat	hugetlb.2MB.max	memory.swap.current
cgroup.subtree_control	hugetlb.2MB.rsvd.current	memory.swap.events
cgroup.threads	hugetlb.2MB.rsvd.max	memory.swap.high
cgroup.type	io.bfq.weight	memory.swap.max
cpu.max	io.latency	pids.current
cpu.stat	io.max	pids.events
cpu.weight	io.stat	pids.max
cpu.weight.nice	memory.current	rdma.current
cpuset.cpus	memory.events	rdma.max
cpuset.cpus.effective	memory.events.local	

The exact path here may change a bit depending on the Linux distribution your Docker server is running on and what the hash of your container is.

You can see that under cgroups, there is a *docker* directory that contains all of the Linux containers that are running on this host. You can't set cgroups for things that aren't running, because they apply only to running processes. This is an important point that you should consider. Docker takes care of reapplying cgroup settings for you when you start and stop containers. Without that mechanism, you are somewhat on your own.

Let's go ahead and inspect the CPU weight (*https://docs.kernel.org/admin-guide/ cgroup-v2.html#cpu-interface-files*) for this container. Remember that we explored setting some of these CPU values in Chapter 5 via the `--cpus` command-line argument to `docker container run`. But for a normal container where no settings were passed, this setting is the default:

```
$ cat /sys/fs/cgroup/docker/dcbb…8e86/cpu.weight
100
```

100 CPU weight means we are not limited at all. Let's tell the kernel that this container should be limited to half that:

```
$ echo 50 > /sys/fs/cgroup/docker/dcbb…8e86/cpu.weight
$ cat /sys/fs/cgroup/docker/dcbb…8e86/cpu.weight
50
```

In production, you should not use this method to adjust cgroups on the fly, but we are demonstrating it here so that you understand the underlying mechanics that make all of this work. Take a look at `docker container update` (*https://dockr.ly/2PPC4P1*) if you'd like to adjust these on a running container. You might also find the `--cgroup-parent` (*https://dockr.ly/2PTLaKK*) option to `docker container run` interesting.

There you have it. We've changed the container's settings on the fly. This method is very powerful because it allows you to set any cgroups setting for the container. But as we mentioned earlier, it's entirely ephemeral. When the container is stopped and restarted, the setting reverts to the default:

```
$ docker container stop dcbb…8e86
dcbb…8e86

$ cat /sys/fs/cgroup/docker/dcbb…8e86/cpu.weight
cat: /sys/fs/…/cpu.weight: No such file or directory
```

You can see that the directory path doesn't even exist anymore now that the container is stopped. And when we start it back up, the directory comes back but the setting is back to 100:

```
$ docker container start dcbb…8e86
dcbb…8e86

$ cat /sys/fs/cgroup/docker/dcbb…8e86/cpu.weight
100
```

If you were to change these kinds of settings in a production system via the */sys* filesystem directly, you'd want to manage that directly. A daemon that watches the `docker system events` stream and changes settings at container startup, for example, is a possibility.

It is possible to create custom cgroups outside of Docker and then attach a new container to that cgroup using the `--cgroup-parent` argument to `docker container create`. This mechanism is also used by schedulers that run multiple containers inside the same cgroup (e.g., Kubernetes pods).

Namespaces

Inside each container, you see a filesystem, network interfaces, disks, and other resources that all appear to be unique to the container despite sharing the kernel with all the other processes on the system. The primary network interface on the actual machine, for example, is a single shared resource. But inside your container, it will look like it has an entire network interface to itself. This is a really useful abstraction: it's what makes your container feel like a machine all by itself. The way this is implemented in the kernel is with Linux namespaces. Namespaces take a traditionally global resource and present the container with its own unique and unshared version of that resource.

Namespaces cannot be explored on the filesystem quite as easily as cgroups, but most of the details can be found under the */proc/*/ns/** and */proc/*/task/*/ns/** hierarchies. In newer Linux releases, the `lsns` command can also be quite useful.

Rather than just having a single namespace, however, by default containers have a namespace on each of the resources that are currently namespaced in the kernel: mount, UTS, IPC, PID, network, and user namespaces, in addition to the partially implemented time namespace. Essentially, when you talk about a container, you're talking about several different namespaces that Docker sets up on your behalf. So what do they all do?

Mount namespaces
> Linux uses these primarily to make your container look like it has its own entire filesystem. If you've ever used a `chroot` jail, this is its more robust relative. It looks a lot like a `chroot` jail but goes all the way down to the deepest levels of the kernel so that even `mount` and `unmount` system calls are namespaced. If you use `docker container exec` or `nsenter`, which we will discuss later in this chapter, to get into a container, you'll see a filesystem rooted on /. But we know that this isn't the actual root partition of the system. It's the mount namespace that makes that possible.

UTS namespaces
> Named for the kernel structure they namespace, UTS (Unix Time Sharing System) namespaces give your container its own hostname and domain name. This

is also used by older systems like NIS to identify which domain a host belongs to. When you enter a container and see a hostname that is not the same as the machine on which it runs, it's this namespace that makes that happen.

 To have a container use its host's UTS namespace, you can specify the --uts=host option when launching the container with docker container run. There are similar commands for sharing the other namespaces as well.

IPC namespaces

These isolate your container's System V IPC and POSIX message queue systems from those of the host. Some IPC mechanisms use filesystem resources like named pipes, and those are covered by the mount namespace. The IPC namespace covers things like shared memory and semaphores that aren't filesystem resources but that really should not cross the container wall.

PID namespaces

We have already shown that you can see all of the processes in containers in the Linux ps output on the host Linux server. But inside the container, processes have a different PID. This is the PID namespace in action. A process has a unique PID in each namespace to which it belongs. If you look in */proc* inside a container, or run ps, you will only see the processes inside the container's PID namespace.

Network namespaces

This is what allows your container to have its own network devices, ports, and so on. When you run docker container ls and see the bound ports for your container, you are seeing ports from both namespaces. Inside the container, your nginx might be bound to port 80, but that's on the namespaced network interface. This namespace makes it possible to have what seems to be a completely separate network stack for your container.

User namespaces

These provide isolation between the user and group IDs inside a container and those on the Linux host. Earlier, when we looked at ps output outside and then inside the container, we saw different user IDs; this is how that happened. A new user inside a container is not a new user on the Linux host's main namespace, and vice versa. There are some subtleties here, though. For example, UID 0 (root) in a user namespace is not the same thing as UID 0 on the host, although running as root inside the container does increase the risk of potential security exploits. There are concerns about security leakage, which we'll talk about in a bit, and this is why things like rootless containers are growing in popularity.

Cgroup namespaces

This namespace was introduced in Linux kernel 4.6 in 2016 and is intended to hide the identity of the cgroup of which the process is a member. A process checking which cgroup any process is part of would see a path that is relative to the cgroup set at creation time, hiding its true cgroup position and identity.

Time namespaces

Time has historically not been namespaced since it is so integral to the Linux kernel, and providing full namespacing would be very complex. However, with the release of Linux kernel 5.6 in 2020, support was added for a time namespace (*https://man7.org/linux/man-pages/man7/time_namespaces.7.html*) that allows containers to have their own unique clock offsets.

At the time of this writing, Docker still does not have direct support for setting the time offset, but like everything else, it can be set directly, if required.

So by combining all of these namespaces, Linux can provide the visual and, in many cases, the functional isolation that makes a container look like a VM even though it's running on the same kernel. Let's explore what some of the namespacing that we just described looks like in more detail.

There is a lot of ongoing work trying to make containers more secure. The community is actively looking into ways to improve support for rootless containers (*https://rootlesscontaine.rs*), which enables regular users to create, run, and manage containers locally without needing special privileges. In Docker, this can now be achieved via rootless mode (*https://docs.docker.com/engine/security/rootless*). New container runtimes like Google gVisor (*https://github.com/google/gvisor*) are also trying to explore better ways to create much more secure container sandboxes without losing most of the advantages of containerized workflows.

Exploring namespaces

One of the easiest namespaces to demonstrate is UTS, so let's use `docker container exec` to get a shell in a container and take a look. From within the Docker server, run the following:

```
$ hostname

docker-desktop
```

Again, remember that you can use the `docker container run --rm -it --privileged --pid=host debian nsenter -t 1 -m -u -n -i sh` command that we originally discussed in Chapter 3 to get access to the Docker host, even if you can't SSH into the server.

And then on your local system, run the following:

```
$ docker container run -ti --rm ubuntu \
    bash -c 'echo "Container hostname: $(hostname)"'

Container hostname: 4cdb66d4495b
```

That `docker container run` command line gets us an interactive session (`-ti`) and then executes the `hostname` command via /bin/bash inside the container. Since the `hostname` command is run inside the container's namespace, we get back the short container ID, which is used as the hostname by default. This is a pretty simple example, but it should clearly show that we're not in the same namespace as the host.

Another example that's easy to understand and demonstrate involves PID namespaces. Let's create a new container:

```
$ docker container run -d --rm --name pstest spkane/train-os sleep 240
6e005f895e259ed03c4386b5aeb03e0a50368cc173078007b6d1beaa8cd7dded

$ docker container exec -ti pstest ps -ef

UID        PID  PPID  C STIME TTY          TIME CMD
root         1     0  0 15:33 ?        00:00:00 sleep 240
root        13     0  0 15:33 pts/0    00:00:00 ps -ef
```

And now let's get Docker to show us the process IDs from the host's perspective:

```
$ docker container top pstest

UID    PID     PPID   C   STIME  TTY  TIME      CMD
root   31396   31370  0   15:33  ?    00:00:00  sleep 240
```

What we can see here is that from inside our container, the original command run by Docker is `sleep 240`, and it has been assigned PID 1 inside the container. You might recall that this is the PID normally used by the `init` process on Unix systems. In this case, the `sleep 240` command that we started the container with is the first process, so it gets PID 1. But in the Docker server's main namespace, we can see that the PID there is not 1 but 31396, and it's a child of process ID 31370.

If you are curious, you can run a command like this to determine what PID 31370 is:

```
$ docker container run --pid=host ubuntu ps -p 31370
PID    TTY  TIME      CMD
31370  ?    00:00:00  containerd-shim
```

Now we can go ahead and remove the container we started in the last example by running the following:

```
$ docker container rm -f pstest
```

The other namespaces work in essentially the same manner, and you probably get the idea by now. It's worth pointing out here that when we were first working with nsenter back in Chapter 3, we had to pass what appeared to be some pretty arcane arguments to the command when we ran it to enter a container from the Docker server. Let's go ahead and look at the nsenter portion of the command docker container run --rm -it --privileged --pid=host debian nsenter -t 1 -m -u -n -i sh.

It turns out that nsenter -t 1 -m -u -n -i sh is exactly the same as nsenter --target 1 --mount --uts --net -ipc sh. So this command really just says, look at PID 1 and then open up a shell in the same mount, uts, net, and ipc namespaces of that process.

Now that we've explained namespaces in detail, this probably makes a lot more sense to you. It can also be educational to use nsenter to try entering different sets of namespaces in a throwaway container to see what you get and simply explore how all of this works in some more detail.

When it comes down to it, namespaces are the primary things that make a container look like a container. Combine them with cgroups, and you have reasonably robust isolation between processes on the same kernel.

Security

We've spent a good bit of space now talking about how Docker provides containment for applications, allows you to constrain resource utilization, and uses namespaces to give the container a unique view of the world. We have also briefly mentioned the need for technologies like Secure Computing Mode, SELinux, and AppArmor. One of the advantages of containers is the ability to replace VMs in several use cases. So let's take a look at what isolation we get by default and what we don't.

You are undoubtedly aware by now that the isolation you get from a container is not as strong as that from a VM. We've been reinforcing the idea from the start of this book that containers are just processes running on the Linux server. Despite the isolation provided by namespaces, containers are not as secure as you might imagine, especially if you are still mentally comparing them to lightweight VMs.

One of the big boosts in performance for containers, and one of the things that makes them lightweight, is that they share the kernel of the Linux server. This is also the source of the greatest security concern around Linux containers. The main reason for this concern is that not everything in the kernel is namespaced. We have talked about all of the namespaces that exist and how the container's view of the world is constrained by the namespaces it runs in. However, there are still lots of places in the kernel where no real isolation exists, and namespaces constrain the container only if it does not have the power to tell the kernel to give it access to a different namespace.

Containerized applications are more secure than noncontainerized applications because cgroups and standard namespaces provide some important isolation from the host's core resources. But you should not think of containers as a substitute for good security practices. If you think about how you would run an application on a production system, that is really how you should run all your containers. If your application would traditionally run as a nonprivileged user on a server, then it should be run in the same manner inside the container. It is very easy to tell Docker to run your container processes as a nonprivileged user, and in almost all cases, this is what you should be doing.

The `--userns-remap` argument to the `dockerd` command and rootless mode both make it possible to force all containers to run within a user and group context that is unprivileged on the host system. These approaches help protect the host from many potential security exploits.

For more information about `userns-remap`, read through the official feature (*https://dockr.ly/2BYfWze*) and Docker daemon (*https://dockr.ly/2LE9gG2*) documentation.

You can learn more about rootless mode in the section "Rootless Mode" on page 308.

Let's look at some common security risks and controls.

UID 0

The first and most overarching security risk in a container is that, unless you are using rootless mode or the `userns-remap` functionality in the Docker daemon, the `root` user in the container is actually the `root` user on the system. There are extra constraints on `root` in a container, and namespaces do a good job of isolating `root` in the container from the most dangerous parts of the */proc* and */sys* filesystems. But if you are UID 0, you have `root` access, so if you somehow get access to protected resources on a file mount or outside of your namespace, then the kernel will treat you as `root` and therefore give you access to the resource. Unless otherwise configured, Docker starts all services in containers as `root`, which means you are responsible for managing privileges in your applications just like if you are on any standard Linux system. Let's explore some of the limits on `root` access and look at some obvious holes. This is not intended to be an exhaustive statement on container security but rather an attempt to give you a healthy understanding of some of the classes of security risks.

First, let's fire up a container and get a bash shell using the public Ubuntu image shown in the following code. Then we'll see what kinds of access we have, after installing some tools we want to run:

```
$ docker container run --rm -ti ubuntu /bin/bash

root@808a2b8426d1:/# apt-get update
…
root@808a2b8426d1:/# apt-get install -y kmod
…
root@808a2b8426d1:/# lsmod
Module                          Size   Used by
xfrm_user                       36864  1
xfrm_algo                       16384  1 xfrm_user
shiftfs                         28672  0
grpcfuse                        16384  0
vmw_vsock_virtio_transport      16384  2
vmw_vsock_virtio_transport_common 28672  1 vmw_vsock_virtio_transport
vsock                           36864  9 vmw_vsock_virtio_transport_common…
```

In Docker Desktop, you may only see a few modules in the list, but on a normal Linux system, this list can be very long. Using lsmod, we've just asked the kernel to tell us what modules are loaded. It is not that surprising that we get this list from inside our container, since a normal user can always do this. If you run this listing on the Docker server itself, it will be identical, which reinforces the fact that the container is talking to the same Linux kernel that is running on the server. So we can see the kernel modules; what happens if we try to unload the floppy module?

```
root@808a2b8426d1:/# rmmod shiftfs

rmmod: ERROR: ../libkmod/libkmod-module.c:799 kmod_module_remove_module() …
rmmod: ERROR: could not remove module shiftfs: Operation not permitted

root@808a2b8426d1:/# exit
```

That's the same error message we would get if we were a nonprivileged user trying to tell the kernel to remove a module. This should give you a good sense that the kernel is doing its best to prevent us from doing things we shouldn't. And because we're in a limited namespace, we can't get the kernel to give us access to the top-level namespace either. We are essentially relying on the hope that there are no bugs in the kernel that allow us to escalate our privileges inside the container. Because if we do manage to do that, we are root, which means that we will be able to make changes if the kernel allows us to.

We can contrive a simple example of how things can go wrong by starting a bash shell in a container that has had the Docker server's /etc bind-mounted into the container's namespace. Keep in mind that anyone who can start a container on your Docker server can do what we're about to do any time they like because you can't configure Docker to prevent it, so you must instead rely on external tools like SELinux to avoid exploits like this.

This example assumes that you are running the docker CLI on a Linux system, which has an */etc/shadow* file. This file will not exist on Windows or macOS hosts running something like Docker Desktop.

```
$ docker container run --rm -it -v /etc:/host_etc ubuntu /bin/bash

root@e674eb96bb74:/# more /host_etc/shadow
root:!:16230:0:99999:7:::
daemon:*:16230:0:99999:7:::
bin:*:16230:0:99999:7:::
sys:*:16230:0:99999:7:::
…
irc:*:16230:0:99999:7:::
nobody:*:16230:0:99999:7:::
libuuid:!:16230:0:99999:7:::
syslog:*:16230:0:99999:7:::
messagebus:*:16230:0:99999:7:::
kmatthias:$1$aTAYQT.j$3xamPL3dHGow4ITBdRh1:16230:0:99999:7:::
sshd:*:16230:0:99999:7:::
lxc-dnsmasq:!:16458:0:99999:7:::

root@e674eb96bb74:/# exit
```

Here we've used the -v switch to tell Docker to mount a host path into the container. The one we've chosen is */etc*, which is a very dangerous thing to do. But it serves to prove a point: we are root in the container, and root has file permissions in this path. So we can look at the */etc/shadow* file on the Linux server, which contains the encrypted passwords for all the users. There are plenty of other things you could do here, but the point is that by default you're only partly constrained.

It is a bad idea to run your container processes with UID 0. This is because any exploit that allows the process to somehow escape its namespaces will expose your host system to a fully privileged process. You should always run your standard containers with a nonprivileged UID.

The easiest way to deal with the potential problems surrounding the use of UID 0 inside containers is to always tell Docker to use a different UID for your container.

You can do this by passing the -u argument to docker container run. In the next example, we run the whoami command to show that we are root by default and that we can read the /etc/shadow file that is inside this container:

```
$ docker container run --rm spkane/train-os:latest whoami
root

$ docker container run --rm spkane/train-os:latest cat /etc/shadow
root:!locked::0:99999:7:::
bin:*:18656:0:99999:7:::
daemon:*:18656:0:99999:7:::
adm:*:18656:0:99999:7:::
lp:*:18656:0:99999:7:::
...
```

In this example, when you add -u 500, you will see that we become a new, unprivileged user and can no longer read the same /etc/shadow file:

```
$ docker container run --rm -u 500 spkane/train-os:latest whoami
user500

$ docker container run --rm -u 500 spkane/train-os:latest cat /etc/shadow
cat: /etc/shadow: Permission denied
```

Another highly recommended approach is to add the USER directive to your *Dockerfiles* so that containers created from them will launch using a nonprivileged user by default:

```
FROM fedora:34
RUN useradd -u 500 -m myuser
USER 500:500
CMD ["whoami"]
```

If you create this *Dockerfile*, and then build and run it, you will see that whoami returns myuser instead of root:

```
$ docker image build -t user-test .

[+] Building 0.5s (6/6) FINISHED
 => [internal] load build definition from Dockerfile              0.0s
 => => transferring dockerfile: 36B                               0.0s
 => [internal] load .dockerignore                                 0.0s
 => => transferring context: 2B                                   0.0s
 => [internal] load metadata for docker.io/library/fedora:34      0.4s
 => [1/2] FROM docker.io/library/fedora:34@sha256:321d…2697       0.0s
 => CACHED [2/2] RUN useradd -u 500 -m myuser                     0.0s
 => exporting to image                                            0.0s
 => => exporting layers                                           0.0s
 => => writing image sha256:4727…30d5                             0.0s
 => => naming to docker.io/library/user-test                      0.0s

$ docker container run --rm user-test
myuser
```

Rootless Mode

One of the primary security challenges with containers is that they often require some root-privileged processes to launch and manage them. Even when you use the --userns-remap feature of the Docker daemon, the daemon itself still runs as a privileged process, even though the containers that it launches will not.

With rootless mode (*https://docs.docker.com/engine/security/rootless*), it is possible to run the daemon and all containers without root privileges, which can do a great deal to improve the security of the underlying system.

Rootless mode requires a Linux system, and Docker recommends Ubuntu, so let's run through an example using a new Ubuntu 22.04 system.

These steps assume that you are logging in a regular unprivileged user and that you already have Docker Engine installed (*https:// docs.docker.com/engine/install/ubuntu*).

The first thing we need to do is make sure that dbus-user-session and uidmap are installed. If dbus-user-session isn't already installed, then we need to log out and log back in after running the following command:

```
$ sudo apt-get install -y dbus-user-session uidmap
…
dbus-user-session is already the newest version (1.12.20-2ubuntu4).
…
Setting up uidmap (1:4.8.1-2ubuntu2) …
…
```

Although, it is not strictly required, if the system-wide Docker daemon is set up to run, it is a very good idea to disable it and then reboot:

```
$ sudo systemctl disable --now docker.service docker.socket

Synchronizing state of docker.service with SysV service script with
  /lib/systemd/systemd-sysv-install.
Executing: /lib/systemd/systemd-sysv-install disable docker
Removed /etc/systemd/system/sockets.target.wants/docker.socket.
Removed /etc/systemd/system/multi-user.target.wants/docker.service.

$ sudo shutdown -r now
```

Once the system is back up, you can SSH back into the server as a regular user and confirm that */var/run/docker.sock* is no longer on the system:

```
$ ls /var/run/docker.sock
ls: cannot access '/var/run/docker.sock': No such file or directory
```

The next step is to run the rootless mode installation script, which is installed in */usr/bin* by the Docker installer:

```
$ dockerd-rootless-setuptool.sh install

[INFO] Creating /home/me/.config/systemd/user/docker.service
[INFO] starting systemd service docker.service
+ systemctl --user start docker.service
+ sleep 3
+ systemctl --user --no-pager --full status docker.service
● docker.service - Docker Application Container Engine (Rootless)
     Loaded: loaded (/home/me/.config/systemd/user/docker.service; …)
…
+ DOCKER_HOST=unix:///run/user/1000/docker.sock /usr/bin/docker version
Client: Docker Engine - Community
 Version:          20.10.18
…
Server: Docker Engine - Community
 Engine:
  Version:         20.10.18
…
+ systemctl --user enable docker.service
Created symlink /home/me/.config/systemd/user/default.target.wants/
  docker.service → /home/me/.config/systemd/user/docker.service.
[INFO] Installed docker.service successfully.

[INFO] To control docker.service, run:
        `systemctl --user (start|stop|restart) docker.service`
[INFO] To run docker.service on system startup, run:
        `sudo loginctl enable-linger me`

[INFO] Creating CLI context "rootless"
Successfully created context "rootless"

[INFO] Make sure the following environment variables are set
       (or add them to ~/.bashrc):
export PATH=/usr/bin:$PATH
export DOCKER_HOST=unix:///run/user/1000/docker.sock
```

 The UID` in the DOCKER_HOST` variable here should match the UID of the user who ran the script. In this case, the UID is 1000.

This script ran a few checks to ensure that our system was ready and then installed and started a user-scoped systemd service file into ${HOME}/.config/systemd/user/docker.service. Each and every user on the system could do the same thing, if desired.

The user Docker daemon can be controlled, like most `systemd` services. A few basic examples are shown here:

```
$ systemctl --user restart docker.service
$ systemctl --user stop docker.service
$ systemctl --user start docker.service
```

To allow the user Docker daemon to run when the user is not logged in, the user needs to use `sudo` to enable a `systemd` feature called `linger`, and then you can also enable the Docker daemon to start whenever the system boots up:

```
$ sudo loginctl enable-linger $(whoami)
$ systemctl --user enable docker
```

This would be a good time to go ahead and add those environment variables to our shell startup files, but at a minimum we need to make sure both of these environment variables are set in our current terminal:

```
$ export PATH=/usr/bin:$PATH
$ export DOCKER_HOST=unix:///run/user/1000/docker.sock
```

We can easily run a standard container:

```
$ docker container run --rm hello-world

Hello from Docker!
This message shows that your installation appears to be working correctly.
...
For more examples and ideas, visit:
 https://docs.docker.com/get-started/
```

However, you will notice that some of the more privileged containers that we have used in earlier sections will not work in this environment:

```
$ docker container run --rm -it --privileged --pid=host debian nsenter \
    -t 1 -m -u -n -i sh

docker: Error response from daemon: failed to create shim task: OCI runtime
create failed: runc create failed: unable to start container process: error
during container init: error mounting "proc" to rootfs at "/proc":
mount proc:/proc (via /proc/self/fd/7), flags: 0xe:
operation not permitted: unknown.
```

And this is because, in rootless mode, the container cannot have more privileges than the user who is running the container, even though, on the surface, the container appears to still have full root privileges:

```
$ docker container run --rm spkane/train-os:latest whoami
root
```

Let's explore this just a little bit more by launching a small container that is running `sleep 480s`:

```
$ docker container run -d --rm --name sleep spkane/train-os:latest sleep 480s
1f8ccec0a834537da20c6e07423f9217efe34c0eac94f0b0e178fb97612341ef
```

If we look at the processes inside the container, we see that they all appear to be running with the user `root`:

```
$ docker container exec sleep ps auxwww
USER        PID %CPU %MEM    VSZ   RSS TTY      STAT START   TIME COMMAND
root          1  0.1  0.0   2400   824 ?        Ss   17:51   0:00 sleep 480s
root          7  0.0  0.0   7780  3316 ?        Rs   17:51   0:00 ps auxwww
```

However, if we look at the processes on the Linux system, we see that the `sleep` command is actually being run by the local user, named me, and not by `root` at all:

```
$ ps auxwww | grep sleep
me    3509 0.0 0.0  2400   824 ?       Ss 10:51 0:00 sleep 480s
me    3569 0.0 0.0 17732  2360 pts/0   S+ 10:51 0:00 grep --color=auto sleep
```

The `root` user inside a rootless container is actually mapped to the user themself. The container processes cannot use any privileges that the user running the daemon does not already have, and because of this, they are a very safe way to allow users on a multiuser system to run containers without granting any of them elevated privileges on the system.

 There are directions to uninstall rootless mode (*https://docs.docker.com/engine/security/rootless/#uninstall*) on the Docker website.

Privileged Containers

There are times when you need your container to have special kernel capabilities (*https://man7.org/linux/man-pages/man7/capabilities.7.html*) that would normally be denied to the container. These could include mounting a USB drive, modifying the network configuration, or creating a new Unix device.

In the following code, we try to change the MAC address of our container:

```
$ docker container run --rm -ti spkane/train-os /bin/bash

[root@280d4dc16407 /]# ip link ls
1: lo: <LOOPBACK,UP,LOWER_UP> mtu 65536 qdisc noqueue state UNKNOWN mode …
    link/loopback 00:00:00:00:00:00 brd 00:00:00:00:00:00
2: tunl0@NONE: <NOARP> mtu 1480 qdisc noop state DOWN mode DEFAULT …
    link/ipip 0.0.0.0 brd 0.0.0.0
3: ip6tnl0@NONE: <NOARP> mtu 1452 qdisc noop state DOWN mode DEFAULT …
    link/tunnel6 :: brd :: permaddr 12b5:6f1b:a7e9::
```

```
22: eth0@if23: <BROADCAST,MULTICAST,UP,LOWER_UP> mtu 1500 qdisc noqueue …
    link/ether 02:42:ac:11:00:02 brd ff:ff:ff:ff:ff:ff link-netnsid 0

[root@fc4589fb8778 /]# ip link set eth0 address 02:0a:03:0b:04:0c
RTNETLINK answers: Operation not permitted

[root@280d4dc16407 /]# exit
```

As you can see, it doesn't work. This is because the underlying Linux kernel blocks the nonprivileged container from doing this, which is exactly what we'd normally want. However, assuming that we need this functionality for our container to work as intended, the easiest way to significantly expand a container's privileges is by launching it with the --privileged=true argument.

 We don't recommend running the ip link set eth0 address command in the next example, since this will change the MAC address on the container's network interface. We show it to help you understand the mechanism. Try it at your own risk.

```
$ docker container run -ti --rm --privileged=true spkane/train-os /bin/bash

[root@853e0ef5dd63 /]# ip link ls
1: lo: <LOOPBACK,UP,LOWER_UP> mtu 65536 qdisc noqueue state UNKNOWN mode …
    link/loopback 00:00:00:00:00:00 brd 00:00:00:00:00:00
2: tunl0@NONE: <NOARP> mtu 1480 qdisc noop state DOWN mode DEFAULT …
    link/ipip 0.0.0.0 brd 0.0.0.0
3: ip6tnl0@NONE: <NOARP> mtu 1452 qdisc noop state DOWN mode DEFAULT …
    link/tunnel6 :: brd :: permaddr 12b5:6f1b:a7e9::
22: eth0@if23: <BROADCAST,MULTICAST,UP,LOWER_UP> mtu 1500 qdisc noqueue …
    link/ether 02:42:ac:11:00:02 brd ff:ff:ff:ff:ff:ff link-netnsid 0

[root@853e0ef5dd63 /]# ip link set eth0 address 02:0a:03:0b:04:0c

[root@853e0ef5dd63 /]#  ip link show eth0
26: eth0@if27: <BROADCAST,MULTICAST,UP,LOWER_UP> mtu 1500 qdisc noqueue …
    link/ether 02:0a:03:0b:04:0c brd ff:ff:ff:ff:ff:ff link-netnsid 0

[root@853e0ef5dd63 /]# exit
```

In the preceding output, you will notice that we no longer get the error, and the link/ether entry for eth0 has been changed.

The problem with using the --privileged=true argument is that you are giving your container very broad privileges, and in most cases, you likely need only one or two kernel capabilities to get the job done.

If we explore our privileged container some more, we will discover that we have capabilities that have nothing to do with changing the MAC address. We can even do things that could cause issues with both Docker and the host system. In the following code, we are going to mount a disk partition from the underlying host system, list all of the underlying Docker-based Linux containers on the system, and explore some of their critical files:

```
$ docker container run -ti --rm --privileged=true spkane/train-os /bin/bash

[root@664a896983d7 /]# mount /dev/vda1 /mnt && \
                        ls -F /mnt/docker/containers | \
                        head -n 10

047df420f6d1f227a26667f83e477f608298c25b0cdad2e149a781587aae5e11/
0888b9f97b1ecc4261f637404e0adcc8ef0c8df291b87c9160426e42dc9b5dea/
174ea3ec35cd3a576bed6f475b477b1a474d897ece15acfc46e61685abb3101d/
1eddad26ee64c4b29eb164b71d56d680739922b3538dc8aa6c6966fce61125b0/
22b2aa38a687f423522dd174fdd85d578eb21c9c8ec154a0f9b8411d08f6fd4b/
23879e3b9cd6a42a1e09dc8e96912ad66e80ec09949c744d1177a911322e7462/
266fe7da627d2e8ec5429140487e984c8d5d36a26bb3cc36a88295e38216e8a7/
2cb6223e115c12ae729d968db0d2f29a934b4724f0c9536e377e0dbd566f1102/
306f00e86122b69eeba9323415532a12f88360a1661f445fc7d64c07249eb0ce/
333b85236409f873d07cd47f62ec1a987df59f688a201df744f40f98b7e4ef2c/

[root@664a896983d7 /]# ls -F /mnt/docker/containers/047d…5e11/

047df420f6d1f227a26667f83e477f608298c25b0cdad2e149a781587aae5e11-json.log
checkpoints/
config.v2.json
hostconfig.json
hostname
hosts
mounts/
resolv.conf
resolv.conf.hash

[root@664a896983d7 /]# cat /mnt/docker/containers/047d…5e11/047…e11-json.log

{"log":"047df420f6d1\r\n","stream":"stdout","time":"2022-09-14T15:18:29.…"}
…

[root@664a896983d7 /]# exit
```

 Do not change or delete any of these files. It could have an unpredictable impact on the containers or the underlying Linux system.

So, as we've seen, people can run commands and get access to things that they shouldn't from a fully privileged container.

To change the MAC address, the only kernel capability we need is CAP_NET_ADMIN. Instead of giving our container the full set of privileges, we can give it this one privilege by launching our Linux container with the --cap-add argument, as shown here:

```
$ docker container run -ti --rm --cap-add=NET_ADMIN spkane/train-os /bin/bash

[root@087c02a3c6e7 /]# ip link show eth0
36: eth0@if37: <BROADCAST,MULTICAST,UP,LOWER_UP> mtu 1500 qdisc noqueue …
    link/ether 02:42:ac:11:00:02 brd ff:ff:ff:ff:ff:ff link-netnsid 0

[root@087c02a3c6e7 /]# ip link set eth0 address 02:0a:03:0b:04:0c

[root@087c02a3c6e7 /]# ip link show eth0
36: eth0@if37: <BROADCAST,MULTICAST,UP,LOWER_UP> mtu 1500 qdisc noqueue …
    link/ether 02:0a:03:0b:04:0c brd ff:ff:ff:ff:ff:ff link-netnsid 0

[root@087c02a3c6e7 /]# exit
```

You should also notice that although we can change the MAC address, we can no longer use the mount command inside our container:

```
$ docker container run -ti --rm --cap-add=NET_ADMIN spkane/train-os /bin/bash

[root@b84a06ddaa0d /]# mount /dev/vda1 /mnt
mount: /mnt: permission denied.

[root@b84a06ddaa0d /]# exit
```

It is also possible to remove specific capabilities from a container. Imagine for a moment that your security team requires that tcpdump be disabled in all containers, and when you test some of your containers, you find that tcpdump is installed and can easily be run:

```
$ docker container run -ti --rm spkane/train-os:latest tcpdump -i eth0

dropped privs to tcpdump
tcpdump: verbose output suppressed, use -v[v]… for full protocol decode
listening on eth0, link-type EN10MB (Ethernet), snapshot length 262144 bytes
15:40:49.847446 IP6 fe80::23:6cff:fed6:424f > ff02::16: HBH ICMP6, …
15:40:49.913977 ARP, Request who-has _gateway tell 5614703ffee2, length 28
15:40:49.914048 ARP, Request who-has _gateway tell 5614703ffee2, length 28
15:40:49.914051 ARP, Reply _gateway is-at 02:49:9b:d9:49:4e (oui Unknown), …
15:40:49.914053 IP 5642703bbff2.45432 > 192.168.75.8.domain: 44649+ PTR? …
…
```

You could remove tcpdump from your images, but there is very little preventing someone from reinstalling it. The most effective way to solve this problem is to determine what capability tcpdump needs to operate and remove that from the container. In this case, you can do so by adding --cap-drop=NET_RAW to your docker container run command:

```
$ docker container run -ti --rm --cap-drop=NET_RAW spkane/train-os:latest \
    tcpdump -i eth0

tcpdump: eth0: You don't have permission to capture on that device
(socket: Operation not permitted)
```

By using both the `--cap-add` and `--cap-drop` arguments to `docker container run`, you can finely control your container's Linux kernel capabilities (*https://man7.org/ linux/man-pages/man7/capabilities.7.html*).

Be aware that in addition to providing access to system calls, there are actually some other things that enabling a specific Linux capability can provide. This might include visibility of all the devices on the system or the ability to change the time on the system.

Secure Computing Mode

When Linux kernel version 2.6.12 was released in 2005, it included a new security feature called Secure Computing Mode, or `seccomp` for short. This feature enables a process to make a one-way transition into a special state, where it will only be allowed to make the system calls `exit()`, `sigreturn()`, and `read()` or `write()` to already-open file descriptors.

An extension to `seccomp`, called `seccomp-bpf`, utilizes the Linux version of Berkeley Packet Filter (BPF) (*https://www.kernel.org/doc/Documentation/networking/filter.txt*) rules to allow you to create a policy that will provide an explicit list of system calls that a process can utilize while running under Secure Computing Mode. The Docker support for Secure Computing Mode utilizes `seccomp-bpf` so that users can create profiles that give them very fine-grained control of which kernel system calls their containerized processes are allowed to make.

By default, all containers use Secure Computing Mode and have the default profile attached to them. You can read more about Secure Computing Mode (*https://docs.docker.com/engine/security/seccomp*) and which system calls the default profile blocks in the documentation. You can also examine the default policy's JSON file (*https://git hub.com/moby/moby/blob/master/profiles/seccomp/default.json*) to see what a policy looks like and understand exactly what it defines.

To see how you could use this, let's use the program `strace` to trace the system calls that a process is making when we try to unmount a filesystem with the `umount` command.

These examples are here to prove a point, but you obviously shouldn't be unmounting filesystems out of your container without knowing exactly what is going to happen.

```
$ docker container run -ti --rm spkane/train-os:latest umount /sys/fs/cgroup
umount: /sys/fs/cgroup: must be superuser to unmount.

$ docker container run -ti --rm spkane/train-os:latest \
  strace umount /sys/fs/cgroup

execve("/usr/bin/umount", ["umount", "/sys/fs/cgroup"], 0x7fff902ddbe8 …
…
umount2("/sys/fs/cgroup", 0)           = -1 EPERM (Operation not permitted)
write(2, "umount: ", 8umount: )          = 8
write(2, "/sys/fs/cgroup: must be superuse"...,
      45/sys/fs/cgroup: must be superuser to unmount.) = 45
write(2, "\n", 1
)                       = 1
dup(1)                        = 3
close(3)                      = 0
dup(2)                        = 3
close(3)                      = 0
exit_group(32)                = ?
+++ exited with 32 +++
```

We already know that mount-related commands do not work in a container with standard permissions, and strace makes it clear that the system returns an "Operation not permitted" error message when the umount command tries to use the umount2 system call.

You could potentially fix this by giving your container the SYS_ADMIN capability, like this:

```
$ docker container run -ti --rm --cap-add=SYS_ADMIN spkane/train-os:latest \
    strace umount /sys/fs/cgroup

execve("/usr/bin/umount", ["umount", "/sys/fs/cgroup"], 0x7ffd3e4452b8 …
…
umount2("/sys/fs/cgroup", 0)           = 0
dup(1)                        = 3
close(3)                      = 0
dup(2)                        = 3
close(3)                      = 0
exit_group(0)                 = ?
+++ exited with 0 +++
```

However, remember that using `--cap-add=SYS_ADMIN` will make it possible for us to do many other things, including mounting system partitions using a command like this:

```
$ docker container run -ti --rm --cap-add=SYS_ADMIN spkane/train-os:latest \
  mount /dev/vda1 /mnt
```

You can solve this problem with a more focused approach by using a `seccomp` profile. Unlike `seccomp`, `--cap-add` will enable a whole set of system calls and some additional privileges, and you almost certainly don't need them all. `CAP_SYS_ADMIN` is particularly powerful and provides way more privileges than any one capability should. With a `seccomp` profile, however, you can be very specific about exactly what system calls you want to be enabled or disabled.

If we take a look at the default `seccomp` profile, we'll see something like this:

```
{
    "defaultAction": "SCMP_ACT_ERRNO",
    "defaultErrnoRet": 1,
    "archMap": [
        {
            "architecture": "SCMP_ARCH_X86_64",
            "subArchitectures": [
                "SCMP_ARCH_X86",
                "SCMP_ARCH_X32"
            ]
        },
    …
    ],
    "syscalls": [
        {
            "names": [
                "accept",
                "accept4",
                "access",
                "adjtimex",
    …
                "waitid",
                "waitpid",
                "write",
                "writev"
            ],
            "action": "SCMP_ACT_ALLOW"
        },
        {
            "names": [
                "bpf",
                "clone",
    …
                "umount2",
                "unshare"
```

```
            ],
            "action": "SCMP_ACT_ALLOW",
            "includes": {
                "caps": [
                    "CAP_SYS_ADMIN"
                ]
            }
        },
    ...
    ]
}
```

This JSON file provides a list of supported architectures, a default ruleset, and groups of system calls that fall within the scope of each capability. In this case, the default action is SCMP_ACT_ERRNO and will generate an error if an unspecified call is attempted.

If you examine the default profile in detail, you'll notice that CAP_SYS_ADMIN controls access to 37 system calls, a huge number that is even larger than the 4-6 system calls included in most other capabilities.

In the current use case, we actually need some of the special functionality provided by CAP_SYS_ADMIN, but we do not need all of those system calls. To ensure that we are adding only the one additional system call that we need, we can create our own Secure Computing Mode policy, based on the default policy that Docker provides.

First, pull down the default policy and make a copy of it:

```
$ wget https://raw.githubusercontent.com/moby/moby/master/\
profiles/seccomp/default.json

$ cp default.json umount2.json
```

 The URL has been continued on the following line so that it fits in the margins. You may find that you need to reassemble the URL and remove the backslashes for the command to work properly in your environment.

Then edit the file and remove a bunch of the system calls that CAP_SYS_ADMIN normally provides. In this case, we actually need to retain two system calls to ensure that both strace and umount work correctly.

The section of the file that we are targeting ends with this JSON block:

```
            "includes": {
                "caps": [
                    "CAP_SYS_ADMIN"
                ]
            }
```

This `diff` shows the exact changes that need to be made in this use case:

```
$ diff -u -U5 default.json umount2.json

diff -u -U5 default.json umount2.json
--- default.json       2022-09-25 13:23:57.000000000 -0700
+++ umount2.json       2022-09-25 13:38:31.000000000 -0700
@@ -575,34 +575,12 @@
                               ]
                       }
               },
               {
                       "names": [
-                               "bpf",
                                "clone",
-                               "clone3",
                                "fanotify_init",
-                               "fsconfig",
-                               "fsmount",
-                               "fsopen",
-                               "fspick",
-                               "lookup_dcookie",
-                               "mount",
-                               "mount_setattr",
-                               "move_mount",
-                               "name_to_handle_at",
-                               "open_tree",
-                               "perf_event_open",
-                               "quotactl",
-                               "quotactl_fd",
-                               "setdomainname",
-                               "sethostname",
-                               "setns",
-                               "syslog",
-                               "umount",
-                               "umount2",
-                               "unshare"
+                               "umount2"
                       ],
                       "action": "SCMP_ACT_ALLOW",
                       "includes": {
                               "caps": [
                                       "CAP_SYS_ADMIN"
```

You are now ready to test your new finely tuned `seccomp` profile to ensure that it can run umount but cannot run mount:

```
$ docker container run -ti --rm --security-opt seccomp=umount2.json \
  --cap-add=SYS_ADMIN spkane/train-os:latest /bin/bash

[root@15b8a26b6cfe /]# strace umount /sys/fs/cgroup
execve("/usr/bin/umount", ["umount", "/sys/fs/cgroup"], 0x7ffece9ebc38 …
close(3)                                = 0
```

```
exit_group(0)                              = ?
+++ exited with 0 +++

[root@15b8a26b6cfe /]# mount /dev/vda1 /mnt
mount: /mnt: permission denied.

[root@15b8a26b6cfe /]# exit
```

If everything went according to plan, your `strace` of the `umount` program should have run perfectly and the `mount` command should have been blocked. In the real world, it would be much safer to consider redesigning your applications so that they do not need these special privileges, but when it cannot be avoided, you should be able to use these tools to help ensure that your containers remain as secure as possible while still doing their jobs.

 You could completely disable the default Secure Computing Mode profile by setting `--security-opt seccomp=unconfined`; however, running a container unconfined is a very bad idea in general and is probably only useful when you are trying to figure out exactly what system calls you may need to define in your profile.

The strength of Secure Computing Mode is that it allows users to be much more selective about what a container can and can't do with the underlying Linux kernel. Custom profiles are not required for most containers, but they are an incredibly handy tool when you need to carefully craft a powerful container and ensure that you maintain the overall security of the system.

SELinux and AppArmor

Earlier, we talked about how containers primarily leverage cgroups and namespaces for their functionality. SELinux (*https://www.redhat.com/en/topics/linux/what-is-selinux*) and AppArmor (*https://apparmor.net*) are security layers in the Linux ecosystem that can be used to increase the security of containers even further. In this section, we are going to discuss these two systems a bit. SELinux and AppArmor allow you to apply security controls that extend beyond those normally supported by Unix systems. SELinux originated in the US National Security Agency, was strongly adopted by Red Hat, and supports very fine-grained control. AppArmor is an effort to achieve many of the same goals while being a bit more user-friendly than SELinux.

By default, Docker ships with reasonable profiles enabled on platforms that support either of these systems. You can further configure these profiles to enable or prevent all sorts of features, and if you're running Docker in production, you should do a risk analysis to determine if there are additional considerations that you should be aware of. We'll give a quick outline of the benefits you are getting from these systems.

Both systems provide *mandatory access control*, a class of security system where a systemwide security policy grants users (or "initiators") access to a resource (or "target"). This allows you to prevent anyone, including root, from accessing a part of the system that they should not have access to. You can apply the policy to a whole container so that all processes are constrained. Many chapters would be required to provide a clear and detailed overview of how to configure these systems. The default profiles are performing tasks like blocking access to parts of the */proc* and */sys* filesystems that would be dangerous to expose in the container, even though they show up in the container's namespace. The default profiles also provide more narrowly scoped mount access to prevent containers from getting hold of mount points they should not see.

If you are considering using Linux containers in production, it is worth seriously considering going through the effort to enable AppArmor or SELinux on these systems. For the most part, both systems are reasonably equivalent. But in the Docker context, one notable limitation of SELinux is that it only works fully on systems that support filesystem metadata, which means that it won't work with all Docker storage drivers. AppArmor, on the other hand, does not use filesystem metadata and therefore works on all of the Docker backends. Which one you use is somewhat distribution-centric, so you may be forced to choose a filesystem backend that also supports the security system that you use.

The Docker Daemon

From a security standpoint, the Docker daemon and its components are the only completely new risk you are introducing to your infrastructure. Your containerized applications are not any less secure and are, at least, a little more secure than they would be if deployed outside of containers. But without the containers, you would not be running dockerd, the Docker daemon. You can run Docker such that it doesn't expose any ports on the network. This is highly recommended and the default for most Docker installations.

The default configuration for Docker, on most distributions, leaves Docker isolated from the network with only a local Unix socket exposed. Since you cannot remotely administer Docker when it is set up this way, it is not uncommon to see people simply add the nonencrypted port 2375 to the configuration. This may be great for getting started with Docker, but it is not what you should do in any environment where you care about the security of your systems. You should not open Docker up to the outside world at all unless you have a very good reason to. If you do, you should also commit to properly securing it. Most scheduler systems run their services on each node and expect to talk to Docker over the Unix domain socket instead of over a network port.

If you do need to expose the daemon to the network, you can do a few things to tighten Docker down in a way that makes sense in most production environments. But no matter what you do, you are relying on the Docker daemon itself to be resilient against threats like buffer overflows and race conditions, two of the more common classes of security vulnerabilities. This is true of any network service. The risk is a lot higher with the Docker daemon because it is normally run as root, it can run anything on your system, and it has no integrated role-based access controls.

The basics of locking Docker down are common with many other network daemons: encrypt your traffic and authenticate users. The first is reasonably easy to set up on Docker; the second is not as easy. If you have SSL certificates you can use for protecting HTTP traffic to your hosts, such as a wildcard certificate for your domain, you can turn on TLS support to encrypt all of the traffic to your Docker servers, using port 2376. This is a good first step. The Docker documentation (*https://docs.docker.com/engine/security/protect-access*) will walk you through doing this.

Authenticating users is more complicated. Docker does not provide any kind of fine-grained authorization: you either have access or you don't. But the authentication control it does provide—signed certificates—is reasonably strong. Unfortunately, this also means that you don't get a cheap step from no authentication to some authentication without also having to set up a certificate authority in most cases. If your organization already has one, then you are in luck. Certificate management needs to be implemented carefully in any organization, both to keep certificates secure and to distribute them efficiently. So, given that, here are the basic steps:

1. Set up a method of generating and signing certificates.
2. Generate certificates for the server and clients.
3. Configure Docker to require certificates with --tlsverify.

Detailed instructions on getting a server and client set up, as well as a simple certificate authority, are included in the Docker documentation (*https://docs.docker.com/engine/security/protect-access*).

 Because it's a daemon that almost always runs with privilege, and because it has direct control of your applications, it is a bad idea to expose Docker directly on the internet. If you need to talk to your Docker hosts from outside your network, consider something like a VPN or an SSH tunnel to a secure jump host.

Advanced Configuration

Docker has a very clean external interface, and on the surface, it looks pretty monolithic. But there are actually a lot of things going on behind the scenes that are configurable, and the logging backends we described in "Logging" on page 150 are a good example. You can also do things like change out the storage backend for container images for the whole daemon, use a completely different runtime, or configure individual containers to run on a different network configuration. Those are powerful switches, and you'll want to know what they do before turning them on. First, we'll talk about the network configuration, then we'll cover the storage backends, and finally, we'll try out a completely different container runtime to replace the default runc supplied with Docker.

Networking

Early on, we described the layers of networking between a Linux container and the real, live network. Let's take a closer look at how that works. Docker supports a rich set of network configurations, but let's start with the default setup. Figure 11-1 shows a drawing of a typical Docker server, where three containers are running on their private network, shown on the right. One of them has a public port (TCP port 10520) that is exposed on the Docker server. We'll track how an inbound request gets to the Linux container and also how a Linux container can make an outbound connection to the external network.

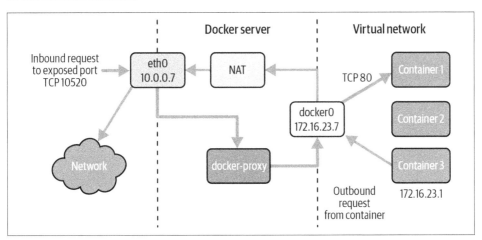

Figure 11-1. The network on a typical Docker server

If we have a client somewhere on the network that wants to talk to the nginx server running on TCP port 80 inside Container 1, the request will come into the eth0 interface on the Docker server. Because Docker knows this is a public port, it has spun up an instance of docker-proxy to listen on port 10520. So our request is passed to the docker-proxy process, which then forwards the request to the correct container address and port on the private network. Return traffic from the request flows through the same route.

Outbound traffic from the container follows a different route in which the docker-proxy is not involved at all. In this case, Container 3 wants to contact a server on the public internet. It has an address on the private network of 172.16.23.1, and its default route is the docker0 interface 172.16.23.7. So it sends the traffic there. The Docker server now sees that this traffic is outbound and that it has traffic forwarding enabled. And since the virtual network is private, it wants to send the traffic from its public address instead. So the request is passed through the kernel's network address translation (NAT) layer and put onto the external network via the eth0 interface on the server. Return traffic passes through the same route. The NAT is one-way, so containers on the virtual network will see real network addresses in response packets.

You've probably noticed that it's not a simple configuration. It's a fair amount of complexity, but it makes Docker seem pretty transparent. It also contributes to the security posture of the Docker stack because the containers are namespaced into individual network namespaces, are on individual private networks, and don't have access to things like the main system's DBus (Desktop Bus) or iptables.

Let's examine what's happening at a more detailed level. The interfaces that show up in ifconfig or ip addr show in the Linux container are actually virtual Ethernet interfaces on the Docker server's kernel. They are then mapped into the container's network namespace and given the names that you see inside the container. Let's take a look at what we might see when running ip addr show on a Docker server. We'll shorten the output a little for clarity and spaces, as shown here:

```
$ ip addr show

1: lo: <LOOPBACK,UP,LOWER_UP> mtu 65536 qdisc noqueue state UNKNOWN group …
    link/loopback 00:00:00:00:00:00 brd 00:00:00:00:00:00
    inet 127.0.0.1/8 brd 127.255.255.255 scope host lo
       valid_lft forever preferred_lft forever
    inet6 ::1/128 scope host
       valid_lft forever preferred_lft forever
2: eth0: <BROADCAST,MULTICAST,UP,LOWER_UP> mtu 1500 qdisc pfifo_fast state …
    link/ether 02:50:00:00:00:01 brd ff:ff:ff:ff:ff:ff
    inet 172.16.168.178/24 brd 192.168.65.255 scope global dynamic …
       valid_lft 4908sec preferred_lft 3468sec
    inet6 fe80::50:ff:fe00:1/64 scope link
       valid_lft forever preferred_lft forever
    …
7: docker0: <BROADCAST,MULTICAST,UP,LOWER_UP> mtu 1500 qdisc noqueue …
    link/ether 02:42:9c:d2:89:4f brd ff:ff:ff:ff:ff:ff
    inet 172.17.42.1/16brd 172.17.255.255 scope global docker0
       valid_lft forever preferred_lft forever
    inet6 fe80::42:9cff:fed2:894f/64 scope link
```

```
        valid_lft forever preferred_lft forever
...
185: veth772de2a@if184: <BROADCAST,MULTICAST,UP,LOWER_UP> mtu 1500 qdisc …
    link/ether 9a:a9:24:b7:5a:31 brd ff:ff:ff:ff:ff:ff link-netnsid 1
    inet6 fe80::98a9:24ff:feb7:5a31/64 scope link
        valid_lft forever preferred_lft forever
```

What this tells us is that we have the normal loopback interface, our real Ethernet interface eth0, and then the Docker bridge interface, docker0, that we described earlier. This is where all the traffic from the Linux containers is picked up to be routed outside the virtual network. The surprising thing in this output is the veth772de2a interface. When Docker creates a container, it creates two virtual interfaces, one of which sits on the server side and is attached to the docker0 bridge, and one that is attached to the container's namespace. What we're seeing here is the server-side interface. Did you notice how it doesn't show up as having an IP address assigned to it? That's because this interface is just joined to the bridge. This interface will have a different name in the container's namespace as well.

As with so many pieces of Docker, you can replace the proxy with a different implementation. To do so, you would use the --userland-proxy-path=<path> setting, but there are probably not that many good reasons to do this unless you have a very specialized network. However, the --userland-proxy=false flag to dockerd will completely disable the userland-proxy and instead rely on hairpin NAT (*https:// www.geeksforgeeks.org/network-address-translation-nat*) functionality to route traffic between local containers. If you need higher-throughput services, this might be right for you.

A hairpin NAT is typically used to describe services inside a NATed network that address one another with their public IP addresses. This causes traffic from the source service to route out to the internet, hit the external interface for the NAT router, and then get routed back into the original network to the destination service. The traffic is shaped like the letter U or a standard hairpin.

Host networking

As we've noted, there is a lot of complexity involved in the default implementation. You can, however, run a container without the whole networking configuration that Docker puts in place for you. And the docker-proxy can also limit the throughput for very high-volume data services by requiring all the network traffic to pass through the docker-proxy process before being received by the container. So what does it look like if we turn off the Docker network layer? Since the beginning, Docker has let you do this on a per-container basis with the --net=host command-line switch. There are times, like when you want to run high-throughput applications, when you might want to do this. But you lose some of Docker's flexibility when you do. Let's examine how this mechanism works.

 Like others we discuss in this chapter, this is not a setting you should take lightly. It has operational and security implications that might be outside your tolerance level. It can be the right thing to do, but you should understand the consequences.

Let's start a container with `--net=host` and see what happens:

```
$ docker container run --rm -it --net=host spkane/train-os bash

[root@docker-desktop /]# docker container run --rm -it --net=host \
                       spkane/train-os ip addr show

1: lo: <LOOPBACK,UP,LOWER_UP> mtu 65536 qdisc noqueue state UNKNOWN group
                             default qlen 1000
    link/loopback 00:00:00:00:00:00 brd 00:00:00:00:00:00
    inet 127.0.0.1/8 brd 127.255.255.255 scope host lo
       valid_lft forever preferred_lft forever
    inet6 ::1/128 scope host
       valid_lft forever preferred_lft forever
2: eth0: <BROADCAST,MULTICAST,UP,LOWER_UP> mtu 1500 qdisc pfifo_fast
                                        state UP group default qlen 1000
    link/ether 02:50:00:00:00:01 brd ff:ff:ff:ff:ff:ff
    inet 192.168.65.3/24 brd 192.168.65.255 scope global dynamic
                                          noprefixroute eth0
       valid_lft 4282sec preferred_lft 2842sec
    inet6 fe80::50:ff:fe00:1/64 scope link
       valid_lft forever preferred_lft forever
…
7: docker0: <NO-CARRIER,BROADCAST,MULTICAST,UP> mtu 1500 qdisc noqueue
                                          state DOWN group default
    link/ether 02:42:9c:d2:89:4f brd ff:ff:ff:ff:ff:ff
    inet 172.17.0.1/16 brd 172.17.255.255 scope global docker0
       valid_lft forever preferred_lft forever
    inet6 fe80::42:9cff:fed2:894f/64 scope link
       valid_lft forever preferred_lft forever
8: br-340323d07310: <NO-CARRIER,BROADCAST,MULTICAST,UP> mtu 1500 qdisc
                                          noqueue state DOWN group default
    link/ether 02:42:56:24:42:b8 brd ff:ff:ff:ff:ff:ff
    inet 172.22.0.1/16 brd 172.22.255.255 scope global br-340323d07310
       valid_lft forever preferred_lft forever
11: br-01f7537b9475: <NO-CARRIER,BROADCAST,MULTICAST,UP> mtu 1500 qdisc
                                          noqueue state DOWN group default
    link/ether 02:42:ed:14:67:61 brd ff:ff:ff:ff:ff:ff
    inet 172.18.0.1/16 brd 172.18.255.255 scope global br-01f7537b9475
       valid_lft forever preferred_lft forever
    inet6 fc00:f853:ccd:e793::1/64 scope global
       valid_lft forever preferred_lft forever
```

```
    inet6 fe80::42:edff:fe14:6761/64 scope link
       valid_lft forever preferred_lft forever
    inet6 fe80::1/64 scope link
       valid_lft forever preferred_lft forever
```

That should look pretty familiar. That's because when we run a container with the host networking option, the container is running in both the host server's network and UTS namespaces. Our server's hostname is docker-desktop, and from the shell prompt, we can tell that our container has the same hostname:

```
[root@docker-desktop /]# hostname
docker-desktop
```

If we run the mount command to see what's mounted, though, we see that Docker is still maintaining our */etc/resolv.conf*, */etc/hosts*, and */etc/hostname* directories. And as expected, the */etc/hostname* directory simply contains the server's hostname:

```
[root@docker-desktop /]# mount

overlay on / type overlay (rw,relatime,lowerdir=/var/lib/docker/overlay2/…)
…
/dev/vda1 on /etc/resolv.conf type ext4 (rw,relatime)
/dev/vda1 on /etc/hostname type ext4 (rw,relatime)
/dev/vda1 on /etc/hosts type ext4 (rw,relatime)
…

[root@docker-desktop /]# cat /etc/hostname
docker-desktop
```

Just to prove that we can see all the normal networking on the Docker server, let's look at the output from ss to see if we can see the sockets that Docker is utilizing:

```
root@852d18f5c38d:/# ss | grep docker

u_str  ESTAB  0  0  /run/guest-services/docker.sock  18086  * 16860
…
u_str  ESTAB  0  0  /var/run/docker.sock             21430  * 21942
```

 If the Docker daemon was listening on a TCP port, like 2375, you could have looked for that as well. Feel free to look for another TCP port on your server port that you know is in use.

If you search for docker in the output of a normal container within its own namespace, you will notice that you get no results:

```
$ docker container run --rm -it spkane/train-os bash -c "ss | grep docker"
```

So we are indeed in the server's network namespace. What all of this means is that if we were to launch a high-throughput network service, we could expect network performance from it that is essentially native. But it also means we could try to bind to ports that would collide with those on the server, so if you do this, you should be careful about how you allocate port assignments.

Configuring networks

There is more to networking than just the default network or host networking, however. The docker network command lets you create multiple networks backed by different drivers. It also allows you to view and manipulate the Docker network layers and how they are attached to containers that are running on the system.

Listing the networks available from Docker's perspective is easily accomplished with the following command:

```
$ docker network ls

NETWORK ID      NAME      DRIVER    SCOPE
5840a6c23373    bridge    bridge    local
1c22b4582189    host      host      local
c128bfdbe003    none      null      local
```

You can then find out more details about any individual network by using the docker network inspect command along with the network ID:

```
$ docker network inspect 5840a6c23373

[
    {
        "Name": "bridge",
        "Id": "5840…fc94",
        "Created": "2022-09-23T01:21:55.697907958Z",
        "Scope": "local",
        "Driver": "bridge",
        "EnableIPv6": false,
        "IPAM": {
            "Driver": "default",
            "Options": null,
            "Config": [
                {
                    "Subnet": "172.17.0.0/16",
                    "Gateway": "172.17.0.1"
                }
            ]
        },
        "Internal": false,
        "Attachable": false,
        "Ingress": false,
        "ConfigFrom": {
            "Network": ""
        },
        "ConfigOnly": false,
        "Containers": {},
```

```
      "Options": {
          "com.docker.network.bridge.default_bridge": "true",
          "com.docker.network.bridge.enable_icc": "true",
          "com.docker.network.bridge.enable_ip_masquerade": "true",
          "com.docker.network.bridge.host_binding_ipv4": "0.0.0.0",
          "com.docker.network.bridge.name": "docker0",
          "com.docker.network.driver.mtu": "1500"
      },
      "Labels": {}
  }
]
```

Docker networks can be created and removed, as well as attached and detached from individual containers, with the network subcommand.

So far, we've set up a bridged network, no Docker network, and a bridged network with hairpin NAT. There are a few other drivers that you can use to create different topologies using Docker as well, with the overlay and macvlan drivers being the most common. Let's take a brief look at what these can do for you:

overlay

This driver is used in Swarm mode to generate a network overlay between the Docker hosts, creating a private network between all the containers that run on top of the real network. This is useful for Swarm but not in scope for general use with non-Swarm containers.

macvlan

This driver creates a real MAC address for each of your containers and then exposes them on the network via the interface of your choice. This requires that you switch gears to support more than one MAC address per physical port on the switch. The result is that all the containers appear directly on the underlying network. When you're moving from a legacy system to a container-native one, this can be a really useful step. There are drawbacks here, such as making it harder when debugging to identify which host the traffic is really coming from, overflowing the MAC tables in your network switches, excessive ARPing by container hosts, and other underlying network issues. For this reason, the macvlan driver is not recommended unless you have a good understanding of your underlying network and can manage it effectively.

There are a few sets of configurations that are possible here, but the basic setup is easy to configure:

```
$ docker network create -d macvlan \
    --subnet=172.16.16.0/24 \
    --gateway=172.16.16.1 \
    -o parent=eth0 ourvlan

$ docker network ls
```

```
NETWORK ID      NAME            DRIVER      SCOPE
5840a6c23373    bridge          bridge      local
1c22b4582189    host            host        local
c128bfdbe003    none            null        local
8218c0ecc9e2    ourvlan         macvlan     local

$ docker network rm 8218c0ecc9e2
```

You can prevent Docker from allocating specific addresses by specifying them as named auxiliary addresses, `--aux-address="my-router=172.16.16.129"`.

There is a lot more you can configure with the Docker network layer. However, the defaults, host networking, and userland proxyless mode are the ones that you're most likely to use or encounter in the wild. Some of the other options you can configure include the container's DNS nameservers, resolver options, and default gateways, among other things. The networking section of the Docker documentation (*https://docs.docker.com/network*) gives an overview of how to do some of this configuration.

For advanced network configuration of Docker, check out Weave (*https://github.com/weaveworks/weave*)—a well-supported overlay network tool for spanning containers across multiple Docker hosts, similar to the `overlay` driver but much more configurable and without the Swarm requirement. Another offering is Project Calico (*https://www.tigera.io/project-calico*). If you're running Kubernetes, which has its own networking configuration, you might also want to familiarize yourself with the Container Network Interface (CNI) (*https://www.cni.dev*) and then look at Cilium (*https://cilium.io*), which provides robust eBPF-based networking for containers.

Storage

Backing all of the images and containers on your Docker server is a storage backend that handles reading and writing all of that data. Docker has some strenuous requirements on its storage backend: it has to support layering, the mechanism by which Docker tracks changes and reduces both how much disk a container occupies and how much is shipped over the wire to deploy new images. Using a copy-on-write strategy, Docker can start up a new container from an existing image without having to copy the whole image. The storage backend supports that. The storage backend is what makes it possible to export images as groups of changes in layers and also lets you save the state of a running container. In most cases, you need the kernel's help in doing this efficiently. That's because the filesystem view in your container is generally a union of all of the layers below it, which are not actually copied into your container. Instead, they are made visible to your container, and only when you make changes does anything get written to your container's filesystem. One place this layering mechanism is exposed to you is when you upload or download a new image from a registry like Docker Hub. The Docker daemon will push or pull each layer separately, and if some of the layers are the same as others it has already stored, it will use the cached layer instead. In the case of a push to a registry, it will sometimes even tell you which image they are mounted from.

Docker relies on an array of possible kernel drivers to handle the layering. The Docker codebase contains code that can handle interacting with many of these backends, and you can configure the decision about which to use on daemon restart. So let's look at what is available and some of the pluses and minuses of each.

Various backends have different limitations that may or may not make them your best option. In some cases, your choices of which backend to use are limited by what your distribution of Linux supports. Using the drivers that are built into the kernel shipped with your distribution will always be the easiest approach. It's generally best to stay close to the well-tested path. We've seen all manner of oddities from various backends since Docker's release. And, as usual, the common case is always the best-supported one. Different backends also report different statistics through the Docker Remote API (*/info* endpoint). This can be very useful for monitoring your Docker systems. However, not all backends are created equal, so let's see how they differ:

Overlay

Overlay (*https://www.kernel.org/doc/html/latest/filesystems/overlayfs.html*) (formerly OverlayFS) is a union filesystem where multiple layers are mounted together so that they appear as a single filesystem. The Overlay filesystem is the most recommended choice for Docker storage these days and works on most major distributions. If you are running on a Linux kernel older than 4.0 (or 3.10.0-693 for RHEL), then you won't be able to take advantage of this backend. The reliability and performance are good enough that it might be worth updating your OS for Docker hosts to support it, even if your company standard is an older distribution. The Overlay filesystem is part of the mainline Linux kernel and has become increasingly stable over time. Being in the mainline means that long-term support is virtually guaranteed, which is another nice advantage. Docker supports two versions of the Overlay backend, `overlay` and `overlay2`. As you might expect, you are strongly advised to use `overlay2` as it is faster, more efficient with inode usage, and more robust.

The Docker community is frequently improving support for a variety of filesystem backends. For more details about the supported filesystems, take a look at the official documentation (*https://docs.docker.com/storage/storagedriver*).

AuFS

Although at the time of this writing it is no longer recommended, `aufs` is the original backend for Docker. AuFS (Advanced multilayered unification filesystem) (*https://aufs.sourceforge.net*) is a union filesystem driver with reasonable support on various popular Linux distributions. It was never accepted into the mainline kernel, however, and this has limited its availability on various distributions. It is not supported on recent versions of Red Hat or Fedora, for example. It is not shipped in the standard Ubuntu distribution but is in the Ubuntu `linux-image-extra` package.

Its status as a second-class citizen in the kernel has led to the development of many of the other backends now available. If you are running an older distribution that supports AuFS, you might consider it, but you should upgrade to a kernel version that natively supports Overlay or Btrfs, which is discussed next.

Btrfs

B-Tree File System (Btrfs) (*https://btrfs.wiki.kernel.org/index.php/Main_Page*) is fundamentally a copy-on-write filesystem, which means it's a pretty good fit for the Docker image model. Like `aufs` and unlike `devicemapper`, Docker is using the backend in the way it was intended. That means it's both pretty stable in production and also a good performer. It scales reasonably to thousands of containers on the same system. A drawback for Red Hat–based systems is that Btrfs does not support SELinux. If you can use the `btrfs` backend, it is worth exploring another option, after the `overlay2` driver. One popular way to run `btrfs` backends for Linux containers without having to give over a whole volume to this filesystem is to make a Btrfs filesystem in a file and loopback-mount it with something like `mount -o loop file.btrs /mnt`. Using this method, you could build a 50 GB Linux container storage filesystem even on cloud-based systems without having to give over all your precious local storage to Btrfs.

Device Mapper

Originally written by Red Hat to support their distributions, which lacked AuFS in Docker's early days, Device Mapper became the default backend on all Red Hat–based distributions of Linux. Depending on the version of Red Hat Linux that you are using, this may be your only option. Device Mapper itself has been built into the Linux kernel for ages and is very stable. The way the Docker daemon uses it is a bit unconventional, though, and in the past, this backend was not that stable. This checkered past means that we recommend picking a different backend when possible. If your distribution supports only the `devicemapper` driver, then you will likely be fine. But it's worth considering using `overlay2` or `btrfs`. By default, `devicemapper` utilizes the `loop-lvm` mode, which has zero configuration and is very slow and generally only useful for development. If you decide to use the `devicemapper` driver, you must make sure it is configured to use `direct-lvm` mode for all nondevelopment environments.

> You can find out more about using the various `devicemap` `per` modes with Docker in the official documentation (*https:// docs.docker.com/storage/storagedriver/device-mapper-driver*). A 2014 blog article (*https://developers.redhat.com/blog/2014/09/30/ overview-storage-scalability-docker*) also provides some interesting history about the various Docker storage backends.

VFS

Of the supported drivers, the Virtual File System (`vfs`) driver is the simplest, and slowest, to start up. It doesn't actually support copy-on-write. Instead, it makes a new directory and copies over all of the existing data. It was originally intended for use in tests and for mounting host volumes. The `vfs` driver is very slow to create new containers, but runtime performance is native, which is a real benefit. Its mechanism is very simple, which means there is less to go wrong. Docker, Inc., does not recommend it for production use, so proceed with caution if you think it's the right solution for your production environment.

ZFS

ZFS, which was created by Sun Microsystems, is the most advanced open source filesystem available on Linux. Due to licensing restrictions, it does not ship in mainline Linux. However, the ZFS on Linux project (*https://zfsonlinux.org*) has made it pretty easy to install. Docker can then run on top of the ZFS filesystem and use its advanced copy-on-write facilities to implement layering. Given that ZFS is not in the mainline kernel and not available off the shelf in the major commercial distributions, going this route requires some extended effort. However, if you are already running ZFS in production, this may be your very best option.

> Storage backends can have a big impact on the performance of your containers. And if you swap the backend on your Docker server, all of your existing images will disappear. They are not gone, but they will not be visible until you switch the driver back. Caution is advised.

You can use `docker system info` to see which storage backend your system is running:

```
$ docker system info
…
 Storage Driver: overlay2
  Backing Filesystem: extfs
  Supports d_type: true
  Native Overlay Diff: true
  userxattr: false
…
```

As you can see, Docker will also tell you what the underlying or "backing" filesystem is if there is one. Since we're running `overlay2` here, we can see it's backed by an `ext` filesystem. In some cases, like with `devicemapper` on raw partitions or with `btrfs`, there won't be a different underlying filesystem.

Storage backends can be swapped via the `daemon-json` configuration file or via command-line arguments to `dockerd` on startup. If we wanted to switch our Ubuntu system from `aufs` to `devicemapper`, we could do so like this:

```
$ dockerd --storage-driver=devicemapper
```

That will work on pretty much any Linux system that can support Docker because `devicemapper` is almost always present. The same is true for `overlay2` on modern Linux kernels. However, you will need to have the actual underlying dependencies in place for the other drivers. For example, without `aufs` in the kernel—usually via a kernel module—Docker will not start up with `aufs` set as the storage driver, and the same is true for Btrfs or ZFS.

Getting the appropriate storage driver for your systems and deployment needs is one of the more important technical points to get right when you're taking Docker to production. Be conservative: make sure the path you choose is well supported in your kernel and distribution. Historically, this was a pain point, but most of the drivers have reached reasonable maturity. Remain cautious for any newly appearing backends, however, as this space continues to change. Getting new backend drivers to work reliably for production systems takes quite some time, in our experience.

nsenter

nsenter, which is short for "namespace enter," allows you to enter any Linux namespace and is part of the core `util-linux` package from kernel.org (*https://mirrors.edge.kernel.org/pub/linux/utils/util-linux*). Using `nsenter`, we can get into a Linux container from the server itself, even in situations where the `dockerd` server is not responding and we can't use `docker container exec`. It can also be used to manipulate things in a container as `root` on the server that would otherwise be prevented by docker container exec. This can be truly useful when you are debugging. Most of the time, docker container exec is all you need, but you should have nsenter in your tool belt.

Most Linux distributions ship with a new-enough util-linux package that it will contain nsenter. If you are on a distribution that does not have it, the easiest way to get hold of nsenter is to install it via the third-party Linux container (*https://github.com/jpetazzo/nsenter*).

This container works by pulling a Docker image from the Docker Hub registry and then running a Linux container that will install the nsenter command-line tool into */usr/local/bin*. This might seem strange at first, but it's a clever way to allow you to install nsenter to any Docker server remotely using nothing more than the docker command.

Unlike docker container exec, which can be run remotely, nsenter requires that you run it on the server itself, directly or via a container. For our purposes, we'll use a specially crafted container to run nsenter. As with the docker container exec example, we need to have a container running:

```
$ docker container run -d --rm  ubuntu:22.04 sleep 600
fd521174d66dc32650d165e0ce7dd97255c7b3624c34cb1d119d955284382ddf
```

docker container exec is pretty simple, but nsenter is a little inconvenient to use. It needs to have the PID of the actual top-level process in your container, which is not obvious to find. Let's go ahead and run nsenter by hand so you can see what's going on.

First, we need to find out the ID of the running container, because nsenter needs to know that to access it. We can easily get this using docker container ls:

```
$ docker container ls

CONTAINER ID   IMAGE         COMMAND        …   NAMES
fd521174d66d   ubuntu:22.04  "sleep 1000" …   angry_albattani
```

The ID we want is that first field, fd521174d66d. With that, we can now find the PID we need, like this:

```
$ docker container inspect --format \{{.State.Pid\}} fd521174d66d
2721
```

You can also get the real PIDs of the processes in your container by running the command docker container top, followed by the container ID. In our example, this would look like the following:

```
$ docker container top fd521174d66d

UID    PID   PPID  C  STIME  TTY  TIME      CMD
root   2721  2696  0  20:37  ?    00:00:00  sleep 600
```

Make sure to update the --target argument in the following command with the process ID that you got from the previous command, then go ahead and invoke nsenter:

```
$ docker container run --rm -it --privileged --pid=host debian \
    nsenter --target 2721 --all

# ps -ef

UID       PID  PPID  C STIME TTY          TIME CMD
root        1     0  0 20:37 ?        00:00:00 sleep 600
root       11     0  0 20:51 ?        00:00:00 -sh
root       15    11  0 20:51 ?        00:00:00 ps -ef
# exit
```

If the result looks a lot like docker container exec, that's because it does almost the same thing under the hood!

The command-line argument --all is telling nsenter that we want to enter all of the namespaces used by the process specified with --target.

Debugging Shell-less Containers

If you want to troubleshoot a container that does not have a Unix shell, then things get a little trickier, but it is still possible. For this example, we can run a container that has a single executable in it:

```
$ docker container run --rm -d --name outyet-small \
    --publish mode=ingress,published=8090,target=8080 \
    spkane/outyet:1.9.4-small
4f6de24d4c9c794c884afa758ef5b33ea38c01f8ec9314dcddd9fadc25c1a443
```

Let's take a quick look at the processes that are running in this container:

```
$ docker container top outyet-small

UID  PID    PPID  C STIME TTY TIME    CMD
root 61033 61008 0 22:43 ?   00:00:00 /outyet -version 1.9.4 -poll 600s …
```

If you try to launch a Unix shell in the container, you will get an error:

```
$ docker container exec -it outyet-small /bin/sh
```

```
OCI runtime exec failed: exec failed: unable to start container process: exec:
   "/bin/sh": stat /bin/sh: no such file or directory: unknown
```

We can then launch a second container that includes a shell and some other useful tools in a way that the new container can see the processes in the first container, is using the same network stack as the first container, and has some extra privileges which will be helpful for our debugging:

```
$ docker container run --rm -it --pid=container:outyet-small \
  --net=container:outyet-small --cap-add sys_ptrace \
  --cap-add sys_admin spkane/train-os /bin/sh

sh-5.1#
```

If you type ls in this container, you will see in the filesystem the spkane/train-os image, which contains /bin/sh and all of our debugging tools, but it does not contain any of the files from our outyet-small container:

```
sh-5.1# ls

bin   dev  home  lib64       media  opt   root  sbin  sys  usr
boot  etc  lib   lost+found  mnt    proc  run   srv   tmp  var
```

However, if you type ps -ef, you will notice that you see all of the processes from the original container. This is because we told Docker to attach to use the namespace from the outyet-small container by passing in --pid=container:outyet-small:

```
sh-5.1# ps -ef

UID  PID PPID C STIME TTY   TIME    CMD
root  1    0 0 22:43 ?      00:00:00 /outyet -version 1.9.4 -poll 600s …
root  29   0 0 22:47 pts/0 00:00:00 /bin/sh
root  36   29 0 22:49 pts/0 00:00:00 ps -ef
```

And because we are using the same network stack, you can even curl the port that the outyet service from the first container is bound to:

```
sh-5.1# curl localhost:8080

<!DOCTYPE html><html><body><center>
  <h2>Is Go 1.9.4 out yet?</h2>
  <h1>

    <a href="https://go.googlesource.com/go/&#43;/go1.9.4">YES!</a>

  </h1>
  <p>Hostname: 155914f7c6cd</p>
</center></body></html>
```

At this point, you could use strace or whatever else you wanted to debug your application, and then finally exit the new debug container, leaving your original container still running on the server.

If you run `strace`, you will need to type Ctrl-C to exit the `strace` process.

```
sh-5.1# strace -p 1

strace: Process 1 attached
futex(0x963698, FUTEX_WAIT, 0, NULL^Cstrace: Process 1 detached
 <detached …>

sh-5.1# exit
exit
```

You'll notice that we could not see the filesystem in this use case. If you need to view or copy files from the container, you can make use of the docker `container export` command to retrieve a tarball of the container's filesystem:

```
$ docker container export outyet-small -o export.tar
```

You can then use `tar` to view or extract the files:

```
$ tar -tvf export.tar

-rwxr-xr-x 0 0   0         0 Jul 17 16:04 .dockerenv
drwxr-xr-x 0 0   0         0 Jul 17 16:04 dev/
-rwxr-xr-x 0 0   0         0 Jul 17 16:04 dev/console
drwxr-xr-x 0 0   0         0 Jul 17 16:04 dev/pts/
drwxr-xr-x 0 0   0         0 Jul 17 16:04 dev/shm/
drwxr-xr-x 0 0   0         0 Jul 17 16:04 etc/
-rwxr-xr-x 0 0   0         0 Jul 17 16:04 etc/hostname
-rwxr-xr-x 0 0   0         0 Jul 17 16:04 etc/hosts
lrwxrwxrwx 0 0   0         0 Jul 17 16:04 etc/mtab -> /proc/mounts
-rwxr-xr-x 0 0   0         0 Jul 17 16:04 etc/resolv.conf
drwxr-xr-x 0 0   0         0 Apr 24  2021 etc/ssl/
drwxr-xr-x 0 0   0         0 Apr 24  2021 etc/ssl/certs/
-rw-r--r-- 0 0   0    261407 Mar 13  2018 etc/ssl/certs/ca-certificates.crt
-rwxr-xr-x 0 0   0   5640640 Apr 24  2021 outyet
drwxr-xr-x 0 0   0         0 Jul 17 16:04 proc/
drwxr-xr-x 0 0   0         0 Jul 17 16:04 sys/
```

When you are finished, go ahead and delete `export.tar`, and then stop the outyet-small container with docker `container stop outyet-small`.

You can explore the container's filesystem from the Docker server by navigating directly to where the filesystem resides on the server's storage system. This will typically look something like */var/lib/docker/overlay/fd5…* but will vary based on the Docker setup, storage backend, and container hash. You can determine your Docker root directory by running docker `system info`.

The Structure of Docker

What we think of as Docker is made of five major server-side components that present a common front via the API. These parts are dockerd, containerd, runc, containerd-shim-runc-v2, and the docker-proxy we described in "Networking" on page 323. We've spent a lot of time interacting with dockerd and the API it presents. It is, in fact, responsible for orchestrating the whole set of components that make up Docker. But when it starts a container, Docker relies on containerd to handle instantiating the container. All of this used to be handled in the dockerd process itself, but there were several shortcomings to that design:

- dockerd had a huge number of jobs.
- A monolithic runtime prevented any of the components from being swapped out easily.
- dockerd had to supervise the lifecycle of the containers themselves, and it couldn't be restarted or upgraded without losing all the running containers.

Another major motivation for containerd was that, as we've just shown, containers are not just a single abstraction. On the Linux platform, they are processes involving namespaces, cgroups, and security rules in AppArmor or SELinux. But Docker also runs on Windows and may even work on other platforms in the future. The idea of containerd is to present a standard layer to the outside world where, regardless of implementation, developers can think about the higher-level concepts of containers, tasks, and snapshots rather than worry about specific Linux system calls. This simplifies the Docker daemon a lot and enables platforms like Kubernetes to integrate directly into containerd rather than using the Docker API. Kubernetes relied on a Docker shim for many years, but nowadays it uses containerd directly.

Let's take a look at the components (shown in Figure 11-2) and see what each of them does:

dockerd
> One per server. Serves the API, builds container images, and does high-level network management, including volumes, logging, statistics reporting, and more.

docker-proxy
> One per port forwarding rule. Each instance handles the forwarding of the defined protocol traffic (TCP/UDP) from the defined host IP and port to the defined container IP and port.

containerd
> One per server. Manages the lifecycle, execution, copy-on-write filesystem, and low-level networking drivers.

```
containerd-shim-runc-v2
```
One per container. Handles file descriptors passed to the container (e.g., `stdin`/`out`) and reports exit status.

```
runc
```
Constructs the container and executes it, gathers statistics, and reports events on the lifecycle.

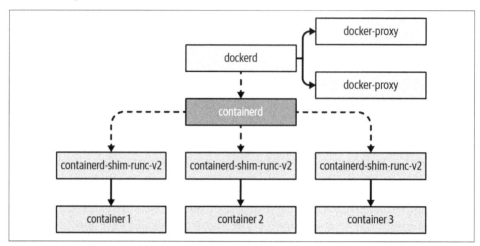

Figure 11-2. Structure of Docker

`dockerd` and `containerd` speak to each other over a socket, usually a Unix socket, using a gRPC API (*https://grpc.io*). `dockerd` is the client in this case, and `containerd` is the server! `runc` is a CLI tool that reads configuration from JSON on disk and is executed by `containerd`.

When we start a new container, `dockerd` will handle making sure that the image is present or will pull it from the repository specified in the image name. (In the future, this responsibility may shift to `containerd`, which already supports image pulls.) The Docker daemon also does most of the rest of the setup around the container, like launching `docker-proxy` to set up port forwarding. It then talks to `containerd` and asks it to run the container. `containerd` will take the image and apply the container configuration passed in from `dockerd` to generate an OCI bundle (*https://www.open containers.org*) that `runc` can execute.[1] It will then execute `containerd-shim-runc-v2` to start the container. This will in turn execute `runc` to construct and start the

---

1 To quote the OCI website: "The Open Container Initiative (OCI) is a lightweight, open governance structure (project), formed under the auspices of the Linux Foundation, for the express purpose of creating open industry standards around container formats and runtime. The OCI was launched on June 22nd, 2015 by Docker, CoreOS and other leaders in the container industry."

container. However, `runc` will not stay running, and the `containerd-shim-runc-v2` will be the actual parent process of the new container process.

If we launch a container and then look at the output of `ps axlf` on the Docker server, we can see the parent/child relationship between the various processes. PID 1 is `/sbin/init` and is the parent process for `containerd`, `dockerd`, and the `containerd-shim-runc-v2`.

 Docker Desktop's VM contains minimal versions of most Linux tools, and some of these commands may not produce the same output that you will get if you use a standard Linux server as the Docker daemon host.

```
$ docker container run --rm -d \
  --publish mode=ingress,published=8080,target=80 \
  --name nginx-test --rm nginx:latest
08b5cffed7baaf32b3af50498f7e5c5fa7ed35e094fa6045c205a88746fe53dd

$ ps axlf
… PID   PPID COMMAND
…
… 5171 1    /usr/bin/containerd
… 5288 1    /usr/bin/dockerd -H fd:// --containerd=/run/cont…/containerd.…
… 5784 5288 \_ /usr/bin/docker-proxy -proto tcp -host-ip … -host-port 8080
… 5791 5288 \_ /usr/bin/docker-proxy -proto tcp -host-ip :: -host-port …
… 5807 1    /usr/bin/containerd-shim-runc-v2 -namespace moby -id …
… 5829 5807 \_ nginx: master process nginx -g daemon off;
… 5880 5829    \_ nginx: worker process
… 5881 5829    \_ nginx: worker process
… 5882 5829    \_ nginx: worker process
… 5883 5829    \_ nginx: worker process
…
```

So what happened to `runc`? Its job is to construct the container and start it running, then it leaves and its children are inherited by its parent, the `containerd-shim-runc-v2`. This leaves the minimal amount of code in memory necessary to manage the file descriptors and exit status for `containerd`.

To help you understand what's going on here, let's take a deeper look at what happens when we start a container. We'll just reuse the `nginx` container that we already have running for this since it's very lightweight and the container stays running when backgrounded:

```
$ docker container ls

CONTAINER ID IMAGE        COMMAND       … PORTS                 NAMES
08b5cffed7ba nginx:latest "/docker-ent…" … 0.0.0.0:8080->80/tcp … nginx-test
```

Let's use the `runc` runtime CLI tool to take a look at its view of the system. We could see a similar view from `ctr`, the CLI client for `containerd`, but `runc` is nicer to work with, and it's at the lowest level:

```
$ sudo runc --root /run/docker/runtime-runc/moby list

ID          PID    …  BUNDLE                                              …  OWNER
08b5…53dd   5829   …  …/io.containerd.runtime.v2.task/moby/08b5…53dd     …  root
```

We normally need root privileges to run this command. Unlike with the Docker CLI, we can't rely on the Docker daemon's permissions to let us access lower-level functionality. With `runc` we need direct access to these privileges. What we can see in the output from `runc` is our container! This is the actual OCI runtime bundle that represents our container, with which it shares an ID. Notice that it also gives us the PID of the container; that's the PID on the host of the application running inside the container:

```
$ ps -edaf | grep 5829

root       5829  5807  …  nginx: master process nginx -g daemon off;
systemd+   5880  5829  …  nginx: worker process
systemd+   5881  5829  …  nginx: worker process
systemd+   5882  5829  …  nginx: worker process
systemd+   5883  5829  …  nginx: worker process
```

If we look in the bundle, we'll see a set of named pipes for our container:

```
$ sudo ls -la /run/docker/containerd/08b5…53dd

total 0
drwxr-xr-x 2 root root 80 Oct  1 08:49 .
drwxr-xr-x 3 root root 60 Oct  1 08:49 ..
prwx------ 1 root root  0 Oct  1 08:49 init-stderr
prwx------ 1 root root  0 Oct  1 08:49 init-stdout
```

You can find a lot of additional files related to your container underneath */run/containerd/io.containerd.runtime.v2.task/moby*:

```
$ sudo ls -la /run/containerd/io.containerd.runtime.v2.task/moby/08b5…53dd/

total 32
drwx------ 3 root root  240 Oct  1 08:49 .
drwx--x--x 3 root root   60 Oct  1 08:49 ..
-rw-r--r-- 1 root root   89 Oct  1 08:49 address
-rw-r--r-- 1 root root 9198 Oct  1 08:49 config.json
-rw-r--r-- 1 root root    4 Oct  1 08:49 init.pid
prwx------ 1 root root    0 Oct  1 08:49 log
-rw-r--r-- 1 root root    0 Oct  1 08:49 log.json
-rw------- 1 root root   82 Oct  1 08:49 options.json
drwx--x--x 2 root root   40 Oct  1 08:49 rootfs
-rw------- 1 root root    4 Oct  1 08:49 runtime
```

```
-rw------- 1 root root   32 Oct  1 08:49 shim-binary-path
lrwxrwxrwx 1 root root  119 Oct  1 08:49 work -> /var/lib/containerd/io…
```

The *config.json* file is a very verbose equivalent of what Docker shows in `docker container inspect`. We are not going to reproduce it here due to size, but we encourage you to dig around and see what's in the config. You may, for example, note all the entries for the "Secure Computing Mode" on page 315 that are present in it.

If you want to explore `runc` some more, you can experiment with the CLI tool. Most of this is already available in Docker, usually on a higher and more useful level than the one available in `runc`. But it can be useful to explore so that you can better understand how containers and the Docker stack are put together. It's also interesting to watch the events that `runc` reports about a running container. We can hook into those with the `runc events` command. During the normal operations of a running container, there is not a lot of activity in the events stream. But `runc` regularly reports runtime statistics, which we can see in JSON format:

```
$ sudo runc --root /run/docker/runtime-runc/moby events 08b5…53dd

{"type":"stats","id":"08b5…53dd","data":{"cpu":{"usage":{"…"}}}}
```

To conserve space, we have removed much of the output from the previous command, but this might look familiar to you now that we've spent some time looking at `docker container stats`. Guess where Docker gets those statistics by default. That's right, `runc`.

At this point, you can go ahead and stop the example container by running `docker container stop nginx-test`.

Swapping Runtimes

As we mentioned in Chapter 2, there are a few other native OCI-compliant runtimes that can be substituted in place of `runc`. As an example, there is crun (*https://git hub.com/containers/crun*), which describes itself as "a fast and low-memory footprint OCI Container Runtime fully written in C." Some other alternative native runtimes, like `railcar` and `rkt`, have been deprecated and largely abandoned. In the next section, we'll talk about a sandboxed runtime from Google, called gVisor (*https:// gvisor.dev*), which provides a user space runtime for untrusted code.

Kata Containers (*https://github.com/kata-containers*) is a very interesting open source project that provides a runtime capable of using VMs as an isolation layer for containers. At the time of this writing, version 3 of Kata works with Kubernetes but does not work with Docker. The Kata developers are working with the Docker developers (*https://github.com/kata-containers/kata-containers/issues/5321*) to try and improve this situation and create better documentation. This may be resolved when Docker 22.06 is publicly released.

gVisor

In mid-2018, Google released gVisor, which is a completely new take on a runtime. It's OCI compliant and can therefore also be used with Docker. However, gVisor also runs in user space and isolates the application by implementing system calls there rather than relying on Kernel isolation mechanisms. It doesn't redirect the calls to the kernel; rather, it implements them itself using kernel calls. The most obvious win from this approach is security isolation since gVisor itself is running in user space and thus is isolated from the kernel. Any security issues are still trapped in user space, and all of the kernel security controls we've mentioned still apply. The downside is that it typically performs worse than Kernel or VM-based solutions.

If you have processes that do not require massive scaling but do require highly secure isolation, gVisor may be an ideal solution for you. A common use case for gVisor is when your containers will be running code provided by your end users and you cannot guarantee that the code is benign. Let's run a quick demo so you can see how gVisor works.

Installation is covered in the gVisor documentation (*https://gvisor.dev/docs/ user_guide/quick_start/docker*). It is written in Go and is delivered as a single executable with no packages required. Once it's installed, you can start containers with the runsc runtime. To demonstrate the different isolation levels offered by gVisor, we'll run a shell using it and compare that to one using a standard container.

First, let's start a shell on gVisor and look around a bit:

```
$ docker container run --rm --runtime=runsc -it alpine /bin/sh
```

That will drop us into a shell running in an Alpine Linux container. One very revealing difference is apparent when you look at the output of the mount command:

```
$ docker container run --rm --runtime=runsc -it alpine /bin/sh -c "mount"

none on / type 9p (rw,trans=fd,rfdno=4,wfdno=4,aname=/,…)
none on /dev type tmpfs (rw,mode=0755)
none on /sys type sysfs (ro,noexec,dentry_cache_limit=1000)
none on /proc type proc (rw,noexec,dentry_cache_limit=1000)
none on /dev/pts type devpts (rw,noexec)
none on /dev/shm type tmpfs (rw,noexec,mode=1777,size=67108864)
```

```
none on /etc/hosts type 9p (rw,trans=fd,rfdno=7,wfdno=7,…)
none on /etc/hostname type 9p (rw,trans=fd,rfdno=6,wfdno=6,…)
none on /etc/resolv.conf type 9p (rw,trans=fd,rfdno=5,wfdno=5,…)
none on /tmp type tmpfs (rw,mode=01777)
```

There is not very much in there! Compare that with the output from a traditional container launched with runc:

```
$ docker container run --rm -it alpine /bin/sh -c "mount"

overlay on / type overlay (rw,relatime,…)
proc on /proc type proc (rw,nosuid,nodev,noexec,relatime)
tmpfs on /dev type tmpfs (rw,nosuid,size=65536k,mode=755,inode64)
devpts on /dev/pts type devpts (rw,nosuid,noexec,relatime,gid=5,…)
sysfs on /sys type sysfs (ro,nosuid,nodev,noexec,relatime)
cgroup on /sys/fs/cgroup type cgroup2 (ro,nosuid,nodev,noexec,relatime)
mqueue on /dev/mqueue type mqueue (rw,nosuid,nodev,noexec,relatime)
shm on /dev/shm type tmpfs (rw,nosuid,nodev,noexec,relatime,…)
/dev/sda3 on /etc/resolv.conf type ext4 (rw,relatime,errors=remount-ro)
…
devpts on /dev/console type devpts (rw,nosuid,noexec,relatime,gid=5,…)
proc on /proc/bus type proc (ro,nosuid,nodev,noexec,relatime)
…
tmpfs on /proc/asound type tmpfs (ro,relatime,inode64)
…
```

This output was 24 lines long, so we truncated it a lot. It should be pretty clear that there is a lot of system detail here. That detail represents the kernel footprint exposed to the container in one way or another. The contrast with the very short output from gVisor should give you an idea of the differing level of isolation. We won't spend a lot more time on it, but it's also worth looking at the output of ip addr show as well. On gVisor:

```
$ docker container run --rm --runtime=runsc alpine ip addr show

1: lo: <LOOPBACK,UP,LOWER_UP> mtu 65522
    link/loopback 00:00:00:00:00:00 brd ff:ff:ff:ff:ff:ff
    inet 127.0.0.1/8 scope global dynamic
2: eth0: <UP,LOWER_UP> mtu 1500
    link/ether 02:42:ac:11:00:02 brd ff:ff:ff:ff:ff:ff
    inet 172.17.0.2/16 scope global dynamic
```

And in a normal Linux container:

```
$ docker container run --rm alpine ip addr show

1: lo: <LOOPBACK,UP,LOWER_UP> mtu 65536 qdisc noqueue state UNKNOWN qlen 1000
    link/loopback 00:00:00:00:00:00 brd 00:00:00:00:00:00
    inet 127.0.0.1/8 scope host lo
       valid_lft forever preferred_lft forever
44: eth0@if45: <BROADCAST,MULTICAST,UP,LOWER_UP,M-DOWN> mtu 1500 qdisc
                                                   noqueue state UP
    link/ether 02:42:ac:11:00:02 brd ff:ff:ff:ff:ff:ff
```

```
    inet 172.17.0.2/16 brd 172.17.255.255 scope global eth0
        valid_lft forever preferred_lft forever
```

Even the Linux */proc* filesystem exposes a lot less in the gVisor container:

```
$ docker container run --rm --runtime=runsc alpine ls -C /proc

1                filesystems    net                sys
cgroups          loadavg        self               thread-self
cmdline          meminfo        sentry-meminfo     uptime
cpuinfo          mounts         stat               version
```

Once more comparing this to a normal Linux container:

```
$ docker container run --rm alpine ls -C /proc

1                fb             mdstat             stat
acpi             filesystems    meminfo            swaps
asound           fs             misc               sys
bootconfig       interrupts     modules            sysrq-trigger
buddyinfo        iomem          mounts             sysvipc
bus              ioports        mpt                thread-self
cgroups          irq            mtd                timer_list
cmdline          kallsyms       mtrr               tty
consoles         kcore          net                uptime
cpuinfo          key-users      pagetypeinfo       version
crypto           keys           partitions         version_signature
devices          kmsg           pressure           vmallocinfo
diskstats        kpagecgroup    schedstat          vmstat
dma              kpagecount     scsi               zoneinfo
driver           kpageflags     self
dynamic_debug    loadavg        slabinfo
execdomains      locks          softirqs
```

Aside from being more isolated, the experience inside the gVisor container is interesting because it looks a lot more like what you might expect to see in an isolated environment. Sandboxed runtimes like gVisor provide a lot of potential for securely running untrusted workloads by providing a much stronger barrier between the application and the underlying kernel.

Wrap-Up

That's a quick tour of some of the more advanced concepts of Docker. Hopefully, it has expanded your knowledge of what is happening behind the scenes and has opened up some avenues for you to continue your exploration. As you build and maintain a production platform, this background should provide you with a broad enough perspective of Docker to know where to start when you need to customize the system.

## CHAPTER 12

The Expanding Landscape

The landscape of tools that are available to interact with Linux containers is constantly evolving, especially with the significant adoption that Kubernetes has experienced for many years.

In this chapter, we are going to take a very quick tour of a few tools that are inspired by Docker but are often focused on improving specific use cases. This is not intended to be a comprehensive list but instead is intended to simply give you a taste of some of the categories and options that are available to explore.

Client Tools

In this section, we are going to introduce three command-line tools: `nerdctl`, `podman`, and `buildah`. All of these tools might be useful to anyone familiar with Docker and its common workflows.

nerdctl

Although `crictl` (*https://oreil.ly/zElq_*)[1] is installed by default in many `containerd`-based environments, `nerdctl` is an easy-to-use Docker-compatible CLI for `containerd`, which is worth checking out. This means that `nerdctl` can provide a very easy migration path for people and scripts that use Docker but need to support `containerd` systems that are not running the Docker daemon.

As a quick example, if you spin up a small Kubernetes cluster with `kind`, which we discussed in "Kind" on page 274, you should end up with a `containerd`-based Kubernetes cluster that is not directly compatible with the `docker` CLI:

---

1 Full URL: *https://github.com/kubernetes-sigs/cri-tools/blob/master/docs/crictl.md*

```
$ kind create cluster --name nerdctl
Creating cluster "nerdctl" …
…

$ docker container exec -ti nerdctl-control-plane /bin/bash
```

You should now be inside the kind/Kubernetes container.

 In the curl command that follows, you must ensure that you are downloading the correct version for your architecture. You will need to replace ${ARCH} with either amd64 or arm64, depending on your system. Also, feel free to try and download the most recent version (*https://github.com/containerd/nerdctl/releases*) of nerdctl.

Once you have edited the following curl command and reassembled it into a single line, you should be able to download and extract the nerdctl client and then try a few commands with it:

```
root@nerdctl-control-plane:/# curl -s -L \
  "https://github.com/containerd/nerdctl/releases/download/v0.23.0/\
nerdctl-0.23.0-linux-${ARCH}.tar.gz" -o /tmp/nerdctl.tar.gz

root@nerdctl-control-plane:/# tar -C /usr/local/bin -xzf /tmp/nerdctl.tar.gz

root@nerdctl-control-plane:/# nerdctl namespace list

NAME      CONTAINERS    IMAGES    VOLUMES    LABELS
k8s.io    18            24        0

root@nerdctl-control-plane:/# nerdctl --namespace k8s.io container list

CONTAINER ID IMAGE                                   … NAMES
07ae69902d11 registry.k8s.io/pause:3.7               … k8s://kube-system/core…
0b241db0485f registry.k8s.io/coredns/coredns:v1.9.3 … k8s://kube-system/core…
…

root@nerdctl-control-plane:/# nerdctl --namespace k8s.io container run --rm \
                     --net=host debian sleep 5

docker.io/library/debian:latest:   resolved    |++++++++++++++++++++++++++++|
index-sha256:e538…4bff:            done        |++++++++++++++++++++++++++++|
manifest-sha256:9b0e…2f7d:         done        |++++++++++++++++++++++++++++|
config-sha256:d917…d33c:           done        |++++++++++++++++++++++++++++|
layer-sha256:f606…5ddf:            done        |++++++++++++++++++++++++++++|
elapsed: 6.4 s                     total:  52.5 M (8.2 MiB/s)

root@nerdctl-control-plane:/# exit
```

In most cases, docker commands can be used with almost no alteration by nerdctl. The one change that might stand out is the need to often provide a namespace value.

This is because `containerd` provides a fully namespaced API (*https://github.com/con tainerd/containerd/blob/main/docs/namespaces.md*), and we need to specify which one we are interested in interacting with.

Once you have exited the `kind` container, you can go ahead and delete it:

```
$ kind delete cluster --name nerdctl

Deleting cluster "nerdctl" …
```

podman and buildah

`podman` (*https://podman.io*) and `buildah` (*https://buildah.io*) are a set of tools from Red Hat that were created early on to provide a container workflow that did not rely on a daemon process, like Docker. It is heavily used within the Red Hat community and rethinks the way that images are built and containers are run and managed.

> You can find a good introduction to `podman` and `buildah` for Docker users on the Red Hat blog (*https://developers.red hat.com/blog/2019/02/21/podman-and-buildah-for-docker-users*).

```
$ kind create cluster --name podman
Creating cluster "podman" …
…

$ docker container exec -ti podman-control-plane /bin/bash
```

> An overview of installing and using `kind` can be found in "Kind" on page 274.

You should now be inside the kind/Kubernetes container:

```
root@podman-control-plane:/# apt update
Get:1 http://security.ubuntu.com/ubuntu jammy-security InRelease [110 kB]
…

root@podman-control-plane:/# apt install -y podman
Reading package lists… Done
…

root@podman-control-plane:/# podman container run -d --rm \
                        --name test debian sleep 120
9b6b333313c0d54e2da6cda49f2787bc5213681d90dac145a9f64128f3e18631
```

```
root@podman-control-plane:/# podman container list

CONTAINER ID   IMAGE                           COMMAND     …  NAMES
548a2f709785   docker.io/library/debian:latest sleep 120   …  test

root@podman-control-plane:/# podman container stop test
test
```

Unlike docker (which interfaces with the Docker daemon) and nerdctl (which interfaces with containerd), podman skips the container engine and instead directly interfaces with an underlying container runtime, like runc.

Although podman build can be used to build containers as well, buildah provides an advanced interface for image building that makes it possible to script the whole image-building process and remove the need to rely on the *Dockerfile* format (or *Containerfile*, as podman calls it).

We won't dig into the details of buildah here, but you can try a very simple example in the kind container, and if you are interested in alternatives to the traditional Dockerfile approach, or the newer alternatives provided by BuildKit's LBB interface (*https://github.com/moby/buildkit#exploring-llb*), you can read more about buildah online via GitHub (*https://github.com/containers/buildah*) and the Red Hat blog (*https://www.redhat.com/sysadmin/building-buildah*).

To try out a buildah script in the kind container, go ahead and run the following commands:

```
root@podman-control-plane:/# cat > apache.sh <<"EOF"

#!/usr/bin/env bash

set -x

ctr1=$(buildah from "${1:-fedora}")

## Get all updates and install the apache server
buildah run "$ctr1" -- dnf update -y
buildah run "$ctr1" -- dnf install -y httpd

## Include some buildtime annotations
buildah config --annotation "com.example.build.host=$(uname -n)" "$ctr1"

## Run our server and expose the port
buildah config --cmd "/usr/sbin/httpd -D FOREGROUND" "$ctr1"
buildah config --port 80 "$ctr1"

## Commit this container to an image name
buildah commit "$ctr1" "${2:-myrepo/apache}"

EOF
```

```
root@podman-control-plane:/# chmod +x apache.sh
root@podman-control-plane:/# ./apache.sh

++ buildah from fedora
+ ctr1=fedora-working-container-1
+ buildah run fedora-working-container-1 -- dnf update -y
…
Writing manifest to image destination
Storing signatures
037c7a7c532a47be67f389d7fd3e4bbba64670e080b120d93744e147df5adf26

root@podman-control-plane:/# exit
```

Once you have exited the kind container, you can go ahead and delete it:

```
$ kind delete cluster --name podman

Deleting cluster "podman" …
```

All-in-One Developer Tools

Although Docker Desktop is a very useful tool, changes in Docker's licensing and the broader technology landscape have led some people and organizations to look for alternative tools. In this section, we will take a quick look at Rancher Desktop and Podman Desktop and how they can be used to provide some of the functionality of Docker Desktop while also bringing some interesting features of their own.

Rancher Desktop

Rancher Desktop (*https://rancherdesktop.io*) is designed to provide a very similar experience to Docker Desktop while focusing specifically on Kubernetes integration. It uses k3s (*https://k3s.io*) to provide a certified, lightweight Kubernetes backend and can use either containerd or dockerd (moby) as the container runtime.

> You should probably quit Docker (and/or Podman) Desktop, if either one is running, before trying out Rancher Desktop, since they all spin up a VM that will consume system resources.

After downloading, installing, and launching Rancher Desktop, you will have a local Kubernetes cluster, which, by default, is using containerd and can be interacted with via nerdctl.

The exact location where Rancher Desktop installs the `nerdctl` binary might vary a bit depending on which operating system you are using. You should initially try and make sure that you are using the version that was packaged with the Rancher Desktop.

```
$ ${HOME}/.rd/bin/nerdctl --namespace k8s.io image list

REPOSITORY       TAG      IMAGE ID      …   PLATFORM      SIZE       BLOB SIZE
moby/buildkit    v0.8.3   171689e43026  …   linux/amd64   119.2 MiB  53.9 MiB
moby/buildkit    <none>   171689e43026  …   linux/amd64   119.2 MiB  53.9 MiB
…
```

Don't forget to quit Rancher Desktop when you are done; otherwise the VM will stay running and consume additional resources.

Podman Desktop

Podman Desktop (*https://podman-desktop.io*) is focused on providing a daemon-less container tool that still provides the seamless experience that developers on all of the major operating systems have grown accustomed to.

You should probably quit Docker (and/or Rancher) Desktop, if either one is running, before trying out Podman Desktop, since they all spin up a VM that will consume system resources.

After downloading, installing, and launching Podman Desktop, you will see an application window on the Home tab. If Podman Desktop does not detect the `podman` CLI on your system, it will prompt you to install it via a button labeled Install. This should walk you through the installation of the `podman` client. When the Podman Desktop VM, which can be controlled from the command line via the `podman machine` command, is not started, click the Run Podman switch, and then wait a few moments. The switch should disappear, and you should see the "Podman is running" message.

The exact location where Podman Desktop installs the `podman` binary might vary a bit depending on which operating system you are using. You should initially make sure that you are using the version that was installed via Podman Desktop.

To test the system, give this a try:

```
$ podman run quay.io/podman/hello

!… Hello Podman World …!

         .--"--.
        / -    - \
       / (O)   (O) \
    ~~~| -=(,Y,)=- |
     .---. /     \   |~~
    ~/  o  o \~~~~.----. ~~
     | =(X)= |~  / (O (O) \
      ~~~~~~~  ~| =(Y_)=-   |
      ~~~~     ~~~|   U      |~~

    Project:   https://github.com/containers/podman
    Website:   https://podman.io
    Documents: https://docs.podman.io
    Twitter:   @Podman_io
```

When you are done exploring Podman Desktop, you can go ahead and shut down the VM by clicking the Preferences tab, selecting Resources → Podman → Podman Machine, and then clicking the Stop button.

At this point, you can go ahead and quit the Podman Desktop application.

You can also start and stop the Podman VM by using the `podman machine start` and `podman machine stop` commands.

Wrap-Up

Docker's place in technology history is well established. There is no doubt that the introduction of Docker took the existing Linux container technology, extended it with the image format, and then made the concepts and technology accessible to engineers all around the world.

We can argue about whether things are better today than they were before Linux containers and Docker, and we can debate about which tools and workflows are better, but in the end, much of that comes down to how each tool is used and how those workflows are designed.

No tools will magically solve all your problems, and any tool can be implemented so poorly that it makes everything much worse than it was before. This is why it is so important to spend significant time thinking about the process workflow that you want to implement from at least three angles. First, what inputs and outputs do we need the workflow to support? Second, how easy will the workflow be for the people who need to use it every day or just once a year? And third, how easy will it be to run and maintain for the people who must ensure that the system runs smoothly and securely at all times?

Once you have a good picture of what you are trying to achieve, then you can start to pick the tools that will help you enable these goals.

CHAPTER 13
Container Platform Design

When implementing any technology in production, you'll often gain the most mileage by designing a resilient platform that can withstand the unexpected issues that will inevitably occur. Docker can be a powerful tool but requires attention to detail to get the whole platform right around it. As a technology that is going through very rapid growth, it is bound to produce frustrating bugs that crop up between the various components that make up your container platform.

If instead of simply deploying Docker into your existing environment, you take the time to build a well-designed container platform utilizing Docker as one of the core components, you can enjoy the many benefits of a container-based workflow while simultaneously protecting yourself from some of the sharper edges that can exist in such high-velocity projects.

Like all other technology, Docker doesn't magically solve all your problems. To reach its true potential, organizations must make very conscious decisions about why and how to use it. For small projects, it is possible to use Docker in a simple manner; however, if you plan to support a large project that can scale with demand, it's crucial that you design your applications and the platform very deliberately. This ensures that you can maximize the return on your investment in the technology. Taking the time to intentionally design your platform will also make it much easier to modify your production workflow over time. A well-designed container platform and deployment process will be as lightweight and straightforward as possible while still supporting the features required to meet all the technical and compliance requirements. A well-thought-out design will help ensure that your software is running on a dynamic foundation that can easily be upgraded as technology and company processes develop.

In this chapter, we will explore two open documents, "The Twelve-Factor App" (*https://12factor.net*) and "The Reactive Manifesto" (*https://www.reactivemanifesto.org*) (a companion document to "The Reactive Principles" (*https://www.reactiveprinciples.org*)), and discuss how they relate to Docker and building robust container platforms. Both documents contain a lot of ideas that should help guide you through the design and implementation of your container platform and ensure more resiliency and supportability across the board.

The Twelve-Factor App

In November of 2011, well before the release of Docker, Heroku cofounder Adam Wiggins and his colleagues released an article called "The Twelve-Factor App" (*https://12factor.net*). This document describes a series of 12 practices, distilled from the experiences of the Heroku (*https://www.heroku.com*) engineers, for designing applications that will thrive and grow in a modern container-based SaaS environment.

Although not required, applications built with these 12 steps in mind are ideal candidates for the Docker workflow. Throughout this chapter, we will explore each of the following steps and explain why these practices can, in numerous ways, help improve your development cycle:

- Codebase
- Dependencies
- Config
- Backing services
- Build, release, run
- Processes
- Port binding
- Concurrency
- Disposability
- Development/production parity
- Logs
- Admin processes

Codebase

One codebase tracked in revision control.

Many instances of your application will be running at any given time, but they should all come from the same code repository. Every single Docker image for a given application should be built from a single source code repository that contains all the code required to build the Linux container. This ensures that the code can easily be rebuilt and that all third-party requirements are well-defined within the repository and will automatically be pulled in during a build.

What this means is that building your application shouldn't require stitching together code from multiple source repositories. That is not to say that you can't have a dependency on an artifact from another repo. But it does mean that there should be a clear mechanism for determining which pieces of code were shipped when you built your application. Docker's ability to simplify dependency management is much less useful if building your application requires pulling down multiple source code repositories and stitching pieces together. It also is not very repeatable if you must know a magic incantation to get the build to work correctly.

A good test might be to give a new developer in your company a clean laptop and a paragraph of directions and then see if they can successfully build your application in under an hour. If they can't, then the process probably needs to be refined and simplified.

Dependencies

Explicitly declare and isolate dependencies.

Never rely on the belief that a dependency will be made available via some other avenue, like the operating system install. Any dependencies that your application requires should be well defined in the codebase and pulled in by the build process. This will help ensure that your application will run when deployed, without relying on libraries being installed by other people or processes. This is particularly important within a container since the container's processes are isolated from the rest of the host operating system and will usually not have access to anything outside of the host's kernel and the container image's filesystem.

The *Dockerfile* and language-dependent configuration files like Node's *package.json* or Ruby's *Gemfile* should define every nonexternal dependency required by your application. This ensures that your image will run correctly on any system to which it is deployed. Gone will be the days when you try to deploy and run your application in production only to find out that important libraries are missing or installed with the wrong version. This pattern has huge reliability and repeatability advantages and very positive ramifications for system security. If to fix a security issue, you update the OpenSSL or *libyaml* libraries that your containerized application uses, then you can be assured that it will always be running with that version wherever you deploy that particular application.

It is also important to note that many Docker base images are larger than they need to be. Remember that your application process will be running on a shared kernel, and the only files that you need inside your image are the ones that the process will require to run. It's good that base images are so readily available, but they can sometimes mask hidden dependencies. Although people often start with a minimal install of Alpine, Ubuntu, or Fedora, these images still contain a lot of operating system files and applications that your process almost certainly does not need, or possibly some files that your application is making use of that you aren't consciously aware of, like compiling your application using the *musl* system library in Alpine versus the *glibc* system library in many other base images. You need to be fully aware of your dependencies, even when containerizing your application. It is also important to consider what support tools, if any, you are including in your images, as there can be a fine line between making things easier to debug and increasing the security attack surface of your application and environments.

A good way to shed light on what files are required inside an image is to compare a "small" base image with an image for a statically linked program written in a language like Go or C. These applications can be designed to run directly on the Linux kernel without any additional libraries or files.

To help drive this point home, it might be useful to review the exercises in "Keeping Images Small" on page 73, where we explored one of these ultra-light containers, `spkane/scratch-helloworld`, and then dived into the underlying filesystem a bit and compared it with the popular `alpine` base image.

In addition to being conscientious about how you manage the filesystem layers in your images, keeping your images stripped down to the bare necessities is another great way to keep everything streamlined and your `docker image pull` commands fast. Applications written with interpreted languages will require many more files because of the large runtimes and dependency graphs you often need to install, but you should try to keep as minimal a base layer as needed for your use case so that you can reason about your dependencies. Docker helps you package them up, but you still need to be in charge of reasoning about them.

Config

Store configuration in environment variables, not in files checked into the codebase.

This makes it simple to deploy the same codebase to different environments, like staging and production, without maintaining complicated configuration in code or rebuilding your container for each environment. This keeps your codebase much cleaner by keeping environment-specific information like database names and passwords out of your source code repository. More importantly, though, it means that you don't bake deployment environment assumptions into the repository, and thus it is extremely easy to deploy your applications anywhere that it might be useful. You also want to be able to test the same image you will ship to production. You can't do that if you have to build an image for each environment with all of its configuration already baked in.

As discussed in Chapter 4, you can achieve this by launching `docker container run` commands that leverage the `-e` command-line argument. Using `-e APP_ENV= production` tells Docker to set the environment variable `APP_ENV` to the value `production` within the newly launched container.

For a real-world example, let's assume we pulled the image for the chat robot Hubot with the Rocket.Chat (*https://www.rocket.chat*) adapter installed. We'd issue something like the following command to get it running:

```
$ docker container run \
  --rm --name hubot -d \
  -e ENVIRONMENT="development" \
  -e ROCKETCHAT_URL='rocketchat:3000' \
  -e ROCKETCHAT_ROOM='general' \
  -e RESPOND_TO_DM=true \
  -e ROCKETCHAT_USER=bot \
  -e ROCKETCHAT_PASSWORD=bot \
  -e ROCKETCHAT_AUTH=password \
  -e BOT_NAME=bot \
  -e EXTERNAL_SCRIPTS=hubot-pugme,hubot-help \
  docker.io/rocketchat/hubot-rocketchat:latest
```

Here, we are passing a whole set of environment variables into the container when it is created. When the process is launched in the container, it will have access to these environment variables so that it can properly configure itself at runtime. These configuration items are now an external dependency that we can inject at runtime.

 There are many other ways to provide this data to a container, including using key/value stores like `etcd` and `consul`. Environment variables are simply a universal option that acts as a very good starting point for most projects. They are the easy path for container configuration because they are well supported by the platform and every programming language in common use. They also aid in the observability of your applications because the configuration can easily be inspected with `docker container inspect`.

In the case of a Node.js application like `hubot`, you could then write the following code to make decisions based on these environment variables:

```
switch(process.env.ENVIRONMENT){
    case 'development':
        console.log('[INFO] Running in development');

    case 'staging':
        console.log('[INFO] Running in staging');

    case 'production':
        console.log('[INFO] Running in production');

    default:
        console.log('[WARN] Environment value is unknown');
}
```

 The exact method used to pass this configuration data into your container will vary depending on the specific tooling that you've chosen for your projects, but almost all of them will make it easy to ensure that every deployment contains the proper settings for that environment.

Keeping specific configuration information out of your source code makes it very easy to deploy the exact same container to multiple environments, with no changes and no sensitive information committed into your source code repository. Crucially, it supports testing your container images thoroughly before deploying to production by allowing the same image to be used in all environments.

```
$ docker container stop hubot
```

 If you need a process for managing secrets that need to be provided to your containers, you might want to look into the documentation (*https://docs.docker.com/engine/swarm/secrets*) for the docker secret command, which works with Docker Swarm mode, and HashiCorp's Vault (*https://www.vaultproject.io*).

Backing Services

Treat backing services as attached resources.

Local databases are no more reliable than third-party services and should be treated as such. Applications should handle the loss of an attached resource gracefully. By implementing graceful degradation in your application and never assuming that any resource, including filesystem space, is available, you ensure that your application will continue to perform as many of its functions as it can, even when external resources are unavailable.

This isn't something that Docker helps you with directly, and although it is always a good idea to write robust services, it is even more important when you are using containers. When using containers, you achieve high availability most often through horizontal scaling and rolling deployments, instead of relying on the live migration of long-running processes, like on traditional VMs. This means that specific instances of a service will often come and go over time, and your service should be able to handle this gracefully.

Additionally, because Linux containers have limited filesystem resources, you can't simply rely on having some local storage available. You need to plan that into your application's dependencies and handle it explicitly.

Build, Release, Run

Strictly separate build and run stages.

Build the code, release it with the proper configuration, and then deploy it. This ensures that you maintain control of the process and can perform any single step without triggering the whole workflow. By ensuring that each of these steps is self-contained in a distinct process, you can tighten the feedback loop and react more quickly to any problems within the deployment flow.

As you design your Docker workflow, you want to clearly separate each step in the deployment process. It is perfectly fine to have a single button that builds a container, tests it, and then deploys it, assuming that you trust your testing processes—but you don't want to be forced to rebuild a container simply to deploy it to another environment.

Docker supports the 12-factor ideal well in this area because the image registry provides a clean handoff point between building an image and shipping it to production. If your build process generates images and pushes them to the registry, then deployment can simply be pulling the image down to servers and running it.

Processes

Execute the app as one or more stateless processes.

All shared data must be accessed via a stateful backing store so that application instances can easily be redeployed without losing any important session data. You don't want to keep any critical state on disk in your ephemeral container or in the memory of one of its processes. Containerized applications should always be considered ephemeral. A truly dynamic container environment requires the ability to destroy and re-create containers at a moment's notice. This flexibility helps enable the rapid deployment cycle and outage recovery demanded by modern, Agile workflows.

As much as possible, it is preferable to write applications that do not need to keep state longer than the time required to process and respond to a single request. This ensures that the impact of stopping any given container in your application pool is very minimal. When you must maintain state, the best approach is to use a remote datastore like Redis, PostgreSQL, Memcache, or even Amazon S3, depending on your resiliency needs.

Port Binding

Export services via port binding.

Your application needs to be addressable by a port specific to itself. Applications should bind directly to a port to expose the service and should not rely on an external daemon like `inetd` to handle that for them. You should be certain that when you're talking to that port, you're talking to your application. Most modern web platforms are quite capable of directly binding to a port and servicing their own requests.

To expose a port from your container, as discussed in Chapter 4, you can launch `docker container run` commands that use the `--publish` command-line argument. Using `--publish mode=ingress,published=80,target=8080`, for example, would tell Docker to proxy the container's port 8080 on the host's port 80.

The statically linked Go Hello World container that we discussed in "Keeping Images Small" on page 73 is a great example of this, because the container contains nothing but our application to serve its content to a web browser. We did not need to include any additional web servers, which would require further configuration, introduce additional complexity, and increase the number of potential failure points in our system.

Concurrency

Scale out via the process model.

Design for concurrency and horizontal scaling within your applications. Increasing the resources of an existing instance can be difficult and hard to reverse. Adding and removing instances as scale fluctuates is much easier and helps maintain flexibility in the infrastructure. Launching another container on a new server is incredibly inexpensive compared to the effort and expense required to add resources to an underlying virtual or physical system. Designing for horizontal scaling allows the platform to react much faster to changes in resource requirements.

As an example, in Chapter 10, you saw how easily a service could be scaled using Docker Swarm mode by simply running a command like this:

```
$ docker service scale myservice=8
```

This is where tools like Docker Swarm mode, Mesos, and Kubernetes truly begin to shine. Once you have implemented a Docker cluster with a dynamic scheduler, it is very easy to add three more instances of a container to the cluster as load increases and then to be able to easily remove two instances of your application from the cluster as load starts to decrease again.

Disposability

Maximize robustness with fast startup and graceful shutdown.

Services should be designed to be ephemeral. We already talked a little bit about this when discussing external state with containers. Responding well to dynamic horizontal scaling, rolling deploys, and unexpected problems requires applications that can quickly and easily be started or shut down. Services should respond gracefully to a SIGTERM signal from the operating system and even handle hard failures confidently. Most importantly, we shouldn't care if any given container for our application is up and running. As long as requests are being served, the developer should be freed of concerns about the health of any single component within the system. If an individual node is behaving poorly, turning it off or redeploying it should be an easy decision that doesn't entail long planning sessions and concerns about the health of the rest of the cluster.

As discussed in Chapter 7, Docker sends standard Unix signals to containers when it is stopping or killing them; therefore, any containerized application can detect these signals and take the appropriate steps to shut down gracefully.

Development/Production Parity

Keep development, staging, and production as similar as possible.

The same processes and artifacts should be used to build, test, and deploy services into all environments. The same people should do the work in all environments, and the physical nature of the environments should be as similar as reasonably possible. Repeatability is incredibly important. Almost any issue discovered in production points to a failure in the process. Every area where production diverges from staging is an area where risk is being introduced into the system. These inconsistencies blind you to certain types of issues that could occur in your production environment until it is too late to proactively deal with them.

In many ways, this advice essentially repeats a few of the early recommendations. However, the specific point here is that any environment divergence introduces risks, and although these differences are common in many organizations, they are much less necessary in a containerized environment. Docker servers can normally be created so that they are identical in all of your environments, and environment-based configuration changes should typically impact only which endpoints your service connects to without specifically changing the application's behavior.

Logs

Treat logs as event streams.

Services should not concern themselves with routing or storing logs. Instead, events should be streamed, unbuffered, to STDOUT and STDERR for handling by the hosting process. In development, STDOUT and STDERR can be easily viewed, whereas in staging and production, the streams can be routed to anything, including a central logging service. Different environments have different exceptions for log handling. This logic should never be hardcoded into the application. Streaming everything to STDOUT and STDERR enables the top-level process manager to handle the logs via whatever method is best for the environment, allowing the application developer to focus on core functionality.

In Chapter 6, we discussed the docker container logs command, which collects the output from your container's STDOUT and STDERR and records it as logs. If you write logs to random files within the container's filesystem, you will not have easy access to them. It is also possible to configure Docker to send logs to a local or remote logging system using tools like rsyslog, journald, or fluentd.

If you use a process manager or initialization system on your servers, like systemd or upstart, it is usually very easy to direct all process output to STDOUT and STDERR and then have your process monitor capture them and send them to a remote logging host.

Admin Processes

Run admin/management tasks as one-off processes.

One-off administration tasks should be run via the same codebase and configuration that the application uses. This helps avoid synchronization problems and code/schema drift problems. Oftentimes, management tools exist as one-off scripts or live in a completely different codebase. It is much safer to build management tools within the application's codebase and utilize the same libraries and functions to perform the required work. This can significantly improve the reliability of these tools by ensuring that they leverage the same code paths that the application relies on to perform its core functionality.

What this means is that you should never rely on random cron-like scripts to perform administrative and maintenance functions. Instead, include all of these scripts and functionality in your application codebase. Assuming that these don't need to be run on every instance of your application, you can launch a special short-lived container, or use `docker container exec` with the existing container, whenever you need to run a maintenance job. This command can trigger the required job, report its status somewhere, and then exit.

Twelve-Factor Wrap-Up

While "The Twelve-Factor App" wasn't written as a Docker-specific manifesto, almost all of this advice can be applied to writing and deploying applications on a Docker platform. This is in part because the article heavily influenced Docker's design, and in part because the manifesto itself codified many of the best practices promoted by modern software architects.

The Reactive Manifesto

Riding alongside "The Twelve-Factor App," another pertinent document was released in July of 2013 by Typesafe cofounder and CTO Jonas Bonér, entitled "The Reactive Manifesto" (*https://www.reactivemanifesto.org*). Jonas originally worked with a small group of contributors to solidify a manifesto that discusses how the expectations for application resiliency have evolved over the last few years and how applications should be engineered to react predictably to various forms of interaction, including events, users, load, and failures (*https://www.lightbend.com/blog/why-do-we-need-a-reactive-manifesto*).

"The Reactive Manifesto" states that "reactive systems" are responsive, resilient, elastic, and message driven.

Responsive

The system responds in a timely manner if at all possible.

In general, this means that the application should respond to requests very quickly. Users simply don't want to wait, and there is rarely a good reason to make them. If you have a containerized service that renders large PDF files, design it so that it immediately responds with a "job submitted" message so that users can go about their day, and then provide a message or banner that informs them when the job is finished and where they can download the resulting PDF.

Resilient

The system stays responsive in the face of failure.

When your application fails for any reason, the situation will always be worse if it becomes unresponsive. It is much better to handle the failure gracefully and dynamically reduce the application's functionality or even display a simple but clear problem message to the user while reporting the issue internally.

Elastic

The system stays responsive under varying workload.

With Docker, you achieve this by dynamically deploying and decommissioning containers as requirements and load fluctuate so that your application is always able to handle server requests quickly, without deploying a lot of underutilized resources.

Message Driven

Reactive systems rely on asynchronous message passing to establish a boundary between components that ensures loose coupling, isolation, and location transparency.

Although not directly addressed by Docker, the idea here is that there are times when an application can become busy or unavailable. If you utilize asynchronous message passing between your services, you can help ensure that your services will not lose requests and that they will be processed as soon as possible.

Wrap-Up

All four of the design features in "The Reactive Manifesto" require application developers to design graceful degradation and define a clear separation of responsibilities in their applications. By treating all dependencies as properly designed, attached resources, dynamic container environments allow you to easily maintain $N+2$ status across your application stack, reliably scale individual services in your environment, and quickly replace unhealthy nodes.

A service is only as reliable as its least reliable dependency, so it is vital to incorporate these ideas into every component of your platform.

The core ideas in "The Reactive Manifesto" merge very nicely with "The Twelve-Factor App" and the Docker workflow. These documents successfully summarize many of the most important discussions about the way you need to think and work if you want to be successful in meeting new expectations in the industry. The Docker workflow provides a practical way to implement many of these ideas in any organization in a completely approachable manner.

## CHAPTER 14

Conclusion

At this point, you have had a solid tour through the Docker ecosystem and have seen many examples of how Docker and Linux containers can benefit you and your organization. We have tried to map out some of the common pitfalls and impart some of the wisdom that we have picked up over the many years that we've run Linux containers in production. Our experience has shown that the promise of Docker is quite achievable, and we've seen significant benefits in our organizations as a result. Like other powerful technologies, Docker is not without its compromises, but the net result has been a big positive for us, our teams, and our organizations. If you implement the Docker workflow and integrate it into the processes you already have in your organization, there is every reason to believe that you can significantly benefit from it as well.

In this chapter, we will take a moment to consider Docker's evolving place in the technology landscape, and then quickly review the problems that Docker is designed to help you solve and some of the power it brings to the table.

The Road Ahead

There is no doubt that containers are here to stay for a very long time, but some people have predicted the ultimate demise of Docker on and off for a long time. Much of this is simply because the word *Docker* represents so many things in so many people's minds (*https://oreil.ly/pvSEl*).[1] Are you talking about the company, which was sold to Mirantis in 2019 and reported $50 million USD in annual recurring revenue (ARR) two years after the restructuring? Or maybe the docker client tool, whose source code can be downloaded (*https://github.com/docker/cli*), modified, and built by

---

[1] Full URL: *https://www.tutorialworks.com/difference-docker-containerd-runc-crio-oci*

anyone who might need it? It is hard to know. People often like to try and predict the future, but reality often lies somewhere in the middle, hidden in the often-overlooked details.

In 2020, Kubernetes announced the deprecation of dockershim (*https://kubernetes.io/blog/2022/02/17/dockershim-faq*), which went fully into effect with the release of Kubernetes v1.24. At the time, lots of people took this to mean that Docker was dead, but the point many people were missing is that Docker has always primarily been a developer tool, not a production component. Sure it can be used on a production system for various reasons, but its true power lies in its ability to streamline much of the software packaging and testing workflow into a consolidated toolset. Kubernetes uses the Container Runtime Interface (CRI) (*https://kubernetes.io/blog/2016/12/container-runtime-interface-cri-in-kubernetes*), which is not implemented by Docker and therefore required them to maintain another piece of wrapper software called `dockershim` to support using Docker Engine via the CRI. This announcement was not given to make some statement about Docker's place in the ecosystem; it was simply given to make maintaining a large volunteer-driven open source project easier. Docker may not run on your Kubernetes servers, but in most cases, this will have no impact at all on the development and release cycle for your software. Unless you are a Kubernetes operator who used the `docker` CLI to directly query the containers running on a Kubernetes node, you are unlikely to notice any change as this transition occurs.

And as it turns out, Docker's parent company has developed and continues to support a new shim, called `cri-dockerd` (*https://github.com/Mirantis/cri-dockerd*), that allows Kubernetes to continue to interface with Docker for those who need that workflow to be supported.

Interestingly enough, Docker is also diversifying into noncontainer technologies, like WebAssembly (*https://docs.docker.com/desktop/wasm*) (Wasm), that can complement containers while improving the developer experience.

So, Docker as a developer-friendly toolset is likely here to stay for a long while, but that doesn't mean that there are not any other tools in the ecosystem that can complement or even replace it if that is something that you want or need. The beauty of the various standards that exist, like the OCI, and their broad adoption, is that many of these tools can interoperate with the same images and containers that other tools generate and manage.

The Challenges Docker Addresses

In traditional deployment workflows, there is often a multitude of required steps that significantly contribute to the overall pain felt by teams. Every step you add to the deployment process for an application increases the risk inherent in shipping it to production. Docker combines a workflow with a simple toolset that is directly targeted at addressing these concerns. Along the way, it squarely aims your development processes toward some of the industry's best practices, and its opinionated approach often leads to better communication and more robustly crafted applications.

Some of the specific problems that Docker and Linux containers can help mitigate include the following:

- Avoiding significant divergence between deployment environments.
- Requiring application developers to re-create configuration and logging logic in applications.
- Using outdated build and release processes that require multiple levels of handoff between development and operations teams.
- Requiring complex and fragile build and deploy processes.
- Managing divergent dependency versions that are required by applications that need to share the same hardware.
- Managing multiple Linux distributions in the same organization.
- Building one-off deployment processes for each application you put into production.
- Needing to treat each application as a unique codebase when it comes to patching and auditing security vulnerabilities.
- And much more.

By using the registry as a handoff point, Docker eases and simplifies communication between operations and development teams, or between multiple development teams on the same project. By bundling all of the dependencies for an application into one shipping artifact, Docker eliminates concerns about which Linux distribution developers want to work on, which versions of libraries they need to use, and how they compile their assets or bundle their software. It isolates operations teams from the build process and puts developers in charge of their dependencies.

The Docker Workflow

Docker's workflow helps organizations tackle really hard problems—some of the same problems that DevOps processes are aimed at solving. A major problem in incorporating DevOps successfully into a company's processes is that many people have no idea where to start. Tools are often incorrectly presented as the solution to what are fundamentally process problems. Adding virtualization, automated testing, deployment tools, or configuration management suites to the environment often just changes the nature of the problem without delivering a resolution.

It would be easy to dismiss Docker as just another tool making unfulfillable promises about fixing your business processes, but that would be selling it short. Docker's power is in the way that its natural workflow allows applications to travel through their whole lifecycle, from conception to retirement, within one ecosystem. Unlike other tools that often target only a single aspect of the DevOps pipeline, Docker significantly improves almost every step of the process. That workflow is often opinionated, but it simplifies the adoption of some of the core principles of DevOps. It encourages development teams to understand the whole lifecycle of their application and allows operations teams to support a much wider variety of applications on the same runtime environment. And that delivers value across the board.

Minimizing Deployment Artifacts

Docker alleviates the pain that is often induced by sprawling deployment artifacts. It does this by defining the result of a build as a single artifact, the Docker image, which contains everything your Linux application requires to run, and it executes this within a protected runtime environment. Containers can then be easily deployed on modern Linux distributions. But because of the clean split between the Docker client and server, developers can build their applications on non-Linux systems and still participate in the Linux container environment remotely.

Leveraging Docker allows software developers to create Docker images that, starting with the very first proof of concept, can be run locally, tested with automated tools, and deployed into integration or production environments without ever having to be rebuilt. This ensures that the application that is launched in production is the same as what was tested. Nothing needs to be recompiled or repackaged during the deployment workflow, which significantly lowers the risks normally inherent in most deployment processes. It also means that a single build step replaces a typically error-prone process that involves compiling and packaging multiple complex components for distribution.

Docker images also simplify the installation and configuration of an application. Every single piece of software that an application requires to run on a modern Linux kernel is contained in the image, and the dependency conflicts you might find in a traditional environment are eliminated. This makes it trivial to run multiple applications that rely on different versions of core system software on the same server.

Optimizing Storage and Retrieval

Docker leverages filesystem layers to allow containers to be built from a composite of multiple images. This shaves a vast amount of time and effort off of many deployment processes by shipping only significant changes across the wire. It also saves considerable disk space by allowing multiple containers to be based on the same lower-level base image and then utilizing a copy-on-write process to write new or modified files into a top layer. This also helps in scaling an application by allowing more copies of an application to be started on the same servers without the need to push the binaries across the wire for each new instance.

To support image retrieval, Docker leverages the image registry for hosting images. While not revolutionary on the face of it, the registry helps split team responsibilities clearly along the lines embraced by DevOps principles. Developers can build their application, test it, ship the final image to the registry, and deploy the image to the production environment, while the operations team can focus on building excellent deployment and cluster management tooling that pulls from the registry, runs reliably, and ensures environmental health. Operations teams can provide feedback to developers and see the results of all the test runs at build time rather than waiting to find problems when the application is shipped to production. This enables both teams to focus on what they do best without a multiphase handoff process.

The Payoff

As teams become more confident with Docker and its workflow, the realization often dawns that containers create a powerful abstraction layer between all of their software components and the underlying operating system. Organizations can begin to move away from having to create custom physical servers or VMs for most applications and instead deploy fleets of identical Docker hosts that can be used as a large pool of resources to dynamically deploy their applications to, with an ease that was previously unheard of.

When these process changes are successful, the cultural impact within a software engineering organization can be dramatic. Developers gain more ownership of their complete application stack, including many of the smallest details, which would typically be handled by a completely different group. Operations teams are simultaneously freed from trying to package and deploy complicated dependency trees with little or no detailed knowledge of the application.

In a well-designed Docker workflow, developers compile and package the application, which makes it much easier for them to focus on ensuring that the application is running properly in all environments, without worrying about significant changes introduced to the application environment by the operations teams. At the same time, operations teams are freed from spending most of their time supporting the application and can focus on creating a robust and stable platform for the application to run on. This dynamic creates a very healthy environment in which teams have clearer ownership and responsibilities in the application delivery process, and friction between them is significantly decreased.

Getting the process right has a huge benefit to both the company and the customers. With organizational friction removed, software quality is improved, processes are streamlined, and code ships to production faster. This all helps free the organization to spend more time providing a satisfying customer experience and delivering directly to the broader business objectives. A well-implemented Docker-based workflow can greatly help organizations achieve those goals.

The Final Word

You should now be equipped with the knowledge that can help you make the transition to a modern, container-based build and deployment process. We encourage you to experiment with Docker on a small scale on your laptop or in a VM to further your understanding of how all of the pieces fit together, and then consider how you might begin to implement it for your organization. Every company or individual developer will follow a different path determined by their own needs and competencies. If you're looking for guidance on how to start, we've found success in tackling the deployment problem first with simpler tools and then moving on to tasks like service discovery and distributed scheduling. Docker can be made as complicated as you like, but as with anything, starting simple usually pays off.

We hope you can now take all of this newfound knowledge and make good on some of Docker and Linux containers' promises for yourself.

Index

About the Authors

Sean P. Kane is the founder of techlabs.sh (*https://techlabs.sh*) and a principal production operations engineer at SuperOrbital (*https://superorbital.io*). Sean specializes in engineering, teaching, and writing about modern DevOps processes, including Kubernetes, Docker, Terraform, and more. He has had a long career in production operations, with many diverse roles across a broad range of industries. Sean is the lead inventor on a container-related patent and spends a lot of his spare time writing, teaching, and speaking about technology. He is an avid traveler, hiker, and camper and lives in the US Pacific Northwest with his wife, children, and dogs.

Karl Matthias is vp of Architecture at Community.com and has previously worked at several well-known tech companies where he held a number of very senior engineering and leadership roles for more than 25 years. He is an enthusiast of hard problems, distributed systems, Go, Ruby, Elixir, scalable datastores, automated infrastructure, and repeatable systems.

Colophon

The animal on the cover of *Docker: Up & Running* is a blue whale (*Balaenoptera musculus*). Blue whales can grow up to 100 feet in length and 200 tons in weight, making them the largest animals on Earth, and the largest animals to ever exist. At birth, a blue whale calf is as large as an adult hippopotamus and can gain up to 200 pounds a day. When fully grown, blue whales are long and thin, with a small dorsal fin, two flippers at their side, and a horizontal tail, also known as a "fluke." Blue whales are named for their bluish-gray coloring.

Blue whales are migratory and can be found in every ocean. They generally feed in colder polar regions and then head to warmer tropical waters to give birth. Blue whales usually travel alone or in pairs and communicate through a series of complex vocalizations. As a member of the rorqual (*balaenopteridae*) family, blue whales feed by straining their prey through bony plates in their mouths known as baleen. Their diet consists almost entirely of krill, a small crustacean similar to shrimp. They require 1.5 million kilocalories of energy every day and can eat up to 7,900 pounds of krill daily. Because of their speed and size, blue whales have practically no natural predators.

Blue whales were once widespread, with a population estimated in the hundreds of thousands. While they were initially too large and fast for whalers to capture, the invention of the harpoon gun in the late 1800s enabled whalers to successfully hunt blue whales. Decades of whaling followed, causing a significant population decline. An international ban on the hunting of blue whales was enacted in 1966, allowing their numbers to recover, although they remain endangered.

Many of the animals on O'Reilly covers are endangered; all of them are important to the world. If you are interested in helping whale populations flourish, please consider volunteering with or donating to whale conservation organizations such as the Whale and Dolphin Conservation Society (*https://whales.org*).

The cover illustration is by Karen Montgomery, based on a black-and-white engraving from *A History of British Quadrupeds, Including the Cetacea*. The cover fonts are Gilroy Semibold and Guardian Sans. The text font is Adobe Minion Pro; the heading font is Adobe Myriad Condensed; and the code font is Dalton Maag's Ubuntu Mono.

Ingram Content Group UK Ltd.
Milton Keynes UK
UKHW050104180423
420195UK00006B/4

9 781098 131821